Invitation to the Dance

Hilary Spurling has written biographies of Ivy Compton-Burnett, Paul Scott and most recently Henri Matisse in two volumes, *The Unknown Matisse* (1998) and *Matisse the Master* (2005). Interim works include a Renaissance cookbook, *Elinor Fettiplace's Receipt Book*; a collection of Vladimir Sulyagin's forbidden portraits of Russian writers and artists, *Paper Spirits*; *La Grande Thérèse*; and *The Girl from the Fiction Department: A Portrait of Sonia Orwell*. She has been Arts and Literary Editor of the *Spectator*, and a regular reviewer for the *Observer*, the *New York Times* and the *Daily T...* to the playwright John Spurling, and has thr...

Praise for HILARY SPURL...

'This checklist of all the characters and main incidents is almost as seductive as the original novels.'

Paul Barker, *The Times*

'Taken together, Hilary Spurling's various indices constitute a work of criticism ... She has brought to her handbook the wit and erudition of Mr Powell himself.'

Francis King, *Sunday Telegraph*

'Spurling's handbook provides an indispensable master-key to the movements of Time for the reader, resolving doubts and confusions perhaps inevitable in a work of one million words with 400 or 500 characters. The bulk of the book is a "Who's Who" of the characters with page references ... Perhaps the most illuminating are the indices on books read or written, paintings looked at and places visited ... Spurling brings out the rich fullness of this feature of the sequence ... an appropriate view of the whole work is X. Trapnel's favourite saying: "Reading novels needs almost as much talent as writing them."'

Financial Times

Also by Hilary Spurling

Ivy When Young:
The Early Life of Ivy Compton-Burnett 1884–1919

Mervyn Peake: Drawings (editor)

Secrets of a Woman's Heart:
The Later Life of Ivy Compton-Burnett 1920–1969

Elinor Fettiplace's Receipt Book

Paul Scott: A Life

Paper Spirits

The Unknown Matisse:
A Life of Henri Matisse, Volume I, 1869–1908

La Grande Thérèse

The Girl from the Fiction Department:
A Portrait of Sonia Orwell

Matisse the Master:
The Conquest of Colour, Volume II, 1909–1954

Invitation
to the Dance

A Handbook to

ANTHONY POWELL'S

A Dance to the Music of Time

HILARY SPURLING

arrow books

This edition published by Arrow Books in 2005

16

Copyright © Hilary Spurling, 1977

Hilary Spurling has asserted her right under the Copyright, Designs
and Patents Act, 1988 to be identified as the author of this work

First published in the United Kingdom in 1977 by William Heinemann Ltd
Later published in 1992 by Mandarin Paperbacks

Arrow Books
The Random House Group Limited
20 Vauxhall Bridge Road, London, SW1V 2SA

Addresses for companies within The Random House Group Limited
can be found at: www.randomhouse.co.uk/offices.htm

Random House Group Limited Reg. No. 954009

www.randomhouse.co.uk

A CIP catalogue record for this book is available from the British Library

ISBN 978 0 09 948436 3

Typeset by SX Composing DTP, Rayleigh, Essex

Penguin Random House is committed to a sustainable future for
our business, our readers and our planet. This book is made from
Forest Stewardship Council® certified paper.

Printed and bound in Great Britain by Clays Ltd, St Ives plc

Contents

Introduction

Throughout the course of a twelve-volume novel, four or five hundred characters, a million words, even the best disposed reader can forget the detail of what went before. Accordingly, on more than one occasion suggestions have been made that some sort of a glossary should be provided for *A Dance to the Music of Time*. This has now been effected with extreme ingenuity by Hilary Spurling.

The novelist is in command of whatever information is set out in a novel, but can only guess at the effect such information may have on its reader. In all the arts extraneous elements interpose themselves between creator and consumer, something that is particularly true of novel-writing. It is an aspect of novels that has always fascinated me; the prerogative of the reader to make an individual judgment, not necessarily the author's, on characters and events.

A Dance to the Music of Time is told, so to speak, over the dinner-table, rather than as recorded history. The narrator, Nicholas Jenkins, is merely a vehicle for expressing how people and happenings struck him during a period of some sixty years; matters on which the opinion of his listeners may differ. The point of view of Jenkins himself inevitably alters with age; at the beginning of the story, fifty seeming decrepitude; later on, an agreeable maturity.

Jenkins's memory is not invariably reliable. He can confuse dates. For example, at the Walpole-Wilsons' dinner-party (which personally I am inclined to place in 1928), guests use as current topics of conversation both occurrences that were taking place in 1929, and also those of the previous year. In 1946, or thereabouts, he reports Sir Magnus Donners, in Sillery's phase, 'gathered to his fathers', when possibly a stroke, or some other affliction, caused Sillery to speculate on the demise of Sir Magnus, who survived until the early 1950s. Polly Duport, it appears, could have been as much as two years older than Jenkins latterly supposed.

But – when the past is discussed – who ever agrees? Hilary Spurling's exhaustive analysis of the novel's characters supplies a master-key for the reader to make a decision on these and many other points.

ANTHONY POWELL

Foreword

The purpose of this book is twofold. I hope it will serve both as a work of reference and as a pleasant bedside companion for readers who simply want to refresh their memories, fill in gaps or check up on the career of an individual character outside his or her fictional framework. The largest item is a Character Index in which I have tried to follow the scheme laid down by Proust's translator, C. K. Scott-Moncrieff, in his note to volume nine of *Remembrance of Things Past*, for 'an index, or "Who's Who" of the characters that figure in the story, each of them studied, as far as possible, in historical sequence . . .' Except in certain cases (such as those of Jean Duport and her lovers Jimmy Stripling, Jimmy Brent and Jenkins, where it seemed essential to preserve the order in which discoveries are made in the text), this has meant a considerable re-arrangement of biographical material; so I have added a simple index at the foot of each entry, for the sake of anyone wanting to check a reference, look up a particular passage or trace the character's pattern as it evolves through the sequence of novels.

I have included virtually every character, factual or fictional (as well as one or two, like Trimalchio, who come from other authors' fictions), largely because it became impossible to decide who should and who shouldn't be left out. Real people have a date or dates attached throughout, to distinguish them from imaginary ones. Anyone who plays the smallest role in the fictional action (like John Constable who painted the Sleafords' ancestral home Dogdene, Edward IV who gave the Tollands their first leg up in the world, or Mrs Simpson who seems to have turned Widmerpool's head in the 'thirties) is included. But so are a great many more marginal cases, scarcely even bit part players: some, like Sun Yat-Sen or the Austrian chancellor Dollfuss, are there because their dates help to fix the timing of fictional events; others, like Ambrose the dance band leader, Mrs Hwfa Williams the Edwardian hostess or a long line of authors from Kierkegaard to Virginia Woolf, may be of interest to students of social or intellectual fashion; and still others, like Fat Boy Gort who failed to find work for Jenkins' father or Sir Gavin Walpole-Wilson's seventeenth-century ancestor Beau Wilson, struck me as so obscure that, if not identified, they risked slipping over the borderline between fact and fiction.

Books read or written, paintings looked at and places visited play such a major part in the sequence that I have added a Book Index (covering literary matters in general), a Painting Index (covering the plastic arts) and a Place Index. The first two are arranged along much the same lines as the Character Index, though entries are not sub-divided except in a few cases (notably Poussin's painting, *A Dance to the Music of Time*) where a composite entry would have been too cumbersome. The Place Index is an altogether more ramshackle affair, since any comprehensive attempt to index places like Bayswater, the Tottenham Court Road or Jenkins' university would degenerate into more or less meaningless lists of page numbers; so, generally speaking, I have simply pointed out the chief descriptive passages.

The essay on structure, which follows this foreword, is an attempt to indicate some of the many aspects of *A Dance to the Music of Time* not touched on in the otherwise largely anecdotal content of this glossary; and the book ends with a Synopsis from which it should be possible to follow the overall pattern of the sequence, as well as to establish the relationship between fictional and factual time in the half century covered by Jenkins' narrative.

Lastly, I should like to thank Anthony Powell for his patience and tolerance in answering my many queries; and to say how very grateful I am to the following for the time and trouble they spent clearing up points which defeated me: John Barron, Charles Chilton, Canon Ivor Davies, Philip French, Madge Garland, Douglas Matthews of the London Library, Leonée Ormonde, Lady Violet Powell, Jean Rhys, John Riley, the Rev. C. T. Spurling and Anthony Thwaite.

HILARY SPURLING.

The Heresy of Naturalism: Some Notes on Structure

'Reading novels needs almost as much talent as writing them' is a favourite saying of X. Trapnel's, and one perhaps specially appropriate to the work in which he figures. For one could hardly find a work of fiction which more clearly demonstrates what Trapnel himself calls 'the heresy of naturalism' than this sequence of novels in which, for the reader, the deepest satisfaction comes less from character and incident than from the structure that supports them both: a structure so contrived that, as it flows, straggles or jerks itself along, by turns farcical and grim, sombre, tumultuous, absurd, reaching out through almost infinite varieties of egotism to embrace the furthest shores of crankiness and melancholia, it seems not so much to shape as to contain the disorderly process of life itself. It is not for nothing that Nicholas Jenkins takes his first name from that specialist in rhythm and design, Nicolas Poussin, whose painting provides both the title and the model for *A Dance to the Music of Time*.

Time, in that painting, smiles a sinister smile as well he may considering that in life and art he has the upper hand. In fiction, or at least in this particular fiction, Time is to the writer what Space is to the painter. Time may be empty or so densely packed that the reader can barely take in more than a few sample details in a hectic corner of the canvas. Time may dawdle or work fast, stretching forward or doubling back to shift a perspective, change an angle, open up one vista, close another, superimpose a further twist on a design already loaded or tweak skew-whiff a whole connecting system of supports. It is Time who disposes of the characters, causing them to topple and collide, tangle, scatter and regroup in new and unexpected couplings. Almost any character will serve to illustrate Time's role. Take, for instance, Milly Andriadis who gives the party in *A Buyer's Market* at which Jenkins first sets foot in that chilly, grasping, power-conscious adult world which will from now on insistently claim his attention.

In the first place, the party is not approached head on but through the disapproving eyes of Uncle Giles who (supposing he were present, which he isn't) would undoubtedly take the gravest exception to his hostess. She herself seems to Jenkins, still largely conventional if increasingly dissatisfied in outlook, only one of many imponderables following one another too close for comfort in the course of a single, eventful midsummer night: 'we came suddenly upon Mrs Andriadis herself, when a further, and enormous, field of speculation was immediately projected into being'. Such stray facts as may be gleaned about her character and history are conveyed by various people in vastly different tones of voice – Mr Deacon's inquisitive but suspicious, Sillery's faintly critical, David Pennistone's sardonic, Barnby's not untinged by a sense of competition. To Dicky Umfraville, whose view we learn later, Mrs Andriadis is simply part of the furniture of his own distant and doubtless murky youth. For her current lover, Charles Stringham, she is already beginning to take on the oppressive lineaments of the two formidable women, his mother and Miss Weedon, whose toils he will never entirely manage to escape. To Jenkins (too bemused to register for several months her resemblance to Stringham's mother and Miss Weedon), she is an enigma, but one which gradually recedes in the later stages of that summer as he moves towards his own decision to settle for the world of the imagination rather than of power. In time she will become a feature of the landscape so unremarkable that when, twenty or thirty years later, she comes to an inevitable bad end, the event itself can be inferred only from casual asides let slip in conversation about other more absorbing topics. But, however modified by hindsight, she will always retain something of the intensity of that first encounter when she seemed a kind of Circe, presiding (as Madame Leroy had done earlier at La Grenadière and Mrs Erdleigh will do a few years later) over a crucial junction in Jenkins' career. Her Hill Street party is the hinge on which *A Buyer's Market* turns, and – together with that other memorable gathering at her Park Lane flat in *The Acceptance World* – provides one of the character friezes of furious activity which punctuate the first of the four movements of the dance.

None of this has, strictly speaking, any place in her *curriculum vitae*. And yet to approach Mrs Andriadis as a character in her own right is to strip her of her single most essential function as a strand in the overall pattern of the sequence. It is much as though one were to describe, say, the sharply individual figure of Eve in Correggio's *Assumption of the Virgin* at Parma without once mentioning that, because she is painted in a tilted perspective on the slanting side of a circular dome eighty feet above the ground, her head is severely foreshortened, her features flattened, her left, apple-bearing forearm massively enlarged and her body invisible from the waist down; while at the same time one failed to take account of her dominant position – slightly above the Virgin, below Christ and facing Adam – in the heaving mass of some fifty Old and New Testament characters, thirty or forty angels and innumerable putti who simultaneously jostle, conceal and support her, all scrambling for a purchase on one another's heads, shoulders and frantically flailing limbs, all enclosed within the harmonious contours of Correggio's master plan.

One might find a parallel case of this foreshortening, brought about by Time rather than Space, in the magician Dr Trelawney whose uncomfortable presence in the second half of *The Music of Time* makes an impact out of all proportion to his actual appearances. We see him face to face only twice, both times in a far from flattering light. He turns up first as a harmless local crackpot running the kind of cult fashionable before the first world war from a gabled villa near the Jenkinses' at Stonehurst. A conspicuous bearded figure in biblical garments, often to be seen out running across the heather with a flock of disconsolate disciples trailing in his wake, he makes a slightly queasy impression on Mrs Jenkins, haunts her son's dreams at night and is politely but firmly sent packing by General Conyers. When next encountered, washed up in a dingy room at the Bellevue a quarter of a century later, he is even less impressive: an ageing semi-invalid, with stained beard and yellow teeth, who has long since become an embarrassment to the management on account of his reluctance to pay his bills, his disobliging attitude to other residents and his habit of getting himself locked in the bathroom at all hours of the night. On this occasion he receives his quietus from Mrs Erdleigh with a hypodermic syringe, administered behind locked doors as his prophecies of doom – 'The slayer of Osiris once again demands his grievous tribute of blood. The Angel of Death will ride the storm . . . The Four Horsemen are at the gate . . .' – degenerate into demented screechings.

In the interval between these two manifestations, which come towards the beginning and end of *The Kindly Ones*, Jenkins has learnt a thing or two from the doctor's fellow Simple Lifer, Mr Deacon (who confirms that, for all his talk of Oneness and the Vision of Visions healing the Blindness of Sight, Trelawney's eye is more firmly on the ball than most when it comes to extracting funds from the faithful, or keeping his disciples on starvation rations); and at second hand from Moreland (who casts light on some rather more sinister proceedings in a necromantic career verging on the criminal). But neither these reports, nor his own taste for cabbalistic dialectic, sufficiently account for Trelawney's palpably unsavoury ambience. Nor is it simply that Jenkins himself is peculiarly susceptible to dabblers in the Black Arts ('I had become increasingly aware of his pervasive, quasi-hypnotic powers, possessed to a greater or lesser degree by all persons – not necessarily connected with occultism – who form little cults devoted primarily to veneration of themselves'). What gives Trelawney a stature not fully warranted by the incomplete, sometimes obscure outlines of his portrait may partly be his relationship to two figures more solidly planted in the novel's foreground, General Conyers and Mrs Erdleigh, each of whom accords him a surprising measure of respect. But the foreshortening effect comes still more from his own position in *The Kindly Ones*, the novel which concludes the first half of the sequence and, of all twelve volumes, covers the widest and most convoluted span of time.

The crowded afternoon on which Trelawney first showed up (it was the day on which the Jenkinses' cook gave notice, the Conyerses came to lunch, the parlourmaid appeared naked in the drawing room and Uncle Giles chose to arrive out of the blue) was also the day in 1914 on which Archduke Franz Ferdinand was assassinated at Sarajevo – a fact to which the reader's attention is drawn in language strongly reminiscent of Trelawney: 'No one yet realized that the Mute with the Bowstring stood at the threshold of the door, that, if they wanted to get anything done in time of peace, they must be quick about it'. He appears for the second and last time on the day in 1939 when Russia and Germany signed their non-aggression pact:

'When the sword of Mithras – to borrow Dr Trelawney's phrase – flashed at last from its scabbard, people supposed London would immediately become the target of bombs. However, the slayer of Osiris did not at first demand his grievous tribute of blood, and a tense, infinitely uneasy over-all stagnation imposed itself upon an equally uncomfortable, equally febrile, over-all activity.'

In each case Trelawney becomes in retrospect a harbinger of war, a figure who gathers to himself the atmosphere of impending catastrophe which pervades *The Kindly Ones*, and who will continue to loom ominously over deaths, dislocations and fresh groupings long after his corporeal body has, in Mrs Erdleigh's words, 're-entered the Vortex of Becoming'. Another quarter of a century later, in the last volume of *The Music of Time*, Trelawney's theories will return to vogue among the cult followers of the late 1960s – an achievement to which Jenkins gives ungrudging recognition: 'It was Dr Trelawney's view – also that of his old friend and fellow occultist, Mrs Erdleigh – that death was no more than transition, blending, synthesis, mutation. To be fair to them both, they seemed to some extent to have made their point'. It is characteristic of the structural complexity of the whole sequence that, in addition to what one might call his surrealistic role, Trelawney remains not only entirely plausible in naturalistic terms – as an ambitious, unscrupulous and exceptionally shrewd mountebank – but also one of the most undilutedly comic characters in fiction.

Indeed, not the least disconcerting thing about *The Music of Time* is precisely its humorous tone. Jenkins himself notes at one point that Shakespeare found it necessary to alternate tragedy with comedy largely because people in everyday life will insist on acting without due regard for procedure; and any reader of Jenkins' own narrative will find again and again that events which seemed hilariously funny at the time become steadily less so in retrospect. A case in point is the scene at the Huntercombes' ball when Barbara Goring drenched Widmerpool with sugar: a surprise attack still sharply etched on Jenkins' imagination thirty years and nine volumes later, on the climactic night in Regent's Park when Pamela Widmerpool mounts her final spectacular assault upon her husband. Other obvious examples are Mrs Foxe's party for Moreland's symphony at which revelations and reversals follow one another with the speed of farce; Sir Magnus Donners' Seven Deadly Sins tableaux at Stourwater a few years later; even the notorious affair of Braddock alias Thorne at school – an escapade which, as it turns out, marks the high point for Stringham whose fortunes afterwards spiral inexorably downwards. Humour in short can go to almost any lengths, given that it works in conjunction with Jenkins' constant awareness of 'the tricks Time can play within its own folds, tricks that emphasize the insecurity of those who trust themselves over much to that treacherous concept'.

The combination governs every part of the design, above all the long series of jolts which make up Jenkins' relationship with Widmerpool. But it can be seen perhaps most clearly in the career of such a relatively minor figure as Stringham's stepfather, the polo-playing sailor, Lieutenant Commander Buster Foxe. Handsome, indolent, pin-headed, a natty dresser slightly younger than his wealthy wife, Buster belongs to a P. G. Wodehouse world of 'twenties chic revolving round fast cars, country houses, smart golf courses and yachting at Cowes. But he also has a less amiable aspect, immediately apparent when Jenkins first sets eyes on him during a visit to Stringham's home from school in the Christmas holidays of 1922:

'Buster was . . . cleaning a cigarette-holder with the end of a match-stick. He was tall, and at once struck me as surprisingly young . . . His turn-out was emphatically excellent, and he diffused waves of personality, strong, chilling gusts of icy air, a protective element that threatened to freeze into rigidity all who came through the door, before they could approach him nearer.

'"Hullo, you fellows," he said, without looking up from his

cigarette-holder, at which he appeared to be sneering, as if this object were not nearly valuable enough to presume to belong to him.'

Stringham, as Jenkins later learns from Dicky Umfraville, loathes Buster's guts; their rivalry supplies a minor theme in *A Question of Upbringing*, provisionally resolved in victory for Stringham. It runs underground for the next three volumes in which Buster disappears from view (though we hear of him from time to time growing fatter, falling out of favour with his wife, taking slimming cures at Tring), only to surface again in foul play at Mrs Foxe's party in *Casanova's Chinese Restaurant* which ends with game, set and match to Buster. But the origins of this feud are disclosed only long afterwards by Buster's old enemy Umfraville, telling the ghastly story of his life and incidentally of Buster's marriage in *The Valley of Bones*. So that it is not until well into the second half of the sequence that the reader is at last in a position to unravel the tensions sensed by Jenkins as a schoolboy on that first morning when Buster, temporarily outflanked by Stringham, went off to ply with hock at Claridge's a man from whom he hoped to buy a Bentley awfully cheap.

Jenkins' attitude to Buster is of course largely coloured by loyalty to Stringham, and by the impression of strain Stringham always gives, whether as a dissident schoolboy, a debauchee in search of ever more exotic haunts of vice, a reprieved alcoholic or on his last appearance as a mess waiter in the second war. Uneasiness in Buster's presence changes to horror at his part in Stringham's disintegration, itself a prototype of the lives of other romantics – Roland Gwatkin, X. Trapnel, to some extent Hugh Moreland – shipwrecked in the gulf between their dreams and an obdurate reality. The same horror deepens and darkens Jenkins' view of Widmerpool (Stringham's butt at school, later indirectly responsible for Stringham's death in a Japanese prisoner-of-war camp, ultimately destroyed by his marriage to Stringham's niece, Pamela Flitton). Whatever the underlying cause of Stringham's troubles – a Hamlet-like temperament exacerbated by his mother's domination, by Buster's machinations, perhaps by the wrongs of his own divorced father – there can be no doubt that they exert a powerful pull on the whole structure of *The Music of Time*: so much so that it is something of a shock when the reader realizes on looking back that, as a friend, Stringham has effectively dropped out of Jenkins' life by the end of the first volume. His disillusionment, his captivating liveliness, his melancholy wit are already so securely established that though from now on he appears at greater intervals – and falls out altogether just over half way through the sequence – large stretches of the action will take place in his shadow.

If Stringham is one of several characters who define the basic framework, others, more often heard than seen, serve so to speak as filters, constantly available to change the lighting of a particular scene or modulate from one incident to another years before or still to come. One thinks of Umfraville's urbane epithets ("'Buster's a contemporary of mine,'" said Umfraville, "'a son-of-a-bitch in the top class'"), Peter Templer's equally pithy turn of phrase, Chips Lovell's gossip, even the grousings of Uncle Giles. Barnby (who starts laying down the law on women some hundred and fifty pages before the reader has the faintest notion who he is, and whose voice continues to make itself heard long after his death in a wartime plane crash) falls into this category, and so does Moreland, whose gradual withdrawal and eventual departure from the scene remove a whole layer of colouring from Jenkins' narrative.

Indeed Jenkins himself may be seen in much the same way, as a convenient device for the adjustment of perspective. It is a device especially noticeable at the beginning of the sequence, where behaviour and events which caused Jenkins no small perplexity at the time – Mrs Andriadis' Hill Street party is one of many instances – are more clearly scrutinized in the light of an understanding arrived at only many years later. It means that the reader sees much of the action in the early volumes as it were in double focus, through the eyes of the narrator and simultaneously through the eyes of his naive younger self: a character hopelessly out of his depth in matters like sex, power and the literary life, equally at sea in his estimate of other people's motives, for ever stubbing his toe on mysteries he is unable to resolve, developments he hadn't anticipated, problems with which he can't begin to cope. The flexibility of this multiple approach is plain in the case of someone like the novelist, St John Clarke, to whom Jenkins' attitude veers through four successive phases (initial dislike, succeeded by a kind of adolescent infatuation which gives way first to the extreme intolerance of youth, later to a more complex mistrust), any or all of which may be called into play at a given moment in the narrative.

It is also perhaps worth noting that there is one unique element in this particular portrait, arising from Jenkins' account of the novelist's work: a technical analysis which in itself amounts to a short course in the art of writing as instructive as it is diverting. St John Clarke's novels are characterized by 'inexactitudes of thought and feeling', 'windy descriptive passages, two-dimensional characterization and . . . the emptiness of the writing's inner content'; their style is 'inept' and 'outworn'; they are 'trivial, unreal, vulgar', 'odiously phrased and "insincere"'; moreover they are slipshod in construction. The very thought of them moves Jenkins by turns to 'savagery' and nausea, reactions altogether different from his lenient appraisal of the work of other artists who fall into roughly the same low category, notably the painters Edgar Deacon, Horace Isbister and Daniel Tokenhouse. As a man St John Clarke may inspire pangs of pity (and once at least a certain reluctant fellow feeling) but not as an author. Even Widmerpool at his most repulsive comes in for nothing comparable to the ruthless and sustained contempt of this purely professional castigation.

Jenkins writes somewhere that he takes a 'hard, cold-blooded, almost mathematical pleasure' in writing and painting. The reverse side of this pleasure is his attitude to Clarke's novels, a rejection framed according to the uncompromising laws of an aesthetic rather than moral or emotional system. It strikes a note not heard elsewhere in a work devoted to exploring, in all their painful and preposterous diversity, the workings of that general rule laid down at a fairly early stage in *The Music of Time*: 'All human beings, driven as they are at different speeds by the same Furies, are at close range equally extraordinary'.

Note

Abbreviations used in the pages which follow:

QU   *A Question of Upbringing*, 1969, 2005 (1951)
BM   *A Buyer's Market*, 1974, 2005 (1952)
AW   *The Acceptance World*, 1972, 2005 (1955)
LM   *At Lady Molly's*, 1971, 2005 (1957)
CCR   *Casanova's Chinese Restaurant*, 1974, 2005 (1960)
KO   *The Kindly Ones*, 1975, 2005 (1962)
VB   *The Valley of Bones*, 1973, 2005 (1964)
SA   *The Soldier's Art*, 1966, 2005
MP   *The Military Philosophers*, 1968, 2005
BDFR   *Books Do Furnish a Room*, 1975, 2005 (1971)
TK   *Temporary Kings*, 1973, 2005
HSH   *Hearing Secret Harmonies*, 1975, 2005

All page numbers and quotations refer to the current, revised editions (dates in brackets are those of first editions, where these are different), published in England by William Heinemann Ltd and in the USA by Little, Brown & Co., and most recently reissued by Arrow Books. Readers using an earlier edition of *A Buyer's Market* will find some slight discrepancy in the pagination of the penultimate chapter but otherwise page numbers are the same in all editions.

To calculate page references to the Minerva four-volume edition, the following sums should be used:

	For Minerva edition, add:
A Question of Upbringing	0
A Buyer's Market	234
The Acceptance World	512
At Lady Molly's	0
Casanova's Chinese Restaurant	242
The Kindly Ones	474
The Valley of Bones	0
The Soldier's Art	248
The Military Philosophers	480
Books Do Furnish a Room	0
Temporary Kings	246
Hearing Secret Harmonies	530

Character Index

ABERAVON, Lord (Rowland) Family name Gwatkin
Father of Lady Walpole-Wilson and Lady Goring; Liverpool shipping magnate, deputy-lieutenant of Shropshire; was made a peer by Queen Victoria shortly before his death (*c.* 1900) and left three-quarters of a million. Said to be directly descended from Vortigern by an incestuous match with one of that prince's own daughters.

Collector and patron of the arts ('Isbister was what he liked. He possessed a large collection of thoroughly bad pictures which we had some difficulty in disposing of at his death': Sir Gavin Walpole-Wilson). A man of vision, according to Mr Deacon from whom he bought the *Boyhood of Cyrus*. Works from his collection highly prized and greatly sought after on the London art market by 1971.

BM 20, 50, 80, 85, 177, 263. AW 109. VB 186–8. HSH 250.

ABLETT, Sergeant
Unusually efficient NCO, in charge of the Mobile Laundry Unit and largely responsible for Lt. Bithel's unexpected survival as its officer. Looks like a veteran of Wellington's campaigns, leading comedian at Divisional concert parties, his trouserless tap dance always a popular item. A great favourite with Stringham.

Posted to Far East with the Laundry in 1941, captured at the Fall of Singapore and survives the Japanese POW camp in which Stringham dies.

SA 8, 181, 217–9, 223–4. TK 206, 209.

ADLER, Professor Alfred 1870–1937
Psychologist for whom General Conyers hasn't much use.

LM 81.

AKWORTH
Very small boy at Jenkins' old school after the second war ('he gave the impression that quite a complicated intellectual programme for ragging Le Bas had been planned').

BDFR 235–6.

AKWORTH, Bertram
Expelled from school *c.* 1918 at the instigation of Widmerpool, who reported him to Le Bas for sending a note to Peter Templer. Atones for this adolescent lapse by a career of almost sanctified respectability in the City; conspires with Farebrother to get Widmerpool sacked from a banking board; knighted for public services. Accosted at his grand-daughter's wedding reception in 1971 by Widmerpool engaged in an act of ritual penance, and fails at first to recognize his old enemy

('Enlightenment.caused a series of violent emotions – deep hatred the most definable – to pass swiftly across his sallow cadaverous features').

QU 13, 131, 223. HSH 187–9, 192–3, 221–3, 229–31.

AKWORTH, Clare
Grand-daughter of above, god-daughter of Flavia Wisebite, only child of a widowed mother distantly related to the Ardglasses. Ed. Stourwater girls' school, later secretary in an advertising agency, m. Sebastian Cutts at Stourwater in 1971 ('Her pleasing *beauté de singe* . . . was of a type calculated to raise the ghost of Sir Magnus Donners in the Stourwater corridors. Perhaps it had done so, when she was a school girl').

HSH 187, 190–1, 200, 205, 221–2, 226, 258–9.

AKWORTH, Rupert
Uncle of above, gives her away on her marriage.

HSH 191.

ALANBROOKE, Field-Marshal Viscount, CIGS 1883–1963
Chief of Imperial General Staff 1941–6:
'[Vavassor's] attention, my own too, was at that moment unequivocally demanded by the hurricane-like imminence of a thickset general, obviously of high rank, wearing enormous horn-rimmed spectacles. He had just burst from a flagged staff-car almost before it had drawn up by the kerb. Now he tore up the steps of the building at the charge, exploding through the inner door into the hall. An extraordinary current of physical energy, almost of electricity, suddenly pervaded the place. I could feel it stabbing through me. This was the CIGS . . .'

Depresses Widmerpool by his habit of sacking anyone he doesn't like the look of ('I saw what he meant. Given the CIGS was easily irritated by the faces of staff-officers, Widmerpool's, where survival was in question, was a bad bet, rather than a good one').

MP 53–5, 110, 142, 174, his will power compared with Field Marshal Montgomery's 183, 239.

ALBERT see CREECH, Albert

ALDREDGE
Quarry director brought to bay in the late 'sixties by the Jenkinses and other conservationists: 'Mr Aldredge, pinched in feature, with a pious expression, seemed at pains to prove that no mere hatred of the human race as such . . . caused him to pursue a policy of wholesale erosion and pollution. He denied those imputations pathetically.'

HSH 150–1.

ALEXANDRA, QUEEN 1844–1926
Once made a double entendre to Lady Bridgnorth's uncle.
AW 199.

ALFORDS
Family of Lord Warminster's first wife, all shortcomings in his ten
children blamed on her Alford blood. A seedy lot, according to Norah
Tolland.
LM 138, 208. KO 10. BDFR 44, 61. HSH 198.

ALFORD-GREEN, Colonel and Mrs Gerald
Hunting types at Sebastian Cutts' wedding.
HSH 227–8, 231.

AL SHARQUI, Major
Rather shy Arab military attaché.
MP 156, 158.

AMBROSE, Bert 1897–1973
Band-leader; playing at the other dance in Belgrave Square on the night
of the Huntercombes' ball in 1928 or '9.
BM 50.

AMESBURY, Lord
Discovered by Miss Weedon one night at Lady Molly's wearing knee
breeches and the Garter and eating scrambled eggs with the vet.
LM 165. KO 234.

AMESBURY, Sybil, Lady
Dowager whose supposedly scurrilous memoirs (which included an
account of the ambassadorial ball wrecked by Lord Vowchurch's
monkeys) greatly disappointed Jenkins as a boy. Later turns out to have
been the elderly intractable relation to whom Mrs Conyers acted as
companion before her marriage. Was the first person to take up
Stringham's mother, making her début as an heiress on the London
marriage market just before the turn of the century.
LM 10, 23. CCR 89.

ANDERS, Lieutenant-General Wladyslaw 1892–1970
Commander-in-Chief of Polish forces in USSR.
MP 17, 55.

ANDRIADIS, Milly (Mrs)
Hostess of long standing and varied experience; lives her life at a furious
rate; once a King's mistress and briefly Stringham's before his marriage
in 1928 or '9. Small, bejewelled, powder grey hair (said by Barnby to
have turned grey 'after her first night with the Royal Personage') and
cockney drawl. Aged about 35 at the end of the 'twenties. Much
married. Has lived in Havana and Paris. Rents the Duports' house in
Hill Street (and raises hell in it, eventually sued for damages by Bob
Duport). Gives the party on the night of the Huntercombes' ball which
culminates in her quarrelling with Stringham and ordering Mr Deacon
onto the street.

Trotskyite convert by 1933, after wholesale rehabilitation at the
hands of her new German boyfriend Werner Guggenbühl. Entertains
Umfraville ('Oh, God, you again, Dicky. Somebody told me you died
of drink in 1929') together with the entire clientèle of Foppa's bar at
her flat in Park Lane. Afterwards moves in left-wing circles frequented
by Erridge, Quiggin, Howard Craggs, etc; solely interested in Spanish
Civil War. Said to be living in a single room in Bloomsbury by 1942,
given over to drink and drugs and later to Second Front propaganda.
D. in Paris in 1957.

BM Wholesale invitation to her party issued by Stringham 94–5; at the
party, chill atmospheric undercurrents 97–9, 101, with Stringham
105–8, Deacon on her racy past 114–7, 122–3, 128, 132, 139–40, row
with Stringham 144–8, and with Deacon 150–2, 160; 165–7, 174,
187–8, 193–4, 205, 210, 212, Deacon's guarded disapproval of 229–30;
242, 251, resemblance to Stringham's mother and Miss Weedon 273.
AW 35, 111, wholesale invitation to her flat issued by Umfraville, her
political conversion and relations with Guggenbühl 157–69; 174. CCR
15, 25, 65, 166, 172, 174. KO 79. VB 110, 125. MP 50, 221. TK Her
death 148.

ANDRIADIS, Mr
Current husband of above ('I imagine him to be a man of almost
infinite tolerance': Deacon), said to have business interests in
Manchester.

BM 116.

ANDRZEJEWSKI, Second-lieutenant
Rosie Manasch's second husband, an elderly invalid Pole who d. in the
second war of an incurable disease soon after the wedding.

BDFR 101.

ANNE, Queen 1665–1714
Raised the Tollands to the peerage.
LM 151.

ANGLESEY, Lord 1768–1854
Commanded the cavalry at Waterloo, only less of a rake than Lord
Erridge according to Wellington.
LM 149.

ARDGLASS, Countess of (Bijou)
A notably fashionable beauty ('Do you know her – probably slept with
her? Most of one's friends have': Chips Lovell). Tall, statuesque, largely
built with china-blue eyes and yellow hair'; not unlike Mona Templer
but has rather more expensive tastes in men. B. 1901 of theatrical
parents ('Do you know, Bijou's father played Abanazar in *Aladdin*
when my mother was Principal Boy in the same show?' Max Pilgrim),
failed to get a job in the chorus and became a model instead before
marrying Lord Ardglass who divorced her soon afterwards.

Baby Wentworth's rival for the favours of Prince Theodoric in the
summer of 1928 or '9; bets placed by Stringham on Bijou who gets
Theodoric briefly that autumn. Turns down an offer to succeed Mrs
Wentworth as Sir Magnus Donners' mistress and breaks up Bob
Duport's marriage to Jean, leaving him when his money runs out round
about 1932. Seen shortly afterwards at the Ritz in mink looking
distinctly older and accompanied by 'two spruce, grey-haired admirers,
at heel like a brace of well-groomed, well-bred sporting dogs' (one of
whom – or another so like as to be indistinguishable – later declines to
buy her portrait by Isbister, even dirt cheap).

Serves under Lady McReith as driver in second war. Killed by a
bomb with all her guests at her fortieth birthday party at the Café de
Madrid in 1941.

BM At Milly Andriadis' party 111, 121, 125–6; 166, 198, 235. AW At
the Ritz, affair with Bob Duport 35, 56–7; at Isbister exhibition,
Jenkins linked to 113–4; Jean Duport on 135–6; 155, 176. LM Her
divorce 16, 29, 42; 68. CCR 158. KO 108. SA War work, invitations
to her party 111–2; 116, 124, 132, Max Pilgrim's account of her death
156–7. MP 188. HSH 256.

ARDGLASS, Earl of, Viscount Kilkeel (Jumbo) Family name
Jamieson.
Brother to Lady Molly Jeavons and Lady Warminster, looked like an
elephant and never denied it. Married as his second wife the mannequin
Bijou, who ran through his money ('The Ardglass family have been

7

hopelessly insolvent since the Land Act': Chips Lovell) and left him; d. without issue by 1933, succeeded by a distant cousin. His paternal grandfather had 97 first cousins and his maternal grandmother 94.

AW 114, 135, 176. LM 16, 18, 25, 28–9, 34, 42.

ASBJØRNSEN, Lieutenant-General
Tall melancholy Scandinavian military attaché who takes part in the trip to inspect allied lines in 1944, and never forgives Jenkins for assisting at his defeat in the affair of Major Prasad's bath.

MP 49, 55–6, 101, 159–66, 221, 224.

ASQUITH, Herbert Henry, first Earl of Oxford and Asquith 1852–1928
Liberal Prime Minister 1908–16. Gave office to Molly Jeavons' first husband Lord Sleaford; and may also have held out hope of political advancement to the young Sillery (who once lunched with him at Downing Street in a suit still going strong after the second war).

QU 169. LM 17, 171. BDFR 9.

ATTLEE, Clement, first Earl 1883–1967
Labour Prime Minister after the General Election of 1945. Is highly thought of by Widmerpool (then a new socialist member of parliament), and confers a peerage on Sillery.

KO 91. BDFR 12, 65. TK 58.

AUDREY
Lady Frederica Budd's good-natured, dumpy, bespectacled maid in the second war; unmarried mother of one and expecting another ('a bit too good-natured or her lenses need adjusting') by different fathers.

VB 146–7.

AVRIL
The most vacant of Bagshaw's three stepdaughters, aged 16 or 17 in 1958 and probably pregnant.

TK 181–2, 192–5.

BAGSHAW, ('Books-do-furnish-a-room') Lindsay
Journalist deeply learned in left-wing lore.
    'Bagshaw was for ever fascinated by revolutionary techniques, always prepared to explain everybody's standpoint, who was a party-member, fellow-traveller, crypto, trotskyist, anarchist, anarcho-syndicalist, every refinement of marxist theory, every subtle distinction between groups. The ebb and flow of subversive forces wafted the breath of life to him,

even if he no longer believed in the beneficial qualities of that tide.'

A seedy figure, seldom in permanent employment. Slightly older than Jenkins who first met him through Moreland (probably responsible for the more fanciful version of how he got his nickname) round about the end of the 'twenties. Professional rebel from schooldays onwards; reckoned to have been engaged to Gypsy Jones at one time; possibly a member of the Communist Party until disillusioned as a reporter in Spain during the civil war. Briefly with the BBC at Savoy Hill before plunging into almost every known form of exploiting the printed word (politics, sport, books, art, fashion, science: 'He would take on anything, and – to be fair – what he produced, even off the cuff, was no worse than what was to be read most of the time. You never wondered how on earth the stuff had managed to be printed').

Balked of a brilliant journalistic career by rows ('A long heritage of awkward incidents accounted for much of the furtiveness of Bagshaw's manner'), loss of jobs and wives (two or more before his last marriage in 1946), drink ('He must have carried in his head the names and addresses of at least two hundred London pubs . . .'), DTs etc. Squadron-Leader in RAF public relations in India during the second war. Edits *Fission* for Quiggin & Craggs immediately afterwards, appointing Jenkins as his third choice for literary editor. Widmerpool determined to winkle him out. Presides over the rise and fall of X. Trapnel; and moves into television (then a 'still mainly unexplored eldorado') on the liquidation of *Fission* at the end of 1947.

Greatly changed when next encountered a decade later: 'One was . . . increasingly aware that he was no longer Books-do-furnish-a-room Bagshaw of ancient days, but Lindsay Bagshaw, the Television "personality", no towering magnate of that order, but, if only a minor scion, fully conscious of inspired status'. House and large worrying family in Primrose Hill. Keen follower of the various stages in Widmerpool's political ruin.

Widower by 1971, dividing his time between his daughters and claiming to be a satisfied Lear. Makes a comeback in the TV series *After Strange Gods*, and has plans to film Murtlock's cult.

Craggs recalled 136–7; 172, 176–7; at home, proposes taking Gwinnett as lodger, his analysis of Widmerpool's impending scandal 180–8; his account of the Pamela Widmerpool affair 191–6; 199, 214, 219, 227, 247, 252. HSH 54, 104, 122, 130.

BAGSHAW, May
Lindsay's wife. In her forties by 1958, dreadfully harassed and rather lame, suffers from migraine. Has children by Bagshaw as well as three difficult daughters (Felicity, Avril and Stella) by a previous marriage.
BDFR 37, 141. TK 180, 182–4, 195.

BAGSHAW, sr.
Lindsay's father, never a notable success in insurance, lives with his son on retirement. Sole eye-witness of Pamela Widmerpool's appearance naked in the small hours on Bagshaw's landing ('What happened was that . . . he muttered an apology, and moved on; his comportment model of what every elderly gentleman might hope to display in similar circumstances') on the night she broke into the bedroom of Bagshaw's lodger, Russell Gwinnett.
TK 182, 191–5.

BALDWYN HODGES, Mrs
Managing director of the fashionable interior-decorating antique dealers, Baldwyn Hodges Ltd; 'a middle-aged, capable, leathery woman, of a type Mr Deacon would particularly have loathed'. Employs Hugo Tolland (generally supposed to be unemployable) on his coming down from Oxford in 1936.
CCR 200–1. KO 144–5, 197.

BARBER, Mary
Shares Jenkins' governess in 1914, her father killed in the first war.
KO 51, 74.

BARKER-SHAW
Field Security Officer at Divisional HQ in 1941, later in MI5, don in civil life.
SA 18, 59. MP 73.

BARNBY, Ralph
Painter and universally acknowledged expert on women, their theory and practice. Introduces Jenkins to Foppa's, the Mortimer, etc. and indirectly to Moreland; it is a first chance encounter with Barnby in the summer of 1928 or '9 which marks Jenkins's release from the 'eternity of

boredom' endured in more conventional circles since leaving Oxford.

B. *c.* 1902, third generation of professional artists (son of a fairly successful academic sculptor who was at the Slade with Edgar Deacon and died young; grandson of a book illustrator in the Tenniel tradition who was not unknown in the 1860s and '70s). An authority on Mr Deacon. Lives over his shop off the Tottenham Court Road before moving, as commissions increase, to a studio in Camden Town and later another near Fitzroy Square in Bloomsbury. Dark, thickset, short stubby hair. Dresses and paints like a Frenchman. An indefatigable lover of the masterful Casanovan (as opposed to Don Juanesque) type. Cuts out Moreland with the waitress Norma ('"Too thin for my taste," said Barnby. "I like a good armful"') at Casanova's Chinese Restaurant; and removes Baby Wentworth without hard feelings on either side from Sir Magnus Donners ('"Of course," Barnby said, "I realize that a poor man competing with a rich one for a woman should be in a relatively strong position if he plays his cards well"'). Affair with Lady Anne Stepney terminated on her marriage to Umfraville in 1933.

Reputation as a painter rising steadily from the end of the 'twenties: 'His own work diffused that rather deceptive air of emancipation that seemed in those years a kind of neo-classicism . . . an atmosphere I can still think of as excitingly peculiar to that time. . . . In some curious manner his pictures seemed to personify a substantial proportion of that wayward and melancholy, perhaps even rather spurious, content of the self-consciously disillusioned art of that epoch.'

Work seems to consist almost exclusively of portraits, generally of women, e.g. Norma, Baby Wentworth, Anne Stepney. Possesses both a naturalistic and a 'more severe', semi-abstract manner after the contemporary Parisian school. Considered daringly modern by the dons of Sillery's college. Patrons include Sir Magnus Donners (who commissioned the frescoes for the Donners-Brebner entrance hall, destroyed by a bomb in the blitz), Sir Herbert Manasch, St John Clarke, Mrs Andriadis, etc.

War artist, later transferring to RAF camouflage ('disguising aerodromes as Tudor cottages') shortly before his death in a plane shot down in June 1941. See also Painting Index.

BM On Deacon 8–9; 25, 87, 106–7; Deacon on 110, 113–4, 116; 146; his scientific approach to women 161–2; first encounter with, pursuing Baby Wentworth, his background, his work 164–74; 176, 189, 192, 202, 207; Mrs Wentworth on 214–5; on Deacon's death, their friendship 227, 229–35; 238, 242–3, 247; summoned by Mrs Wentworth, reflections on his role as link between the worlds of power and imagination 250–6; 268. AW 14, 16, as lover, on St John Clarke's conversion to modernism 23–9; 55, on portraying women, start of his affair with Anne Stepney recalled

68–74; 112, 136, 140, 144; at Foppa's with Anne, and at Mrs Andriadis' 148–50, 154, 156–8, 160, 163, 169; end of his affair with Anne 172; 176, 213. LM 32, 68, 181. CCR Compared and contrasted with Moreland 3–4, 7–12; his part in the pattern of Jenkins' life 15–16; evening at the Mortimer and conquest of Norma recalled 25–39; 46, 131, 135, 158, 210, 215. KO 76, 79, 109, 113, 243, 248. VB 13, 89, encounter with in RAF uniform, envy of 110–3; 123, 126, 183. SA His Donners-Brebner frescoes destroyed 5; his plane shot down 228. MP 113. BDFR 51, 53, 57, 100. TK 26–7, 70, 72, 104, 114, 121, 152, 172, 230, 259. HSH 206, 247.

BARRY
A slip-up of Frederica Budd's maid Audrey in the war, useful as spare man and escort for the infant Caroline Lovell.

VB 139, 146.

BASSET, Sergeant
Sound but slow, replaces Pendry as Jenkins' platoon-sergeant.

VB 211.

BELKIN, Dr
Widmerpool's 'cultural' contact in E. Europe, a shadowy figure known also to Ferrand-Sénéschal. Is denounced for Stalinist sympathies at the time of his country's anti-Stalinist coup in 1958; and fails to keep an appointment with Widmerpool in Venice (where he had for years passed himself off to the socialist-realist Tokenhouse as a politically sound art-lover, purchasing one of Tokenhouse's paintings and using his address as a convenient poste restante for undercover packages). His downfall (or possibly defection) responsible for Widmerpool's exposure the following year as a communist spy. Presumably one of the old Stalinist pals who blackmailed Widmerpool (and also Ferrand-Sénéschal) into supplying secret information.

TK 107–10, 112, 141, 145–7, 187–8, 211(?), 247(?), 262–3.

BERNHARD of the Netherlands, Prince b. 1911
The kind of minor royalty with whom Lt-Col Finn likes to hobnob.

MP 48.

BERTHE
The more talkative and less prepossessing of Mme Leroy's two nieces at La Grenadière during Jenkins' visit to France in 1923, 'a plump brunette . . . watching life through sly, greenish eyes set far apart in a face of fawn-coloured rubber'.

QU 113, 122, 3, 126, 137–8, 142, 148, 152, 159–60. BM 69.

BIGGS, Captain

Jenkins' morose and aggressive companion in F Mess at Divisional HQ in 1941; Sports Officer, Physical Training; sports organizer at a seaside resort in civil life:

'A captain with '14–'18 ribbons, bald as an egg, he had perhaps been good-looking in a heavy classical manner when younger; anyway, had himself so supposed. Now, with chronically flushed cheeks, he was putting on flesh, his large bulbous nose set between fierce frightened eyes and a small cupid's bow mouth that kept twitching open and shut like a rubber valve. Muscular over-development of chest, shoulder and buttock gave him the air of a strong man at a circus – a strong woman almost.'

Suffers from persecution mania, currently divorcing his wife, rags Captain Soper. Takes exception to Stringham as Mess Waiter ('Something wrong with that bloke . . . Man's potty. You can see it'), and helps to get him removed ('"Glad that bugger's gone," he said. "Got me down"'). Hangs himself a month later ('In the cricket pav, of all places, and him so fond of the game': Soper).

SA 4, 10–11, 19–20, 64–71, 76–8, 168–71, 176, 190, 226–8. MP 223.

BILL

Lesbian who asked herself to Louis Glober's party in they late 'twenties. TK 69, 71.

BILLSON, Doreen (?)

The Jenkinses' misanthropic parlourmaid ('"Just like a man," Billson used to say, in her simile for human nature at its lowest, most despicable') at Stonehurst in 1914. Nervous temperament, inclined to hysteria, has seen the Stonehurst ghost twice. Driven by unrequited love for Albert the cook to hand in her notice naked one afternoon in the drawing room ('There can be no doubt whatever that the scene was disturbing, terrifying, saddening, a moment that summarized, in the unclothed figure of Billson, human lack of co-ordination and abandonment of self-control in the face of emotional misery').

Taken in charge by General Conyers, and returned to her relatives in Suffolk a few weeks before the outbreak of the first war. May possibly be the elderly daily called Doreen employed at the end of the second war by Rosie Udall (née Manasch).

KO 3–6, 12–13, 15–20, 26, 28, 32–4, 42–4, 49–50, 52–3; her crisis 57–63, 71–2; 74, 133, 151–2, 199, 217. TK 196.

BISCHOFFSHEIM

Old Boy in Le Bas' house.

BDFR 233.

13

BITHEL, Lieutenant ('Bith')

Elderly (late thirties) Territorial lieutenant posted to the same Welsh regiment as Jenkins in 1940. Said to have played rugger for Wales and be brother to a VC:

'This officer had a large, round, pasty face and a ragged moustache, the tangled hairs of which glistened with beer. His thick lips were closed on the stub of a cigar . . . [he] had an extraordinary air of guilt which somehow suggested juvenility; a schoolboy wearing a false moustache . . . who only a few minutes before had done something perfectly disgusting, and was pretty sure that act was about to be detected by the headmaster with whom he had often been in trouble before.'

A cross between the Walrus and the Carpenter to look at, fearfully dilapidated uniform, astonishingly ill-fitting false teeth, face pitted and blotched like the surface of a Gruyère cheese. Confirmed alcoholic. Son of a possibly crooked provincial auctioneer; drifts from one odd job (preferably theatrical, front of house, walk on parts etc) to another in peace time; wangled a commission on the strength of the footballer and the VC, though in fact related to neither. Deeply respectful of Jenkins' literary leanings ('I was a great reader as a lad. One of those thoughtful little boys. Never kept it up as I should'). Former Scoutmaster ('I threw it up in the end. Some of them are little brutes, you know . . . I was surprised they knew about such matters. And their language among themselves. You wouldn't credit it'). Dotes on his batman Daniels.

Loathed by Captain Gwatkin who has him arrested for kissing an Other Rank. Transferred to Divisional HQ, on the enthusiastic recommendation of his CO, as commander of the Mobile Laundry Unit in which Stringham later serves as private. Miraculously escapes court-martial over a dud cheque in 1941. Discovered dead drunk, rescued by Stringham ('a' varsity man like yourself, Nick . . . got some fine boys in the Laundry . . . proud to command them'), and promptly ejected from the army with considerable relish by Widmerpool.

Turns up thirty years later as a filthy, grey-bearded, half-cracked follower of Scorpio Murtlock's cult. Worships Murtlock who saved him from destitution and imposed a monstrous penance on Widmerpool; his arrival marks the turning point of their power struggle in Murtlock's favour. Eyewitness of the events leading up to Widmerpool's death that autumn; accuses Murtlock of murder and swears never to return; sent back by Henderson to Murtlock.

VB 15–16, first encounter with, ragged by his fellow officers, his violently grotesque reaction and ghastly state next morning, confidences about his past 24–37, 41; Gwatkin's contempt for 49–50; his type and character elucidated, relations with Daniels 68–73; 79–80, 193–5; arrested by Gwatkin 198–206, 213–16; 224, Widmerpool looks forward

14

to meeting 243. SA His impending downfall at Div. HQ 7–18; 67; Stringham's rescue attempt foiled by Widmerpool 176–8; his disgrace visited on Stringham 190, 193, 219. BDFR 214. MP 223. TK 135. HSH 142, unidentified straggler on Widmerpool's ritual run 211–12; Widmerpool's account of his joining the cult and its consequences 215–22, 224; drinking 226, 233, Widmerpool blamed by Murtlock for his drunken state 238–9; Henderson on his role inside the cult 251, 258–61; his account of Widmerpool's death 263–71.

BLACKHEAD, Mr
Civil servant famed for his supremacy in the field of bureaucratic procrastination, obstruction and passive resistance ("'Blackhead is a man apart," said Pennistone. "Even his colleagues are aware of that. His minutes have the abstract quality of pure extension.'"). A notable handicap to the war effort. Working in some obscure capacity with the military authorities and virtually uncontrolled by his own superiors: 'It was as if Blackhead, relatively humble though his grading might be, had become an anonymous immanence of all their kind, a fetish, the Voodoo deity of the whole Civil Service to be venerated and placated, even if better – safer – hidden away out of sight: the mystic holy essence incarnate of arguing, encumbering delaying, hair-splitting, all for the best of reasons.'

Bearded in his lair under the leads by Jenkins; challenged and routed by Pennistone in the matter of Polish Women's Corps, soap issue for.

MP 32–3, 38–46, 56, 85, 140, 192, 218. BDFR 7.

BLAIDES
Family name of Lord Vowchurch.

BLAIDES, Hon Bertha see CONYERS

BLAIDES, Hon Mildred
Handsome and rackety youngest daughter of Lord Vowchurch (the last of her parents' many unsuccessful and eventually abandoned attempts to produce a male heir); sister to Bertha Conyers and distant cousin to Baby Wentworth. Aged about twenty in 1916. A decided figure of romance to Jenkins as a boy on account of her smoking thirty gaspers a day, her stories about Tommies getting tight and her habit of beetling off in glad rags to shows.

Red Cross nurse at Dogdene, then made over into a military hospital, and friend of its châtelaine, the young Lady Sleaford (later Lady Molly Jeavons). Turns out long afterwards to have been the unknown VAD who gave the glad eye to Ted Jeavons one night on a wartime leave, and spent the rest of it with him. M. 1) a Flying Corps officer called M'Cracken who was killed soon after the wedding. Thrills her slightly younger contemporary Frederica Tolland as a dashing war widow but is thought to be flighty and fast and 'about to go to the bad in a spectacular manner' by people like Jenkins' parents.

M. 2) an Australian businessman named Haycock who d. *c.* 1933, leaving her his money, his villa on the Riviera and two sons regularly expelled from school. Has 'slept with every old-timer between Cannes and St Tropez' (Chips Lovell); once seen about with Buster Foxe. In the neighbourhood of forty and looks no younger. Engaged to Widmerpool ('"I do not mind informing you that my lady mother thinks well of my choice," he said') by 1934, but breaks off the engagement after a disastrous night at Dogdene in which he fails to come up to scratch as a lover. Returns to the South of France.

LM At Mrs Conyers' flat in 1916, her daring 7–10; 23; produced nearly twenty years later as his fiancée by Widmerpool, her intervening career 39–49; Widmerpool's nervousness about, on the score of sex 54–62; 67; Jenkins cross-examined by her anxious relatives 70–4, 81–2, 85; 87; Molly Jeavons on the engagement 159–61; Miss Weedon on the same 165–7; Jeavons reveals his wartime encounter with 175–7, 179; with Widmerpool at Umfraville's night club, her reunion with Jeavons 184–93, 195–205; her engagement cancelled 215–17; General Conyers' explanation 227–34; and Widmerpool's 237–9. CCR 86, Widmerpool on 128; 194. KO Widmerpool sweats at memory of 223. MP 109, 231. TK 14, Baby Wentworth's resemblance to 114.

BLESSINGTON, Lady 1789–1849
Beauty and blue-stocking, the friend of Byron and Hercules Mallock.
VB 170.

BLUM, Léon 1872–1950
French socialist statesman, supported by both Erridge and Widmerpool in the 'thirties.
CCR 64, 128.

BOBETTY (Lord Salisbury) 1893–1972
Leader of the Conservative party in the House of Lords.
KO 91.

BOBROWSKI, Major-General
Humorous and highly excitable Polish military attaché; exiled at the end of the war and eventually run down by a taxi.
MP 17, 26–7, 29, 33, 64–5, 93, 103, 159–64, 181, 214. HSH 1, 19–20.

BOBS see, Field-Marshal Earl ROBERTS

BORDA
Kernéval's assistant.

MP 238–9.

BORRIT
Wartime colleague of Jenkins, looks after the Netherlands in Allied
Military Liaison, wholesale fruiterer in civil life. Melancholy middle-
aged widower, never had a free poke in his life. Deeply impressed by
Pamela Flitton. D. soon after the war on the point of marrying a widow
('I wondered whether on this final confrontation Borrit had brought off
the never realized "free poke", before the grave claimed him').

MP 30–4, 74, 109, 198–9, 223, 237. TK 151.

BRABAZON, Major-General Sir John Palmer ('Bwab') 1843–1922
Victorian dandy who 'said he couldn't remember what regiment he
had exchanged into – after leaving the Brigade of Guards because it was
too expensive – but "they wore green facings and you got to them by
Waterloo Station"'; source of Alfred Tolland's only story about Lord
Vowchurch and Edward VII.

LM 87–8.

BRACEY, Private
Captain Jenkins' soldier-servant ('He was a great favourite with my
father, who may have recognized in Bracey something of his own
uncalm, incurious nature'). 'A man of unparalleled smartness of
turnout', looks like a fox terrier and suffers from melancholia; his
'funny days' a source of alarm and despondency in the kitchen at
Stonehurst. Sweet on and spurned by the parlourmaid Billson. Killed
on the retreat from Mons in 1914.

KO 3–6, 10–28, 32–4, 37, 49, 61, 70, 72–4, 86, 151. 158. VB 67, 71, 193.

BRADDOCK alias THORNE
Bald, bespectacled, villainous-looking criminal wanted for fraud and
closely resembling Jenkins' housemaster Le Bas who is in fact mistaken
for him and arrested by the police, acting on a tip off from Stringham,
in the summer of 1922.

QU 35–7, 45, 70, 131, 224, 227. AW 185.

BRAGADIN, Jacky
Owner of the several Bragadin palaces in Venice, one of which
contains Tiepolo's *Candaules and Gyges* ceiling. Son of a Venetian who

m. a Macwatters of Philadelphia ('one of the big American fortunes of the last century'), and founder of the Bragadin cultural foundation.

In his fifties, small, nervous, fidgety, harassed. Host in 1958 to the horrific house party ('Jacky certainly can take it on the chin, Baby and Pamela Widmerpool under the same roof': Rosie Stephens) at which Glober hits Widmerpool on the jaw with a peach, Pamela is credited with murder, and Widmerpool with espionage. Weak heart and does not long survive this gathering.

TK 42–3, 60–3, 74–6, 78, 93, 107, 112–16, 150–2, 161–2, 167–8, 246, 255, 269. HSH 57, 246.

BRAGADIN, Matteo Giovanni d. 1767
Casanova's bachelor patron, ancestor ('though not, of course, in the legitimate line') of above.

TK 42.

BRANDRETH, Dr
Fashionable physician in the 'thirties, son of a medical baronet, takes charge when Le Bas passes out at a house reunion dinner. St John Clarke's medical man. Treats Widmerpool for boils. Recommended by Members ('a typical piece of malice on his part') to Moreland, who sacks him after the second war. Gossip the passion of his life; puts Moreland on the rack about music; famous composers' ailments his speciality ('Wagner, a chronic sufferer, I understand, from some form of dermatitis, though he finally succumbed, I believe, to a cardiac lesion – unlike Schubert with his abdominal trouble . . .').

AW 176, 195, 197, 201, 203. CCR 98–105, 124–5, 198. KO 134–5. BDFR 120.

BRAYBROOK, Dolly
Dicky Umfraville's first wife, an absolute stunner, daughter of a former commander of his regiment known as Bloody Braybrook. Married just after the first war and was happy as the day is long for a year or so till she fell in love with Buster Foxe, and poisoned herself when he married Amy Stringham instead. Cause of Umfraville's lifelong feud with Buster.

AW 158. VB 145, 152–4.

BREEN, Jo
Jockey ('the chap who was suspended one year at Cheltenham for pulling Middlemarch') who ran away with Umfraville's second wife, and afterwards kept a pub with her in the Thames valley.

VB 155.

BREEZE, Lieutenant Evan (Yanto)
Platoon commander in Captain Gwatkin's company in 1940. Newly married, nearly twenty-five, an accountant in civil life; tall, shambling, 'looks like an old hen in uniform'; an able officer, liked by his men.

Teases Gwatkin who hates him on account of his sister Gwenllian as well as for slackness and mockery. Unjustly blamed by Gwatkin for Sergeant Pendry's death and applies for transfer to an anti-tank company; promoted captain in traffic control on the day of Gwatkin's military downfall.

VB 16–19, 24–7, 29, 40, 45–6, 49, 51, 68, 73–8, 80, 82, 93, 98–101, 191, 220. SA 30.

BREEZE, Gwenllian
Yanto's older sister. Gwatkin was 'once so stuck on Gwenllian Breeze you would have thought he had the measles', but she wouldn't look at him and married a college professor from Swansea instead.

VB 17–18, 191.

BRENT, Jimmy
Unprepossessing City friend of Peter Templer's, first encountered with Bob Duport on a visit to the university in 1924 ('They accepted some of Stringham's sherry, and Brent, whose manners seemed on the whole better than Duport's, said: "What do they rush you for this poison?"') Several years older than Jenkins. Fat, bespectacled, almost falsetto voice. Talks incessantly of women and insists on picking up two girls on a disastrous jaunt in Templer's Vauxhall which ends up in a ditch.

Only less of a lout than Jimmy Stripling, according to Duport. Turns out long afterwards to have been Jean Duport's lover at the time of her affair with Jenkins ('Even in retrospect this was a frightful piece of information'). Would have preferred to settle for the little coloured cigarette seller at the Old Plantation night-club ('more in my line, though it cost me a small fortune to get her'), if Jean had not pursued him, ditching Jenkins for his sake. Travels out on business to South America with the Duports in 1933 but can't quite see his way to obliging Jean by running away with her. Bob Duport his ideal of manhood. Returns to England with a commission on the outbreak of war and confides the story of his affair with Jean to Jenkins, recalling Moreland's theories on the attraction exercised over women by men to whom they can safely feel superior ('Remember Bottom and Titania. The Bard knew.')

Grown fatter than ever by 1946, has fixed up Bob in oil and is about to marry a widow with two grown-up sons.

QU At Oxford, precipitates Templer's car accident 191–200. BM 141.

AW 42. KO 164–5, Duport's graphic account of his affair with Jean, mortifying reflections on 177–9, 181. VB On Aldershot training course 118–20, his own account of his affair with Jean 122–34; 169. BDFR Jean on 99.

BRIAN
Red-faced, loud-mouthed army friend of Odo Stevens.

SA 149–51.

BRIDGNORTH, Countess of (Mary)
Mother of John Mountfitchet, Peggy and Anne Stepney. Daughter of a Scottish duke dimly connected to the Walpole-Wilsons. St John's Ambulance Brigade in first war; bitter foe to members of the Red Cross faction such as Molly Sleaford (later Lady Molly Jeavons); afterwards engages in terrible wars on the hospital front with Stringham's mother Mrs Foxe. Shares her husband's resigned attitude to their daughters.

QU 227–8. BM 44, 212, 222, 224–6. AW 72, 149–50, 187, 199. LM 8. CCR 88. MP 113.

BRIDGNORTH, Major the Earl of, late the Royal Horse Guards (Eddie) Family name Stepney
Distantly related to the Tollands; house in Grosvenor Square*; country seat Mountfichet. 'A stout red-faced man . . . notable for having owned a horse that won the Derby at a hundred to seven' (probably Yellow Jack on which Dicky Umfraville made a packet). 'His is a name to conjure with on the Turf. When I was married to his elder daughter, the beautiful Peggy, I was often to be seen conjuring with it on the course at Epsom and elsewhere, but with little success' (Charles Stringham).

Not specially cheerful at Peggy's wedding to Stringham, who thinks him the most conceited pompous man in the world; philosophical about his younger daughter Anne's defection to socialism and loose morals; consoled by Peggy's divorce; makes the best of Anne's subsequent marriage to his old racing chum Umfraville.

His butler once offered macaroni cheese to the Duke of Connaught without giving him a plate to put it on.

QU 227–8. BM 44, 212, 222, 224–6. AW 72, 149–52, 163, 187, 199. LM 165, 182–3. CCR 176–7. KO 234. SA 76. MP 113.

BRIGHTMAN, Dr Emily
Formidably coy lady don noted for her ability to reduce her pupils to

* And/or Cavendish square, see QU 228, BM 224.

tears and her distinguished work on the Triads. First encountered at the
international writers' conference in Venice in 1958: 'She briskly shook
the crop of short white curls cut close to her head. They looked like a
battery of coiled wire (like the Dark Lady's) galvanising an immensely
powerful dynamo'. Old friend of Russell Gwinnett. Lectures on
Tiepolo's painting of Candaules and Gyges, and bores its owner to
distraction. Takes a fancy (apparently not reciprocated) to 'that
charming little Ada Leintwardine'; and another to Pamela Widmerpool
('in spite of her naughtiness').

Later pub. a controversial study of Boethius; created DBE 1966; on
Magnus Donners prize committee 1968.

TK First impressions of 4–5, relations with Gwinnett 18–20, 41–51; at
Bragadin palace 75–82, lectures on Tiepolo 85–90, 92, 97–8, 100,
112–13, 115–16, 132, 138, 148, 156, 174–5, 177–8, 196; at Soviet
embassy luncheon 214–9; 277. HSH On prize committee 56–9, 65–70,
72–5, 87; at prize-giving 93, 98–100, 102, 105–6, 112–13; 181.

BRIGHTMAN, Harold
History don unsympathetic to Sillery, who loses no opportunity of
running down his lectures, tutorial abilities, unfulfilled early promise
etc. At Quiggin's college. Helps organize Sillery's nineteenth birthday
party in the late 'fifties. Some sort of cousin to Dr Emily.

QU 170, 179, 201, 208–12. BM 239. AW 112. CCR 200. BDFR 9, 27.
TK 5.

BRIGHTMAN, Revd. Salathiel
Augustan ancestor of Emily, Harold and scores of other learned
Brightmans; expert on weights and measures (said to have
revolutionized contemporary thinking on the cochlearion and
oxybaphon); immortalized by Pope in the *Dunciad*.

TK 5.

BROUGHAM, Lord 1778–1868
Defended Queen Caroline at her trial; and was shrewdly put down by
the 4th Lord Erridge.

LM 149.

BROWNRIGG, Lt-General Sir Douglas b. 1886
Member of the Army Council in 1939, but fails to bring off anything
in the way of a job for Jenkins' father.

KO 207.

BRUMMEL, George Bryan ('Beau') 1778–1840
Regency leader of fashion. Widmerpool's hopes of becoming the, of

the new reign, blasted by Edward VIII's abdication. Paid the first Earl of Warminster the compliment of asking who made his driving-coat.

CCR 195. BDFR 44.

BRUYLANT
Musical Belgian, replaces Kucherman as military attaché.

MP 215, 218.

BUDD
Captain of the Eleven at school, not above criticism at cricket but film star teeth and noble brow, scores a bull's eye on Widmerpool with a ripe banana.

QU 11–12, 14. BM 34, 72–3. SA 56.

BUDD, Colonel
Uncle of above, father of Margaret; holds a minor appointment at Court; house in Sussex Square. The elderly gentleman with an eyeglass and medals at Mrs Andriadis' party; quite unchanged when next encountered nearly twenty years later shepherding the royal party at the Victory Day service in St Paul's ('White-moustached, spruce, very upright, he glanced about him with an air of total informality, as if prepared for any eventuality from assassination to imperfect acoustics').

BM 18, 100, 109–12, 114, 121. LM 5. MP 221.

BUDD, Lady Frederica (née Tolland)
Lord Warminster's eldest daughter, named after the Empress Frederick of Prussia. Scorned for her dreadful correctness by Molly Jeavons. M. 1) Robin Budd by whom she had two sons, Edward and Christopher. A somewhat forbidding widow by 1934: 'She was dressed in a manner to be described as impregnable, like a long, neat, up-to-date battle-cruiser. You felt that her clothes were certainly removed when she retired for the night, but that no intermediate adjustment, however minor, was ever required, or would, indeed, be practicable'.

Lady-in-Waiting at court (or possibly Extra Woman of the Bedchamber); a great crony of Mrs Conyers. Disapproves of Erridge's activities, associates and shocking neglect of Thrubworth Park, but is in point of obstinacy the closest to him of all the Tollands. On cordial terms with her brother George, squabbles at sight with her sister Norah, comes increasingly to feel herself the custodian of her family's social and moral standards.

Moves just before the second war to a country vicarage ('The place had that same air of intense respectability Frederica's own personality conveyed') near Thrubworth. Rapidly overrun by evacuees, including her sisters Priscilla Lovell and Isobel Jenkins; not far from forty; said to have turned down a proposal from the elderly widower Jock Udney. Transformed by her engagement to Dicky Umfraville ('Do you realize she'll be my fifth? Something wrong with a man who keeps marrying like that. Must be. But I really couldn't resist Frederica. That prim look of hers') who swears to turn over a new leaf, and does so under Frederica's management.

LM 30–1, at the Conyerses', her rigid self-control analysed, her unconcealed disapproval of Norah's ménage with Eleanor Walpole-Wilson 75–97; 115, 117, 135–6, 211. CCR 60, 66, 135–6, 153, her mutual understanding with Erridge 198; visit to, on St John Clarke and Erridge 221–8. KO 88, moves to the country, Isobel staying with 204, 213, 224, 239. VB 110, weekend leave spent with, her guests, her inexplicable excitement, produces Umfraville as her fiancé 134–47, Umfraville on 149, 151 & 156, 158–63, 167, 169. SA 107–8, 126, 148. BDFR Erridge's executor 38–9; at the funeral, coping with Widmerpool and assorted hangers-on 60–3, 67, 72, 78–80, 89–90, 172. TK Never tired of Umfraville 3. HSH With him at Cutts' wedding 189–90, wartime encounter with recalled by Flavia Wisebite 201–2.

BUDD, Margaret
A beauty, cousin to the cricketer, already in her third or fourth season and showing no signs of getting engaged by the time of the Huntercombes' ball in 1928 or 9:
'She was, as it were, the female equivalent of Archie Gilbert: present at every dance, always lovely, always fresh, and yet somehow quite unreal. She scarcely spoke at all, and might have been one of those huge dolls which, when inclined backwards, say "Ma-ma" or "Pa-pa": though impossible to imagine in any position so undignified as that required for the mechanism to produce these syllables: equally hard to conceive her dishevelled, or bad-tempered, or, indeed, capable of physical passion – though appearances may be deceptive in no sphere so much as the last.

M. 1) an elderly ill-tempered hypochondriacal Scottish landowner in the whisky trade by whom she has at least two children by 1932; and 2) the Pole Horaczko in 1945.

BM 33–5, 39, 41–2, 54, 110. AW 34–5. LM 30. MP 244.

BUDD, Robin
Frederica Tolland's first husband, brother or cousin of Margaret, d. in a hunting accident at the end of the 'twenties; looked a little like his contemporary, Frederica's second husband, Dicky Umfraville.

LM 30. VB 136, 145.

BUM
Mme Leroy's wire-haired terrier at La Grenadière, on poor terms with his colleague Charley

QU 121–2, 150–1, 164.

BURDEN, Mr and Mrs
Couple running the Templers' house at Maidenhead when Mona leaves Peter for Quiggin.

AW 40, 139.

BURGESS, Guy 1911–63
Foreign Office employee who defected with Donald Maclean to Moscow in the 'fifties, thought by some to have been acting on a tip-off from Widmerpool.

TK 39.

BUSHMAN, Francis X. 1883–1966
Silent movie star christened Francis Xavier like X. Trapnel ('Watching an old western starring Francis X. Bushman in a cowboy part, it struck me we'd both been called after the same saint, and, if he could suppress the second name, I could the first').

BDFR 110

CABALLERO, F. L. 1869–1946
Spanish left-wing politician who headed a coalition government 1936–7.

CCR 95.

CAGLIOSTRO, Count 1743–95
Venetian charlatan, not essentially different from Dr Trelawney.

KO 85, 197.

CADWALLADER, CSM
Captain Gwatkin's efficient and dependable company-sergeant major in 1940: 'Cleanshaven, with the severely puritanical countenance of an Ironside in a Victorian illustration to a Cavalier-and-Roundhead romance, CSM Cadwallader was not as old as he looked, nor for that matter . . . nearly so puritanical . . . Like the rest of the "other ranks" of the Battalion, he was a minor. His smooth skull, entirely hairless, was streaked with an intricate pattern of blue veins, where coal dust of accumulated years beneath the ground had found its way under the skin, spreading into a design that resembled an astrological nativity – his

own perhaps – cast in tattoo over the ochre-coloured surface of the cranium.

VB 1, 3–6, 8–10, 43–5, 52, 62, 64–7, 77, 99, 101, 112, 172, 174–5, 177–8, 195–6, 210, 224, 231–2, 235–6.

CALTHORPE
The 'young friend' visited in his room at school by Pamela Widmerpool after the second war. Son or nephew to one of below.

BDFR 238.

CALTHORPE, Major and Minor.
Boys at school with Jenkins in 1922, their parents the first to be informed about the affair of Braddock alias Thorne ('"I sat straight down and wrote off a letter to my people about Le Bas having been removed to prison at last," Calthorpe Major was saying. "They never liked him"').

QU 48–9. BDFR 238.

CALVERLEY, Charles Stuart 1831–84.
Poet and parodist, a relation of Parkinson.

QU 222.

CAMPBELL, Mrs Patrick 1865–1940
Actress, a passionate memory of Alfred Tolland's youth.
LM 37–8.

CAMPBELL-BANNERMAN, Sir Henry 1836–1908
Liberal Prime Minister; Chips Lovell's first Sleaford Uncle held office under.

LM 17.

CAROLO
Violinist; pale and drawn with romantic raven locks and an air of slighted genius; somewhat older than Moreland whose first musical memory is of hearing him play at the Wigmore Hall as an ageing infant prodigy bursting out of his lace-collared black velvet suit. Comes from the North Midlands. Real name Wilson or Wilkinson or Parker. Only interested in making money ('Daydreams of wealth or women must have given Carolo that faraway look which never left him; sad and silent, he contemplated huge bank balances and voluptuous revels').

Turns out to have been Matilda Wilson's first husband; was already having trouble with her when first encountered at the Mortimer in

1928 or 9; divorced shortly afterwards. Fallen on hard times by 1936. Lodges with the Maclinticks and runs away with Audrey Maclintick a few days before her husband's suicide. Leaves her for a repertory actress on the outbreak of war.

Last encountered as stand-in violin at the Stevens' Mozart party in 1959; his hair now snow white and long as Liszt's, to whom he bears some slight resemblance.

CCR 4, first encounter with, his past history 14–15, 20, 24–5; 32; lodging with the Maclinticks 111–16, 118–19, 121–3; at Mrs Foxe's party 142, 151, Matilda on their marriage 156–9, 186–7; absconds with Mrs Maclintick 203–4, 206–7, 210–11, 214, 217. KO 78–9. SA 118–19. TK At the Stevens' party 238–41, 249. HSH 64.

CASANOVA, Giacomo de Seingalt 1725–1803.
Professional seducer not unlike Barnby in Moreland's estimation ('If you hope to rise to the top class in seducing, you must appeal to the majority') but very different from Don Juan. Played the violin in early life like Carolo. His *Memoirs* full of endless good things in Moreland's view. See also Place Index under CASANOVA'S CHINESE RESTAURANT.

CCR 28–9, 32–5, 210–11. TK 42, 90, 178. HSH 84.

CASTLEMAINE, Countess of 1641–1709
Charles II's mistress, pursued by Chips Lovell's ancestor Lord Sleaford.
LM 11.

CASLTEMALLOCK, fourth or fifth Marquess of Family name Mallock.
The fellow who removed Umfraville's second wife Joy Grant in Kenya, twice her age and 'looked like an ostler suffering from a dose of clap'; when he turned out to be impotent as well, she left him for a jockey. Distant connection of the Ardglasses, and descendant of the Lord Chief Justice of Ireland who built Castlemallock in N. Ireland where Jenkins' company is stationed during the second war.

VB 155, 170–1.

CATTLE
Disobliging porter in Le Bas' house at school.
QU 24–5.

CAVENDISH
Guest at the Huntercombes' ball.
BM 57.

CHAMBERLAIN, Neville 1869–1940
Tory Prime Minister 1937–40.
KO 114, 123.

CHANDLER, Norman
'An actor. Also dances a bit. Rather a hand at the saxophone'
(Moreland). The last of Mr Deacon's *petites folies*, first encountered at
the Mortimer a week before Deacon's fatal accident in 1928 or 9: 'Sad-
eyed and pert, he was an urchin with good looks of that curiously
puppet-like formation which designates certain individual as actors or
dancers; anonymity of feature and flexibility of body fitting them from
birth to play an assumed part'. Met Deacon perfectly respectably
through his mother ('A most agreeable, sensible woman I found her,
quite devoted to her boy') after a vegetarian communal holiday.
Chorus-boy drawl, 'half Cockney, half drawing-room comedy';
trained to dance in panto but already looking to higher things than
Drury Lane.
    Makes a name for himself in the next few years as an actor
specializing in unusual small parts; meets Matilda Wilson at a lesbian
party given by Heather Hopkins and helps her get theatrical work;
plays Bosola to her Julia in *The Duchess of Malfi* in 1934. Pure Picasso,
according to Moreland ('one of those attenuated, androgynous
mountebanks of the Blue Period, who haven't had a meal for weeks').
Picked up at a charity performance by Stringham's mother, Mrs Foxe
('Of course by the nature of things he can only be a son to her':
Stringham), and takes over her household, doing the flowers, mixing
drinks, rearranging the furniture, choosing her hats and library books,
even making her read one of Jenkins' novels ('"I liked it very much."
She looked a bit pathetic when she said that, making me feel in this
respect perhaps Chandler had gone too far in his exercise of power').
Buster Foxe and Stringham both devoted to him.
    Enlists on the outbreak of war. Encamped in Essex where Mrs Foxe
takes a workman's cottage to be near him and proposes divorcing
Buster. Commissioned by 1941 ('Won't he look wonderful in a Sam
Browne belt – that waist': Stringham).
    Old friend of Moreland with whom he shares a passion for
mechanical pianos; also of Max Pilgrim and the music critic Gossage.
Flat in Ted Jeavons' house after the war. Takes to directing at the end
of his career (including Polly Duport in Strindberg). Last encountered
at the centenary show of Bosworth Deacon's paintings in 1971:
'Goodness, don't these bring Edgar back?'
    CCR With Deacon in the Mortimer 13–14, 21–3, 34; in *Duchess of
Malfi*, pursued by Mrs Foxe 40, 44–5, 48–54; relationship with Mrs

27

Foxe 88, 90–1; friendship with Matilda 132–3; at Mrs Foxe's party, Buster's admiration for 141–8, and Stringham's 164–5, with Mrs Foxe 170–2, 187–8. VB In the army 165–6. SA Stringham on 79; 113–14. TK At the Stevens' musical party 226, 237–40, 247–8. HSH 59–60, 64–5, at the Deacon exhibition 252–7.

CHARLEY
Dog at the Leroys', 'so named on account of the really astonishing presumption that he looked like an English dog; whereas his unnaturally long brown body, short black legs, and white curly tail, made it almost questionable whether he was indeed a dog at all, and not a survival of a low, and now forgotten, form of prehistoric life'.

QU 121–2, 150–1.

CHEESMAN, Lieutenant
Officer in charge of the Mobile Laundry Unit in which Stringham serves as private, posted to Far East and captured after the fall of Singapore. The ma who wore a waistcoat under his service-dress tunic. Accountant in civil life. Turns up at a military reunion dinner in 1959 and gives a noncommittal account of being a Japanese prisoner of war ('for a brief second, something much shorter than that, something scarcely measurable in time, there shot, like forked lightning, across his serious unornamental features that awful look, common to those who speak of that experience. I had seen it before. Cheesman's face reverted – the word suggests too extended a duration of instantaneous, petrifying exposure of hidden feeling – to a habitual sedateness'), and of Stringham's death in the camp.

SA 215–19, 223–5. MP 222. TK 204–10.

CHIANG KAI-SHEK, Generalissimo 1887–1975
Leader of the Kuomintang, Colonel Chu d. fighting under him at Mukden.

MP 155.

CHU, Colonel
Chinese military attaché in wartime, exacting, unpopular and vain; enjoys his attachment as cadet at Sandhurst so much that he demands to go to Eton ('I told him thirty-eight is regarded as too mature in this country to be still at school. It was no good. All he said was "I can make myself young"'; Finn). Returns to China and d. in battle commanding a Nationalist division.

MP 55, 155, 178, 181.

CHUCK
Barnabas Henderson's burly cockney boyfriend, ditched when
Henderson joined Murtlock's cult. Driver in Clare Akworth's
advertising agency. Reunited with Henderson at her wedding and
twice rescues him from Murtlock.

HSH 212, 219, 232–7, 250–9, 262.

CHURCHILL, Winston 1874–1965.
Prime Minister 1940–5. Sir Magnus Donners has the ear of; comes into
contact with Widmerpool at the Cabinet Offices.

KO 91. VB 179, 239. SA 4, 191. MP 20, 51, 62, 189, 193, 195.

CIGS see ALANBROOKE and SLIM

CLANWAERT
Amusing fellow living in Jenkins' block of flats in wartime, works for
the Belgian military attaché, former Elephant Officer in the Congo.
Huge moustache and nose like Cyrano de Bergerac's.

MP 90, 94–6, 122–3, 129, 138, 158.

CLAPHAM
St John Clarke's publisher in the 'thirties, doesn't mind admitting he
was moved to tears by *Fields of Amaranth*. Neighbour of Widmerpool
after the war and chairman of the firm which takes over Quiggin &
Craggs; dead by 1958; succeeded by Quiggin.

AW 109–11. BDFR 115, 155, 174, 207, 238. TK 135

CLAPHAM, Evadne
Lesbian novelist, niece of above, boasts of a 'success' with Ada
Leintwardine (' "Evadne Clapham's coiffure always reminds me of that
line of Arthur Symons, 'And is it seaweed in your hair?'" said Ada').
Short story in *Fission*'s first number. Snubbed by X. Trapnel in the
Hero of Acre. Changes her style in favour of copying Ada's after *Golden
Grime* (1947) but reverts to her earlier manner for her thirty-fifth novel,
Cain's Jawbone, with which she makes something of a comeback at the
end of the 'sixties.

BDFR 115–16, 127–8, 138, 145, 147, 149, 151, 186, 194, 239. TK 17,
31, 34, 92, 214. HSH 95, 101, 114.

CLARINI, Signor
Baby Wentworth's second (subsequently estranged) husband, the
celebrated Italian film director who makes a film in the 'fifties with
Polly Duport.

AW 25, 58. LM 199. TK 104, 113, 151, 268.

29

CLARINI, Signora see WENTWORTH, Baby

CLARKE, E. St John
Prolific and popular Edwardian novelist, slightly younger than Wells
and Barrie, his fame at its height before the first war. Has hopes (not
entirely unfounded) of the Nobel Prize. Reputation in eclipse by the
late 'twenties, briefly revived by a timely leftwing conversion, slumped
again by 1936:
'Something about St John Clarke put him in the category – of which
Widmerpool was another example – of persons at once absurd and
threatening. St John Clarke's head recalled Blake's, a resemblance no
doubt deliberately cultivated, because the folds and crannies of his face
insistently suggested a self-applauding interior activity, a desire to let
everyone know about his own "mental strife" . . .'
Humble origins, champion snob, bitterly envious of the public
honours showered on his boyhood friend Isbister. Indifferent to all
women save literary hostesses ('"I don't think St John Clarke is
interested in either sex," said Barnby. "He fell in love with himself at
first sight and it is a passion to which he has always remained faithful."')
Rich and notoriously mean with money. Strong taste for public
controversy (campaigned against the Post-Impressionist show in 1910,
for the erection of Peter Pan on the Serpentine, against Rima in the
bird sanctuary; joins issue in *The Times* over the Haig war memorial in
1929).
Employs a series of young men on the make as secretaries ('You
know, what St J. really wants is a son. He wants to be a father without
having a wife': Members), including in quick succession: Mark
Members who introduces him to modernism, whereupon he buys a
painting from Barnby and makes favourable mention in a New York
paper of Jenkins' first novel; J. G. Quiggin who converts him to
communism, whereupon he takes part in the Hunger Marchers'
demonstration in Hyde Park, yelling slogans from a wheel-chair and
subsequently joining 'that group of authors, dons and clergymen
increasingly to be found at that period on political platforms of a
"Leftish" sort'; and Werner Guggenbühl who reconciles Members and
Quiggin in mutual disgust by converting him to Trotskyism.
Abandoned by all three in his last years ('"The man has got it in him
to be a traitor to any cause", Quiggin said'), dropped by the intellectual
left, 'forgotten by the critics but remembered fairly faithfully by the
circulating libraries'. D. 1937, and commended chiefly for 'his deep
love for the Peter Pan statue in Kensington Gardens and his
contributions to Queen Mary's Gift Book.' Leaves his money
(£16–17,000) to Erridge whose friendship, both as peer and as political

mentor, had consoled him at the end: 'If St John Clarke had been often provoked by Members and Quiggin during his life, the last laugh had to some extent fallen to St John Clarke after his death'.

Author of *Fields of Amaranth* (enjoyed in its day by Lady Warminster, made its publisher Clapham weep), *Match Me Such Marvel* (Bithel's favourite, homosexual undercurrent according to Ada Leintwardine), *Dust Thou Art* ('rather a recondite one about the French Revolution', admired by Lady Anne Stepney), *The Heart is Highland, Never to the Philistines, E'en the Longest River, Mimosa* etc. Also of an introduction to *The Art of Horace Isbister*, rashly undertaken for Jenkins' firm before its author came under the influence of Members, re-cast under Quiggin as an essay on artistic decadence in a capitalist society, and eventually published as a pamphlet on Socialist Realism in painting ('not without merit' according to Daniel Tokenhouse).

Mona Templer, Mrs George Tolland and Mrs Conyers among his many fans. Represents literature itself to Widmerpool. Isobel Jenkins and X. Trapnel both expert on the more obscure aspects of his novels; his work tirelessly plugged by Ada Leintwardine throughout the 'sixties ('St John Clarke is no back number. His style may seem a little old-fashioned today, but there is nothing old-fashioned about his thought. He is full of compassion . . .'). Subject of a TV rehabilitation in 1968, largely devoted to Members, Quiggin and Gainsborough (formerly Guggenbühl) quarrelling about his possibly homosexual relationship with Isbister.

For further discussion of his style and fluctuating reputation, see Book Index.

BM 39, 46, employs Members as secretary, his literary standing 243–5; AW Trouble over his introduction to Isbister book, his career, Jenkins' former weakness for 16, 18–23; his conversion to modernism 25–9; further delay over Isbister introduction 30, 33, 36, 39–40; sacks Members for Quiggin, his Marxist conversion 48–50, 52–3; Mona Templer and Jean Duport on 61; 70, Quiggin at loggerheads with Members over 74–7, 80, 98–101; Clapham on 110–11; 113, Quiggin on, Members' bitterness towards, takes part in Hyde Park demonstration 115–27, 129–32, 139; meets Guggenbühl 165, 167–8; sacked Quiggin for Guggenbühl 173–4; 183, 214. LM 80, Erridge a tougher proposition than 116; introduced Quiggin to Erridge, abandoned by Guggenbühl 124–5; 214, 221. CCR Lunches with Lady Warminster 64, 68, his political backsliding, his character, his literary and political standing, relations with Erridge 72–5, 77–86, 91–6; 102, 105, 118; his death, obituaries 190–3, 196; 216; Erridge his heir 222–9. KO *Never to the Philistines* at Stonehurst 60, 203. SA Bithel on 13. MP *Fields of Amaranth* 94. BDFR *Dust Thou Art* 4; 17, his meanness possibly not proof against

31

Trapnel 152–4; 174; has a word for Pamela Widmerpool 192; 235. TK 3, 9, 55, his haggling over Isbister introduction recalled 65–6, 68; Glober persuaded to film *Match Me Such Marvel* 134–6, 149, 220, 229, 234–6; film abandoned 268. HSH TV documentary on 36–40, 47, 52.

CLAUSEWITZ, Karl von 1780–1831
Prussian general and military writer, an able fellow according to Jenkins' father.
KO 54.

CLAY
Undergraduate son of a consul in the Levant through whom Sillery succeeds in making trouble for Brightman.
QU 169–70.

CLEMENTS, Private
Member of Jenkins' platoon in 1940.
VB 97.

CLINTON, Mrs Arthur
One of the few hostesses prepared to countenance Widmerpool at a dance in the 'twenties.
BM 77.

CLIPTHORPE, Tim
Solicitor struck off the roll the year the *Titanic* went down, habitué of the Hero of Acre and Trapnel's legal adviser after the second war.
BDFR 158.

COBB, Colonel
American assistant military attaché, gifted raconteur and stern disciplinarian, known throughout the US army as 'Courthouse Cobb'. Takes part in the trip to inspect allied lines in 1944, and accidentally draws Jenkins' attention to the fact that the party's first stopping place was Cabourg, Proust's Balbec.
MP 70–2, 166–8, 218. TK 113.

COBBERTON, Rev.
Housemaster at school, old enemy of Le Bas, instrumental in releasing him from police custody in the affair of Braddock alias Thorne. Hastens Templer's removal by reporting him for smoking.
QU 50, 71. BDFR 232.

COCKSIDGE, Captain Jack
Intelligence officer at Divisional HQ in 1941, carries obsequiousness to extreme and imaginative lengths, rising at dawn to warm the General's butter ration etc: 'the mind of Cocksidge was perpetually afire with fresh projects for the self-abasement before the powerful'.

SA 28, 35–8, 41–2, 171–2, 193–4. MP 143.

COLLINS, Angus
George Tolland's stepson, becomes a journalist in industrial relations.

CCR 72, 75. HSH 192, 194.

COLLINS, Fred
Veronica Tolland's alcoholic first husband, father of Angus and Iris; a businessman in Lagos, divorced ('"Native women," said Chips Lovell, "also some trouble about a cheque"') by the early 'thirties.

CCR 72, 76, 131. TK 200. HSH 192.

COLLINS, Iris
Daughter of above, m. one of the Vowchurches

CCR 72, 75. HSH 192, 194.

COLLINS José (Lady Robert Innes Ker) 1887–1958
Musical comedy star, married into the aristocracy like Ted Jeavons and was appearing in *The Maid of the Mountains* at Daly's Theatre in 1917 on the night he got the glad eye from the Hon. Mildred Blaides.

LM 176.

COMBERMERE, First Viscount 1773–1865
One of Wellington's generals but not such a damned fool as the fourth Lord Erridge.

LM 149.

CONCHITA
Model used by Barnby and Augustus John, described by Moreland as 'antithesis of the pavement artist's traditional representation of a loaf of bread, captioned *Easy to Draw but Hard to Get*'.

TK 70. HSH 206.

CONNAUGHT, Duke of 1850–1942.
Third son of Queen Victoria; Lord Bridgnorth's complexion, richly tinted at the best of times, resembled Dutch bulb fields in bloom when his butler offered macaroni cheese to HRH without a plate to eat it off.

SA 76.

CONYERS, General Aylmer

First-rate soldier, family friend of Jenkins' grandparents and a distant cousin on Jenkins' mother's side. Tall, inquisitive, very bright blue eyes; famous for the variety of his interests, the antiquity of his links with the past ('he was . . . one of the last to my knowledge to speak of the Household Cavalry as "the Plungers"'), and his determination to keep abreast of modern thought. Little short of an octogenarian by 1934: 'he was a man who gave the impression, rightly or wrongly, that he would stop at nothing. If he decided to kill you, he would kill you; if he thought it sufficient to knock you down, he would knock you down: if a mere reprimand was all required, he would confine himself to a reprimand'.

Served in Afghanistan and Burma as a subaltern, also in the Sudan, India and South Africa ('Went in for jobs abroad. Supposed to have saved the life of some native ruler in a local rumpus. Armed the palace eunuchs with rook rifles. Fellow gave him a jewelled scimitar – semi-precious stones, of course': Uncle Giles). Took part in French's cavalry charge across the Modder river, and was a notable success at the capture of Pretoria ('Just a bit of luck things turned out as they did for him – due mostly to Boer stupidity, I believe': Captain Jenkins). Rather a gay spark in his youth and always a notorious womaniser. Rose to Brigadier-General and was expected to go much higher when he m. at nearly fifty the Hon. Bertha Blaides, and sent in his papers eighteen months later. One daughter Charlotte. Had long predicted a German war, and perhaps got tired of waiting for it.

Gentleman-at-Arms in the Body Guard on retirement, plays the 'cello and trains poodles as gun dogs. Flat in Sloane Square and small house in Hampshire. Owns a motor car by 1914 and is rumoured to have been up in a flying machine. Occult interests. Old acquaintance of Dr Trelawney. Takes charge of the parlourmaid Billson on the afternoon of her appearance naked in the Jenkinses' drawing room, and foresees trouble on hearing of the assassinations at Sarajevo ('"Mark my words," said General Conyers, "this is a disaster"'). Minor job, 'respectably graded in the rank of major-general', in first war.

Takes up psychoanalysis in the early 'thirties. An interested spectator of Mrs Haycock's disastrous night with Widmerpool at Dogdene ('a touch of exaggerated narcissism. Is that Widmerpool's trouble? . . . Can't help wondering about the inhibiting action of the incest barrier though – among other things'). Widower by 1934 or 5, forcibly retired from his post at court. M. c. 1939 2) Geraldine Weedon, former governess to Stringham's sister ('If he could handle Billson naked, he could probably handle Miss Weedon clothed – or naked, too, if it came to that').

Air-raid warden in second war. D. on duty of a heart attack while pursuing raiders in the street: 'He died, as he had lived, in active, dramatic, unusual circumstances; such, one felt, as he himself would have preferred'.

LM Uncle Giles' account of his military career, his marriage 1–7, 9–10, 23; falls from poodles' food loft 39; 42, 47–8, 58, Widmerpool's prospective brother-in-law 65–6; tea at his flat, on Widmerpool and Mrs Haydock 68–76, 78–81, 84–7; 139, 169, 191–2, his account of Widmerpool's broken engagement, his Boer war reminiscences 224–37. KO Invited to lunch at Stonehurst in 1914, mixed feelings of Jenkins' parents 8–10, 34–6, 38–42, 47–8; his arrival 50–8, takes command of Billson, encounter with Trelawney, reaction to news from Sarajevo 61–70, 73–4, 133, 152; visit to in 1939, produces Miss Weedon as his bride, disgust of Jenkins' parents 207–18; 231. VB 70, marriage going well 158–9. SA 6. Stringham on 80. MP His death 77; 219, his diagnosis of Widmerpool recalled 230–1. BDFR 147. TK 17, 57, 277. HSH 21, 31, 119.

CONYERS, Hon. Bertha (née Blaides)
Wife of above, eldest of the six daughters of Edward VII's friend Lord Vowchurch: 'In appearance Mrs Conyers retained, no doubt from her childhood, the harassed, uncertain expression of those who have for many years had to endure close association with persons addicted to practical joking. Like the rest of her sisters, she must have suffered in no small degree from her father's love of horse-play . . . Although never exactly handsome, Mrs Conyers was not without a look of sad distinction'.

Twenty years older than her youngest sister Mildred Haycock, and twenty years younger than her husband; thought to have reorganized his life much for the better after their marriage. Crony of Lady Frederica Budd, and one of the very few friends whose company is enjoyed by Jenkins' mother. Doesn't at all mind admitting she is old-fashioned. D. in the early 'thirties.

LM Her marriage, her history, visit to her flat in 1916, her disapproval of Mildred's flightiness 3–10; at the Jeavonses' in 1934, 22–6, 31, 33–4, her agitation over Widmerpool's engagement to Mildred 39–44, 47, 58–9; 66, tea with, her continued anxiety over Widmerpool 68–87; compared with Mildred 191, 200; 211, 224–5, 227–8. KO 9, her friendship with Jenkins' mother 34–6, 40–2; 47–8, at Stonehurst in 1914 50–3, 56–7, 63, 65, 67–70, 72–3; her death 208–9, 217.

CONYERS, Charlotte
Rather colourless only child of General and Mrs Conyers, made a poor impression on Jenkins as a boy; m. a naval lieutenant-commander and

has children; advent of Miss Weedon as stepmother considered very awkward for her by Jenkins' parents.

LM 6, 22, 86. KO 209, 217.

CONYERS, Geraldine see WEEDON, Geraldine.

CORDEREY
Le Bas' predecessor as housemaster, Alfred Tolland and Dicky Umfraville at school under him.

AW 154, 182, 185. BDFR 64.

CRADDOCK, Lieutenant Lyn
Fat and energetic Messing Officer in Gwatkin's company, killed at Caen in 1944.

VB 12, 46, 51, 220. MP 175.

CRAGGS, Howard
Left-wing publisher, 'randy as a stoat' (Pamela Flitton), 'has the most loathsomely oily voice in the whole of Bloomsbury' (Jenkins). Tall, baldish, early middle aged by the late 'twenties. Managing director of the Vox Populi Press next door to Mr Deacon's shop. Employs Gypsy Jones ('duties alleged by Barnby to be contingent on "sleeping with Craggs"'); has the girls from the 1917 Club; attends the Merry Thought fancy-dress ball as Adam to Gypsy's Eve.

Takes over Boggis & Stone ('books about Lenin and Trotsky and Litvinov and the Days of October and all that'), finding jobs for Quiggin and later Members at low points in their respective fortunes. Becomes one of Erridge's hangers-on in the 'thirties, and gets quite a bit of money out of him before dropping Erridge's Sedition Bill in favour of his own good causes (German refugees, South American arms embargoes, 'Smash Fascism' etc. 'He wants to be doing the latest thing all the time, whether it's the independence of Catalonia or free meals for school-children': Erridge).

Ministry of Information ('Rationing paper, was it? Something of the sort') during the war, knighted 1943. One of Pamela Flitton's would-be lovers and early victims. M. Gypsy at the end of the war.

Co-founder of Quiggin & Craggs (incorporating 'the good will of Boggis & Stone, together with such Left Wing steadies as survive'). Employs Ada Leintwardine ('I hope she's aware of Howard Craggs's little failings. Just as bad as ever, even at the advanced age he's reached, so I'm told': Sillery). In his sixties at Erridge's funeral in 1947, haggard, bent, bald, notably self-satisfied; his developed something of Mr Deacon's 'wandering demented appearance . . . a touch of the Mad

Hatter mingling with that of King Lear'. Fellow traveller of long standing. Not without a certain commercial shrewdness as publisher but has 'no great affection for authors as men – for that matter, unless easily seducible, as women'. Quarrels with Quiggin and is bullied by Gypsy ('Howard's afraid of her – actually physically afraid': Bagshaw) over the firm's choice of books. Goes into semi-retirement on the closing down of Quiggin & Craggs, d. by 1958.

BM Running Vox Pop. Press, employs Gypsy Jones 233; making fairly free with her at Mr Deacon's party 247–50; presumably her lover 259. AW Director of Boggis & Stone 49; swaps Quiggin for Members as literary adviser 118–19, 122. LM Quiggin disparaging on 109–10; Erridge disappointed in 113, 118–19; 137, relations with Erridge 154, 204. CCR 197. KO 227–8, 250. VB 212. MP Humiliated by Pamela Flitton 73; knighted 113. BDFR Starting Quiggin & Craggs, Sillery on 8–9; m. to Gypsy, Bagshaw on 35; at Erridge's funeral 45, 49, Pamela Widmerpool on 71, conciliatory attitude to Gypsy 80; 115–16, his approach to publishing 117; at *Fission* party 122, 124, 129–30, tolerates Gypsy's lovers 132; 136, his rows with Quiggin 142, 146, 157–8, 168–9; retired 209–11. TK Dead 135; 148. HSH 104.

CREECH, Albert
The Jenkinses' cook (formerly hall-boy to Jenkins' grandmother) at Stonehurst in 1914: 'Albert, fleshy, sallow, blue-chinned, breathing hard, sweating a little, fitted an iron bar into sockets . . . Rolled shirt-sleeves, green baize apron, conferred a misleadingly business-like appearance, instantly dispelled by carpet-slippers of untold shabbiness which encased his large, chronically tender feet. All work except cooking abhorrent to him, he went through the required movements with an air of weariness, almost of despair'.

Middle to late thirties; moody, timorous, sceptical, cruelly persecuted by women; his fear of suffragettes ('Don't want any of them Virgin Marys bursting in and burning the place down') makes a keen impression on the young Jenkins. Beloved by the parlourmaid Billson who is herself beloved by the soldier-servant Bracey: 'Albert, for his part, possessed that touch of narcissism to be found in some artists whatever their medium – for Albert was certainly an artist in cooking – and apparently loved nobody but himself'. Precipitates Billson's breakdown by his engagement to another, and gives notice ('"Madam," he said, "I've been goaded to this"') on the day of the Conyerses' visit. Joins up ('firm as ever in his fight for the quiet life') as canteen cook.

Hotel chef between the wars: 'He had now settled down to be a fat man, with the professional fat man's privileges and far from negligible status in life. He still supported a chronic weariness of spirit with an irony quite brutal in its unvarnished view of things . . . He could have passed for a depressed, incurably indolent member of some royal house (there was a look of Prince Theodoric) in hopeless exile'. Turns up again in 1939 running the Bellevue where Uncle Giles dies, Dr Trelawney gives trouble and General Conyers proposes spending his second honeymoon.

Gone forth in his cerements, according to Mrs Erdleigh, by 1944.

KO His background and temperament 1–7, 9–11, 13; triangular relationship with Billson and Bracey 15–18, 20–1, 26–8, 32–5; pleasure in the Conyers' visit 40; engaged, gives notice 43–6, 49–50, 53; his part in Billson's crisis, his subsequent career 55–62, 70–4; his effect on Billson compared to Peter Templer's on his wife 133; running the Bellevue 140–2; barely able to recall Stonehurst 147–55; 162, 165, Bob Duport on 167–8; his agitation over Dr Trelawney 183–5, 187–9; 191, 196, his stoical approach to war 201–2; 215. VB 193. MP His death 137–8.

CREECH, Mrs
The 'girl from Bristol' whose long threatening letters forced Albert into marriage. Takes his career in hand ('The dreaded marriage turned out – as Albert himself put it – "no worse than most"'), bears him a son and daughter, housekeeps at the Bellevue. M. as her second husband a Pole with whom she runs a boarding house at Weston-super-Mare.

KO 6–7, 44, 50, 141, 147–8, 150, 152–4, 183–4, 187, 201. MP 137–8.

CROWDING, Malcolm
Committed poet in the late 'forties and early 'fifties, has a poem in *Fission*'s first number, afterwards abandons verse to teach English 'in a spirit of severest literary puritanism' at Widmerpool's newish university. His account of X. Trapnel's last night at the Hero of Acre probably the best in existence ('He had been there in person. Besides, his own works proclaimed him a writer of little or no imagination. He could never have invented such a story').

BDFR 115, 127, 151. TK 29–35, 91. HSH 43.

CROXTON
Officer who annoys Odo Stevens and is punished for it at Aldershot.

VB 121.

CUNEDDA fl. 450 AD
Ancient Briton, and ancestor of Jenkins.

VB 3

CURTIS, Corporal
Clerk to Pennistone and Jenkins at the War Office, 'a henchman of

notable efficiency and wide interests', improves the time on fire duty by summarising the plot of *Adam Bede*.

MP 28, 146, 149.

CUTTS, Lady Augusta
Mother of Roddy and Mercy, 'rather a terror' according to her future daughter-in-law Susan Tolland, gave debutante dances attended by Erridge.

BM 57, 77. LM 139. CCR 73.

CUTTS, Fiona
Jenkins' niece, youngest child of Roddy and Susan Cutts, b. 1947 (in token of her parents' reconciliation after a wartime affair of Roddy's). A difficult subject from earliest years but never in the same class as Pamela Flitton.

Runs away from various schools, has some sort of affair with Etienne Delavacquerie and works briefly in glossy journalism before joining Scorpio Murtlock's cult. Wholly under Murtlock's thumb, assumed to be sleeping with him (Hugo Tolland doubts this), singled out by him for gutting crayfish on the cult's caravan expedition to the Jenkinses in 1968. Takes part two years later in the naked stagmask dance as preliminary to ritual sex with Murtlock, Widmerpool and other cult members. Watched by Gwinnett. Leaves the cult and moves in with Etienne's father, Gibson Delavacquerie (himself now thought to be in love with her). M. Gwinnett shortly afterwards.

BDFR Her birth 182. HSH Murtlock's disciple, her past history 1–18, 23–4, 28–9; former girlfriend of Etienne Delavacquerie 78–9; 118, Gwinnett's account of stagmask dance 164–9; Gibson Delavacquerie on negotiations with Murtlock for her release 175–86; still at his flat 189, 193; m. to Gwinnett 196–8; with him at Stourwater, encounter with cult members 207–15, 219–21, 224–7, 231–3, encounter with Murtlock 234–9; Delavacquerie on her marriage 239–42; 259.

CUTTS, Jonathan
Fiona's eldest brother, 'married, several children, rising rapidly in a celebrated firm of art auctioneers . . . Both the Cutts sons were tireless conversationalists in their father's manner, uncheckable, informative, sagacious, on the subject of their respective jobs'.

HSH 6, 190–1, 225–6.

CUTTS, Mercy
Aunt of above; made a family joke of Widmerpool as dancing partner in her debutante days; 'rather a plain girl' in Widmerpool's view.

BM 57. CCR 85. BDFR 73.

CUTTS, Roddy

The ambitious young Tory who m. Lady Susan Tolland in 1934; father of Jonathan, Sebastian, Fiona; Jenkins' brother-in-law. Banking family, in the City, widely tipped as a coming man. MP for a northern constituency by 1936: 'Tall, sandy-haired, bland, Roddy smiled ceaselessly. The House of Commons had, if anything, increased a tendency, probably congenital, to behave with a shade more assiduity than ordinary politeness required; a trait that gave Roddy some of the bearing of a clergyman at a school-treat. Always smiling, his eyes roved for ever round the room, while he offered his hosts their own food, and made a point of talking chiefly to people he did not know, as if he felt these could not be altogether comfortable if still unacquainted with himself'. Holds strong but absolutely noncommittal views on the Spanish Civil War in 1936. Abstains with Churchill's faction over Munich in 1938. Commissioned on the outbreak of war in his own county yeomanry (later transformed into Reconnaissance corps). Falls for a girl decoding cyphers at GHQ Persia/Iraq and astounds his relatives by writing home for a divorce.

Subsequently abandoned by the cypherine; barely scrapes a seat at the 1945 General Election; greatly chastened by his wife: 'She made him toil like a slave . . . His handsome, rather too large features were now marked with signs of stress, everything about him a shade less strident, even the sandy hair. At the same time he retained the forceful manner, half hectoring, half subservient, common to representatives of all political parties, together with the politician's hallmark of getting hold of the wrong end of the stick. He was almost pathetically thankful to be back in the House of Commons'. Makes no great mark on politics thereafter.

LM His engagement 139–40, 145, 152. CCR At Lady Warminster's, his professional manner and rivalry with George Tolland 72–3, 77, 85–7, on Spain 95–6; on the abdication 135. KO Entertains Widmerpool to dinner, his political views 90–3; on Donners 114; his unctuousness 226; 239. VB 112. MP His wartime romance 68. BDFR At Erridge's funeral, Susan's domination of 38–40, charmed by Pamela Widmerpool 47, 77–80, assists in the disposal of her vomit 85–6; on Widmerpool 87–8; dinner with at House of Commons 169–70, at Widmerpool's flat on the night of Pamela's departure, his total incuriosity 171–82. HSH His attitude to his children 5–7, 10, 78, 193–4; at Sebastian's wedding, on Widmerpool, on Fiona's marriage and murky past 195–7; 260.

CUTTS, Sebastian

Roddy's younger son, in computers, m. Clare Akworth at Stourwater

in 1971. Has inherited his father's sandy hair and political ambitions.
HSH 6, 190–1, 215, 221, 226.

CUTTS, Lady Susan, see TOLLAND, Lady Susan

DAISY
Old bitch, lost by her owner Mr Gauntlett and recovered through a
notable piece of guesswork, or prophecy, on Scorpio Murtlock's part.
HSH 20–3, 153, 173.

DANIELS, Private
Bithel's batman ('I call him the priceless jewel . . . Besides, he's as clean
as a whistle. A real pleasure to look at when he's doing PT, which is
more than you can say for some of them in the early morning');
formerly boot-boy at the Green Dragon in Bithel's home town;
generally regarded as unreliable, lightfingered and sly.

VB 32, 50, 70–2, 195.

DARLAN, Admiral J. 1881–1942
French High Commissioner in Algiers, assassinated on Christmas Eve
1942.
MP 84.

DAVIES, Blodwen, see GWATKIN, Blodwen

DAVIES, Col.
CO of Jenkins' Welsh regiment.
HSH 265.

DAVIES, E; DAVIES, G; DAVIES, J; DAVIES, L.
Privates in Jenkins' regiment.
VB 97, 112.

DEACON, Edgar Bosworth
Painter ('"Some people hold that as a bad painter Edgar carries all
before him," said Barnby. "I know good judges who think there is
literally no worse one'") given to enthusiasms. Intermittent advocate of
Esperanto, decimal coinage, vegetarianism, Hygienic Clothing, etc.
Looks upon himself 'as a figure almost Promethean in spirit of
independence – godlike, and following ideals of his own, far from the
well-worn tracks of fellow men'.
   B. 1871 (under the Archer). Modest private income. At the Slade
with Barnby's father; afterwards supported by faithful patrons (including

Lord Aberavon and Quiggin's uncle), mostly drawn from business circles in the Midlands. Had a studio before the first war in Brighton, where he met Captain and Mrs Jenkins ('My parents legitimately considered Mr Deacon an eccentric, who, unless watched carefully, might develop into a bore') and gave their son a wooden paintbox. By no means a failure in life. Loathes the Royal Academy, dislikes the Impressionists and Post-Impressionists almost equally, prefers to close his eyes to the existence of modern painting. His own works invariably huge, and classical in theme: 'Mr Deacon, in the words of his great hero, Walt Whitman, used to describe them as "the rhythmic myths of the Greeks, and the strong legends of the Romans"'.

Dubious reputation; 'incurable leanings towards the openly disreputable'; ancient antagonist of Dr Trelawney, and probably also of Sillery. Shuns what Dicky Umfraville used to call 'the female form divine'. Considers youth the only valid criterion in any field. Relies in all circumstances on an artist's traditional innocence of heart. Obliged to leave the country after 'a bit of trouble' in Battersea Park before or just after the start of the first war ('the course of which he seemed scarcely to have noticed'). Settles in Paris and goes downhill. Abandons painting in favour of antique dealing. Tall, lean, grey-haired, rather bent, possibly corseted; looks a little like an actor made up to play Prospero, 'the face heavily lined and grave, without conveying any sense of dejection'.

Turns up again at the end of the 'twenties, running a junk shop (and not above marketing the odd volume of curiosa, 'eroticism preferably confined to the male sex') off the Tottenham Court Road. Turned pacifist. Active in the cause of disarmament. Puts up Gypsy Jones at the back of his shop and lets the attic to Barnby. Overbearing and sarcastic in manner to anyone held to be frivolous, philistine, wealthy or favourably disposed towards the establishment ('He looked upon himself as the appointed scourge of all such persons, amongst whom he had immediately classed Widmerpool'). Still inclined to indulge in minor indiscretions with young friends, including a supposed 'ex-convict from Devil's Island', a would-be Venetian gondolier and the cockney dancer Norman Chandler. Loses his temper in a row with Max Pilgrim at Milly Andriadis' party. Introduces Jenkins to Moreland shortly afterwards in the Mortimer:

'His long arthritic fingers curled round half a pint of bitter, making an irregular mould or beading about the glass, recalling a mediaeval receptacle for setting at rest a drinking horn. The sight of Mr Deacon always made me think of the Middle Ages because of his resemblance to a pilgrim, a mildly sinister pilgrim, with more than a streak of madness in him, but then in every epoch a proportion of pilgrims must have been sinister, some mad as well. I was rather snobbishly glad that the streets had been too wet for his sandals.'

Falls downstairs at the Bronze Monkey nightclub on the night of his birthday party a week later, and d. of internal injuries on the day of Stringham's wedding.

His works include *Boyhood of Cyrus*, *Pupils of Socrates* and *By the Will of Diocletian*. Also studies of Spartan youth at exercise, Olympic runners, 'a boy-slave reproved by his toga-enveloped master whose dignified figure was not without all resemblance to Mr Deacon himself in his palmy days' etc. See also Painting Index.

BM Four of his canvases recalled, up for auction long after his death 1–3; early acquaintance with in Brighton, his character and career, his work analysed 4–9; encounter with in Paris after the first war 10–14; his *Boyhood of Cyrus*, its eventual significance for Jenkins 15–16, 20, 29–30; 36; encounter with in 1928 or '9 on Grosvenor Place with Gypsy Jones, his instant dislike of Widmerpool and sympathy with Stringham 83–94; 97, at Milly Andriadis' party 99, 101–2, 107–10, incensed by Max Pilgrim 113–20, Sillery on 122, Gypsy in search of 126–8, 138, row with Pilgrim, ordered from the house by Mrs Andriadis 147–52; his shop and its neighbourhood, Barnby on his work and recent history 161–8, 171; 174, 177, 192, 207; his death 224, 226–32; his birthday party recalled 233–50; his funeral 250–2, 254–5, 258–9, 272. AW St John Clark has a look of 22; 24, his party recalled 54–5; 70, 77, 85, his *Boyhood of Cyrus* 109; his young men 128, 164–5; 210. LM 104, his technique recalled by décor of Soho gin palace 168–9; 183, 222. CCR 5, encounter with in the Mortimer recalled, his career surveyed, his introduction of Moreland and relations with Chandler 9–24; 27, 36, 40, 44; St John Clark's resemblance to 80; 134, 144, 201. KO His dim view of Dr Trelawney 30–1; relations with the Jenkinses in his Brighton period 80–1; 148, 180, 218, 227–8. VB 186. SA 146. MP 221. BDFR 55, 60. TK 32, contrasted with Tokenhouse 57–8; his trade in pornographic books 67, 69. HSH His *Boyhood of Cyrus* 1; 119, 148; his centenary exhibition, its critical and commercial success, Jenkins' revised attitude to his paintings 244–51; Chandler's nostalgia for 255–6.

DEANERY, Lieutenant-Colonel Ivo, MC
Sunny Farebrother's protegé, the cavalryman appointed to command the Divisional Reconnaissance Corps in 1941 to the consternation of Widmerpool and Hogbourne-Johnson (each of whom had tried to double-cross the other by backing his own candidate).

Commands the Recce Unit with a great deal of bash until blown up by a landmine within a few days of the German surrender; but apparently sustains no lasting injury since he turns up in the late 'fifties as Major-General at a military reunion dinner.

SA 202–3, 206, 211–13. TK 204, 213.

DELAVACQUERIE, Etienne
Hardworking, humdrum son of Gibson Delavacquerie, jilted by Fiona Cutts. Contemporary of the Quiggin twins at the university of which Widmerpool is chancellor.

HSH 76–9, 90, 175–7, 182, 184.

DELAVACQUERIE, Gibson
Poet and public relations officer at Donners Brebner. Small, dark, dry; widower in his late forties by 1968; flat in Islington. Secretary to the Magnus Donners Prize committee, useful as a contact within the firm to Matilda Donners, thought by some to have been her lover.

Ex-colonial (British citizen of French descent from the West Indies); one of the few, perhaps the sole, holder of a Donners Brebner fellowship at an English university in the 'thirties; Royal Signals in Middle East and India during the war. Afterwards worked for a shipping firm before joining Donners Brebner. His early verse rhymed and scanned; poem published in *Fission*; new book due in 1971.

Polly Duport's long-term lover, and one of Jenkins' prime informants on the Gwinnett-Murtlock-Widmerpool entanglement. Probably in love with his son's former girlfriend Fiona Cutts but is obliged to settle instead for marriage to Polly.

HSH Background, career, involvement in the Magnus Donners prize 51–6; submits Gwinnett's biography of X. Trapnel to prize committee, copes successfully with libel difficulties concerning Widmerpool 66–80, 87–90; organizes prize dinner 91–3, 97–8, 100–1, 105, 110, 113; Polly's lover 123–4, 141; contemplating marriage, reports Gwinnett's dealings with Widmerpool 143–8; Gwinnett on 165–6; confides his tangled relations with Fiona, and through her with Murtlock 174–86; in love with Fiona 189; Fiona still his lodger 193–4; Fiona married to Gwinnett, his reaction 196, 207, 239–42; about to marry Polly 255.

DEMPSTER
Officer responsible for Norwegian liaison in Jenkins' War Office section; accomplished pianist, timber merchant in civil life, remotely related to Ibsen; 'looked like an immensely genial troll come south from the fjords to have a good time'.

MP 24–5, 29, 83, 150, 198, 215. TK 202.

DERWENTWATERS
Parties involved in a much publicized divorce case (in which Baby
Wentworth figured, 'though not culpably') at the end of the 'twenties;
their marriage annulled by the Vatican, courtesy of Sillery.

QU 170, BM 125, 187.

DIANA, Lady (Lady Diana Manners, afterwards Cooper) b. 1892.
Contemporary of Lady Molly Jeavons, inhabiting the kind of smart
world in which Lady Molly was never at ease.

LM 158.

DICKINSON
Boy at school who witnessed Widmerpool's seizure with contortions
of the bottom.

QU 10.

DIETRICH, Marlene b. 1901
May have had her life saved (unless it was Hepburn or Harlow) in
Hollywood by Louis Glober.

TK 63.

DIPLOCK, Mr, Warrant Officer, Class One
Chief clerk and sole partisan of the evil-tempered Colonel Hogbourne-
Johnson at Divisional HQ in N. Ireland in 1941, 'one of the major
impediments to the dynamic improvement of this formation' in
Widmerpool's view:
'His woolly grey hair, short thick body, air of perpetual busyness,
suggested an industrious gnome conscripted into the service of the
army; a gnome who also liked to practise considerable malice against
the race of men with whom he mingled, by making as complicated as
possible every transaction they had to execute through himself.
Diplock . . . could have taken on the whole of the Civil Service,
collectively and individually, in manipulation of red tape; and emerged
victorious.'

Proof of his criminal activities tirelessly pursued and eventually secured
by Widmerpool ('Through the backwoods of this bureaucratic jungle
. . . Widmerpool was hunting down Mr Diplock in relentless safari') as
a means of revenge on Hogbourne-Johnson. Obtains a day's leave to
clear himself and deserts across the border.

Hopelessly outclassed in the field of military obscurantism by
Blackhead of the War Office: 'To transact business even for a few
minutes with Blackhead was immediately to grasp how pitifully

deficient Diplock had, in fact, often proved himself in evolving a really impregnable system of obstruction and preclusion; awareness of such falling short of perfection perhaps telling on his nerves and finally causing him to embezzle and desert'.

SA 29, 58–64, 74, 85, 97, 173, 209–11, 213–15. MP 39, 140.

DOLLFUSS, Englebert 1892–1934
Austrian Chancellor, murdered by the Nazis July 25, 1934.

LM 63.

DOLLY SISTERS (Jennie and Rosie) 1892–1941 and 1892–
Dancers, one of them held by Stringham to be the mother of the other.

QU 38.

DONNERS, Sir Magnus ('The Chief')
Immensely rich industrialist and patron of the arts; head of Donners Brebner; his supposedly unconventional sexual tastes a source of constant speculation and jocularity. Middle fifties by 1928 or '9 but looks at least ten years younger. Tallish, green eyes, good-looking rather than the reverse. Something odd about the set of his mouth: 'Apart from that his features had been reduced, no doubt by laborious mental discipline, to a state of almost unnatural ordinariness. He possessed, however, a suggestion about him that was decidedly parsonic: a lay-reader, or clerical headmaster: even some distinguished athlete, of almost uncomfortably rigid moral convictions, of whose good work at the boys' club in some East End settlement his own close friends were quite unaware . . . A touch of sadness about his face was not unprepossessing.'

Said to be the son of an eminently solid figure of German or Scandinavian extraction; ed. 'at some quite decent university' (Sir Gavin Walpole-Wilson), probably the Sorbonne. Member of the government during first war, lost his seat by 1924. Employs Bill Truscott and Charles Stringham as private secretaries; also Widmerpool (whom he is eventually obliged to sack for intriguing). Negotiates base metal concessions from Prince Theodoric in the Balkans. Regularly seen about with Baby Wentworth; turned down by Bijou Ardglass; taken on instead by Matilda Wilson at the beginning of the 'thirties. His girls will admit to no more than accepting presents. Seat: Stourwater Castle.

Early patron of Barnby (murals for Donners Brebner entrance hall) and Moreland (incidental music for the highbrow film *Lysistrata*). Fond of *Parsifal* and sheds tears over the sufferings of the Chinese slave girl in *Turandot*. His collections of paintings (Toulouse-Lautrec, Conder,

Steer, Sickert, John, Wyndham Lewis, Barnby, etc.), furniture, china and armour housed at Stourwater. Taste in literature stops short at standard authors. Renowned for his unrivalled grasp of cliché: 'When he spoke, it was as if he had forced himself by sheer effort of will into manufacturing a few stereotyped sentences to tide over the trackless wilderness of social life . . . Like most successful men, he had turned this apparent disadvantage into a powerful weapon of offence and defence, in the way that the sledge-hammer impact of his comment left, by its banality, every other speaker at a standstill, giving him as a rule complete mastery of the conversational field. A vast capacity for imposing boredom, a sense of immensely powerful stuffiness, emanated from him, sapping every drop of vitality from weaker spirits.'

Proposes to Matilda before her marriage to Moreland. Doesn't know what jealousy means. Living with Lady Anne Umfraville by 1938. Fixes up the Morelands in a cottage on his Stourwater estate that autumn, and photographs them with the Jenkinses and Templers in tableaux of the Seven Deadly Sins ('He had become more than ever like an energetic, dominating headmaster, organising extempore indoor exercise for his pupils on an afternoon too wet for outdoor games. A faint suggestion of repressed, slightly feverish excitement under his calm, added to this air, like some pedagogue confronted with aspects of his duties that gratify him almost to the point of aberration'). Rumours of his voyeurism – 'Disgusting stories. Totally untrue, of course, but mud sticks' – deplored by Widmerpool.

Removes Matilda from Moreland a year later; m. to her by 1941. Member of Churchill's war cabinet; is heavily attacked in they press but has the ear of the Head Man. Looks no older after the war ('The set of Sir Magnus's mouth, always a trifle uncomfortable to contemplate, had become very slightly less under control, increasing the vaguely warning note the rest of his appearance implied'). Dead by 1946*. His voyeurism ('It was Donners' thing, you know': Moreland) generally agreed to have been indulged by all his mistresses except Matilda. See also Book Index under Magnus Donners Memorial Prize.

QU Truscott in search of a young man for 186–90; Stringham selected 204–6. BM Business dealings with Prince Theodoric 44, 47; 104; Donners Brebner fellowships 123–4; proposing to recruit Widmerpool, attends Milly Andriadis' party with Baby Wentworth, their relationship, his colourless correctitude 132–9; Barnby's patron and rival in love, speculations on his sex life 165, 172–4; gives a luncheon

---

* BDFR 10; but TK 272, HSH 50 and 214 put his death somewhat later, round about the beginning of the 'fifties.

party at Stourwater, his background 181–3, 186, 193–4, his conversation 195–6, his guided tour of the dungeons 198–202, 204–5, 209–13, his sunken lawn wrecked by Widmerpool 216–8, 221–2; 235, 253; Widmerpool on 270. AW Has exchanged Mrs Wentworth for Matilda Wilson 24–5; and sacked Widmerpool 45–6; Jean Duport on, mystery of his sexual proclivities 58, 91, 135; 154. LM Widmerpool on 50, 64; 200. CCR Moreland's patron 7, 15; and Barnby's 38; affair with Matilda over 41–2; 47, 99; Widmerpool on his shortcomings as businessman 124; Veronica Tolland's account of his first encounter with Matilda 131; 133; Matilda on his advantages and drawbacks as a lover 157–9. KO As man of action, Moreland on 77–9, 84; lends the Morelands a cottage 89–90; his political and industrial activities, his patronage of the arts 92–3; Moreland's ambivalence towards, Matilda's former interest in 95–101; dinner at Stourwater with, Anne Umfraville installed as châtelaine 103–4, 107–18, 120, photographs tableaux of the Seven Deadly Sins 122–9; approves Widmerpool's arrangements for employing Bob Duport 131–8; 156, Duport on his business activities and sexual tastes 166–7, 170, 172–4, 200; Widmerpool on his frivolity 225–6; Matilda returns to him 242, 245–8, 250. VB Not yet in office 118–9; 172; appointed to ministerial post 179. SA 35; married to Matilda 93. MP At Widmerpool's cabinet office meeting 15; 22; Theodoric on his power and influence 50–1; his power to put to the test over Belgian resistance 88–9, 187, 193–5; at Indian embassy party, his puppet-like appearance 206–9. BDFR Dead 10; his pictures sold 101–2. TK 80, 104, 113–4, his voyeurism compared to Candaules' by Pamela Widmerpool 151–3; 160, 208, 217; Moreland on his sexual tastes, his youthful spurt to become cultured and his marriage to Matilda 270–5. HSH Stourwater dinner party recalled 45; prize founded in his memory, his will 48–53; 56, 59; his Stourwater photographs of the Seven Deadly Sins produced 61–4; 73, 101, 105, publicly denounced by Widmerpool at prize dinner 108–9; his ghost at Stourwater 191–2; 195, 206, 214–5, 217; Widmerpool's revised opinion of his enlightened sexual practices 225; 233.

DONNERS, Matilda see WILSON, Matilda

DOOLEY, Father Ambrose
Roman Catholic chaplain attached to Jenkins' Welsh battalion, famed for the wit and license of his lavatory jokes.

VB 19–25, 27–8.

DORIS
Odo Stevens' aunt, m. to an estate agent near Thrubworth.

VB 134–5, 143.

D'ORSAY, Count 1801–52
The intimate companion of Lady Blessington and friend of Hercules Mallock.

VB 170.

DRUM, Bertha, Lady
Gave one of the few dances for which Widmerpool got a card in the 'twenties.

BM 77.

DUBUISSON, Madame
Stocky, loquacious, elderly newly-wed enjoying a cheap holiday at La Grenadière during Jenkins' visit to France on leaving school. Thought to have long been her husband's mistress before obliging him to marry her. Mistaken by Jenkins for Mme Leroy's niece Suzette in compromising circumstances, and accepts his halting romantic declaration without the least surprise.

QU 115–8, 122–6, 142, 160, 164–6, 172.

DUBUISSON, Monsieur
Even older ('afterwards I discovered M. Dubuisson was only about forty') husband of above. Rank, grey, almost lavender-coloured hair, look of immense and ineradicable scepticism: 'His long upper lip and general carriage made me think of a French version of the Mad Hatter'. Twice wounded, four citations. Worked with Sunny Farebrother at the Paris peace conference; not to be thought of as merely a commercial gent; freely admits to mastery of finance, politics, literature and the English language: 'I did not know in those days that it was impossible to convince egoists of Monsieur Dubuisson's calibre that everyone does not look on the world as if it were arranged with them – in this case Monsieur Dubuisson – at its centre . . .'

QU 115–8, 123–6, 142–8, 151, 157, 160–1, 163–4. AW 193.

DUFF (Sir Alfred Duff Cooper, first Viscount Norwich) 1890–1954.
First Lord of the Admiralty, resigned over Munich in 1938.

KO 91.

DULLES, John Foster 1888–1959
American Secretary of State, imitated in his galoshes by Heather Hopkins in the Hero of Acre.

TK 31.

DUNCH, Ernie

Neighbour of the Jenkinses in the country, quite a young fellow, farms the land on which the Devil's Fingers stand. Grandson of old Seth Dunch who wouldn't go near the Fingers after dark. Gets in a fearful taking after seeing four horned dancers ('Ernie swears they were naked as the day they were born – if they were human and were born') at the Fingers on Midsummer Eve while shooting rabbits from his landrover. HSH 153–60, 171.

DUPORT, Bob

Aggressive and contradictious City friend brought by Peter Templer to call on Stringham at the university in 1924, when Jenkins takes against him at sight. Tall, thin, sandy-haired, coarser even than Jimmy Brent. Notorious since leaving school (the year before Jenkins went there) for drunkenness, car crashes, etc.; sent down in his first term at Cambridge; gets a black eye in Templer's motor accident. Already pursuing Jean Templer.

Married to her by 1928 or '9 ('I've had worse brothers-in-law although, God knows, that's not saying much. Still, Bob *is* difficult': Templer); flourishing in the City ('one of those men money likes'); owner of the sumptuous if vulgar house in Hill Street where Mrs Andriadis holds her party. Source of no small jealousy to Jenkins on all three counts.

Leaves Jean the year after for Bijou Ardglass, who drops him when the money runs out during one of his periodic financial crises. Sells his house and goes abroad (scrap metal scheme, angling for the Balkan agency from Donners Brebner), leaving a trail of girl friends and bad debts behind him. Patches up his marriage (and incidentally puts a stop to Jenkins' affair with Jean) on his return in 1933 with a new job fixed by Widmerpool. Sails for South America where he brings off some smart deals in manganese; is cuckolded by Jimmy Brent; and leaves Jean again for another girl. Divorced by 1938. Dispatched to Turkey for chromite by Donners.

Turns up in hiding from creditors (his chromite scheme ditched by 'that château-bottled shit, Widmerpool') at the Bellevue on the outbreak of war, and reveals that Jean's second lover in 1933 was the fat slob Jimmy Brent. Jenkins loathes him and gives him Uncle Giles' copy of *The Perfumed Garden or The Arab Art of Love*. Afterwards proves to have been Brent's lifelong hero on account of his wizardry in business, terrific gifts with women, and the flawless taste in art exemplified at his Hill Street house ('absolute perfection in my humble opinion': Brent).

Spends the war in censorship in Egypt, where he picks up gyppy tummy, and later with Civil Affairs in Brussels. Importing crude oil to

Canada by 1946; 'rather a wreck' according to Jean. Still 'in the crude' ten years later ('This seemed an enormously suitable calling, whatever it was, for Duport to follow').

Last seen in a wheel chair at the beginning of the 'seventies, inspecting sales of the Robert Duport collection of Victorian seascapes with his ex-wife and daughter Polly. A rather ghastly sight, ill-tempered, semi-invalid, memory gone to pot, still plagued by gyppy tummy: 'I feel I liked him better than I used'.

See also Painting Index under DUPORT, Robert, collection; and Place Index under HILL STREET.

QU At Oxford 191–200. BM His house, his marriage, Jenkins' successive pangs of envy and deep vexation 140–1, 143; Jean on being married to 192–4, 215; gone abroad 234. AW Lost his money and left Jean 42–3; Widmerpool roped in to lend a hand with 46; affair with Bijou Ardglass 57, 114, 134–5; never mentioned between Jean and Jenkins 141–2; 155–6; sold his house 160; back in England 175–6; not yet fixed up by Widmerpool 197–8; Jenkins' affair with Jean threatened by his return 213–4. LM Job fixed by Widmerpool, in South America with Jean 53; Jenkins' jealousy of 67–8, 184, 187; gone off with a new girl 199. KO 100; divorced, Donners' business dealings with 108, 136–7; at the Bellevue, Jenkins' indissoluble link with, his account of Widmerpool's treachery and Jean's affair with Brent 162–82, rescues Dr Trelawney from locked bathroom, their unexpected friendship 183–96, 198, up a gum tree on outbreak of war 199–202; Widmerpool on his stupidity and ingratitude 224–5; 246. VB 110, 113; meeting with Jimmy Brent recalls memories of 118–20; Brent's unbounded admiration for 124–7, 131–3; 169. MP Encounter with in Brussels, his account of Templer's death 185–90; 210, 234. BDFR 96, Jean on his misfortunes 99. TK 73, 152–3; Polly on 235. HSH Been ill, looked after by Polly 145; 206; at Barnabas Henderson gallery inspecting sales 251–6.

DUPORT, Jean see TEMPLER, Jean

DUPORT, Polly
Actress. Only child of Bob and Jean Duport, born* round about the time of her parents' first separation. Brought up by her mother and stepfather in South America. Quite famous (not a very interesting talent) by the late 'fifties. Married to and separated from a well-known

* The old-fashioned upbringing 'that made her seem older than her age' presumably accounts for some slight discrepancy between her date of birth (Jean was in the early stages of pregnancy by the autumn of 1928 or 9, BM 234) and her various ages: 'twelve or thirteen' in 1940 (VB 133), 'about seventeen or eighteen' in 1945 (MP 233), 'in her thirties' by 1958 (TK 234).

actor; dedicated to her profession; lives like a nun. Succeeds Pamela Widmerpool as Louis Glober's mistress and prospective star of his (eventually abandoned) film of *Match Me Such Marvel*. Prettier and much nicer than her mother, 'but without, so far as I myself was concerned, any of her mother's former bowling-over endowments'.

Stars in Ibsen and Strindberg at the end of the 'sixties. Long-standing affair with Gibson Delavacquerie, marriage pending in 1971.

BM Conceived 234. AW In London during Jenkins' affair with her mother 43, 114, 133. VB Said to have tipped off Bob about Jean's affair with Jimmy Brent 133. MP With her mother and stepfather in London, reminds Jenkins of Jean when young 232–4. BDFR Going on the stage 98. TK Starring in Hardy film, her career 51–2; 168–9; to star in Glober's film 220–2; with him at the Stevens' party, on her parents 234–6; taunted by Pamela Widmerpool 253–4, 256–9, 266; to star in Clarini's film 268; with Glober 278. HSH Directed by Chandler 59–60; in Ibsen revival 120; affair with Delavacquerie 123–4, 141; Delavacquerie on, plays Celia in *The Humorous Lieutenant* 145–6; contemplating marriage 148; marriage postponed on account of Delavacquerie's affair with Fiona Cutts 174, 176–8, 182, 186; at Barnabas Henderson gallery with her parents, about to marry Delavacquerie 252–7.

EDITH
Nurse to Jenkins as a small boy at Stonehurst in 1914; suffers from terrible sick headaches and has heard mysterious rappings in the night nursery.

KO 3–5, 12–13, 16–20, 26, 28, 33–4, 43–5, 49, 55, 58, 63, 71, 74.

EDWARD IV, King 1442–83
Knighted one of the Tollands.

LM 151.

EDWARD VII, King 1841–1910.
Was a friend to Lord Vowchurch and regularly forgave him for horseplay, practical jokes and rudeness at the bridge table.

LM 4–5, 47, 87–8. KO 40, 82, 214.

ELLIS, Private
Member of Jenkins' platoon in 1940.

VB 97.

ELYSTAN-EDWARDS
VC in Jenkins' former regiment.

MP 177.

EMMOTT, Private
The burly and despondent mess waiter kissed by Lt. Bithel at
Castlemallock, greatly cheered by Bithel's subsequent arrest.
VB 173–4, 202–5, 214–15, 221.

ENA
One of two girls picked up in Templer's car at Oxford in 1924; kicks
Stringham in the face, gives Duport a black eye, knees Jenkins on the
nose and complains of a broken arm in the ensuing accident.
QU 194–9. AW 42. KO 164–5. VB 118.

ENOCH (Rt Hon. Enoch Powell) b. 1912
Tory Member of Parliament.
HSH 105.

ERDLEIGH, Myra (Mrs)
Clairvoyante; 'a conspicuous, perhaps even a sinister figure'; the first
woman apart from members of his own family ever seen in Uncle
Giles' company. Reads the cards for Jenkins and his uncle one day at
the Ufford in the early 'thirties. Largely built, dark red hair, huge liquid
eyes and rapturous smile: 'Her movements, too, were unusual. She
seemed to glide rather than walk across the carpet, giving the
impression almost of a phantom, a being from another world . . . Scent,
vaguely Oriental in its implications, rolled across from her in great
stifling waves'. Indeterminate age, probably between forty and fifty.
Born under Scorpio. Widow (husband employed out East: 'Chinese
customs, was it? Burma police?' or possibly Yangtze pilot). Suspected
by the family of marital designs on Uncle Giles.
   Turns up with Jimmy Stripling for lunch at the Templers' house in
Maidenhead some eighteen months later, and presides over planchette.
Has Stripling thoroughly under her thumb. Afterwards reported to be
'fairly skinning Jimmy'. All knowledge of her existence denied by
Uncle Giles round about this time. Rated highly as an oracle by Lady
Warminster ('"Lady Warminster was a woman among women," said
Mrs Erdleigh. "I shall never forget her gratitude when I revealed to her
that Tuesday was the best day for the operation of revenge"').
   Turns up again in the seaside town where Uncle Giles d. at the
Bellevue in 1939. Known to have paid him frequent visits; sole
mourner (apart from Jenkins) at his funeral; and sole legatee under his
will. 'Looks as if she kept a high-class knocking shop' (Bob Duport).
Associate of Dr Trelawney; shares his taste for cabbalistic dialectic and
familiarity with the sages and mages (Trismegistus, Cornelius Agrippa,
Thomas Vaughan – 'Eugenius Philalethes, as we know him' – Eliphas

Levi, Desbarrolles etc.); supplies him with drugs behind locked doors in the period leading up to his own death at the Bellevue.

Moved to Jenkins' block of flats in Chelsea by 1944; often to be seen burning incense on the roof; prophesies during an air raid concerning the respective fates of Pamela Flitton and Odo Stevens.

In Venice during the various Widmerpool scandals of 1958. Encountered the following summer with Stripling (a couple bound together 'without marriage, probably without sexual relationship') at the Stevenses' musical party:

'She looked very old indeed, yet old in an intangible, rather than corporeal sense. Lighter than air, disembodied from a material world, the swirl of capes, hoods, stoles, scarves, veils, as usual encompassed her from head to foot, all seeming of so light a texture that, far from bringing an impression of accretion, their blurring of hard outlines produced a positively spectral effect, a Whistlerian nocturne in portraiture, sage greens, sombre blues, almost frivolous greys, sprinkled with gold . . . She smiled her otherworldly smile, misted hazel eyes roaming over past and future, apportioning to each their substance and shadow, elements to herself one and indivisible'.

Foretells her own death, or re-entry into the Vortex of Becoming, and takes credit for predicting Jenkins' marriage (a claim he is reluctant to dispute: 'Sorceresses, more than most, are safer allowed their *amour propre*'). Smiles her unnerving smile ('one I would rather not have played on myself': Moreland) at Pamela Widmerpool, and pronounces a final warning during the scene between the Widmerpools in Regent's Park after the party: 'My dear, beware. You are near the abyss. You stand at its utmost edge . . . Court at your peril those spirits that dabble lasciviously with primaeval matter, horrid substances, sperm of the world, producing monsters and fantastic things, as it is written, so that the toad, this leprous earth, eats up the eagle'. Vanishes with Stripling in the ensuing commotion ('taking off, no doubt, on her broomstick, the tall elderly vintage-car-bore riding pillion': Moreland).

Never seen again, though her spirits, returning 'somewhat in the manner of Hamlet's father', presides over the revival among cults such as Murtlock's in the late 'sixties of her own and Dr Trelawney's views on the insignificance of death: 'To be fair to them both, they seemed to some extent to have made their point'.

AW At the Ufford, tells Uncle Giles' and Jenkins' fortunes 5–18; 34; at the Templers' with Stripling, bewitches Mona Templer 81–7, 88–94, 98–102; 115, 140, 157; Uncle Giles admits no recollection of 182–3; her lovers 213. CCR Relations with Lady Warminster 73. KO Visits Uncle Giles on his deathbed, installs Trelawney at the Bellevue 152–4, 156, 174–5, supplying Trelawney with special pills 184–5, 187–9, soothes his frenzy with a hypodermic 195–8; at Uncle Giles' funeral, inherits all his money 202; 213, 217. MP Living in Jenkins' flats, encounter with Pamela Flitton and Odo Stevens 129–38. TK 102; in Venice 115; at Stevens' party with Stripling, foresees trouble for the Widmerpools 241–6, brings her full force to bear on Pamela 256, 259–61, departs 264, 266. HSH Her views revived by contemporary cults 35–6; 81; her resemblance to, and acquaintance with, Canon Fenneau 127, 134.

ERRIDGE, Viscount, Earl of Warminster (Alfred) Family name Tolland.
Erratic and high-minded social revolutionary; egoist of the first water; supports large number of spongers and left-wing hangers-on in the 'thirties. Eldest of the ten Tollands (and eventually Jenkins' brother-in-law), succeeded his father in the late 'twenties* but is invariably known in the family by his second title as Erridge, or 'Erry' Seat: Thrubworth Park. His exploits (living as a tramp in the Midlands etc.) a source of inexhaustible gossip to his disapproving relations. Turns up as Quiggin's patron and landlord in the country in 1934:
'The man who came into the room was, I suppose, in his early thirties. At first he seemed older on account of his straggling beard and air of utter down-at-heelness. His hair was long on top of his head, but had been given a rough military crop round the sides. He wore a tweed coat, much the worst for wear and patched with leather at elbows and cuffs; but a coat that was well cut and had certainly seen better days. An infinitely filthy pair of corduroy trousers clothed his legs . . . It seemed at first surprising that such an unkempt figure should have announced himself by knocking so gently, but it now appeared that he was overcome with diffidence . . . At last, by taking hold of himself firmly, he managed to pass through the door, immediately turning his sunken eyes upon me with a look of deep uneasiness, as if he suspected – indeed, was almost certain – I was plotting some violently disagreeable move against himself. By exercising this disturbed, and essentially disturbing, stare, he made me feel remarkably uncomfortable; although, at the same time, there was something about him not at all unsympathetic: a presence of forcefulness and despair enclosed in an envelope of constraint.'
Had previously crossed Jenkins' path as a gloomy, cadaverous schoolboy ('Angular, sallow and spotty, he was usually frowning to

* Various references (LM 28–9, 112 etc) and the ages of his brothers and sisters suggest that Erridge was born round about 1901, certainly not later than 1904, and had not yet become Lord Warminster when he attended the Huntercombes' dance in 1928 or 9 (BM 57); CCR 58 puts his father's death 'eight or nine years' before the outbreak of the Spanish Civil War in 1936 (a date more or less confirmed by LM 147). But see CCR 59: 'Erridge had been less pleased to find himself head of the family at the age of eighteen or nineteen . . .'

himself . . .') and later as a hot, cross misfit at debutante dances. Spent his youth in loneliness and boredom 'a vague, immature, unhappy young man, taking flats and leaving them, wandering about the Continent, buying useless odds and ends, joining obscure societies, in general without friends or interest') until taken in hand at the beginning of the 'thirties by Quiggin, who met him pottering about one afternoon in a bookshop on the Charing Cross Road. Promptly sets himself a stiff programme of reading, undertakes a one-man survey on unemployment, distributes pamphlets, subsidizes societies ('sums that would make you gasp': Quiggin), sets up committees and proposes founding a political paper with Quiggin as joint-editor. Always more at home with causes than individuals, but may possibly have had some sort of affair with Gypsy Jones.

Frugal habits, mean with drink, taste for holding on to his money. Lives like a hermit in ghastly discomfort in one room at Thrubworth attended by his dipsomaniac butler Smith, keeping the house under dustsheets, letting the estate go to ruin, entertaining his guests on sausages and mash and barley water. *Chums* and the *Boy's Own Paper* ('the pages of which he would turn unsmiling for hours at times of worry and irritation') his only vice.

Sails for China at the end of 1934, taking Quiggin's girlfriend Mona Templer with him ('the question of marriage now loomed steeply for his relations'). Returns alone and dissatisfied some months later. Harassed by death duties, also by gross mismanagement of the estate in his absence; seriously overdrawn. Shuts himself up in the country, replacing Quiggin as confidant with the ageing novelist St John Clarke (' "At Thrubworth," said St John Clarke reverently. 'We talked there until the wee small hours'"), and escaping thankfully to Spain on the outbreak of civil war. Returns shortly afterwards with dysentery but without having got to the front or met Hemingway. Inherits a small fortune from St John Clarke. Thought by his more hopeful relations to be fed up with Spain and going to spend the money on saving the woods at Thrubworth instead. Never a member of the Communist Party; beginning to lose his enthusiasm for Soviet Russia.

His opposition to Nazi Germany complicated by his increasingly keen pacificism. Retreats into hypochondria. Bordering on a chronic invalid by 1939. Derives much solace throughout the war from a running fight with the military authorities who take over Thrubworth, providing him with a series of legitimate grievances missing since birth ('Erridge, a rebel whose life had been exasperatingly lacking in persecution, had enjoyed independence of parental control, plenty of money, assured social position, early in life. Since leaving school he had been deprived of all the typical grudges within the grasp of most young men. Some of these grudges, it was true, he had later developed with fair success by artificial means, grudges being, in a measure, part and parcel of his political approach').

Turns from contemporary politics to the Anabaptists and revolutionary movements of the Middle Ages. About to provide funds for the leftwing magazine *Fission* when he d. suddenly of coronary thrombosis in 1946, leaving directions for certain books that had influenced him to be reprinted by Quiggin & Craggs under the Warminster Trust. Succeeded by his brother George's posthumous son Jeremy. For ancestry, see TOLLANDS, and WARMINSTER, Earls of.

BM At Huntercombes' ball 57. AW Succeeded to the title 187. LM His eccentricities discussed by his relations at Lady Molly's 21, 27–30, 38; and by his sister Frederica at the Conyerses' 79–80; and at his sister Norah's 93–4; Quiggin's mysterious socially conscious landlord 108–10; at Quiggin's cottage, forms taken by his egoism, relations with Quiggin 112–25; supper with at Thrubworth 126–30, duel with Smith over sherry 131–4, duel with Smith over champagne 135–48, his tour of the house 149–52; Quiggin on his good works 153–5; sails for China with Mona 203–6; Jenkins cross-examined by Lady Warminster on 208–11; 213; 218–19, Members' account of the start of his affair with Mona 221–3; 238. CCR His role in the family 59–60; abandoned by Mona, leaves for Spain, speculation among his relations 63–8, 70–1, 76–8; 81, 87; St John Clarke entrusted with his politico-literary affairs 91–4; further speculation by friends and relations 97, 131, 137, 139, 170; back from Spain, takes to his bed 195–9, 201–2; St John Clarke's heir 227–9. KO At Thrubworth, in poor health, his political outlook 142–4; enjoys being requisitioned 203–6; General Conyers' diagnosis of 211. VB 150–1, 161, 167. SA Boys' comics his only vice 13–14. BDFR His death, his last years 27–8; his plans for *Fission* 34–6; his funeral, his indisposition a few months earlier at his brother George's, his ancestry 38–44, Widmerpool a mourner with the Craggses 45, fitness of Widmerpool, Quiggin and Craggs to consign him to the tomb, his character and fate contrasted unfavourably with George's 49–51, 53–4, Mona a mourner, her account of travelling dry with him to Hong Kong 55–6, Alfred Tolland on 58, 63–5, Widmerpool on his will 60–2, his flat at Thrubworth, his life reviewed 65–9, Craggs and Quiggin on 74–7, his family on 79, 86–7; 106, 131, his trust fund 171–3, 176–7. TK 135.

ETHEL
Milly Andriadis' elderly lady's-maid.

AW 161–2.

EVANGENLINE (Mrs David Bruce) b. *c.* 1918
Wife of the American ambassador in London, 1961–9.

HSH 197

EVANS
Checkweighman in the mine, said to be having an affair back home
with Sergeant Pendry's wife after the regiment moves away in 1940.

VB 54–6.

EVANS, Private J.
Oddly shaped soldier in Gwatkin's company.

VB 181.

FAREBROTHER, Captain A. Sunderland ('Sunny'), DSO, OBE
Business friend of Peter Templer's father (and distant relation of Mrs
Templer), already famous for his charm when first encountered by
Jenkins as a schoolboy staying with the Templers in 1923. Aged 30 to
35; tall, dark, ascetic; his war record (on the Somme, 'rather a good
DSO') a source of extreme vexation to Jimmy Stripling. Frayed tie,
dilapidated suit, battered leather baggage, 'almost unnecessarily
ingratiating manner'; mean with tips; thought to be decidedly rich and
'doing just about as nicely in the City as anyone could reasonably
expect'. Superficial resemblance to Buster Foxe, and also to Mrs Foxe's
secretary Miss Weedon ('both had in common some smoothness, an
acceptance that their mission in life was to iron out the difficulties of
others: a recognition that, for them, power was won by self-
abasement'). Demolishes six of Jimmy Stripling's collars in his patent
collar-turning device, and foils Stripling's attempted revenge in the
matter of the green chamber pot. 'A downy old bird', according to
Peter Templer.
    Turns up again in 1939 (London unit of Yeoman cavalry) as Brigade-
Major of Widmerpool's Territorials; and later as Widmerpool's
opposite number at command at Divisional HQ in N. Ireland:
'Middle-age caused him to look more than ever like one's conception
of Colonel Newcome, though a more sophisticated, enterprising
prototype of Thackeray's old warrior. Sunny Farebrother could never
entirely conceal his own shrewdness, however much he tried. He was
a Colonel Newcome . . . offered a seat on the East India Company's
Board, rather than mooning round the precincts of the Charterhouse
. . . Above all, he bestowed around him a sense of smoothness,
ineffable, unstemmable smoothness, like oil flowing ever so gently
from the spout of a vessel perfectly regulated by its pourer, soft
lubricating fluid, gradually, but irresistibly, spreading; and spreading, let
it be said, over an unexpectedly wide, even a vast area.'
Engages throughout the war in a running feud with Widmerpool,
dating back to their days together in the City. Promoted Lt.-Col. in
1941 and transferred to 'one of the cloak-and-dagger shows' (probably
Baker Street) responsible for dropping British agents behind enemy
lines. Ambitious as hell, according to Pennistone. Recruits Templer to

his secret service outfit; his activities not unconnected with the resistance in Prince Theodoric's Balkan country; arranges Szymanski's escape from British detention for secret purposes of his own. Unstuck in consequence ('Disciplined, demoted in rank, shunted off to a bloody awful job') on Widmerpool's personal intervention.

Restored in rank with a promising job in Civil Affairs by 1944. M. General Conyers' widow, the former Miss Weedon ('A wonderful woman. Couldn't believe my ears when she said she'd be mine'). Flat in London after the war, cottage in the country; rather proud of his roses. Manages to get Widmerpool sacked from a banking board in collaboration with Sir Bertram Akworth, and anticipates 'no mean revenge' at the time of Widmerpool's disgrace in 1959.

Last encountered as a widower, verging on 80 and looking much younger ('Top-hole form, top-hole. Saw my vet last week. Said he'd never inspected a fitter man of my age'), on his way back from Jimmy Stripling's funeral in the late 'sixties.

QU At the Templers', negotiating a foreign loan with Templer sr., his appearance, demeanour and resemblance to Col. Newcome 74–9, baited by Stripling, disapproves of Gwen McReith, Templer on 81–7, incident of the collar-turner 88–92, Stripling's revenge 94–9, his stinginess, his doubts of Stripling's mental health 100–105; 124; Widmerpool on 132; M. Dubuisson at Paris Conference with 145–6; 220. BM Something in common with Archie Gilbert 57; 152. AW His obituary of Templer sr. 37; Stripling's ragging of recalled 76, 82, 90, 99. CCR 71. KO 24, Widmerpool's Brigade-Major 221. VB Widmerpool's opposite number at Command 243. SA Widmerpool's old enmity towards 22–3, 63; his smoothness, transferred to secret service, his triumph over Widmerpool 194–209, 214. MP His undercover activities. Finn's disapproval of 9–10; his hatred of Widmerpool, Templer hoping for a job with 12–16, 18–19; Pennistone on his arse-licking, in touch with Theodoric 48–9, 51, 54; engineers Szymanski's escape, thereby infuriating Finn 92; Widmerpool gloats over his downfall 111; his own account of the same, unable to bring himself to salute Widmerpool, his views on the nobility of women 114–19; 124; forgiven by Finn, engaged to Mrs Conyers 151; 185, 197; on his fiancée 199–201. TK 79, at military reunion dinner, gloats over Widmerpool's impending ruin 203–4, 210–13; 216–7. HSH Last encounter with recalled 80–3; Widmerpool on their old enmity 223.

FAREBROTHER, Geraldine see WEEDON, Geraldine

FARINELLI
Moreland's tabby cat (named after the famous 18thC castrato singer).
KO 98, 238, 240.

FEINGOLD
Jewish colleague at Jenkins' film studio in the 'thirties; mauve suit and crimson tie; newly graduated from the cutting room and still enthusiastic about script treatments. Settles down to write a satirical novel about the film business with help from Jenkins.

LM 13–14, 28, 168, 212.

FELICITY
Eldest of Bagshaw's three adolescent stepdaughters ('That one's rather a worry too. Young people are nowadays. It's either Regan or Goneril': Bagshaw)

TK 186, 192–5.

FELIX, Prince of Luxembourg 1893–1970
Another of the minor royalty with whom Finn enjoys hobnobbing.

MP 48

FENNEAU, Revd Canon Paul
Fashionable London clergyman with plump pink cheeks and grey curls encountered at a Royal Academy dinner in 1969:
'For some reason Canon Fenneau made me feel a little uneasy. His voice might be soft, it was also coercive. He had small eyes, a large loose mouth, the lips thick, a somewhat receding chin. The eyes were the main feature. They were unusual eyes, not only almost unnaturally small, but vague, moist, dreamy, the eyes of a medium. His cherubic side, increased by a long slightly uptilted nose, was a little too good to be true, with eyes like that. In the manner in which he gave you all his attention there was a taste for mastery.'
Dabbles in the Black Arts ('what might be called the scholarly end of Magic'). Turns out to have been present at Sillery's Oxford tea party in the 'twenties as a frightened freshman (less than the dust beneath Mark Members' chariot wheels); also to have come off best at one point in a brush with Dr Trelawney. Was the first to spot talent in the young Scorpio Murtlock, whose occult powers found encouragement during a stint in the choir of Fenneau's South London church ('"Mystical studies – my Bishop agrees – can be unexpectedly valuable in combating the undesirable in that field". Fenneau's mouth went a little tight again at mention of his Bishop, the eyes taking on a harder, less misty surface. It was permissible to feel that the Bishop himself – elements of exorcism perhaps out of easy reach at that moment – could have agreed, not least from trepidation at prospect of being transformed into a toad, or confined for a thousand years within a hollow oak'). Has since been obliged to dissociate himself from Murtlock's cult, and pronounces a stern warning against him to Widmerpool.

Afterwards proves to be Murtlock's undercover link with the respectable world, useful in occasional tight spots such as the disposal of Widmerpool's body two years later.

QU At Sillery's tea party 176, 179, 189. HSH At RA dinner, his Oxford reminiscences, his marked resemblance to Dr Trelawney and Mrs Erdleigh and previous acquaintance with both, his account of Murtlock's career, his warning to Widmerpool 120, 123–41; 242; acquaintance with Mr Deacon 251; useful to Murtlock 259; summoned by Murtlock after Widmerpool's death 269, 271.

FENWICKS
Children who shared Jenkins' governess at Stonehurst in 1914, their father killed in the first war.

KO 51, 74.

FERRAND-SENESCHAL, Léon-Joseph
Well-known French Marxist intellectual ('an interesting sub-species of fellow traveller': Bagshaw); prolific author of novels, plays, philosophical and economic studies, political tracts etc. Thick lips, closely set eyes, ruminatively brutal expression. Old friend of Widmerpool to whom he bears a certain facial resemblance.

Much in evidence as a Man of the Left at the time of the Spanish Civil War; spent the second war very comfortably in America (showing 'rather exceptional agility in sitting on the fence that divided conflicting attitudes of the Vichy administration from French elements, in France and elsewhere, engaged in active opposition to Germany'), returning on the cessation of hostilities with a greatly enhanced reputation. First met Widmerpool in 1947. Probably responsible for Widmerpool's subsequent contacts with an E. European communist regime, also for furthering his sexual education in a Paris brothel ('I'm not sure what Ferrand-Sénéschal is himself supposed to like – being chained to a crucifix, while a green light's played on him – little girls – two-way mirrors – I've been told, but I can't remember': Bagshaw).

D. in his sixtieth year of a stroke in a Kensington hotel in 1958. Hints of suppressed scandal on the day of his death involving Pamela Widmerpool published in French popular press under the headline 'L'APRES MIDI D'UN MONSTRE?'

Turns out to have been for years playing the same 'under-the-counter Communist games' as Widmerpool, passing information to the Stalinists via Dr Belkin and others. Attended call-girl parties in London with Widmerpool. Had arranged to hide Widmerpool in his hotel room at the time of his appointment with Pamela, and d. in bed with her in the course of this visit. His secret activities afterwards betrayed by Widmerpool as the price of escaping trial for espionage.

TK 8–19, 44–7, 60, 91, 93–4, 107–11, 151, 154, 158, 167, 188, 196, 200, 261–3.

FETTIPLACE-JONES
Tall, dark and handsome, moon-faced Tory MP; former captain of house in Jenkins' first term at school; later develops 'that ingratiating, almost cringing manner some politicians assume to avoid the appearance of thrusting themselves forward'. Friend and contemporary of Roddy Cutts ('His untiring professional geniality rivalled even Roddy's remorseless charm of manner').

AW 176–8, 190, 195–6. CCR 85. KO 91–3, 114. BDFR 233–4, 236.

FETTIPLACE-JONES, Mrs
Wife of above, 'an eager little woman with the features of the Red Queen in *Alice*'.

KO 91.

FETTIPLACE-JONES, Jocelyn
Son of above? M. to a good-looking black girl by 1971, his mother was an Akworth.

HSH 194.

FIELD-MARSHAL, the, see, MONTGOMERY, Field-Marshal

FINES
Family name of Lord Sleaford.

FINN, Major Lysander, VC, Légion d'Honneur, Croix de Guerre avec Palmes, etc.
Jenkins' commanding officer at the War Office, 1941–5, in charge of the Section responsible for liaison with Allies and Neutrals, 'an unusually likeable man' in Jenkins' view. 'Finn's as brave as a lion, as straight as a die, but as hard as nails' (Farebrother).

First War hero, put up an excellent show under General Liddament and afterwards left the City to make an equally good thing out of the cosmetics trade in Paris. Keeps a wife and children hidden away. Re-employed by the army in his middle fifties with the Free French mission in London (and makes a hit with de Gaulle), later moving to the War Office as Lt.-Colonel. Noted for his panache, his unpredictable fusion of agitation with calm, and his remarkable histrionic gifts:
'Had Finn, in fact, chosen the stage as a career, rather than war and commerce, his personal appearance would have restricted him to "character" parts. Superficial good looks were entirely absent. Short,

square, cleanshaven, his head seemed carved out of an elephant's tusk, the whole massive cone of ivory left more or less complete in its original shape, eyes hollowed out deep in the roots, the rest of the protuberance accommodating his other features, terminating in a perfectly colossal nose that stretched directly forward from the totally bald cranium. The nose was preposterous, grotesque, slapstick, a mask from a Goldoni comedy.'

Takes his other assistant David Pennistone into his cosmetics firm after the war, retires shortly afterwards, d. by 1958.

SA Jenkins recommended to by Gen. Liddament 49–50, 85–6; Jenkins interviewed and turned down by 89, 92, 95, 99–106, 172. MP At War Office 2; his character, career and methods of work 4–10, 16, 29; 33, with Prince Theodoric, his brand of snobbery contrasted with Farebrother's 46–9, 51–2; his efficiency in action 54–6; makes a filthy French joke 64–5; 70–1, 85, 87–8; his fury with Farebrother over the Szymanski affair 90–3; his distress over Katyn 103–4; Farebrother's compunction towards 114–5; 139; makes it up with Farebrother 150–2; on trip to continent 155–6, 158, 165–6, 170, 172, 178–80, 183, 191; 192–5, 198, 214, 218–19, 227–9, 236–7. TK Dead 202.

FITZ, Mrs fl. 1920s
Renowned proprietess of a house for tarts in the Piccadilly area.

BM 145.

FITZWITH
Old Boy in Le Bas' house.

BDFR 233.

FLANNIGAN-FITZGERALD
Undergraduate, brother to the Papal chamberlain who provides Sillery with strings to pull at the Vatican.

QU 170.

FLETCHER, F. F.
Boy at school.

QU 48.

FLITTON, Captain Cosmo
Flavia Stringham's first husband ('a well-known criminal with one arm': Peter Templer), father of Pamela (but see below). Heavy drinker, professional gambler, alleged to be none too scrupulous in business dealings. Lost his arm in first war, joined the Happy Valley set in Kenya with Dicky Umfraville ('My God, Cosmo was a swine. A real swine')

and Boffles Stringham, and married the latter's daughter (said to be pregnant by Umfraville at the time, a claim Jenkins rejects: 'Pamela Flitton, it might be thought, carried all the marks of being Cosmo Flitton's daughter'). Ran away with Baby Wentworth but declined to marry her after their respective divorces. Tuberculosis probably the least of the diseases Pamela inherited from him.

M. an American wife after the second war and runs a dude ranch in Montana.

QU 9, 69. CCR 87. VB 146, 150, 156. SA 79. MP 58, 74, 83, 196. BDFR 91–2. TK 150, 163. HSH 200, 227.

FLITTON, Flavia see WISEBITE, Flavia

FLITTON, Pamela
Stringham's niece, only child of his sister Flavia's marriage to Cosmo Flitton. Sick in the font as a 6 or 7 year old bridesmaid ('That child's a fiend') at Stringham's wedding in 1928 or 9. Always in a class by herself from her earliest days.

Turns up in 1942 as a driver briefly attached to Jenkins' War Office section ('it was clear that this AT possessed in a high degree that power which all women – some men – command to a greater or lesser extent when in the mood, of projecting round them a sense of vast resentment. The girl driving, I noticed, was able to do this with quite superlative effect'). Pale eyes, dead white complexion and black hair. Announces Stringham's capture at Singapore, and claims to have been close to him as a child. Leaves the ATS after trouble with a lung. Rumours of devastation among her lovers in the next year or so: 'She appeared . . . scarcely at all interested in looks or money, rank or youth, as such; just as happy deranging the modest home life of a middle-aged air-raid warden, as compromising the commission of a rich and handsome Guards ensign recently left school. In fact, she seemed to prefer "older men" on the whole, possibly because of their potentiality for deeper suffering. Young men might superficially transcend their seniors in this respect, but they probably showed less endurance in sustaining that state, while, once pinioned, the middle-aged could be made to writhe almost indefinitely.'

Operates also in more or less lesbian women drivers' circles (Norah Tolland one of her early victims; seen about with Gwen McReith; friend of Ada Leintwardine). Possibly Prince Theodoric's mistress. Has inside knowledge of the Szymanski affair (and may have been Szymanski's mistress). Generally agreed to have driven Peter Templer to such desperation that he volunteers for what turns out to be a fatal mission in the Balkans.

Posted as secretary to a secret outfit in Cairo where Widmerpool meets her at Groppi's and makes a fool of himself. Said to have been stuffed by Bob Duport against a shed at Cairo airport. Back in London by the summer of 1944, pursuing Widmerpool ("She sent me a postcard – and what a postcard." Widmerpool giggled violently, then recovered himself'), and simultaneously living with Odo Stevens: 'Pamela Flitton gave the impression of being thoroughly vicious, using the word not so much in the moral sense, but as one might speak of a horse – more specifically, a mare'. Temper her chief charm in Stevens' view ('makes her wonderful in bed'). Under Scorpio, according to Mrs Erdleigh, 'and possesses many of the scorpion's cruellest traits'.

Engaged to Widmerpool by July 1945. Inherits Stringham's gold shares (and is said long afterwards by her mother to have fallen madly in love with him when she was a little girl). Publicly accused Widmerpool of murdering Templer, and marries him that autumn ('Why did she do it? How could she? Find the most horrible man on earth, and then marry him?': Flavia Wisebite).

Disrupts Erridge's funeral after the war, and vomits into a Chinese vase at Thrubworth. Leaves Widmerpool for the novelist X. Trapnel in the spring of 1947, suggesting a possible explanation of why she had married Widmerpool in the first place: 'She had done it, so to speak, in order to run away with Trapnel. I do not mean that she had thought it out in precise terms . . . but the violent antithesis presented by their contrasted forms of experience, two unique specimens as it were brought into collision, promised anarchic extremities of feeling of the kind at which she aimed; in which she was principally at home. She liked – to borrow a phrase from St John Clarke – to 'try conclusions with the maelstrom".' Torments Trapnel about his writing. Her love-making (a 'blend of frigidity with insatiable desire') afterwards described by him in nightmarish terms; her hold over Widmerpool alleged to exclude sexual relationship ('She told me he only tried a couple of times. Gave it up as a bad job': Trapnel). Destroys the manuscript of Trapnel's new novel by dumping it in the Regent's Park canal, and returns to Widmerpool that autumn.

Rapid turnover in lovers during the next decade, culminating in sensational press rumours of debauch with the Marxist intellectual Ferrand-Sénéschal on his deathbed in 1958. Turns up the week after with the film tycoon Louis Glober in Venice ('She had the gift of making silence as vindictive as speech'). Said to have agreed to marry Glober in exchange for the lead in his next film. Keenly stimulated by Tiepolo's painting of King Candaules exhibiting his naked wife to a friend, and uses it freely as a means of taunting Widmerpool with impending sexual and political scandal ('The look he gave her suggested that, of all things living, she was the most abhorrent to him'). Lays herself out to impress Trapnel's biographer, Russell Gwinnett, who remains proof against her 'unvarying technique of silence, followed by violence'.

Discovered later that autumn by night on the landing of Gwinnett's lodgings in London ('Perhaps the Tiepolo picture had done something to disturb the balance of Pamela's mind'). Drives Gwinnett into hiding. Tracks down his whereabouts on the day of the Stevenses' musical soirée and mounts a final public assault on Widmerpool afterwards, accusing him of having been hidden in the room on the day Ferrand-Sénéschal died in bed with her, and claiming that both had long been communist agents as well as sexual collaborators. Swallows drugs almost immediately afterwards and d. in bed with Gwinnett at his hotel. The more scandalous aspects of this affair ('Tell me, Nicholas, did not Pamela Widmerpool take an overdose that she might be available to the necrophiliac professor?') hushed up at the inquest; her death reported briefly as suicide of life peer's wife.

BM At Stringham's wedding 225–7. VB 146. MP ATS driver 33–4; identifies herself to Jenkins and announces Stringham's capture at Singapore 57–61, 63–4; notorious in Polish military circles 65–7; reports havoc among her lovers 72–4; brought by Norah Tolland to Ted Jeavons' party, identified as the girl who tormented Templer 79–82; at *Bartered Bride*, with Theodoric, Widmerpool asks her name 98–102; said to be Theodoric's mistress 111; unidentified girl over whom Widmerpool lost his head in Cairo 116; with Odo Stevens, her part in the Szymanski affair, Mrs Erdleigh foretells her future, assaults Stevens 123–37; blamed by Duport for Templer's death 188–90; engaged to Widmerpool 196; his account of their courtship, and her inheritance from Stringham 202–5; at Indian embassy party, blames Widmerpool for Templer's death 209–13, 230 her marriage 244. BDFR Sillery on her prospects of ruining Widmerpool's career 14–16; friendship with Ada Leintwardine 21–3; represents Death itself at Erridge's funeral, 46–8, disrupts the service 52–3, Widmerpool's anxiety over 60–3, Alfred Tolland's enthusiasm for 65; at Thrubworth 69–74, flirts with Roddy Cutts, sick in the Chinese vase 77–85; Tollands on her marriage 88–9; Umfraville lays dubious claim to her paternity 91–2; at *Fission* party, cuts Stevens 128–9, 132, takes an instant dislike to Trapnel 135–7, 139; Trapnel's account of falling for her 160–6; runs away with Trapnel, her departure discovered by Widmerpool 174–84; summons Jenkins to Trapnel's flat, relations with Trapnel, excited by Widmerpool's visit 188–205; reported row with Trapnel 212–3; his account of her technique of persecution 219; turns out to have destroyed his manuscript and left him, his account of her sexual proclivities 223–7; returns to Widmerpool, closeted with a schoolboy 237–8. TK Reflections on her role in the destruction of Trapnel, difficulty of conveying it to Gwinnett 25, 27–9; her married life 36–40; press hints of debauch with Ferrand-Sénéschal 43–7; at Bragadin Palace with Glober, her affinity with and interest in Tiepolo's painting 76–90, snubs Ada Leintwardine 92–5, drawn to Gwinnett over Trapnel, her feelings aroused only by dead lovers 99–103, scene with Widmerpool 104–5, 107–12; makes an assignation with Gwinnett 116; her plans for Glober's Trapnel film undermined by Ada 134–5, 143; Ada on Glober's plan to marry her, and her strange behaviour at dinner the night before 149–52; Gwinnett's account of their assignation 154–9; Odo Stevens on 161–2; at Florian's with the Stevenses 164–9; pursuing Gwinnett, boasts of the destruction of Trapnel's manuscript 170–4, 176–7; last sight of her in Venice 178–9; speculations on Gwinnett's relations with 189–90; mysterious affair of her nakedness at the Bagshaws' 192–6; Gwinnett on 199–200; ditched by Glober, in pursuit of Gwinnett 219–22; at Stevenses' party 230–3, on Gwinnett 236–7; 242; after the party 250–2, scene with Polly Duport and Glober 254–9, defies Mrs Erdleigh's ultimatum 260–1, final onslaught on Widmerpool 262–3; her death 267, 269–70, 276; Widmerpool on 280. HSH Her suicide recalled 41–2; 57, 61; possible reference to in lines from *The Revenger's Tragedy* prefixed to Gwinnett's life of Trapnel 71–3; speculation on her motives, and Gwinnett's 75–6; 94, 98, 100, 109, 118; almost certainly legitimate 200; her mother on her marriage, and her passion as a child for Stringham 202–5.

FLORA
Night club hostess who caused some sort of grievance to Jimmy Brent.
QU 193–4.

FLORES, Colonel Carlos, CBE
Jean Duport's second husband, Latin American army officer and nephew to the President of his country, some years younger than his wife. 'Looks like Rudolph Valentino on an off day' (Bob Duport).

Posted with his wife and stepdaughter to London as military attaché immediately after the second war; spruce, shrewd, genial, rich; comparable to Theodoric and Farebrother in point of smoothness ('All the same I liked him'). Recalled by new government the following year to take up a major military command with political implications. Dictator by the end of the 'fifties. Assassinated by urban guerrillas ten years later.

AW 31, 33. KO 181. MP 219–21, 228–9, 231–6. BDFR 94–8. TK 51, 234–5. HSH 60, 145–6, 252, 254–5.

FLORES, Signora see TEMPLER, Jean

FOCH, Marshal Ferdinand 1851–1929
Commander of Allied Forces in France 1917–18. 'What was it Foch said? War not an exact science, but a terrible and passionate drama? Something like that. Fact is, marriage is rather like that too' (General Conyers).

LM 234–5.

FOPPA
Italian proprietor of the club over a restaurant in Soho to which Barnby introduces Jenkins in the late 'twenties ('one of the merits of the place was that no one either of us knew ever went there'), and where Jean Duport later likes to play Russian billiards. Would have looked remarkably like Victor Emmanuel II if he had grown his moustache and added an imperial to his chin: 'Foppa was decidedly short, always exquisitely dressed in a neat blue, or brown, suit, his tiny feet encased in excruciatingly tight shoes of light tan shade. The shoes were sharply pointed and polished to form dazzling highlights. In summer he varied his footgear by sporting white brogues picked out in snakeskin . . . He was a man of great good nature and independence, who could not curb his taste for gambling in high stakes; a passion that brought him finally, I believe, into difficulties'.

Long settled in London, British army cook in first war, at best a lukewarm supporter of Mussolini. Competes in trotting races; met Umfraville on the course at Greenford; playing piquet with him on the night Barnby brings Anne Stepney to the club ('and before you could say Jack Robinson, the next thing I knew was that the Lady Anne had become my fourth wife': Umfraville). His club avoided by Jenkins after Jean's defection; later a favourite haunt of the Jenkinses and Morelands in the early years of their respective marriages. See also Place Index under FOPPA's.

AW 29, 143–8, 150–1, 153–4, 156–7, 160. LM 14–15, 180–1. CCR 27, 130, 133. KO 85. VB 129, 149, 156. SA 113–14.

FOPPA, Miss
Melancholy and beautiful daughter of above, member of the local Fascist party, never seen in the club.

AW 145–7.

FOXE, Amy
Stringham's mother, daughter of a South African gold millionaire. M. (1) Lord Warrington who d. soon afterwards (2) Boffles Stringham by whom she had two children, Flavia and Charles, divorcing him c.

1920 in favour of (3) Lieutenant-Commander Buster Foxe.

Dazzling, dominating, very decorative, accustomed to fascinate from her first appearance in London as a young and marriageable heiress taken about by old Lady Amesbury. Life interest in her first husband's estate, stud and country seat, Glimber. House near Berkeley Square, and later a place at Sunningdale. Moves at a rapid pace in a smart political and social set (Bill Truscott, Sir Magnus Donners and Sillery all anxious to get in with her in the 'twenties). Old friend of Lady Warminster, and an old enemy in the hospital world of Lady Bridgnorth. Spends money like water; thought to have run through her own fortune and be well on the way to getting through Lord Warrington's by the mid 'thirties.

Said to have led Stringham's father a dance before exchanging him for the no less handsome and even younger Buster. Gave Flavia a baddish time. Too busy (balls, parties, committees, charity work, Red Cross etc.) from earliest years for Charles: 'his mother seemed to exhaust his energies and subdue him. This was not surprising, considering the force of her personality . . .'

Beginning to tire of Buster long before she falls at sight, c. 1934, for the cockney dancer Norman Chandler: 'It looked as if he might be made her prisoner. This was an unguessed aspect of Mrs Foxe's life, a new departure in her career of domination'. Constantly seen about with him thereafter, 'linked in a relationship somewhere between lover with mistress and mother to son'; almost certainly no physical basis to this affair ('just one of those fascinating mutual attractions between improbable people that take place from time to time': Moreland). Devotes her resources exclusively to furthering the interests of Chandler and his friends. Gives the party for Moreland's symphony at which Stringham (now an alcoholic) is forcibly removed by her former secretary Miss Weedon, and Moreland's affair with Priscilla Tolland is made public.

Leaves London on the outbreak of war to be near Norman's army camp, moving into a labourer's cottage in Essex, rising at 5.30 a.m. each morning to cook his breakfast, and serving notice of divorce on Buster. Money troubles. Dies shortly after the war in greatly reduced circumstances, her entailed estate (South African securities now showing every sign of recovery) passing via Stringham to her grand-daughter Pamela Flitton.

QU Her photograph in Stringham's room at school 9; Uncle Giles on her family 20; luncheon with, force of her personality 54, 59–62; Templer on her family life 69–70; Widmerpool on her vast wealth 130; Sillery's interest in 175–6; Truscott and Donners hangers-on of 190; against Stringham leaving Oxford 206–9; at lunch in Stringham's rooms, won over by Sillery 212–14, 216–19. BM Said to be tiring of Buster 61, 103; Mr Deacon's recollections of 119–20; Donners' connection with 137; reaction to Stringham's wedding 197, 222, 225–6; resemblance to Milly Andriadis 273. AW Barnby not averse to 72; her photograph in Stringham's flat 206. LM Miss Weedon's relations with 161–2, 167. CCR At the *Duchess of Malfi*, start of her passion for Norman Chandler 43–4, 49–54; Lady Warminster on her background, speculation on her relationship with Chandler 87–91; giving a party for Moreland 133–5; at her party, on Stringham, Chandler's domination of 140–9, with Stringham, his approval of Chandler's influence on 161–6, her negotiations to get Stringham removed 170–3, 180, 187–9. KO Her party recalled 104–5, 247. VB Umfraville's account of how she fell for Buster 154; Buster on her proposal to divorce him 164–5. SA Money troubles, Stringham on her life with Norman 79; her party recalled 72, 222–3. TK 227. MP Helping with Red Cross libraries 59; Widmerpool on her death, and her fortune 204–5. HSH Her tears at Stringham's wedding recalled 205.

FOXE, Lieutenant-Commander Buster, RN
Stringham's mother's third husband, an immensely chic polo-playing sailor several years younger than his wife. 'A son-of-a-bitch in the top class' (Dicky Umfraville).

Not at university; DSC in first war; same generation as Umfraville whose first wife killed herself when Buster ditched her to marry Amy Stringham for money in 1920. On terms of mutual hostility with his stepson ('Charles hated Buster's guts': Umfraville) and with his wife's secretary Miss Weedon. In the Admiralty. Tall, fit, exquisitely turned out, does himself pretty well; savage sneer and icy personality; almost preternaturally small head. Makes Jenkins feel remarkably ill at ease as a schoolboy introduced to the house by Stringham:
'I was conscious that some sort of duel had been taking place, and that Stringham had somehow gained an advantage by, as it were, ordering Buster from the room . . . Like a man effortlessly winning a walking race, he crossed the carpet with long, easy strides: at the same time separating from himself some of the eddies of cold air that surrounded him, and bequeathing them to the atmosphere of the room after he had left it. I was relieved at his departure.'

Grown distinctly fatter and less juvenile in appearance when next encountered in 1924 ('It was clear that he accepted the fact that in the presence of his wife he was a subordinate figure, wherever he might rank away from her. Mrs Foxe's ownership of Buster seemed complete when they were in a room together'). Thwarted in plans for Stringham to settle in Kenya, and in further schemes to prevent his leaving

Oxford. 'Much humbled' according to Stringham by the end of the 'twenties; left the navy; his wife reported to be contemplating divorce. Retires to bed ('perhaps physically incapacitated by anguish of jealousy') on the say of Stringham's wedding.

Solely interested in dieting (cures at Tring) by the early 'thirties according to his old enemy Miss Weedon. Once pinched Matilda Moreland's leg, and has been seen about with Mildred Haycock. Chastened to the point of obsequiousness at his wife's party (where he is mistaken by Maclintick for the butler). Enthusiastic about her infatuation for Norman Chandler. Gloats openly over having rid the house at last of Stringham. Takes a beautiful revenge, when Stringham drops in unexpectedly to tease him, by tipping off Stringham's gaoler Miss Weedon.

Re-joins the navy on the outbreak of war, stationed with a top-secret outfit at Thrubworth Park and turns up in 1941 ('Good looks, formerly of neat film-star quality, had settled down in middle-age to an appearance at once solid and forcible, a bust of the better type of Roman senator') at Lady Frederica Budd's:
'When people really hate one another, the tension within them can sometimes make itself felt throughout a room, like atmospheric waves, first hot, then cold, wafted backwards and forwards, as if in an invisible process of air conditioning, creating a pervasive physical disturbance. Buster Foxe and Dicky Umfraville, between them, brought about this state. Their really overpowering mutual detestation dominated for a moment all other local agitations . . . At the same time, to anyone who did not know what horrors linked them together, they might have appeared a pair of old friends, met after an age apart.'

Under threat of divorce, his wife having apparently stopped his allowance, locked up both her houses and gone off to be with Norman ('taking the keys with her, so that I can't even get at my own suits and shirts'). Subsequently promoted Captain. Parts company with his wife. Dead by 1958: 'There hasn't been a good laugh since that horse-box backed over Buster Foxe at Lingfield' (Umfraville).★

QU At home, his glacial manner, relations with his wife and stepson 54–61, 63, 69; Claudius to Stringham's Hamlet 73; resemblance to Farebrother 75, 77; jealousy of, and machinations against Stringham 174–6, 206, 208, 214, 216; with his wife at Oxford, outmanoeuvred by Sillery 217–19. BM Out of favour with Mrs Foxe 61, 103–4; Mr Deacon on 119; reaction to Stringham's wedding 197, 224–5. AW Resemblance to Umfraville 151, 156. LM Miss Weedon on 166–7.

★ An exaggeration on Umfraville's part: 'Captain Foxe's end . . . was less dramatic, though certainly brought about by some fatal accident near the course . . .'

CCR Moreland on 135; at his wife's party 140, on Stringham's fate, his boundless admiration for Chandler 144–8, 153, greatly put out by Stringham's arrival 162–5, 168, his revenge 186–7. KO Claims to be great pals with Stringham 104–5; rejoins the navy 215. VB Umfraville's account of being framed by 150–6; at Frederica Budd's house to register complaints about his wife, Umfraville's revenge 160–7. SA Parted from his wife, Stringham on 79. TK Umfraville on his death 3.

FRANCO, General Francisco 1892–1975
Nationalist C-in-C during Spanish Civil War, 1936–9; St John Clarke thinks he can't win, George Tolland inclines to think he can, Mrs Maclintick hopes to God he doesn't.

CCR 95, 119, 121, 200.

FRANZ FERDINAND, Archduke d. 1914
Heir to the thrones of Austria and Hungary, assassinated with his morganatic wife in the Bosnian capital Sarajevo on June 28, 1914, in a nasty affair reported that very afternoon by Uncle Giles ('Heard the news in Aldershot. Fellow I went to see was told on the telephone') to Captain and Mrs Jenkins at Stonehurst.

KO 69–70.

FRED
Beefy talkative barman at the Royal in the same seaside town as the Bellevue, provides girls for Bob Duport.

KO 167–8, 171, 181–2, 193.

FREDERICK, Empress 1840–1901
Widow of Frederick, Emperor of Germany; shared an interest in painting with a great-uncle of her namesake, Frederica Budd.

LM 26, 211.

FRENCH, Field-Marshal Sir John 1852–1925
Hero of Jenkins' childhood on account of his Boer War exploits, notably the cavalry charge on Kimberley in which General Conyers took part as a young man ('What was it like? Just have to think for a moment. Long time ago, you know. Have to collect my thoughts. Well, I think I can tell you exactly. The fact was there had been some difficulty in mounting me . . . Ride rather heavy, you know. As far as I can remember, I had the greatest difficulty in getting my pony out of a trot. I'm sure that was what happened. Later on in the day, I shot a Boer in the shin': Conyers).

LM 2–3, 235.

FREUD, Sigmund 1856–1939
Pooh-poohed by St John Clarke but taken up in the early 'thirties by General Conyers who diagnoses the case histories of Widmerpool, Jenkins, Erridge etc. in the light of his psychoanalytical principles. Chips Lovell also recently (1937) been told about.

AW 127. LM 81, 221, 226–30, 235–6. CCR 201, 215. KO 211.

GAINSBOROUGH, Dr Vernon see GUGGENBÜHL, Werner

GAITSKELL, Hugh 1906–63
Leader of the Labour party, probably had a hand in Widmerpool's peerage.

TK 39.

GANDHI, Mahatma 1869–1948
Sillery once a keen propagandist for.

QU 169.

GARBO, Greta b. 1905
Film star, Alfred Tolland thought she was a man.

LM 137.

de GAULLE, General Charles A. J. M. 1890–1970
Leader of Free French forces in second war, likes Major Finn.

LM 5. SA 104. MP 84–5, 141, 235.

GAUNTLETT, Mr
Ancient neighbour of the Jenkinses in the country, professional rustic and local sage of some standing. Yeomanry in first war, once rode through the Khyber Pass; slight resemblance to General Conyers; lives alone in haunted house near the Devil's Fingers and is sceptical about Scorpio Murtlock's transcendental powers.

HSH 18, 20–3, 25–7, 152–60, 173, 243.

GEDDES
Name of Widmerpool's paternal grandfather, a Lowland Scott who m. a Miss Widmerpool and changed his name to hers on account of her higher social standing.

QU 135. LM 84.

GEORGE IV 1762–1830
Dogdene painted white and gold from top to bottom when he came to stay.

LM 214.

GHIKA
Old Boy at Le Bas' house reunion dinner; 'He fixed his huge black eyes on Widmerpool, concentrating absolutely on his words, but whether with interest, or boredom of an intensity that might lead even to physical assault, it was impossible to say'.

AW 176, 184–5, 195. BDFR 233.

GILBERT, Archie
Immaculate spare man invariably present at London dances in the 'twenties, has partnered every one of the three or four hundred debutantes in circulation and is approved without exception by their mothers. Dines with the Walpole-Wilsons on the night of the Huntercombes' ball. Said to do something with base metals in the City: 'He himself never referred to any such subordination, and I used sometimes to wonder whether this putative job was not, in reality, a polite fiction, invented on his own part out of genuine modesty, of which I am sure he possessed a great deal, in order to make himself appear a less remarkable person than in truth he was: even a kind of superhuman ordinariness being undesirable, perhaps, for true perfection in this role of absolute normality which he had chosen to play with such *éclat*. He was unthinkable in everyday clothes; and he must, in any case, have required that rest and sleep during the hours of light which his nocturnal duties could rarely, if ever, have allowed him.'

Not seen again till 1945, when he and Jenkins run into one another collecting demob outfits at Olympia. Gunner captain in an anti-aircraft battery in north London ('One pictured a lot of hard, rather dreary work, sometimes fairly dangerous, sometimes demanding endurance in unexciting circumstances. Perhaps experience in the London ballrooms had stood him in good stead in the latter respect'), where he met and married a girl from across the road.

BM At the Walpole-Wilsons' 26–7, 31, 33–5, 38, 41, 46–7, 49–51; gives rise to a terrible suspicion 54–7; at the Huntercombes' 62, 78; compared to Truscott 131; and to Donners 136; 159, 195. CCR 61. MP 242–4.

GIRAUD, General H. H. 1879–1949
Succeeds Darlan as C-in-C of French forces in N. Africa at Christmas 1942.

MP 84, 141.

GITTINS, Lance-Corporal Gareth
Storeman in Gwatkin's company, brother-in-law to CSM Cadwallader, an eccentric and forceful personality who holds a nightly salon for friends and relations in the store-room.

SA 35, 50–2, 85–7, 207–8. HSH 141–3.

GLADSTONE, William Ewart 1809–98
Liberal Prime Minister, once insulted by Lord Vowchurch; salmon always makes Sillery think of.

QU 169, 214. AW 126. LM 34.

GLOBER, Louis
American publisher, playboy and film tycoon. A tall, bald, melodramatic character ('looking as if he's going to play Long John Silver in a Christmas production of *Treasure Island*': Moreland). Rather intelligent and far from unsympathetic. Early sixties by 1958, staying with Jacky Bragadin in Venice and anxious to marry Pamela Widmerpool.

Son of emigré Russian Jews from the Bronx (where his father made a sizeable pile as a builder). Previously encountered at the end of the 'twenties as a dynamic young publisher from New York. Looked like a Byzantine emperor ('His quietly forceful manner suggested a right to command, inexhaustible funds of stored up energy, overwhelming sophistication, inexhaustible funds of stored up energy, overwhelming sophistication, limitless financial resource. At that age I did not notice a hard core of melancholy lurking beneath these assets'), and made love to Mopsy Pontner on the table after a fairly sticky dinner party at his hotel ('One rather odd thing about Glober, he insisted on taking a cutting from my bush – said he always did that after having anyone for the first time': Mrs Pontner). His firm sold up the year after.

Subsequently made and lost several fortunes, married and left several beautiful wives. Regularly figures in gossip columns on both sides of the Atlantic as socialite, sportsman (noted rider, shot, golfer, yachtsman, racing car driver) etc.; secret philanthropist; collects paintings (including one of only two Daniel Tokenhouses ever sold) and vintage cars.

Pursued by Baby Clarini (formerly Wentworth) in Venice with a view to marriage. Plans to film Pamela's version of X. Trapnel's *Profiles in String* with herself in the starring role; hits Widmerpool on the jaw with a ripe peach during a game of cricket at the Bragadin palazzo; and is cut out with Pamela by Russell Gwinnett. Plans to film St John Clarke's *Match Me Such Marvel* with Polly Duport as star.

Turns up with Polly the following summer at the Stevenses' party and breaks Widmerpool's glasses during the commotion caused by Pamela afterwards. Killed in 1960 in a car accident on the Moyenne Corniche.

TK In Venice, his career and public image 61–4; previous encounter with recalled 64–72; compared to Trapnel 73–4; at Bragadin palace with Pamela 79–82, 85–9, meets Gwinnett, comparison between the two as American types 95–101, his Trapnel film plans, with Baby Clarini 103–4,

113–16; at Biennale with Ada Leintwardine, lunches with Jenkins and Tokenhouse, his character contrasted with Gwinnett's, buys a painting 128–48; Ada on his plans to marry Pamela 149–52; 155, 159; his past exploits, Pamela's disobliging attitude to 162–6, 168; 171, 173, 216; has dropped Pamela and Trapnel for Polly and St John Clarke 219–22; at the Stevens' party 229, 233–6, 245, 251; and afterwards 253–9, 262, 264–6; his death 268–9; last sight of in vintage car rally recalled 278–9. HSH 63, 115, Duport charmed by his treatment of Widmerpool 254.

GOERING, Hermann 1893–1946
Presents no obstacle to Widmerpool's peace plans for Nazi Germany in the 'thirties ('I expect he is a bit of a snob – most of us are at heart – well, ask him to Buckingham Palace. Show him round. What is there against giving him the Garter? After all, it is what such things are for, isn't it?').

LM 64.

GOLDNEY, Mr
Ally of the Jenkinses and others in the great quarry battle of 1968; secretary to the local archaeological society; colonial service, retired; looks like a 'twenties film star making a comeback.

HSH 151–2, 172.

GOLLOP, Mr
The younger and more pugnacious of two quarry directors scheming to build a waste tip on the Devil's Fingers site in the late 'sixties; makes no concession in the direction of appeasement, speaking instead 'in a harsh rasping voice about the nation's need for nonskid surfacing on its motorways and arterial roads'; temporarily thwarted by a government enquiry.

HSH 150–2, 172.

GOMEZ, General
Head of a South American republic, his rise to (or possibly fall from) power indirectly responsible for an inglorious close to Sir Gavin Walpole-Wilson's diplomatic career.

BM 19.

GORING, Hon. Barbara
Pretty and popular daughter of Lord and Lady Goring, granddaughter of Lord Aberavon, cousin to Eleanor Walpole-Wilson. Jenkins tormented by love of her from an afternoon at the Albert Memorial in June, not long after leaving Oxford ('I must have been about twenty-

one or twenty-two at the time, and held then many rather wild ideas on the subject of women'), until the Huntercombes' ball the following summer, when his feelings are abruptly quenched by her emptying a sugar castor over Widmerpool.

Small, dark, dishevelled, noisy, fond of ragging: 'her restlessness was of that deceptive kind that usually indicates a fundamental deficiency, rather than surplus, of energy . . .' Gives Jenkins little to show for their affair ('Such scuffles as had, once in a way, taken place between us . . . were not exactly encouraged by her') beyond wakeful nights, frightful jealousy of potential rivals such as Tompsitt, and a legacy of painful sensations ever afterwards associated with Mr Deacon's *Boyhood of Cyrus* which had hung in her aunt Lady Walpole-Wilson's hall, 'representing on my arrival in front of it a two-to-one chance of seeing Barbara at dinner'.

Turns out to have been simultaneously beloved by Widmerpool, who was for years prevented from proposing only by lack of funds and is finally disabused, like Jenkins, by her behaviour at the Huntercombes'. Engaged to Johnny Pardoe later that summer.

Immured in the country on Pardoe's estate by the early 'thirties, thought to be having a difficult time coping with his melancholia and a baby that went wrong. Has a seventeen-year-old granddaughter, newly m. to a pop star by 1968.

BM Jenkins' feelings for, recalled by Mr Deacon's paintings 1, 15–16; start of his obsession with 17–19; unsatisfactory course of their affair 23–5; 34; at the Walpole-Wilsons', Jenkins' jealousy 36–40, 42, 47, 49–50, 54–5; acquaintance with Widmerpool 60; at the Huntercombes', pours sugar over Widmerpool 62–74; his reactions 79–82; compared to Gypsy Jones, as object of Widmerpool's desire 127, 130, 170–1; Jenkins' growing indifference to 141, 143, 152–3, 175–6, 181, 191, 224; Widmerpool's ditto 206, 208, 222; compared to Gypsy, as object of Jenkins' desire 257–8; the Widmerpools on, her engagement 263–4, 266–71. AW Afternoon in Hyde Park with recalled 120; sugar incident recalled 178. LM Sugar pouring recalled 29, 46; Widmerpool on 55–7; her marriage, reversal of roles between herself and Eleanor 92–3. CCR Sugar pouring recalled 85. VB Her family connection with Rowland Gwatkin 186, 189. SA Hogbourne-Johnson's brutality to Widmerpool recalls hers 56. MP 109, 244. TK 158, her assault on Widmerpool compared to his wife's 263. HSH Her behaviour recalled by Quiggin twins 46–7.

GORING, Hon. David
Barbara's younger brother, still a schoolboy at the time of her association with Jenkins (and not much of a hand at his books, according to Mrs Widmerpool).

BM 16, 124.

GORING, Lady (Constance)
Mother of Tom, Barbara and David, sister of Lady Walpole-Wilson, daughter of the shipping magnate Lord Aberavon; brought her husband half his fortune ('without the Gwatkin money they would never be able to keep up Pembringham Woodhouse as they do': Widmerpool). Reluctant hostess, semi-invalid from nerves. Used to ask the Widmerpools over quite often when Kenneth's father worked for her husband.

BM 21, 33, 59–60, 80–81. HSH 47.

GORING, Lord (George)
Barbara's father; no connection with the baronets of the same name ('of course, the Gorings have not produced a statesman of the first rank since their eighteenth-century ancestor – and he is entirely forgotten': Widmerpool). Once showed promise in the House of Lords but held no office and has since sunk into political obscurity. Shuns London. Seat: Pembringham Woodhouse. Pioneer in scientific approach to agriculture, owns a fruit farm 'rather famous for daring methods'. Bought his liquid manure from Widmerpool's father, and supplied the Widmerpools with a house on his estate while experimenting with fertilizers.

BM 21, 33, 58–9, 80–1. LM 84–5. HSH 47.

GORING, Brigadier the Hon. Tom
Elder son of above, contemporary of Jenkins at school; rifleman commanding a brigade in second war, crony of George Tolland.

BM 16, 24. BDFR 41, 51.

GORT, General Lord ('Fat Boy Gort') 1886–1946
CIGS and commander of British Expeditionary Force in 1939, fails to find a job for Jenkins' father.

KO 207.

GOSSAGE
Weekly music critic, first encountered in the Mortimer with Moreland and Maclintick at the end of the 'twenties: 'He was a lean, toothy little man, belonging to another common musical type, whose jerky movements gave him no rest. He toyed nervously with his bow tie, pince-nez and moustache, the last of which carried little conviction of masculinity. Gossage's voice was like that of a ventriloquist's doll . . .' It was Gossage who unwittingly brought Maclintick and his wife Audrey together, having picked up a musical bank clerk named Stanley who turned out to be her brother. Helps Moreland clear up the mess

seven years later after Audrey's elopement and Maclintick's suicide.

Barely changed, 'a trifle more dried up and toothy than formerly', at the Stevenses' musical party in 1959.

CCR In the Mortimer 14–15, 18–19, 22–5; 43, 54–5, 107, 139, 142, 146, 148–52; Maclintick's account of meeting Audrey through 208–10; 217–18. SA 135. TK 226, 230, 237–40, 247–8. HSH 64.

de GRAEF, Captain Gauthier
Belgian assistant military attaché.

MP 86–7, 90, 156, 158, 178–80, 184, 200.

GRANT, Joy
Lady of the town and the second of Dicky Umfraville's five wives; had slept with practically every brother officer in the regiment before consoling him for the death of his first round about 1920. Umfraville obliged to send in his papers on marrying her and emigrate to Kenya, where she left him for Lord Castlemallock, eloping almost immediately with the jockey Jo Breen. Afterwards keeps an infamously expensive pub in the Thames valley.

AW 158. VB 145, 154–5, 170.

GREENING, Robin
General Liddament's pink-cheeked, fair-haired ADC in 1941, 'one of the most agreeable officers in those headquarters'. About twenty, blushes easily, unlikely to rise far. Badly wounded at Anzio.

Deeply impressed by Widmerpool's brutality to Bithel, and turns up as a forestry consultant in 1969 bringing news of the takeover of Widmerpool by Murtlock's cult ('A new lot . . . who wore even stranger togs, and went in for even gaudier monkey tricks').

VB 94–5, 97. SA 35, 50–2, 85–7, 207–8. HSH 141–3, 218.

GUGGENBÜHL, Werner
Milly Andriadis' new young boyfriend in 1933 ('He was dark . . . and not bad looking in a very German style. His irritable expression recalled Quiggin's'); owner of the grey pyjamas in which she receives Umfraville and party at her Park Lane flat; responsible for her political conversion ('His uncompromising behaviour no doubt expressed to perfection the role to which he was assigned in her mind: the scourge of frivolous persons of the sort she knew so well').

'Patrician background but turned early to the Left' (Sillery). 'Smart enough to see Hitler coming and get out of Germany' (Quiggin). Didactic, ambitious, disobliging. Writing a socially conscious play ('Drama as highest of arts we Germans know. No mere entertainment, please'). His malevolence disconcerts even Umfraville. Ousts Quiggin later that summer as secretary to St John Clarke, whom he turns into a Trotskyite. Has moved on to something more paying by 1935.

Becomes a fellow (political theory) of Sillery's college after the war, and changes his name to Vernon Gainsborough. Affair with Lady Craggs (formerly Gypsy Jones). Recants from Trotskyism in his book *Bronstein: Marxist or Mystagogue?* ('It's a real *apologia pro vita sua*': Bagshaw), pub. Quiggin & Craggs 1947.

Puts in a somewhat sour appearance on the TV rehabilitation of St John Clarke in 1968, trying unsuccessfully to divert Quiggin and Members from sex to politics.

AW 162, 164–9, 174. LM 125, 154. CCR 74, 226. BDFR 21, 70, 132, 135, 239. HHS 39–40.

GUINAN, Texas 1884–1933
Night club queen and minor Hollywood star, on whose account Louis Glober once burst a methusalem of champagne.

TK 63.

GULLICK
The Jenkinses' morose and wizened gardener at Stonehurst in 1914, born out of wedlock ('Gullick, as if gloomily contemplating the accident of his birth, was usually to be found pottering among the vegetables, foretelling a bad season for whichever crop he stood among').

KO 8–9, 42, 73.

GULLICK, Mrs
Wife of above, helps in the house at Stonehurst, 'a small elderly, red-faced woman, said to "give Gullick a time", because she considered she had married beneath her'. Sceptical about the Stonehurst ghost. Has it for a fact on the outbreak of war that Dr Trelawney has been shot as a spy in the Tower of London.

KO 3, 6, 8, 20, 33, 42–3, 61, 74.

GWATKIN
Family name of Lord Aberavon.

GWATKIN, Blodwen
Rowland Gwatkin's wife ('Blodwen Davies that had lived next door all their lives'), whom he married for want of a better when jilted by Yanto Breeze's sister, and who eventually succeeds in saddling him with his mother-in-law as well.

VB 18, 102, 191, 232–3. MP 176.

GWATKIN, Captain Rowland

Jenkins' company commander in the Welsh battalion posted to N.
Ireland in 1940. Smallish with a little black moustache and angry little
black eyes ('I judged him to be about my own age, perhaps a year or
two younger'). Works in a local bank like the rest of the battalion's
officers and is not expected to go far. Father in insurance, grandfather
a tenant farmer on the estate of Lord Aberavon (another Rowland
Gwatkin, with whom there may or may not be a remote family
connection). M., no children.

Stern, even Stendhalian sense of destiny. Dedicated to making his
company the best in the battalion. Outraged by slackers such as
Lieutenants Breeze and Bithel. Spends hours poring over his *Field
Service Pocket Book, Infantry Training, Manual of Military Law* etc., and is
wildly over-ambitious in attempts to put their theory into practice.
Confides a secret admiration for the Roman centurion in *Puck of Pook's
Hill*, and for Kipling's 'Hymn to Mithras' (' "Those lines make you
think," said Gwatkin slowly . . . "Make you glad you're married . . .
Don't have to bother about women any more"'). Jenkins increasingly
fascinated by the gulf between his comparatively modest practical
abilities ('Criticism from above left him dreadfully depressed') and his
romantic aspirations:

'He had draped a rubber groundsheet round him like a cloak, which,
with his flattish-brimmed steel helmet, transferred him into a figure
from the later Middle Ages, a captain-of-arms of the Hundred Years
War, or the guerrilla campaigning of Owen Glendower. I suddenly saw
that was where Gwatkin belonged, rather than to the soldiery of modern
times, the period which captured his own fancy. Rain had wetted his
moustache, causing it to droop over the corners of the mouth, like those
belonging to effigies on tombs or church brasses. Persons at odds with
their surroundings not infrequently suggest an earlier historical epoch.
Gwatkin was not exactly at odds with the rest of the world. In many
ways, he was the essence of conventional behaviour. At the same time,
he never mixed with others on precisely their own terms. Perhaps
people suspected – disapproved – his vaulting dreams.'

Begins to lose his grip after the company's move to Castlemallock in
May. Lost in daydreams of a local barmaid Maureen, for whom his
feelings are too sacred to describe. Puts the alcoholic Bithel under arrest
('Bithel *kissed* an Other Rank'), and is severely reprimanded by the
Castle commandant. Makes 'an imperial balls-up' over codewords, and
is further humiliated by the Adjutant. Relieved of his command.
Discovers Maureen in a clinch with one of his own corporals. Ordered
to return to the ITC (Infantry Training Centre) to await a posting.
Hears from his wife that her mother may move in with them. Invalided

out of the army shortly afterwards ('Kidneys, was it? Or something to do with the back? Flat feet, it might have been') and reported to have returned to banking:

'The thought of Gwatkin and his mother-in-law had sometimes haunted me; the memory of his combined horror and resignation in face of this threatened affliction. To have his dreams of military glory totally shattered as well seemed, as so often in what happens to human beings, out of all proportion to what he had deserved, even if these dreams had, in truth, been impracticable for one of his capacity.'

Dead by the end of the 'sixties, having taken an active interest in Territorial and ex-Service organizations to the end.

VB First impressions of 3, 8–13, 15, 31; hatred of Lt. Breeze 17–18; excitement at the move to Ireland 40, 42, 45; contradictions in his character analysed 46–51; his nocturnal panic over codewords, his weakness for Kipling 56–9; his vain attempt to reform Private Sayce 60–5; his pep talk on rifles 66–8; 70; his vaulting dreams, his misplaced enthusiasm on divisional exercise ends in disaster 73–82; handsome behaviour to Jenkins, on Kipling and on women 85–92; self-confidence restored, blames Breeze for Pendry's death 93–5, 97–102; his company quartered at Castlemallock 168, 170; startling change in him 175–9; glamour of army life still indimmed for him, his infatuation with Maureen 179–93, 197–8; puts Bithel under arrest 199–206; muddle over codewords, in trouble over Bithel, relieved by her with Corporal Gwylt 223–31; his dignity at parting 232–7; 239, 242. SA His love of Kipling recalled 15; Widmerpool's behaviour compared to 58; and contrasted with 187–8. MP Left the army 174–6. BDFR Compared to X. Trapnel 167. HSH His death 134; a dim memory to Bithel 264–5.

GWINNETT, Button 1735–1777
Signer of the American Declaration of Independence, collateral ancestor of below.

TK 49, 97–8. HSH 197.

GWINNETT, Professor Russell
American academic (English literature at a well-known US women's college) writing a doctoral dissertation on the life and works of X. Trapnel: 'Nothing about the Trapnel story was simple. Although Gwinnett was quick to grasp things, nothing about his own personality was simple either. He was an altogether unfamiliar type'.

First encountered at the international writers' conference in Venice in 1958. Early thirties, slight, sallow, neat black moustache, tinted spectacles; well-disposed towards Jenkins' novels ('That was an excellent start') but otherwise markedly unforthcoming. Possibly eaten up with donnish vanity: 'There was also something not at all self-satisfied about him, an impression of anxiety, a never ceasing awareness of impending disaster . . . It might be that he was a reprieved alcoholic. He had some of that sad, worn, preoccupied air that suggests loneliness'.

Old friend and protegé of Dr Emily Brightman. Impeccable New England lineage, grandson of a successful lawyer, son of some sort of spendthrift and bad lot. Good at racquets, skating, ski-ing, had hoped to be a poet, draws well ('Almost always portraits of himself'). Deep-seated Gothic tastes. Obsessed with death from early college days when he broke into a mortuary to obtain access to the body of a girlfriend who had committed suicide.

Intrigued by Pamela Widmerpool's part in Trapnel's downfall, and shows impressive ability in handling her; unmoved by her Trapnel impersonations; indifferent to physical assault ('He seemed . . . to have accomplished a transformation of roles, in which she stalked him, rather than he her'). In London that autumn, sampling the various sleazy hotels where Trapnel lived, tracing Trapnel's girlfriends etc. Moot point as to whether his attempts at reconstructing Trapnel's life will stop short of an affair with Pamela. Interviews L. O. Salvidge, Bagshaw etc. and moves into Bagshaw's house as lodger, leaving at Christmas after a mysterious episode in which Pamela possibly broke into the house, probably spent several hours alone with him in his bedroom, and was certainly discovered naked outside it in the small hours. Moves into another of Trapnel's hotels near St Pancras; and is visited by Pamela who d. in bed with him from an overdose of drugs. Abandons his career, shelves his Trapnel book, takes a job as water-ski-ing instructor at a Spanish coastal resort.

Next heard of when his biography of Trapnel, *Death's-Head Swordsman*, wins the Magnus Donners prize in 1968. Thickset, shaven skull, unrecognisable. Has returned to academic life (obscure American college with exceptionally severe student trouble). Working on a new book, *The Gothic Symbolism of Mortality in the Texture of Jacobean Stagecraft*.

Back in London for research purposes in 1970. Highly esteemed in occult circles as necromancer and necrophiliac ('in modern times almost making magical history') on account of the circumstances of Pamela's death. Invited severally by Widmerpool and Scorpio Murtlock to inspect their joint cult activities. Takes notes throughout the Midsummer Eve rites in which naked cult members, including Fiona Cutts, attempt to raise Dr Trelawney's ghost, and Murtlock knifes Widmerpool. M. Fiona the following spring ('if he had done some dubious things in his time, so too had she'), and returns to the Middle West.

TK In Venice, preliminary diagnosis of his character, difficulty of conveying any but the most superficial truths about Trapnel to 19–24, has Trapnel's Commonplace Book, 36, 40–1; his friendship with Dr Brightman, intrigued by deathbed connection between Pamela Widmerpool and Ferrand-Sénéschal 41–5, 47; Dr Brightman on his background and eccentricities 48–51; at Bragadin palace, on Glober 60–4, 73–5, meets Glober, their dissimilarity and likeness 95–9, approaches Pamela over Trapnel 100–105, 108–9, 111–12, 116; contrasted as an American type with Glober 138–9; Glober's jealousy of 149, 152; dinner with, his report of a startling encounter with Pamela in the Basilica 154–9; at Florian's, meets Pamela 162–4, 166–7; proof against her dramatic attempts to impress him 169–75; gives Jenkins Trapnel's Commonplace Book 176–7, 181; Bagshaw's plans to entice him as a lodger 184–6; his attempt at retracing Trapnel's steps, incident with Pamela at the Bagshaws' 189–91, 193–6; lunch with in the New Year, his Trapnel researches, enigma of his relations with Pamela 197–201, 214–15; Pamela in pursuit of 221; and discovers his address 236–7; 251–2; enigmatic letter from him a year later, speculations on his part in Pamela's death 267–70, 276. HSH His part in Pamela's death recalled 41–2, 57–8; his life of Trapnel submitted for Donners prize, its cryptic epigraph 66–77; his biography assessed, and awarded the prize 86–8, 90–2, 94–5; at prize dinner 97–101, 105, his speech 106–7, 109, 113, approached by Widmerpool 114–15; back in London, proposing to visit Widmerpool and Murtlock 143–4, 146–8; at the Devil's Fingers, his account of the night's rites 161–174; Delavacquerie's account of Murtlock's means and motives in getting hold of him 177–86, 198; married to Fiona Cutts 196–9; at Stourwater with her, encounter with Widmerpool and cult members 207–15, 220, 227, 231–7; Delavacquerie's reaction to his marriage 239–40; his transcendental powers, Murtlock's interest in 260.

GWITHER, Lance Corporal
Squat and swarthy cook to F Mess at Divisional HQ in 1941, plasterer's mate in civil life, gets on well with the mess waiter Charles Stringham.

SA 71, 77.

GWYLT, Corporal Ivor
NCO in Jenkins' platoon in 1940, 'one of the company's several wits, tiny, almost a dwarf, with a huge head of black curly hair'. His jokes, songs, gossip about girls, Dai and Shoni stories etc. a welcome distraction from the tedium of army life. Discovered by Captain Gwatkin embracing the barmaid Maureen, Gwatkin's beloved, in Lady Caro's Dingle at Castlemallock.

VB 41–5, 51, 54–6, 74–5, 82, 84–6, 88, 92, 97, 121, 175, 195–6, 211–12, 229–32, 235–6.

HACKFORTH, Captain
Guest at the Huntercombes' ball.
BM 57.

HARDICANUTE
Moreland's black cat, successor to Farinelli.
TK 153.

HARLOW, Jean 1911–37
See DIETRICH, Marlene.

HARMER, Sergeant
In charge of Defence Platoon temporarily commanded by Jenkins at Divisional HQ in 1941, 'a middle-aged man with bushy eyebrows, largely built, rather slow, given to moralizing', foreman in a steel works in peace time.
SA 42–3, 49, 52, 107, 186.

HARRIET
One of Jenkins' great-aunts, said by Uncle Giles to have narrowly missed a proposal from General Conyers when young.
LM 3.

HAW-HAW, Lord (William Joyce) 1906–46
Nazi radio propagandist during second war, provides food for thought at Lance-Corporal Gittins' salon in the store room.
VB 52–4. SA 148.

HAWKINS, Brigadier
Tall, lean, energetic commander of artillery at Divisional HQ in 1941, old friend of General Liddament and one of the few members of his staff 'who set about his duties with the "gaiety" which, according to Dicky Umfraville, Marshal Lyautey regarded as the first requirement of an officer'.
SA 28, 50–1, 54.

HAYCOCK
Mildred Blaides' second husband, a fairly rich, retired, rather rough Australian business man. Owned a villa in the south of France, spent much of his time travelling round the world, got on quite well with his

wife and made no bones about her lovers ('They were – as one might say – a very modern married couple': Widmerpool). D. the year before her engagement to Widmerpool. Two sons.

LM 40, 57, 59–60.

HAYCOCK, Mrs see BLAIDES, Hon Mildred

HEGARTY
Jenkins' colleague at the film studio in the early 'thirties: 'He had been a script-writer most of his grown-up life – burdened by then with three, if not four, wives, to all of whom he was paying alimony – and he possessed, when reasonably sober, an extraordinary facility for constructing film scenarios. That day, he could not have been described as reasonably sober . . . We were working on a stage play that had enjoyed a three-weeks West End run twenty or thirty years before, the banality of which had persuaded some director that it would "make a picture". This was the ninth treatment we had produced between us. At last, for the third time in an hour, Hegarty broke out in a cold sweat. He began taking aspirins by the handful. It was agreed to abandon work for the day.'

LM 13–14, 212.

HEPBURN, Katharine b. 1909
See DIETRICH, Marlene

HENDERSON, Barnabas
Drop-out with certain conventional aspects ('notably a father killed in the war, who had left enough money for his son to buy a partnership in a small picture-dealing business'). Disciple of Scorpio Murtlock, probably paying for the cult's caravan jaunt chez Jenkins in 1968. Late twenties, blue robe, amulet, shoulder length ringlets, yellow plastic spectacles and Chinese magician's moustache. Said to have abandoned a promising career to follow this less circumscribed way of life ('Perhaps that was a wrong identification, the new life desirable because additionally circumscribed, rather than less so').

In love with Murtlock. Defects three years later to return to his former boyfriend Chuck. Discovers Mr Deacon's work. A new man when next encountered at the inauguration of his gallery near Berkeley Square with an immensely successful combined show of Victorian seascapes (Robert Duport collection) and the Bosworth Deacon Centenary Exhibition. Eventual owner of Charles Stringham's Modigliani drawing.

HSH Crayfishing with Murtlock, his appearance and background 3–6,

11, 15, 17, 23, 28–9; 33, 164; at Stourwater, defies Murtlock 211–12, 219–20, 232–7; at his gallery 246–53, his reminiscences of cult life, with Bithel 256–71.

HENRY VIII 1491–1547
Employed a Tolland as Esquire of the Body.

LM 151.

HERNANDEZ
Replaced by Colonel Flores as military attaché in London.

MP 219.

HERTFORD, Lord 1800–70
Founder of the Hertford–Wallace collection, outbid by Lord Sleaford for Tipoo Sahib's necklace.
KO 146.

HEWETSON
Jenkins' predecessor in charge of Belgian and Czechoslovak liaison at the War Office, and neighbour in the block of Chelsea flats managed by the warlike Miss Wartstone. Goes white at mention of her name. Posted to N. Africa in 1943. Solicitor in civil life.

MP 69–70, 72, 86–7, 96. TK 202.

HITLER, Adolf 1889–1945
Inspires considerable sympathy in Uncle Giles ('"I like the little man they've got in Germany now," he would remark, quite casually'), as well as a shared sense of personal persecution.

LM 55, 63, 125, 170. CCR 95. KO 94, 113, 123, 142, 192, 200–1, 229. VB 54, 63, 66, 185. MP 144.

HLAVA, Colonel
Musical Czech military attaché, flying ace, test pilot, much decorated for gallantry in first war; likes a mild joke; incomparably easy to work with. Returned to Prague by 1945, promoted Major-General, shortly afterwards placed under house arrest and d. of heart failure.

MP 9, 24, 86, 90, 96–8, 100–1, 153, 178, 183, 215, 229.

HOGBOURNE-JOHNSON, Colonel Derrick, MC
One of Major Widmerpool's principal enemies at Divisional HQ in 1941. Foul temper. Disliked by all ranks, including the General and excluding only his trusty chief clerk Diplock: 'he was tall, getting decidedly fat, with a small beaky nose set above a pouting mouth

turning down at the corners. He somewhat resembled an owl, an angry, ageing bird, recently baulked of a field-mouse and looking about for another small animal to devour'.

Regular soldier, line regiment, decorated in first war; some sort of setback between the wars ('Still thinks he'll get a Division. If he asked me, I could tell him he's bound for some administrative backwater, and lucky if he isn't bowler-hatted before the cessation of hostilities': Widmerpool). Prides himself on his sparkling performance as a man of the world, and once wrote a parody of *Omar Khayyám*.

His intelligence fatally underrated by Widmerpool during rival intrigues to promote their respective candidates (both eventually bypassed) for command of the Divisional Recce Unit. Publicly humiliates Widmerpool by ticking him off ('You're not fit to organize an outing for a troop of Girl Guides in the vicarage garden . . . I want an immediate explanation of the muddle your infernal incompetence has made') for failure to control the traffic on divisional exercise. Punished by Widmerpool's vendetta against Diplock. Relegated to London training branch, and pursued even in Whitehall by Widmerpool's gloating over his downfall.

SA His character, origins of his feud with Widmerpool 27–41, 43–4, 51–8; Widmerpool's revenge over Diplock 58–61, 85, 173; 64–5, 67, 99; final reckoning with Widmerpool 208–15; 225. MP Widmerpool on 112. TK 207.

HONTHORST, Chester
American Rhodes Scholar at Sillery's Oxford tea party, bird-like appearance and millionaire stock on both sides of his family.

QU 176–8, 180, 183.

HOPKINS, Heather ('Hoppy')
Plays the piano most nights at the Merry Thought. Chelsea neighbour of Norah Tolland and Eleanor Walpole-Wilson in the early 'thirties. Small, gnarled, dumpy, middle-aged; horn-rimmed spectacles and bulging blue flannel trousers; strong line in barrack-room slang. Makes a dim impression on Lady Frederica Budd.

Accompanies Max Pilgrim ('Hopkins struck a few bars on the piano with brutal violence') at Umfraville's night club after their act proves a flop at the Café de Madrid. Has dropped the girls because Eleanor said a very unkind thing. Gives lesbian parties at one of which Matilda Wilson first met Norman Chandler. Roman Catholic convert by 1938. Her fancy-dress get-up for cabaret at the Merry Thought brought to mind by Widmerpool in army uniform.

Last seen in the late 'fifties by Evadne Clapham, entertaining the clientèle of the Hero of Acre with an impersonation of John Foster Dulles

LM At Eleanor and Norah's 94–7; at Umfraville's night club 182–6, 190, 199–201. CCR 132. KO 97, 134. VB 141. TK 31.

HORABINS
Hosts at the dance in 1923 where Jenkins first realized his feelings for Jean Templer, 'for long after . . . momentous to me simply for that reason'.

QU 93, 98.

HORACZKO, Second-Lieutenant
Assistant to the Polish military attaché, cavalry officer who began the second war at the head of a troop of lancers and made a dramatic escape through Hungary. Formerly executive in a Galician petroleum plant, has the air of a juvenile lead in drawing-room comedy. M. as her second husband Margaret Budd in 1945.

MP 27–9, 65–6, 72, 101, 244.

HUGFORD, Miss
Eighteenth-century heiress (only child of a Lord Mayor) who m. the then Lord Erridge and brought him Thrubworth Park.

BDFR 43.

HUMBLE
Undergraduate at Short's luncheon party.

QU 209.

HUMPHRIES, Sergeant
Expected to replace CSM Cadwallader.

VB 231.

HUNTERCOMBE, Lady (Sybil)
Gave the dance in 1928 or 9 at which Barbara Goring poured sugar over Widmerpool. Dinner at her house (according to St John Clarke who was only ever asked twice) possessed 'two dramatic features – the wine was a farce and the food a tragedy'.

Dresses in clothes more striking than fashionable designed to emphasize her resemblance to Gainsborough's Mrs Siddons ('She nodded at once in such a way as to indicate enthusiasm, the rather reckless gaiety of a great actress on holiday, one of the moods, comparatively limited in range, to which her hat and general appearance committed her'). Considered dreadfully slow by Mrs Foxe. Mother of Venetia Penistone and at least one other daughter.

BM Her dance 24, 50, 54, 56, 62, 78, 93, 97–9, 105, 110; at Stourwater 187, 195, 199–200, 202, 221; 226. AW 121, 126, 214. LM 29, 46, 82. CCR 12, 51, 140, 143–4, 153, 161, 187, 191. MP 98, 244. BDFR 88. TK 263. HSH 46.

HUNTERCOMBE, Lord (Walter) Family name Penistone
'A small man, very exquisite in appearance and possessing a look of ineffable cunning'. House in Belgrave Square, neighbour in the country of sir Magnus Donners and the Walpole-Wilsons. Lord Lieutenant of his county, trustee of one or more public galleries, active on cultural committees. Rich as Croesus according to Mr Deacon. Connoisseur and collector, a man to be reckoned with in the art field. Picks the lock of Mrs Foxe's china cabinet and finds a forgery within; gets the better of Smethwyck in a matter of attribution; and once told Erridge's father that his eighteenth-century Chinese vases were nineteenth-century fakes.

BM His wife's dance 24, 50, 54, 56, 62, 78, 93, 97–9, 105, 110; at Stourwater 187, 196, 211, 215, 221. AW 214. LM 29, 46, 82. CCR 12, at Mrs Foxe's party 143, 162, 169–71, 189; 191. MP 98, 244. BDFR 67, 82, 88. TK 263. HSH 46.

IRVING, Sir Henry 1838–1905
Actor-manager, alleged to have slept (unless it was Tree) with old Mrs Maliphant.

TK 70.

ISBISTER, Horace, RA
The British Franz Hals. Fashionable portrait painter in the early years of the century, specializing in businessmen, ecclesiastics and mayors. Studio in St John's Wood. M. his model Morwenna (a lesbian, according to Mark Members) from whom he later separated. His reputation already on the wane by the time of his death c. 1932.

   Early struggles shared with his contemporary and friend, the novelist St John Clarke whom he frequently painted (and whose proposed introduction to *The Art of Horace Isbister*, commissioned by Jenkins' artbook firm, causes nothing but trouble until eventually abandoned). His success a special grievance to Mr Deacon, and a source of extreme secret bitterness to St John Clarke:
' "Isbister was beloved of the gods, Mark," he had cried aloud, looking up with a haggard face from *The Times* of New Year's Day and its list of awards, "RA before he was forty-five – Gold Medallist

at the Paris Salon – Diploma of Honour at the International Exhibition at Amsterdam – Commander of the Papal Order of Pius IX – refused a knighthood. Think of it, Mark, a man the King would have delighted to honour. What recognition have I had compared with these?"

"Why did Isbister refuse a knighthood?" Members had asked.

"To spite his wife.'"

His technique in portraiture distinguished by a combination of shrewd commercialism with hints of inner madness, murky brushwork, aggressive use of paint and unswerving obsequiousness towards the sitter. Works include portraits of Peter Templer's father (' "Of course I know about Isbister, RA," [Templer] said. "He painted that shocking picture of my old man. I tried to pop it when he dropped off the hooks, but there were no takers"'); Lord Aberavon ('painted in peer's robes over the uniform of a deputy-lieutenant, different tones of scarlet contrasted against a crimson velvet curtain; a pictorial experiment that could not be called successful. Through french windows behind Lord Aberavon stretched a broad landscape . . . in which something had gone seriously wrong with the colour values'); Cardinal Whelan ('the only picture I had ever heard Widmerpool spontaneously praise'); Lord Sleaford in Garter robes; Sir Horrocks Rusby, KC; the diplomat Saltonstall; *The Countess of Ardglass with Faithful Girl*. Also genre paintings such as *The Old Humorists, Clergyman Eating an Apple* (long afterwards evinced by Members, on account of the sitter's supposed resemblance to St John Clarke when young, as evidence of homosexual relations between the painter and his old friend – 'perhaps more than friend').

Reputation rising steadily by 1968. See also Painting Index.

QU His portrait of Templer's father 76. BM Mr Deacon and Widmerpool on 87; his portrait of Lord Aberavon 177. AW *The Art of Horace Isbister*, St John Clarke's introduction to 16, biographical content of, delays over 18–19, 22–3, probable modernistic complexion of 25–7; dies 30; introduction further delayed 33; Templer on 39–40; Quiggin on 53–4, 80; his memorial exhibition: his style, its peculiar fascination for Jenkins 106–14; Clarke's introduction, probable Marxist complexion of 115–18. LM 17. CCR His ancient rivalry with St John Clarke 190–1. MP His style 37–8. TK 65, 68. HSH His relations with St John Clarke 40; his reputation 65.

ISBISTER, Morwenna
Widow of above, featured in his obituaries (' "Those photographs the Press resurrected of Morwenna standing beside him looking out to sea," said St John Clarke, "they were antediluvian – diluvian possibly.

It was the Flood they were looking at, I expect. They'd been living apart for years when he died'").

CCR 191. HSH 40.

JACQUELINE
One of X. Trapnel's mistresses, afterwards married to a foreign correspondent.

TK 198.

JAMIESON
Family name of Lord Ardglass.

JEAN-NEPOCUMENE
The younger and quieter of Mme Leroy's two young relatives, perhaps great-nephews, at La Grenadière in 1923. Possible author of the crude but not unaccomplished drawing of Widmerpool etched on the wall of the *cabinet de toilette*.

QU 114–5, 122–3, 137–8, 142, 156, 159, 161, 164.

JEAVONS, Lil
Wife of Ted Jeavons' brother Stanley, suggested by Janet Walpole-Wilson as a suitable tenant for Widmerpool's mother in the country on the outbreak of war. Gets on with all sorts but is not a success with Mrs Widmerpool.

KO 223–4, 251, 253. SA 84.

JEAVONS, Lady Molly
Erratic and easy-going hostess, will put up with anyone, her drawing-room a social no-man's land. Sister of Jumbo, Earl of Ardglass, and Katherine, Lady Warminster. Aunt of Chips Lovell (by her first marriage to his uncle John, Lord Sleaford) and of the ten Tollands (her sister's stepchildren). Runs her ramshackle house in South Kensington as a kind of free rest home for human and animal strays. Cordially returns the disapproval of her 'frightfully correct' relations such as Frederica Budd. Gives the party for Widmerpool's engagement to Mildred Haycock in 1934 at which Jenkins first hears talk of the Tollands; and gives another that autumn for his own engagement to Isobel Tolland.

Friend and contemporary of Mildred Haycock. M. Lord Sleaford *c.* 1907 ('Molly married him from the ballroom. She was only eighteen. Never seen a man before': Chips Lovell); retiring and very shy in those days, never showed the slightest desire to cut a dash; known to have entertained royalty at Dogdene, also St John Clarke and Dicky

Umfraville in his gilded youth. Red Cross work in first war, came across Ted Jeavons as a patient in the military hospital which occupied all but the east wing at Dogdene. No affair ('Between you and me, she's not a great one for bed': Jeavons) until the death of her husband in 1919, when she met Jeavons again and m. him six months later. Prefers dull dogs as husbands; no child by either marriage; maintains unquestioned sway over Jeavons. Chronically hard up, not known what they live on (Jeavons being incapable of earning a living, the Sleafords notoriously mean to their widows and the Ardglasses hopelessly insolvent).

Handsome, noisy, good-natured, quite reckless in her judgement of people, endlessly kind to former dependents and aged or ailing relatives. Owner of two budgerigars, four principal dogs, at least as many cats and the monkey Maisky. A born tease ('perhaps the only outward indication that her inner life was not altogether happy; since there is no greater sign of innate misery than a love of teasing'). Old friend of Miss Weedon, who cures Charles Stringham of drink in her top-floor flat in the 'thirties.

In her element on the outbreak of the second war: 'Dark, large, still good-looking at fifty, there was something of the barmaid about her, something of the Charles II beauty, although Molly, they said, had never been exactly a 'beauty' when younger, more from lack of temperament to play the part, than want of physical equipment'. Returns briefly to Dogdene to help run an evacuated girls' school. Back in London by 1941; killed by a bomb which destroys the back part of her house on the same night as the raid on the Madrid.

LM At Dogdene in 1916 8–9; Chips Lovell on her history and background 15–19; party at her house 21, ragging Alfred Tolland, her temperament 24–43, 45, 47, 49; 57–8, 70; Frederica Budd on 75, 77–9; 106, 124, 130; her household, her marriages, her character explored 155–9; at her house, Miss Weedon on her ménage 159–65, 168; 171–3, 175, 177; Jeavons on their marriage 179–80; 182–3, 189, 192–3, 197; compared to her sister 206–7, 211; her Dogdene days 214; her party for Jenkins' engagement 216–21, 223–5, 236–8. CCR Her household compared to her sister's 58; 61, 68, 73–4; St John Clarke's dim view of 80–1; Miss Weedon and Stringham moved in with 86–7, 89, 102, 145, 163; 201, 223. KO Her distress at her sister's death, their points in common 145–6; 213–4; fixing a lodger for Widmerpool's mother 223–4, at her house 231–8, relations with Moreland 240–3, 249, 251. VB 137, 170. SA 84, Priscilla Lovell staying with 111; 132, 158; her death 160–2, 164–6, 222. MP 23; her provision for Ted 75–6; 102. BDFR 62–3, 89. TK 226. HSR Hugo Tolland's likeness to 10.

JEAVONS, Stanley

Ted's brother, accountant in Nottingham, his existence unsuspected even by Chips Lovell until 1939. 'The sight of Jeavons' brother . . . brought home to one the innate eccentricity of Jeavons . . . He was far more anonymous than Jeavons: older, solider, greyer, quieter, in general more staid.' War Office staff captain, three first war ribbons; in charge of army reservists' applications; succeeds (where General Conyers and Widmerpool signally failed) in fixing a commission for Jenkins.

KO 231–2, 235–8, 240, 251–4.

JEAVONS, Ted

Lady Molly's second husband, slightly younger than his wife, first encountered at one of her parties in 1934: 'It was at once apparent that he was something left over from the war . . . He stood there, scanning everyone's face closely, as if hoping for some explanation of the matter in hand; perhaps even of life itself, so intense was his concentration: some reasonable explanation couched in terms simple enough for a plain man to understand without undue effort. He also gave the impression of an old dog waiting to have a ball thrown to retrieve, more because it was the custom in the past than because sport or exercise was urgently required.'

Enlisted in the Green Howards, commissioned into Duke of Wellington's regiment, transferred to Machine Gun Corps, wounded in the stomach at La Bassée, has suffered horribly with his inside ever since. Military Cross; feels bilious most of the time. Quite unemployable. Picked up by Lady Sleaford while acting as car polisher at the Olympia Motor Show ('I can't remember which make, but not a car anyone would be proud to own. That represented just about the height of what he could rise to in civil life': Chips Lovell). Charlie Chaplin moustache, dark shiny corkscrew curls, speaks in a faint croak; fine singing voice and wide repertoire drawn from the musical comedy songs of his youth. Can be slow at grasping the point of a story. Given to impenetrable silences alternating with half-hearted attempts to palm off unsaleable gadgets (automatic bootjack, petrol-saving device etc.) on his wife's guests. Encyclopaedic knowledge of her relations. Widely considered a bore (e.g. by Widmerpool, Chips Lovell, Mrs Conyers, Mark Members, Dicky Umfraville) though not by Jenkins: 'On the contrary, he seemed to me, in his own way, rather a remarkable person'.

His marriage an unexpected success apart from an occasional urge to kick over the traces on solitary pub crawls; said once to have brought a tart home for a drink ('the story, even if untrue, impressed me as of interest in its bearing on a sense of strain suffered, perhaps continuously, by Jeavons himself. At worst, the supposed introduction of a "tart" into his house was a myth . . . which represented in highly-coloured terms a long since vanquished husband's vain efforts publicly to demonstrate his own independence from a wife's too evident domination'). Once spent a wartime leave with Mildred Haycock ('"I suppose it's a story a real gent wouldn't tell," said Jeavons. "But then I'm not a real gent"'); meets her again nearly twenty years later at Umfraville's night club; and takes to his bed for a week after this debauch.

Greatly appeals to Stringham, also long afterwards to Peter Templer (briefly his lodger in 1942). Air raid warden in second war ('There could be no doubt that the war had livened him up. He felt at home within its icy grasp'). Hair turns quite white after Molly's death. Fifty in the offing. Dislikes butlers in general, and Erridge's butler Smith in particular ('Of course, I was brought in contact with butlers late in life. Never set eyes on them in the circles I came from. I may have been unlucky in the butlers I've met . . .'). Converts his house in S. Kensington into flats after the war, and lets one to Norman Chandler. D. by 1968.

LM Chips Lovell on his marriage, his advantages and drawbacks 16–18; pouring drinks at his wife's party 21–2, 34, 36–7, 43, 46–7, 49; the Conyers on 70, 78; his relations with Molly 155–9; 161, 165, his peculiar interest for Jenkins, his wartime memories of Mrs Haycock, his philosophy of life 167–83; reunion with Mrs Haycock 185–98, 200–2; aftermath of this episode 216–8; party at his house, makes a poor impression on Mark Members 220–1, 223–4, 237–8. CCR Iller than ever 58; 71, 81, on the mend 86–7, 89; Stringham on 163–4, 178, 182. KO 145–6; 192; air raid warden 213–4, 225; at his house, transformed by war, contrasted with his brother 231–6, 238–41, 251, 253–4. VB 104, 140. SA 84; survives the bomb which kills his wife 160–3, 165, 222. MP Templer his prospective lodger 22–4; his reactions to Molly's death, holds a party, his view of Templer and Pamela Flitton 75–82; 123. BDFR At George Tolland's funeral 41; and Erridge's 47, 63, on Templer 85–6, 88–91. TK 46, friendship with Chandler 226. HSH Dead 60.

JEFF
The Air Vice Marshal ('*Burdened* with gongs') who m. Mona Templer as her second husband.

BDFR 55–6.

JENKINS family
Descent from the hero of the war of Jenkins' Ear (England v. Spain, 1739) unproven. Small Welsh landowners who produced quite a

handful of unnoticed officers of Marines or the East India Company in the mid-nineteenth century but no name of the least distinction for three or four hundred years before that. Of some account in war in medieval times, tracing back through remote Celtic kings ('One wondered what on earth such predecessors had been like personally; certainly not above blinding or castrating when in the mood') to Llywarch the Old and ('though only in the female line') Cunedda.

QU 24. VB 1–3.

JENKINS, Captain
Father of Nicholas, regular soldier, contemporary at Sandhurst of the publisher Daniel Tokenhouse. Attached to a cavalry regiment before the first war near Brighton where he met Mr Deacon. Stationed at Aldershot by 1914 and takes a short lease on the bungalow Stonehurst. Shipped to France with British Expeditionary Force in the first weeks of the war; wounded in Mesopotamia; spell of duty in Cairo; job ('something to do with disarmament') at Paris Peace Conference. On the staff of a Corps HQ in the West of England by 1922. Invalided out of the army with the rank of Lt-Colonel *c.* 1927.

No stranger to depression. Innate fretfulness of spirit not cured by happy marriage. Peculiarly prone to domestic misfortune: 'His temperament, a craft of light tonnage, borne effortlessly into heavy seas no matter how calm the weather on setting sail, was preordained to violent ups and downs . . .' Testy, argumentative, a confirmed maker of mysteries, dislikes imparting information of any but a didactic kind ('If forced to offer an exposé of any given situation, he was always in favour of presenting the substance of what he had to say in terms of more or less oracular . . . My father really hated clarity'). Handicapped in his military career by a chronic dislike of authority: 'He did his best to conceal this antipathy, because the one thing he hated, more than constituted authority itself, was to hear constituted authority questioned by anyone but himself. This is perhaps an endemic trait in all who love power, and my father had an absolute passion for power, although he was never in a position to wield it on a notable scale . . .'

On poor terms with his brother Martin; relations almost completely severed with his brother Giles. Much the youngest in his family and claims to have been neglected as a child; son of an unappeasable fox-hunter; dislikes any form of outdoor sport. Dyspeptic, abstemious, poor health. Eye-glass on account of extreme short sight. Unpredictable aesthetic tastes, tolerates Mr Deacon as an entertaining freak, deplores any form of achievement in the arts as something of a social aberration. Considers writing, along with painting, sculpture, music etc., 'an unusual, not wholly desirable profession in an acquaintance.' Dislikes books that make him think ('In due course, as he grew older, my father became increasingly committed to this exclusion of what made him think, so that he finally disliked not only books, but also people – even places – that threatened to induce this disturbing mental effect').

Drifts into a life of extreme seclusion on retirement. Infuriated by Giles' ill-timed death (' "Awkward to the end," my father said, "though I suppose one should not speak in that way"'); outraged by General Conyers' second marriage (' "No fool like an old fool," my father said. "I shouldn't have believed it of him, Bertha hardly cold in her grave"'); quarrels irretrievably with most of his old friends and never speaks again to Tokenhouse after a bitter disagreement over Munich. Obsessed with hopeless attempts to get himself re-employed by the army at the start of the second war. Dead by the late 'forties.

QU Dim view of his brother Giles, mutual hostilities over Family Trust 17–18, 21–4; 60, 63, 85, 108, 119, 145. BM Acquaintance with Mr Deacon in Brighton 4, 6–8, and in Paris after the first war 10–13, 19, 157. AW 17. LM Friendship with General Conyers 1, 3, 5; 40, 69. KO at Stonehurst: 5, 8, devotion of his soldier-servant Bracey 11–12, 14–15, 17, 21, 23, his temperament 26–7, mixed reactions to General Conyers, his character analysed, relationship with Giles 35–49, host to the Conyerses, nonplussed by Billson incident 51–7, 60, 63, with Giles 65–7, 69–71; shipped to France 73–4; dubious view of the arts 80; on Giles' death 146–7, 151, 203; desperate to rejoin the army in 1939, disgust at Conyers' remarrying 206–8, 210–12, 216–18. VB 15, 71, 114. SA 63. MP 89–90. TK His character, fondness for continental travel, ancient friendship and final row with Tokenhouse 1, 52–8; Tokenhouse on 120; his favourite anecdote 274.

JENKINS, Captain Giles Delahay ('Uncle Giles')
Older brother of above; 'captain' probably a more or less honorary rank; his activities a source of perpetual foreboding and curiosity to his numerous relatives. Career punctuated by debts, shady business deals ('His mastery of the hard-luck story was of a kind never achieved by persons not wholly concentrated on themselves'), reckless mismanagement on the Stock Exchange ('Even those who, to their cost, had known him for years, sometimes found difficulty in estimating the lengths to which he could carry his lack of reliability – and indeed sheer incapacity – in matters of business'), indiscriminate dealings with the opposite sex etc.: 'Like many people whose days are passed largely in a state of inanition, when not of crisis, Uncle Giles prided himself on his serious approach to life, deprecating nothing so much as what he called "trying to laugh things off"; and it was true that a lifetime of laughter would scarcely have sufficed to exorcise some of his own fiascos.'

Obliged to leave the army at the turn of the century on account of two separate rows ('somebody's wife, and somebody else's money'); his plans to settle in Cape Town scotched by a very nearly disastrous miscalculation over diamonds; works instead for a bucket-shop (outside broking).

Intriguing, not wholly unromantic figure to Jenkins as a boy. Turns up at Stonehurst on the day of the Conyerses' visit in 1914, bringing news of a nasty accident in a motor car at Sarajevo. Rejected by the army on grounds of ill health ('trouble with the old duodenal'), employed by Ministry of Munitions, later Ministry of Food, ends up supplying comforts to US troops. Fondly hoped by his relatives to have emigrated after the war. Aged about 50 in 1921; deprecating expression, small fair moustache, well-worn rather sporting tweed suit. Involved with a lady in Reading ('some said a manicurist: others the widow of a garage proprietor'), threatens marriage at one point. In the paper business by the end of the 'twenties, afterwards administers a charity in the home counties. Fond of Sussex.

'A bit of a radical', urgent advocate of the dissolution of the British Empire, later a keen supporter of Hitler and the Nazi party. Unhesitating contempt for all human conduct but his own. Chronically suspicious of wealth (with a possible exception in favour of the *nouveaux riches*, 'provided the money had been amassed by owners safely to be despised . . . and by methods commonly acknowledged to be indefensible. It was to any form of long-established affluence that he took the gravest exception'), rank and privilege; also of coloured persons and Bohemians. No friend to up-to-date thought.

Aimless existence ('Dedicated, perhaps, to his own egotism; his determination to be – without adequate moral or intellectual equipment – absolutely different from everyone else') passed mostly in seedy residential hotels such as the Ufford in Bayswater. Has some sort of connection with Mrs Erdleigh in his sixties, supposed by Jenkins to be her lover, possibly still contemplating marriage. Subsequently denies all knowledge of her existence. Under Aries, Saturn in the Twelfth House. D. of a stroke at the Bellevue private hotel in August 1939, giving some offence within the family by leaving his unexpectedly large estate (£7,300) to Mrs Erdleigh ('"Giles was always an unreliable fellow," said my father, "but we mustn't speak ill of him now"').

QU Calls on Jenkins at school, smokes a forbidden cigarette, his character and career 14–25; Le Bas' tiresomeness about his smoking 26–9, 31, 35, 43; 52; contemplating marriage, his disastrous past, his philosophy of life 63–7; 80, 110, 122, 135–6, 172–3, summons Jenkins to dine 219–20, 228–30. BM Compared to Mr Deacon 6–7; and to Sir Gavin Walpole-Wilson 20–1, 28, 54, 183; his habit of wholesale condemnation, promising material for supplied by Milly Andriadis' party 96–101, 123; encountered at dawn in Shepherd Market 154–8; 230. AW Tea with at the Ufford, introduces Mrs Erdleigh, his fortune told, speculations on his relationship with Mrs Erdleigh 1–18; 41, 81, 97, 120, 151; denies acquaintance with Mrs Erdleigh 182–4; very probably her lover 213. LM His unflattering account of General Conyers 1–6; 12, 18, 69, 169, 173, 199, 205, 235. CCR 58, 73, 98. KO 35, 37–9, threatens arrival at Stonehurst in 1914 46–9, 53, 55–6, 58; 62; at Stonehurst with the Conyerses and Dr Trelawney 66–71; 74, staying at the Bellevue in the late 'thirties, his taste in seedy hotels 141–3; dies, his effects, his horoscope, his character and achievements surveyed 146–62; 164, 167, 169, 174, 184, Dr Trelawney on 191, 195–7; his funeral 199, 201–3; 212, 216. VB 1, 84. SA 63. MP Residence at the Ufford recalled 27, 61–2; 65, 130–1, 137, 187. TK 55, 58, 214. HSH 117.

JENKINS, Hannibal
Ancestor, of Cwm Shenkin, paid Hearth Tax in 1674.
QU 24.

JENKINS, Lady Isobel see TOLLAND, Lady Isobel

JENKINS, Martin
Brother of Giles and of Nicholas' father, quarrelled with both. Killed in the second battle of the Marne, leaving an unsatisfactory will which exacerbates hostilities over the Family Trust.
QU 21–2. KO 36, 48.

JENKINS, Mrs
Nicholas' mother, remotely related to General Conyers. Ascetic inclinations; taste for the occult; has sensed ghostly presences at Stonehurst. Keen enough on balls and parties before her marriage but afterwards develops a dislike even greater than her husband's for worldly amusements. Almost morbid horror of 'regimental' officers' wives. Makes a rare exception in favour of gossiping with Bertha Conyers. Habitually denies herself all forms of self-indulgence ('except perhaps indulgence of an emotional kind, even that rather special in expression'). Invariably tender of other people's susceptibilities ('always felt warmly towards hopeless characters like Uncle Giles when they were in difficulties'). Fond of continental travel ('She enjoyed sightseeing, to which she brought a good deal of general knowledge, wholly untouched by intellectual theory; except possibly as provided by a much earlier, almost pre-Victorian tradition of upbringing'). Firm believer in candour and tact, the last freely called on not only by her husband ('my mother, distressed as ever by the absolutely unredeemed state of misery and rage that misfortune always provoked in my father's

spirit . . .') but also by exceptionally severe servant trouble at Stonehurst before the first world war.

BM Acquaintance with Mr Deacon 7–11, 13; and with the Walpole-Wilsons 19. AW 17. LM 5, visit to Mrs Conyers in 1916 recalled, her disapproval of Mildred Blaides 6, 9; 40, 69. KO At Stonehurst 4–7, 11–12, 14–16, 22–3, 26–31, 33, 35–6, Conyers' visit 40–53, her account of Billson's breakdown 55–60, 63, 65–70, 74; 80, 140, 207–8, 211–12, 217–18. TK Holiday with in Venice recalled 1, 53, 56.

JENKINS, Nicholas
(This entry has no reference section, since a full index would be too unwieldy for practical consultation. The information below comes from the volume indicated in brackets after the item to which it refers. Anyone requiring page numbers may find the Synopsis helpful, or other entries in the Character Index.)

Narrator, novelist. B. 1906 or 7, only child of Captain and Mrs Jenkins. Solitary upbringing, spent mostly in furnished houses near his father's various army posts. Ambition to be a soldier. Educated at home by the local governess Miss Orchard in 1914 (KO); away at prep school during first war.

Spends five years in Le Bas' house at public school, messing in his last two years with Stringham and Templer; slightly junior to Widmerpool. Leaves school in the summer of 1923 and pays a weekend visit to the Templers, during which he is initiated into an unsuspected world of adult physical sensation while foxtrotting with Lady McReith; and acknowledges romantic feelings for Peter's younger sister Jean. Sent to France to learn the language as paying guest of the Leroys at La Grenadière, where he experiences romantic feelings for Mme Leroy's niece Suzette; and is cross-examined by Widmerpool on his future prospects ('I made several rather lame remarks to the effect that I wanted one day "to write": an assertion that had not even the merit of being true, as it was an idea that had scarcely crossed my mind until that moment'). Up at university that autumn, reading history; contemporary of Quiggin and Members (QU).

Moves to London, rooms in Shepherd Market beside an all-night garage and opposite a block of flats inhabited almost exclusively by tarts. Works for a publisher specializing in art books [dogsbody in Daniel Tokenhouse's firm, TK]. Advised by Widmerpool to look for something more promising. Debutante dances and dinner with the Walpole-Wilsons. Age 21 or 22, still holds decidedly romantic views on women, love and power, politics etc. Embarks on an unsatisfactory passion for Barbara Goring, terminated by her pouring sugar over Widmerpool at the Huntercombes' ball in May, 1928 or 9. Crosses a threshold at Milly Andriadis' party ('I was . . . more than half aware that such latitudes are entered by a door through which there is, in a sense, no return'). Pangs of envy and vexation roused by Bob Duport's lavish possessions, successful City career and marriage to Jean Templer; unfavourable contrast with his own hand-to-mouth existence, 'dreary, even monotonous' job and lovelorn state ('left, emotionally speaking, high and dry on a not specially Elysian coast'). Meets Barnby later that summer. Meets Jean again at Stourwater. Somewhat idealistic notions of the literary life; has even toyed with a first novel ('this matter of writing was beginning to occupy an increasing amount of attention in my own mind'). Sleeps with Gypsy Jones at the back of Mr Deacon's shop. (BM)

Friendship with Barnby that summer leads almost immediately to a meeting with Moreland, and final escape from the conventional social round of dances and unexciting outings with former undergraduate acquaintances ('The hiatus between coming down from the university and finding a place for myself in London had comprised, with some bright spots, an eternity of boredom') into the more congenial world of painters, musicians, journalists and literary hangers-on, all more or less on the make, to be found throughout the 'thirties in such relatively sleazy spots as the Mortimer, Foppa's, Casanova's Chinese Restaurant etc. (CCR)

First novel published *c.* 1931,* working on another. Still in publishing, makeshift love-life. Under Sagittarius, fortune told by Mrs Erdleigh (' "You live between two worlds," she said. "Perhaps even more than two worlds. You cannot always surmount your feelings . . . You are thought cold, but you possess deep affections, sometimes for people worthless in themselves . . . You expect too much, and yet you are also too resigned. You must try to understand life"'). Regards himself as tremendously intelligent, according to Peter Templer. Desperately in love with Jean Duport, who becomes his mistress early in 1933. Shaken by her revelation of a previous affair with Jimmy Stripling ('I was . . . overcome with a horrible feeling of nausea, as if one had suddenly woken from sleep and found oneself chained to a corpse'). Anticipates difficulties on Bob Duport's return to England that autumn. (AW)

Moved from publishing to a fairly low-grade British film company by 1934, scriptwriter making second features for the Quota ('It may lead to something better. If you are industrious, you get on. That is true of all professions, even the humblest': Widmerpool). Age of thirty in sight; 'aware for the first time that a younger generation was close on my heels'; has written a couple of novels. A grey hair. Broods on memories of Jean ('For a moment the thought of her reunited to

* AW 23 and CCR 82; but see also AW 179, which seems to suggest a publication date some eighteen months later.

Duport . . . brought to the heart a touch of the red-hot pincers'). Meets and knows at sight that he will marry Lady Isobel Tolland. Engaged to her that autumn. Psychoanalysed by General Conyers ('"You are an introvert, of course," he said . . . "Introverted intuitive type, do you think? I shouldn't wonder. . . . Anyway," said the General, "keep an eye on not over-compensating"'). (LM)

Hard, cold-blooded, almost mathematical pleasure in writing and painting. Married for two years by 1936 ('To think at all objectively about one's own marriage is impossible . . . Objectivity is not, of course, everything in writing; but, even after one has cast objectivity aside, the difficulties of presenting marriage are inordinate'). Sacked by film studio. Two or three novels published; book reviewer for a national daily; occasional contributor to the weekly of which Members is assistant literary editor. Widmerpool thinks it a pity he can't find regular work. (CCR)

In lowish water by 1938; jobs hard to come by; finding it almost impossible to work in face of approaching war. Plays Sloth in Sir Magnus Donners' tableaux of the Seven Deadly Sins at Stourwater. Appalled to learn for the first time that Jimmy Brent had been Jean's lover at the height of his own affair with her; loathes Bob Duport who told her. Writing out of the question, name on army reserve. Angling for a commission; applies in vain to Widmerpool; eventually fixed up in the Welsh line regiment of his choice by Stanley Jeavons. (KO)

Commissioned second-lieutenant round about the end of 1939, platoon commander in Captain Gwatkin's company, serving in N. Ireland. Has written three or four novels, incapable of writing another ('Whatever inner processes are required for writing novels, so far as I myself was concerned, war now utterly inhibited'). Dismayed at further light on Jean's treachery cast by Jimmy Brent. Birth of a son, 1940. Stationed at Castlemallock School of Chemical Warfare ('At Castlemallock I knew despair . . . Like a million others, I missed my wife, wearied of the officers and men round me, grew to loathe a post wanting even the consolation that one was required to be brave'). Posted in June to General Liddament's Divisional HQ, F Mess ('low, though not the final dregs of the divisional staff'), as assistant to Major Widmerpool, DAAG: 'I saw that I was now in Widmerpool's power. This, for some reason, gave me a disagreeable, sinking feeling within'. (VB)

Spends a dismal year ('it was often necessary to remind oneself that low spirits, disturbed moods, senses of persecution, were not necessarily the consequence of serving in the army . . .') bottle-washing for Widmerpool. Middle thirties. Turned down by Major Finn of the Free French mission. Annoyed, 'even disgusted', by Widmerpool's callousness to Stringham; intercedes in vain on his behalf. His 'mediocre qualities as a staff officer' itemized (and his promotion prospects

102

ditched) by Widmerpool. Posted to the War Office, June 1941. (SA)

Gazetted Captain, Intelligence Corps, spends the rest of the war on Finn's section of the General Staff, dealing with Allied Liaison. Assistant to David Pennistone in Polish liaison (later put in charge of Belgians and Czechs, promoted Major, takes over France and Luxembourg as well; Finn's second in command by 1945). Lives in a single room on the eighth floor of a Chelsea tenement, visits Isobel once a fortnight, preoccupied with the seventeenth century, reading Proust. Conducts party of allied military attachés on trip to continent. Fails to recognize Jean when introduced to her as Mme Flores. Demobilized (MP)

Spends three months getting through his army gratuity in the country; aged forty; briefly back at the university for research on a book about Robert Burton (*Borage and Hellebore*, eventually pub. 1947). Living in London. Reputation rising, early books long out of print but now better known after nearly seven years of literary silence ('This was a more acceptable side of growing older'). Rocky financial situation, becomes part-time literary editor of *Fission* ('We'd have liked Bernard Shernmaker . . . but everyone's after him. Then we tried L. O. Salvidge. He'd been snapped up too. Bagshaw suggested you might like to take the job on': Quiggin). Second son born 1946. Attends a party at the Floreses', and is relieved to find himself at last wholly unmoved by contact with Jean. A son going to school. (BDFR)

In his fifties ('One felt oneself taking more interest than formerly in the habits and lineaments of old age'); trouble with a book ('Writing may not be enjoyable, its discontinuance can be worse . . .'). Attends international writers' conference in Venice in 1958. Ranks Tiepolo with Poussin among his most admired masters. A son nearing age for military service. (TK)

Moved to the country. In his sixties. Makes intermittent attempts to stave off reclusion, work taking an increasing stranglehold. On Magnus Donners prize committee, and Royal Academy guest list. Recalls his performance as Sloth ('Sloth means Accidie too. Feeling fed up with life. There are moments when I can put forward claims'). Signs of madness among his contemporaries ('As one gets older, one gets increasingly used to encountering this development in friends and acquaintances; causing periods of self-examination in a similar connexion'). Reflections on Poussin's *Dance to the Music of Time*. (HSH)

See also Book Index.

JODRILL, Dr
Erridge's GP and sole confidant at Thrubworth, attributes his coronary thrombosis to distress at his brother George's death.

BDFR 41.

JONES, Private A.
Soldier with ring-worm in Gwatkin's company.

VB 10.

JONES, Private D.
Soldier with a singing voice of heart-breaking melancholy; sea-sick, accident prone, killed in the retreat before Dunkirk ('"Always an unlucky boy, Jones D.," said CSM Cadwallader').

VB 4, 6–7, 42, 78, 82, 96–7, 195–6.

JONES, Gypsy
'La Pasionaria of Hendon Central' (Moreland). Truculent young pacifist colleague of Mr Deacon, selling *War Never Pays!* with him when first encountered on Grosvenor Place after the Huntercombes' ball in 1928 or 9. Small and grubby ('She looked like a thoroughly ill-conditioned errand boy'). Rasping, though not entirely unattractive voice. Short skirt, bare knees, Eton crop; dressed like the Fool to Deacon's Lear.

Daughter of a schoolmaster in Hendon, shorthand typist to Howard Craggs. Sleeps at the back of Mr Deacon's shop when not sleeping with Craggs at the Vox Populi Press next door. Toast of the 1917 Club. World revolution her aim. Older than you'd think, according to Barnby; Deacon in search of an abortionist on her behalf. Takes Widmerpool's fancy on the rebound from Barbara Goring. Not without appeal for Jenkins:

'Her egotism was of that entirely unrestrained kind, always hard to resist when accompanied by tolerable looks, a passionate self-absorption of the crudest kind, extending almost far enough to threaten the limits of sanity: with the added attraction of unfamiliar ways and thought.'

Pursued that summer by Widmerpool, who pays for her operation ('I wondered what unthinkable passages had passed between them') but enjoys no favours in return. Tries on her costume for the Merry Thought fancy-dress party (Eve to Craggs's Adam) on the day of Mr Deacon's funeral and sleeps with Jenkins at the back of the shop.
Member of the Communist Party; highly regarded in its ranks by the early 'thirties; Erridge thought to be keen on her round about this time. Widmerpool still trembles at the sight of her haranguing an anti-war meeting from a soap-box in the street in 1939. Has lost a front tooth but otherwise not greatly changed.

M. Craggs at the end of the war. Said to have been once engaged to Bagshaw. Member of Widmerpool's delegation at Erridge's funeral ('short, wiry, her head tied up in a red handkerchief, somehow calling to mind Soviet posters celebrating the Five Year Plan. Too stocky and irritable in appearance, in fact, to figure in pictorial propaganda, she had the right sort of aggressiveness'). In her forties. Affair with Vernon Gainsborough (formerly Guggenbühl), also with Len Pugsley. Puts pressure on Quiggin & Craggs to toe the party line; intimidates Craggs ('He knows about one or two things Gypsy's arranged in her time. So do I. I don't blame him': Bagshaw); and outflanks Quiggin in the matter of Odo Stevens' memoirs by liquidating the manuscript ('You can't help admiring the way Gypsy does things. Good old hard-core stuff': Bagshaw).

Widowed by 1958, moves in with Len Pugsley, retaining her style as Lady Craggs. D. suddenly in Czechoslovakia in 1968.

BM Encountered on Grosvenor Place with Mr Deacon, Widmerpool much taken by 83–5, 87–91, 93–4; at Milly Andriadis' party 99, 101–2, Mr Deacon on 107–10 & 113–14, drunk and disorderly, her overwhelming effect on Nana 126–30, 146–7, 150, 153; 164; Barnby's lack of enthusiasm for and account of Widmerpool's attentions to 167–71; 174; Widmerpool confesses to procuring her abortion 206–8; Barnby's version of this transaction 231–4; at Mr Deacon's party 237–9, 242, on Craggs' lap, her account of Widmerpool's paying up 247–51; sleeps with Jenkins, compared to Barbara Goring 255–9, 264, 270; Widmerpool puts her behind him 271–2. AW 87, 96, well looked on by the Party 119; 128, 210. LM 46, Widmerpool on 56; Erridge's interest in 123. KO addressing street meeting, Widmerpool's terror of 226–31, 237. SA 120, 214. MP 109, 123. BDFR Association with Bagshaw 30–1; married to Craggs 35–7; at Erridge's funeral 45, 48–50, 55, 59–60, 70–1, 79–80, 83; at *Fission* party 124, 129, relations with Gainsborough 132; bullies Craggs 142, 168–9; destroys Stevens' ms 209–11. TK Widowed 136–7; 187. HSH Dead 104.

JUDY
Bagshaw's secretary at *Fission*, shares an outhouse with him at the far side of Quiggin & Craggs' backyard, not at all stupid but unreliable on spelling.

BDFR 115, 184, 187, 189.

JUNG, Carl Gustav 1875–1961
One of General Conyers' favourite authors ('Don't tie myself down to Freud. Jung has got some interesting stuff too'); his ideas well illustrated by Widmerpool's disastrous night with Mrs Haycock at Dogdene.

LM 81, 226, 230.

KAMENEV, Lev 1883–1936
Arraigned with Zinoviev and others at Moscow show trial, his
execution approved by Widmerpool.

CCR 84.

KARLOFF, Boris (William Henry Pratt) 1887–1969
Film star specializing in monsters and mad magicians, X. Trapnel
famous for his impersonations of.

BDFR 108, 112, 114. TK 33.

KAROLYI, Count 1875–1955
Hungarian statesman at Paris Peace Conference, one of the men of the
middle of the road in whom Sir Gavin Walpole-Wilson senses a
fundamental reciprocity of thought.

BM 221.

KEDWARD, Lieutenant Idwal
Platoon commander in Captain Gwatkin's company in 1940, senior to
Jenkins ('Although he had assured me he was nearly twenty-two,
Kedward's air was that of a small boy who had dressed up for a lark in
officer's uniform, completing the rag by rubbing his upper lip with
burnt cork. He looked young enough to be the Sergeant-Major's son,
grandson almost'). Efficient, practical, ambitious, unimpressed by
Gwatkin's abilities as leader of men. Has been to London twice, works
in a bank, engaged to the manager's daughter. Replaces Gwatkin as
company commander, and welcomes Jenkins' departure ('I was a little
worried about having you on my hands, to tell the truth') with
unconcealed relief.

Sees action near Caen; m. by 1944 and father of two girls; fails to
recognize Major Jenkins when next encountered during the allied
advance into Germany.

VB First impressions of 1, 3–6, 8–19; takes part in ragging of Bithel
24–7, 29–31; 39–40, 46, 51, 59, his and Gwatkin's mutual distrust of
one another 68; 72, doubts Gwatkin's efficiency 76–80; 93, 98, 115,
168, 175–80, 193, 198; his part in the troubles leading up to Gwatkin's
downfall 200–2, 204–8, 210, 212–4; replaces Gwatkin 216–21, 223–6,
230–2, 234; 237, 242. MP With the battalion at the front, on Gwatkin
173–7.

KEEF, Captain, DAPM (Deputy-Assistant Provost-Marshal)
Gnarled foxy little officer commanding military police at General
Liddament's HQ.

SA 54, 212–14, 228.

KERNEVEL, Lieutenant
Chief clerk to French military attaché in London; founder member of
the Free French; middle-aged Breton with a taste for conviviality.
Takes a dim view of Proust ('"Doesn't he always write about society
people?' was Kernével's chilly comment').

MP 139–41, 190–1, 237–41.

KIELKIEWICZ, General
Polish Chief of Staff in exile.

MP 17, 26–7, 29, 33, 64, 66–7, 214.

KILLICK, Professor
Hearty rugby-playing don of Jenkins' college, goes to Manchester on
the day he invited Jenkins to dine in Oxford.

BDFR 4.

KITCHENER, Field-Marshal Earl of Khartoum, 1850–1916
Shared his passion for porcelain with Stringham's mother's first
husband Lord Warrington.

QU 61. CCR 169. KO 73. MP 51, 54.

KLEIN, Jimmy
Cousin of Rosie Manasch; in love with Peggy Stepney before her
marriage to Stringham; eventually becomes her third husband. Cited in
the 'thirties by Widmerpool ('I myself possess a number of Jewish
friends, some of them very able men – Jimmy Klein, for example') as
reason for some mild objection on his part to Hitler's anti-semitism.

BM 61. LM 63. MP 114. BDFR 101.

KLEIN, Peggy see STEPNEY, Lady Peggy

KUCHERMAN, Major
Belgian military attaché, industrial magnate and well-known
international figure, eighteenth-century looks ('the French abbé style').
Once lunched at Stourwater before the war and solves the problem of
his country's resistance army, thereby averting civil war in Belgium,
with indirect assistance from Jenkins. Member of the Belgian cabinet
by 1945.

MP 85–6, 87–90, 94, 104, 144–6, 155, 156, 179, 187, 191–5, 215.

KYDD, Alaric
Amateur pornographer with a slipshod prose style. One of Quiggin &
Craggs' new authors ('A lot was expected from Kydd') immediately

after the second war. Lured away from Clapham's rival publishing firm but proves a liability on account of his novel *Sweetskin* ('Trapnel was specially contemptuous of Kydd's attempts at eroticism. To be fair, *Sweetskin* was in due course the object of prosecution, so presumably someone found the book erotic . . .'). His impending trial for obscenity one of several clouds gathering over Quiggin & Craggs before its abrupt demise in the autumn of 1947. Eventually acquitted. Emigrates in the 'sixties.

BDFR 117, 125, 151–2, 155–7, 159, 167–8, 186, 207, 240. TK 8, 214. HSH 92, 107, 110.

LAKIN
Nondescript undergraduate whose family connection with a senior Trades Union official gives Sillery unexpected strings to pull during the General Strike of 1926.

QU 170.

LAMB, Lady Caroline 1785–1828
Byron's mistress, exiled on his account by her family in 1812 to Bessborough and Lismore in Ireland; gave her name to Lady Caro's Dingle in the grounds at Castlemallock during the course of this trip.

VB 170–1, 225, 228–9.

LANNOO
Kucherman's predecessor as Belgian military attaché.

MP 87.

LE BAS, Lawrence Langton
Jenkins' housemaster at school ('At the time . . . he merely seemed to Stringham and myself a dangerous lunatic, to be humoured and outwitted'). Tall, bald, untidy; red eyes and rimless spectacles; slight lisp. Fresh air fiend. No sex life.
'On some occasions, especially when vexed, he had the habit of getting into unusual positions, stretching his legs far apart and putting his hands on his hips; or standing at attention with heels together and feet turned outwards so far that it seemed impossible that he should not overbalance and fall flat on his face. Alternatively, especially when in a good humour, he would balance on the fender, with each foot pointing in the same direction. These postures gave him the air of belonging to some highly conventionalised form of graphic art: an oriental god, or knave of playing cards.'

Poet and oarsman (once won the Diamond Sculls, later relegated to a Duffers' Eight) who failed to live up to his boundless promise in youth. Has a pronounced weakness for late Victorian Hellenistic poets, and is frequently to be found reading them aloud to his pupils, or alone in the fields beyond the railway line ('He crouched there in the manner of a large animal – some beast alien to the English countryside, a yak or sea-lion – taking its ease: marring, as Stringham said later, the beauty of the summer afternoon'). Makes rather a favourite of Stringham. Never quite happy about Widmerpool. Identified to the police by Stringham as the wanted criminal Braddock alias Thorne and arrested in the summer of 1921. Is chronically suspicious of Templer, with good reason, and moves heaven and earth to get him removed from school.

Holds an annual dinner party for Old Boys in London at one of which he collapses, possibly from impotence and rage, during an unsolicited speech by Widmerpool.

Last encountered in the school library immediately after the second war; in his eighties, looking well, 'leathery, saurian; dry as a bone'.

QU His house rules 8, 18–19; expulsion of Akworth 13; his personality and strange postures, his objectionable behaviour over Uncle Giles' smoking and Templer's trip to London, his early promise 26–35; episode of Braddock alias Thorne 36–7, 39–43, 44–51; 60; his redoubled persecution of Templer 70–2; relations with Widmerpool 129–31, 134; compared to Sillery 169; 172, 207; visits Jenkins at Oxford and gives him a piece of advice 221–7. BM His daydreams of Hellas compared to Mr Deacon's 9; 93, 102; mistakes Stringham for Umfraville at Cowes 104; 106, 142; Mrs Widmerpool on 262. AW His views on St John Clarke 20; 37, 42, 44, 93, 152, Umfraville left school at request of 154–5; his Old Boys' dinner at the Ritz 170, 176–7, 179–82, 184–5, his speech 187–91, his collapse during Widmerpool's 194–7, 179–82, 184–5, his speech 187–91, his collapse during Widmerpool's 194–7, 201–3, 214. LM Alfred Tolland a regular at his reunions 24–5, 29. CCR His seizure recalled 99, 101, 125, 214; 141. SA 176. MP Exchange with Stringham over Lord de Tabley's *Medea* recalled 62–3; 105. BDFR 56–7, 64, last encounter with 231–6. HSH 108, 193.

LEBEDEV, General
Soviet military attaché, 'at all times a stranger to laughter'.

MP 24, 26, 151–2, 166–7. TK 218.

LEINTWARDINE, Ada
Novelist, near bestseller. First encountered as Sillery's secretary after the second war; 'decidedly pretty . . . in her twenties, fair, with a high colour, a shade on the plump side, though only enough to suggest changes in the female figure then pending'; typing his diaries for publication. Local doctor's daughter with literary ambitions, at work

on a first novel. Sole female friend of Pamela Widmerpool, from ATS days together. Abandons Sillery ('His annoyance, together with Miss Leintwardine's now very definitely troubled manner, confirmed that in a peculiar way they must have been having some sort of flirtation, an hypothesis scarcely to be guessed by even the most hardened Sillery experts') to join the new publishing firm of Quiggin & Craggs.

Makes herself rapidly at home on the London literary scene; her sex life hotly debated (the novelist Evadne Clapham and the critic Nathaniel Sheldon both claiming some success in this direction); extract from her novel published in *Fission*. Specialises in dealing with awkward customers such as X. Trapnel ('for someone who liked running other people's lives so much as Ada, to get on with Trapnel, who liked running his own, was certainly a recommendation for tact in doing business'). Reforms Quiggin's taste in dress and m. him on the collapse of the firm in the autumn of 1947. Alleged to prefer her own sex (notably by Bernard Shernmaker, possibly out of pique at having his own advances rejected) in spite of twin daughters born soon after the marriage ('their identical, almost laughable, resemblance to their father scotching another of Shernmaker's disobliging innuendos').

First novel, *I Stopped at a Chemist's*, pub. 1947; followed, on Quiggin's advice, by two dull domestic chronicles; reputation and sales retrieved in the 'fifties by *Bedsores* and *The Bitch Pack Meets on Wednesday*.

Shrewd, inquisitive, effusive; a dab hand at extracting and retailing gossip; gives notorious literary dinner parties. Increasingly busy on committees, signing protests, making speeches etc. Makes rather a hit at the writers' conference in Venice in 1958 ('she was no thinner, but carried herself well, retaining that air of blonde, bright, efficient, self-possessed secretary, who knows the whereabouts of everything required in a properly run office, much too sensible to allow more than just the right minimum of flirtatious behaviour to pervade business hours'). Charms Dr Emily Brightman (their Italian holiday together not a success).

Abandons writing in the 'sixties in favour of taking an active interest in Quiggin's publishing activities. Spends ten years attempting to rehabilitate the forgotten Edwardian novelist St John Clarke, and eventually brings off a 40 minute documentary on TV in 1968. Fifty in sight.

BDFR At Sillery's, speculations on their relationship, deserts him for Quiggin & Craggs 16–17; Bagshaw on 36–7, 71; prospers in London 115–16; at *Fission* party 122, 137–8; 141; skill in managing Trapnel 157–8; 160, 162–3, 165; incredulous over Pamela's affair with Trapnel, relations with Quiggin 183–5, 187; 208; marriage to Quiggin 210–11;

novel published 239. TK At Venice conference 8; at Bragadin Palace, her career and reputation, snubbed by Pamela 90–5, 98–101, 103, 116; with Glober, her plans for a St John Clarke film, her skill in managing Tokenhouse 131–7, 140, 142–3, 147–52; Pamela on 165; Dr Brightman's enthusiasm for 174, 177; and subsequent chilliness to 213–14; on Pamela, and Glober's film plans 219–23. HSH Her part in St John Clarke TV programme, her marriage 36–8, 40; 58; at Magnus Donners prize dinner 93–6, 103–4, 109, 112, 113.

LEROY, Commandant
Retired infantry officer, host at La Grenadière in Touraine to Jenkins and Widmerpool during the summer they spent there learning French in 1923. Small, semi-invalid (gassed at Ypres), bullied by his wife and rarely speaks. Liked by Jenkins, despised by Widmerpool.

QU 108, 112–13, 119, 123–4, 142, 145, 152–3, 162. MP 141. HSH 222.

LEROY, Madame
Masterful wife of above, aunt of Berthe and Suzette. In her sixties. 'Had evidently been a handsome proposition in her youth'. A kind of sorceress. Much admired and possibly feared by Widmerpool, who sees in her a likeness to his own mother.

QU 108–22, 142, 150, 152–3, 157, 159, 161–2. BM 29, 31, 69, 262. SA 103. MP 141. TK 14. HSH 222.

LIDDAMENT, Major-General H de C, DSO, MC
The new Divisional Commander in N. Ireland in 1940. Carries a hunting horn and wand, accompanied by two small cross dogs ('Widmerpool was not above saying "wuff-wuff" to the pair of them, if their owner was in earshot, which he would follow up by giving individual, though unconvincing pats of encouragement. 'Thank God, the brutes aren't allowed out on exercise," he said'). Thin, clean-shaven; ascetic features, air of a scholar rather than a soldier, touch of Sir Magnus Donners; young for his rank and determined to ginger things up.

Considered a buffoon by Widmerpool who nonetheless admits him to be the only man beside himself fit to command the division. Fond of teasing. Takes an unexpected interest in the art of the novel. Recommends Jenkins to Major Finn (who served under him in first war), and is prevented in the nick of time from ruining Widmerpool's career over the Recce Unit affair by his own sudden departure to command a corps in June, 1941.

A success in the N. African campaign of 1943; on Army Council by the late 'fifties.

VB His first move as divisional commander 74; snap inspection of Gwatkin's company, staggered by the men's virtually unanimous dislike of porridge 93–7; Jenkins joins his staff 238; Widmerpool despairs of 240–1. SA 5, Widmerpool's low opinion of 26–8, 31–2; dinner in his mess, likened to Pharaoh guarded by his colonels as animal-headed deities 34–7, falls into a trance 41–2; his stern views on Trollope, startling intervention in Jenkins' career 44–52, 79, 84–6; 89, 95, 100, Jenkins fails to justify his confidence 102–3, 172–4; enraged by Widmerpool's intriguing 207–9, 211, 214; given command of a corps 227–8. MP 111, 181. TK 202, 212.

LILIENTHAL
Bearded second-hand bookseller with a shop round the corner from Mr Deacon's in the late 'twenties; frequenter of the Mortimer; later Mopsy Pontner's second husband.

TK 67–9, 71, 80.

LILIENTHAL, Xenia
First wife of above, 'small with ginger corkscrew curls and a beseeching expression'; at Louis Glober's party with a heavy cold in the head; afterwards goes off with an Indian doctor.

TK 66–9, 71, 80.

LINDA
One of X. Trapnel's mistresses.

TK 198.

LINTOT
Travel agent and former officer in the same War Office section as Jenkins; client of the accountant, Mr Cheesman, who was a Japanese POW with Stringham.

TK 203–7, 209–10.

LIPTON, Sir Thomas, Bt 1850–1931
Grocer and yachtsman; present on the Squadron Lawn at Cowes when Lord Vowchurch made one of his stinging ripostes to Edward VII.

LM 87.

LISZT, Franz 1811–86
Added a touch of the sublime to the humdrum home backyard of Moreland whose uncle once saw him passing through Sydenham. Colonel Hlava has a look of him, and so has Carolo in later life.

CCR 4. MP 97. TK 240.

LLOYD GEORGE, Earl, of Dwyfor 1863–1945
Liberal statesman and Prime Minister, conferred a baronetcy on Peter
Templer's uncle.

QU 68. KO 1, 18, 30, 248.

LLYWARCH the Old d. 646
Bard who retired in disgust from King Arthur's court and afterwards
lived to be 150 years old; ancestor of Jenkins.

VB 3.

LONSDALE, Fifth Earl of 1857–1944
Celebrated sportsman with whom St John Clarke was once forced to
play croquet during a weekend at Dogdene before the first war.

CCR 191.

LOVELL, Caroline
Jenkins' niece, only child of Priscilla and Chips Lovell. Orphaned 1941;
ed. at Dr Brighman's university; m. to a soldier serving in N. Ireland
by 1971.

KO 88. VB 137, 139, 146. SA 106, 111–12, 166. TK 5. HSH 225–6.

LOVELL, Chips
Scriptwriter in the early 'thirties ('To be a scriptwriter was at that
period the ambition of almost everyone who could hold a pen') at the
same film studio as Jenkins. Aged about twenty-three or four. Means
to marry money and work on a gossip column. Son of a painter who
eloped with Lord Sleaford's sister; nephew by marriage of Lady Molly
Jeavons; has designs on Priscilla Tolland. Ingenuous, hard-headed, odd
mixture of realist and romantic, unerring instinct for the obvious. A
success with both sexes. Daily instalments of the doings of his vast
horde of relations ('He had that deep appreciation of family
relationships and their ramifications that is a gift of its own, like being
musical, or having an instinct for the value of horses or jewels')
provides one of the few redeeming features of Jenkins' life at the studio.

Job on a Fleet Street gossip column by 1936. M. to Priscilla, one
daughter Caroline. Settles down to be a model husband. Doing well
('Like everyone else of his kind he was writing a play . . . "I never get
time to settle down to serious writing," he used to say, thereby making
what amounted to a legal declaration in defining his own inclusion
within an easily recognizable category of non-starting literary
apprenticeship').

Joins the Marines on outbreak of war, posted to East coast (later
promoted Captain at Combined Ops HQ in Whitehall). Greatly

distressed by Priscilla's affair with Odo Stevens; hoping for a reconciliation at Bijou Ardglass's birthday party; killed that night by the bomb on the Café de Madrid.

LM 5; at film studio, his character and ambitions, his relations, introduces Jenkins to his Aunt Molly, his interest in Priscilla Tolland 12–21, 23–4, 26–9, 31–2, 34, 36, 42, 49; 57; by no means universally liked 78, 89; 112; his stories about Erridge 140–1, 147, 151; and about the Jeavonses 155–9, 164, 170, 198; further extracts from his family saga, his technique analysed 212–16; 236. CCR On the Ardglasses and Tollands 59–61, 70, 72, 77; now a gossip columnist, still interested in Priscilla 193–6; 199, 201, 222; engaged to Priscilla 225, 227, 229. KO 35; has a child, marriage a success 86–8; 146, 231–2, 234, 239. VB 88; joined the Marines 112; resemblance to Odo Stevens 115, 117; 138; stationed on E. coast without Priscilla 143, 146–8; 196. SA Rumours of her indiscretion in his absence 74, 88–90; reflections on his character, career and marriage 90–2; at Café Royal, his account of Priscilla's affair with Odo, hoping to patch things up 106–17; speculations on this prompted by Priscilla's arrival with Odo 124–8, 130–2, 134, her feelings for 142–3; 148; killed 157, 160, 163–4, 166, 169. MP 76, Stevens' synthetic compunction over 124–6; 185. TK 22. HSH 225.

LOVELL, Lady Priscilla see TOLLAND, Lady Priscilla

LUNDQUIST
Swede with complete confidence in his own powers of pleasing. En pension with the Leroys in France; makes a distressing scene after being insulted on the tennis court by the Norwegian M. Örn. First inklings of Widmerpool's quest for power provided by his prodigious efforts at reconciling the feud between these two Scandinavians.

QU 114–15, 126–7, 134, 137–44, 146, 148–9, 152–8, 184. MP 162.

LYAUTEY, Marshal 1854–1934
French Colonial administrator, held gaiety to be the first essential in an officer. Admired by Dicky Umfraville who was about to take a leaf out of his book when framed by Buster Foxe after the first war.

VB 152, 172. SA 51. MP 140.

MACDONALD, Ramsay 1866–1937
Labour Prime Minister and leader of the National Government 1931–5, torn to shreds in Fettiplace-Jones' maiden speech.

AW 190.

MACFADDEN
Feverishly keen officer on Aldershot training course in 1941, schoolmaster in civil life, regularly volunteers for optional extras like crawling miles through mud.

VB 122–4, 128, 134.

MACFIE, Major, DADMS (Deputy-Assistant Director Medical Service)
Regular soldier in Royal Army Medical Corps, one of Jenkins' companions in the notorious F Mess at Divisional HQ in 1941, 'gaunt, glum, ungenial, rarely spoke at meals or indeed at any other time'.

SA 65–6, 68, 71, 168, 225–6, 228.

MACGIVERING
At army reunion dinner in 1959.

TK 203.

MACLEAN, Donald b. 1913
See BURGESS, Guy

MACLINTICK
Stout caustic middle-aged music critic; one of the earliest champions of Moreland's music in the 'twenties; a regular at the Mortimer and the Nag's Head, passion for Irish whisky and the Russian composers. 'Maclintick's calculatedly humdrum appearance, although shabby, seemed aimed at concealing Bohemian affiliations. The minute circular lenses of his gold-rimmed spectacles, set across the nose of a pug dog, made one think of caricatures of Thackeray or President Thiers, imposing upon him the air of a bad-tempered doctor'.

Splenetic hag-ridden temperament. Disapproves of Deacon, dislikes Barnby, despises Gossage, can't stick Carolo. Hero-worships Moreland. Working on a great tome about musical theory. Son of a musical, half-Jewish mother; father and grandfather in the linen trade; ed. at same German university (probably Bonn) as Dr Trelawney. Full of carefully concealed romanticism. Hates all women except whores. Terrified of being thought sentimental. Small squalid terrace house near Victoria ('He says his mood is for ever Pimlico'). Rows incessantly with his wife Audrey: ' The Maclinticks . . . as a married couple gave the impression of being near the end of their tether. When, for example, Mona and Peter Templer had quarrelled . . . the horror had been less acute, more amenable to adjustment, than the bleak despair of the Maclinticks' union'.

Looks in at Mrs Foxe's party for Moreland's symphony in 1936, and pities Buster Foxe for being married to such a wife. Deserted by Audrey the following spring, sacked by his editor in the same week. Drinking hard, kidney trouble, almost certainly broke. Is advised by Moreland to get some sleep, and makes 'that harrowing remark that established throughout all eternity his relationship with Moreland. "I obey you, Moreland," he said, "with the proper respect of the poor interpretative hack for the true creative artist"'. Gasses himself two or three days later, having first torn up the manuscript of his book and stopped the lavatory with it.

CCR 5, 7; first encounter with in the Mortimer in 1928 or 9 14–15, his temperament, his devotion to Moreland 17–19, 22–5, 27–8; at Casanova's Chinese restaurant 30–5, 37–8; Moreland on 55; first visit to his house in 1936, grim relations with his wife 104–23; at Mrs Foxe's party 142, on Moreland's symphony, brutal exchange with his wife 147–53, 156–7, 159–60, her complaints about 167–8 & 175–6 & 178, 186, 188–9; lost his wife and job, second visit with Moreland to his house, his account of his marriage 203–15; his suicide 216–21. KO Acquaintance with Trelawney 84; 246. SA Moreland living with his widow, their respective reminiscences of 117, 119–21, 123, 125, 135, 145, 152, 159. BDFR 119, 191, 228. TK 14.

MACLINTICK, Audrey

Wife of above, m. for seven years by 1936: 'When she opened the door to us, her formidable discontent with life swept across the threshold in scorching, blasting waves. She was a small dark woman with a touch of the gypsy about her, this last possibly suggested by sallow skin and bright black eyes. Her black hair was worn in a fringe. Some men might have found her attractive. I was not among them . . .'

Jealous of Moreland. Entertains him with Jenkins in her basement on cold mutton and pickles, and eventually drives them from the house after a running diatribe on Maclintick's disgusting personal habits, professional shortcomings and lamentable performance as a husband ('There was a moment . . . when I thought she might pick up one of the battered table knives and stick it into him'). Tamed by Stringham after another vicious row with Maclintick at Mrs Foxe's party that autumn. Runs away shortly afterwards with her lodger Carolo, leaving Moreland to clear up the mess after her husband's suicide. Turns out to have first met Maclintick at a concert at which neither spoke, and after which he doggedly pursued her ('You know, Audrey was my ideal in a sort of way': Maclintick).

Abandoned after three years by Carolo. Works in a canteen. Moves in with Moreland at the time of his divorce, despondency and general retreat from perfectionism ('there could be no doubt Mrs Maclintick herself was an element in this retreat. In her case, indeed, so far as Moreland was concerned, withdrawal from perfectionism had been so unphased as to constitute an operation reasonably to be designated a rout'). Aged about forty, and marginally less disagreeable than before, when next encountered at the Café Royal in 1941: 'Small, wiry, aggressive, she looked as ready as ever for a row, her bright black eyes and unsmiling countenance confronting a world from which perpetual hostility was not merely potential, but presumptive'. Gives Moreland a companionable feeling that Maclintick is still about.

Supervises his work, checks his drinking and nurses him efficiently during the years of ill health leading up to his death at the end of the 'fifties. Never married to him.

CCR Acrimonious relations with her husband 27; visit to her house, her comparative amiability to Carolo, her complaints of and quarrel with Maclintick 105–22; at Mrs Foxe's party 142, row with Maclintick 150–3, 156–7, 159–60, charmed by Stringham 166–8, 171, 173–9, defeated by Miss Weedon in battle over Stringham, leaves with Carolo 181–7; runs away with Carolo, Maclintick's reactions and account of their courtship 203–13, 218. SA Living with Moreland, at Café Royal with him, speculations on their relationship 117–27, charmed by Odo Stevens 129–31, 133, 135–9, 141–2, 144–5, 148–51; at home, maternal feelings for her lodger Max Pilgrim 152–3, 155–9; Stringham's memories of 222–3. BDFR Making Moreland work 102. MP On provincial tour with Moreland 35; 208; Pamela Flitton's ill humours compared with hers 57, 123, 125. TK 81, 153, at Stevens' party with Moreland 227–8, 231, flustered by Carolo's presence, momentary revelation of her feelings for Moreland 237–9 & 241, 248–9, 253–4, 256, 266; visiting Moreland on his deathbed 275.

MAELGWYN-JONES
Adjutant of Jenkins' Welsh battalion in 1940, 'an efficient, short-tempered Regular, whose slight impediment of speech became a positive stutter when he grew enraged'. Largely responsible for booting out Bithel, also for relieving Captain Gwatkin of his command after an imperial balls-up over the codeword Fishcake.

VB 8, 48, 65–6, 73–4, 93–4, 102, 194, 207–9, 211–12, 222–5, 238. SA 58.

MAIDEN
One of the organisers of Le Bas' dinners for Old Boys; in the margarine business; 'yellowish, worried face, which seemed to have taken on sympathetic colouring from the commodity he marketed'.

AW 176–7, 181–2, 191, 195–7. BDFR 233.

MAISKY

Lady Molly's monkey, bought in Soho in 1934 and named for the then Soviet Ambassador. Receives homage at the Jeavons' party ('There was something of Quiggin in his seriousness and self-absorption: also in the watchful manner in which he glanced from time to time at the nuts, sometimes choosing one specially tempting to crack'); and brings out Miss Weedon's anti-simianism.

Later bites Erridge's butler Smith who d. after trying to filch a biscuit from him: 'Silly thing to do, to take issue with Maisky. Of course Smith came off second-best. Perhaps they both reached out for the biscuit at the same moment. Anyway, Maisky wouldn't have any snatching and Smith contracted septicemia with fatal results. Meant the end of Maisky to, which wasn't really just. But then what is just in this life?' (Ted Jeavons). Far outclassed by Sillery in point of devastating monkey-like shrewdness.

LM 160–1, 163–4, 167–8. KO 235. MP 78–9. BDFR 7.

MALIPHANT, Mrs

On the stage in the 1870s ('alleged to have slept with Irving; some said Tree; possibly both'), rambles on about old Chelsea days at Louis Glober's party half a century later.

TK 70–1.

MALLOCK, Hercules

Second Marquess of Castlemallock, friend of d'Orsay and Lady Blessington, alleged by Caroline Lamb to be her lover and by Byron to prefer his own sex. D. hard up and unmarried at a great age in Lisbon, succeeded by a great-nephew, father or grandfather of the Castlemallock who ran away with Dicky Umfraville's second wife.

VB 170–1.

MANASCH, Sir Herbert and Lady

Rosie's parents. Wealthy and hospitable patrons of the arts between the wars. Bought paintings from Barnby, found work for Moreland at musical parties but failed to provide anything spectacular in the way of plunder for Mark Members when he tried to involve them in literature too.

BM 44. AW 71, 149. LM 220. CCR 38, 177. BDFR 100. TK 255–6.

MANASCH, Isadore

Relative of above, published a slim volume of Symbolist verse and was painted in the background of a café scene by Toulouse-Lautrec; an embarrassment to his side of the family.

BDFR 101.

MANASCH, Leopold
Rosie's uncle, sold Stourwater to Sir Magnus Donners on the grounds that the hunting wasn't good enough.

BM 183.

MANASCH, Rosie
A 'Lively, gleaming little Jewess in a scarlet frock' at debutante dances in the 'twenties: 'She looked quite out of place in this setting; intended by nature to dance veiled, or perhaps unveiled, before the throne of some Oriental potentate . . .' Daughter of Sir Herbert Manasch, contemporary of Eleanor Walpole-Wilson and a great favourite with Eleanor's father Sir Gavin. Chained to a staple by Johnny Pardoe during Sir Magnus Donners' tour of the dungeons at Stourwater. M. 1) the newspaper proprietor Jock Udall, and has trouble with him. Hated like poison by Peggy Stringham. Widowed in the war, m. 2) an elderly invalid Pole, Andrzejewski, and reverts to her maiden name on his death a few months later.

Succeeds Erridge as *Fission*'s backer in 1946. Aged forty or so. Decides, possibly on sight, to marry 3) Odo Stevens, and precipitates *Fission*'s collapse by withdrawing her money after the row over his book *Sad Majors*. Involved in fierce skirmishings with Matilda Donners for possession of Odo, who may or may not have given her a black eye during this troubled period and whom she afterwards keeps on a short string ('imposing idleness on her husband as a kind of eternal punishment for the brief scamper with Matilda'). Two or three children by this marriage.

House in Regent's Park. Gives the musical party in 1959 at which Moreland collapses, and after which Pamela Widmerpool ('far from popular with her hostess') stages her last savage scene with Widmerpool.

BM At dinner with the Walpole-Wilsons 33, 35, 39, 41, 44–5, 48–9, 54–5; and at the Huntercombes' ball 60–2; staying with the Walpole-Wilsons 176, 180, 183–4, at Stourwater luncheon party 188, 190, 195, visits the dungeons 200, 202 & 209–10, 217, 221–2. LM 178. CCR 177. KO 72. MP 244. BDFR *Fission*'s anonymous backer 76, 93; at the Flores' party, her background and marital career, her charms 99–103; her party for *Fission*'s first number 120, Odo Stevens takes a fancy to 130; returns his interest 143; affair with Stevens 208; withdraws support from *Fission* 210; has his book serialized in Fleet Street 240. TK In Venice with Odo, their courtship and marriage 159–64, 166–9; her musical party 225–6, 227, 229, 231–3, 241, 247–9. HSH 62.

MANTLE, Corporal
Energetic NCO in Jenkins' Defence Platoon in 1941, becomes a pawn in Widmerpool's schemes for spiting Col. Hogbourne-Johnson.

SA 7, 18, 42–5, 73, 186, 215.

MARINKO
Jugoslav military attaché, supporter of Mihailovich's resistance movement, out of a job under Tito's partisans.

MP 166–7, 169, 215.

MARTHE
Girl with a goitre who did the cooking ('and did it uncommonly well') at La Grenadière.

QU 121, 160.

MARX, Karl 1818–83
Summoned by planchette and leaves a message for Quiggin after Sunday luncheon at the Templers' in 1933.

AWA 94–8, 116, 126. KO 31. BDFR 21, 138.

MARY I, Queen 1516–58
Sacked the Tolland who was Esquire of the Body to Henry VIII.

LM 151.

MASHAM, Captain
Ardent Francophil, Finn's assistant at the start of the second war in liaison with the Free French.

SA 94–6, 98–9, 101, 104. MP 84–5.

MAUREEN
Short, squat, blackhaired barmaid at Castlemallock, Captain Gwatkin's ideal of womanhood ('I thought her good-looking, with that touch of an animal, almost a touch of monstrosity, some men find very attractive . . . Barnby would certainly have liked this girl'). Ruins Gwatkin's military career, and afterwards betrays him with Corporal Gwylt.

VB 182–6, 189–93, 197–8, 209, 212, 221, 226–7, 229–31, 233, 236. BDFR 167.

M'CRACKEN
Mildred Blaides' first husband; Flying Corps officer in first war, killed soon after the wedding in a raid over Germany.

LM 40.

McREITH, Lady (Gwen)
Old friend of the Templers (widow of one of Peter's father's business partners, who died of shock ten days after being knighted). First encountered at their house by Jenkins as a schoolboy in the summer of 1923: 'a figure whose origins and demeanour suggested enigmas I could not, in those days, even attempt to fathom'. Tall, slight, fair-skinned, heavily lip-sticked, drenched in scent. Rags Jimmy Stripling and is inseparable from his wife, Peter's elder sister Babs ('demonstrative kissing took place between them at the slightest provocation'). Makes Sunny Farebrother morally uncomfortable. Accidentally responsible, while demonstrating a fox-trot step with Jenkins, for revealing to him a whole range of staggering new sexual possibilities:

'The transaction took place so swiftly, and, so far as Lady McReith was concerned, so unselfconsciously, that Peter and Stripling did not look up from their game; but – although employed merely as a mechanical dummy – I had become aware, with colossal impact, that Lady McReith's footing in life was established in a world of physical action of which at present I knew little or nothing . . .'

Sleeps with Peter on the last night of this visit.

Present ten years later at the Carlton Grill dinner where Peter's younger sister Jean (then Jenkins' mistress) first met and fell for Jimmy Brent. Lesbian. Runs an odd female organisation in second war, supplying drivers to the Belgians or Poles in London and employing Norah Tolland, Eleanor Walpole-Wilson and Bijou Ardglass. Last seen in uniform in 1943 ('thinner than ever, almost a skeleton, the blue veins more darkly shaded on her marble skin'), escorting Pamela Flitton at the opera and not in the best of humours.

QU At the Templers, her unsettling effect on Jenkins 80–4, ragging Farebrother, Jenkins' revelation while dancing with 88–93, sleeps with Peter 94–6, 99–101; 124, 172. KO 206. VB Turns out to have been present at Brent's first encounter with Jean, Jean's subsequent lies about her recalled by Jenkins 128–30. SA 111. MP 81, 99, 101, 210.

MEMBERS, Lenore
American author and journalist, a few years older than Mark Members whom she m. as her fourth husband in the 'fifties; away in US more often than not, reports the rumour about Widmerpool's being framed by the CIA.

TK 6, 17. HSH 39, 42–3, 46, 93, 117.

MEMBERS, Mark
Poet, critic, man-of-letters. Contemporary of Jenkins at university, and already a freshman of some standing ('on account of a poem published

121

in *Public School Verse* and favourably noticed by Edmund Gosse') when first encountered at one of Sillery's tea parties in 1924:

'Up to that afternoon I had only seen Members hurrying about the streets, shaking from his round, somewhat pasty face a brownish uneven fringe that grew low on his forehead and made him look rather like a rag doll, or marionette: an air augmented by brown eyes like beads, and a sprinkling of freckles.'

Tall, willowy, Byronic collar and loosely knotted tie. Cultivates the Scholar Gypsy look. Aesthete ('Sillers, it is too clever of you to buy a suit the same colour as your loose covers') with an eye to the main chance. Comes from the same Midlands town as J. G. Quiggin; may even be related to him; their life-long rivalry possibly springs from seeds of mutual suspicion and dislike sown by Sillery at this tea party. Fails to secure his expected First.

Secretary to the novelist St John Clarke by the end of the 'twenties. Has abandoned his Romantic movement overtones in favour of something more spruce: 'His slim waist and forceful, interrogative manner rather suggested one of those strong-willed elegant young salesmen, who lead the customer from the shop only after the intention to buy a few handkerchiefs has been transmuted into a reckless squandering on shirts, socks and ties of patterns later to be found fundamentally unsympathetic'. Writing for one of the weeklies; four books in hand; Quiggin markedly respectful ('This was to be a race neck-and-neck, though whether the competitors themselves were already aware of the invisible ligament binding them together in apparently eternal contrast and comparison, I do not know').

Revolutionises St John Clarke's attitude to modernism. Energetic social life; active womaniser; no truth in rumours of a sexual hold over his employer. Has already published several books of verse by the time of Jenkins' first novel ('I found myself unable to consider him without prejudice') and made some name for himself as a critic. Usurped by Quiggin as secretary to St John Clarke at the end of 1932. Takes over Quiggin's old job at Boggis & Stone (not a living wage), retains a pittance from St John Clarke ('scarcely enough . . . to cover my bus fares'). Goes downhill. Shabby, emaciated and bitterly resentful of Quiggin's treachery until mollified by St John Clarke's sacking Quiggin too.

A goodish poet. Modelled his early verse on Browning, afterwards toys with the Symbolists, takes on Freudian overtones by the early 'thirties ('Unfortunately his *oeuvre* is at present lacking in any real sense of social significance': Quiggin), later flirts half-heartedly with communism, later still switches to German influence and becomes one of the first to take up Kierkegaard ('Members, no fool, was always a little ahead of the fashion'). Beginning to retrieve lost ground by 1936. Lecture tour in US; popular spare man at intellectual dinner parties; his travel book *Baroque Interlude* a notable success. Becomes assistant literary editor on a weekly paper, thereby putting both Quiggin and Jenkins to some extent in his power as reviewers. Talk of his marrying an heiress.

Ministry of Information in second war. Hair worn long and turned snow white by 1946 ('Gives just that air of distinction required by the passing of youth – and nobody got more out of being a professional young man than Mark when the going was good': Sillery). Lectures at Oxford on *Kleist, Marx, Sartre, the Existentialist Equilibrium*. Finds his vocation arranging virtually free holidays abroad for himself and other intellectuals at symposia on 'The Writer's Position in Society' etc. His talents wasted on authorship.

Has become a hardened veteran of cultural congresses (and picked up a wife, Lenore, at one of them) by the late 'fifties; organizes the international writers' conference at Venice in 1958; and sits on the Magnus Donners prize committee ten years later (his inclusion almost statutory on any award-giving panel). Modest prize for his own *Collected Poems*, 'a volume which brought together all his verse from *Iron Aspidistra* (1923) to *H-bomb Eclogue* (1960)'. Air of an eighteenth-century sage too high-minded to wear a wig. Putting away more drink than he used. Admits at last to being Quiggin's second-cousin but is not above gloating over his old friend's domestic vexations.

QU at Sillery's tea party, takes against Quiggin, butters up Bill Truscott 176–7, 179–83, 185–6, 189–90; Quiggin's curiosity about 201–3; his dislike of Quiggin 209–11. BM At Mr Deacon's birthday party with Quiggin, change in him analysed, his literary standing, attitude to St John Clarke and indissoluble bond with Quiggin 237, 240–7. AW 16, 21–3; his part in converting St John Clarke to modernism 26–9; 30; meditations on, Jenkins' prejudice against 32–3, 35–6; replaced by Quiggin as St John Clarke's secretary 47–54; various opinions of his poetry 60–1, 74–5, 86–7; 77, temporarily reinstated with St John Clarke 100–101; Sillery on 113; 115–16, with Boggis & Stone 118–19; encountered in Hyde Park, his career reviewed, his account of Quiggin's treachery, his despair at sight of St John Clarke in protest march 120–32; reconciled with Quiggin 172–3. LM 105, 125, 204; at Lady Molly's, appalled by the company she keeps, his career to date, his account of Mona's leaving Quiggin 218–24. CCR 42–3, assistant literary editor 64; 74–5, on St John Clarke 79–82; 92, 105, 136; his obituary for St John Clarke 190–2; 196, 226. KO His brush with Dr Trelawney 85; 249–51. BDFR Sillery on 8, 21; 100, at *Fission* party 126–7, 130; 147, 151, 153–4; witness at Quiggin's wedding 211. TK Organizing Venice conference, his career to date, his marriage 6–9, 11; 17, 159, 214. HSH On St John Clarke TV programme 37–40; 48; on

Donners prize committee 56–8, 66–70, 72–5, 87; at prize dinner 91, teasing Quiggin 93–6, 98–9, his speech 105–7; at RA dinner, on Quiggin's family troubles 120–2, Canon Fenneau on his fame as an undergraduate 125, 128; 134.

MENJOU, Adolphe 1890–1963
Movie actor who once sat next to Lady Molly.

LM 37.

MERCY
Disobliging young housemaid at Stonehurst in 1914; belongs to a local sect numbering some twenty persons, all related to one another, who hold the rest of the world to be damned.

KO 4–5, 19–20, 33, 43, 61.

MICHAEL
Sailor on one of Widmerpool's Cabinet committees.

MP 105–7.

MICHALSKI
One of General Kielkiewicz's ADCs; Jenkins' principal informant on Polish personnel at the Titian and on the havoc wrought there by Pamela Flitton.

MP 27, 29, 66–7, 73.

MIHAILOVICH, Draza 1893–1946
Leader of Jugoslav resistance movement in rivalry with Tito's communist partisans, loses British support in 1944, subsequently captured and shot by Tito.

MP 167, 215.

MOFFET ('the murderer')
Stringham's scout at Oxford, and a prime reason for his leaving the university.

QU 215–9.

MOLLY, Lady see JEAVONS, Lady Molly

MONA
The strapping black-haired artist's model and friend of Gypsy Jones who brought Mark Members to Mr Deacon's birthday party in 1928 or 9. Nearly six feet tall and beautiful by any standards. Painted by Barnby among others. Said by Members to have emotional leanings towards her own sex.

Afterwards dyes her hair peroxide blonde and moves on to more lucrative commercial work, advertising toothpaste on the front of every London bus. Claims to be partly Swiss, father (dead) an engineer in Birmingham. Picked up by Peter Templer at a roadhouse near Staines, and m. to him by 1933. Something appealing about her artistic aspirations, and her absurdly artificial social manner:
'She was like some savage creature, anxious to keep up appearances before members of a more highly civilized species, although at the same time keenly aware of her own superiority in cunning. There was something hard and untamed about her, probably the force that had attracted Templer and others.'

Invites Jenkins to stay at Maidenhead for the weekend which sees the start of his affair with Jean Duport. Bored by married life ('Mona's sulkiness cast a gloom over the house. Although obviously lazy and easy-going in her manner of life, she possessed also an energy and egotism that put considerable force behind this display of moodiness'). St John Clarke her favourite author. Still hankers after the Bohemian company of her youth. Takes a fancy to J. G. Quiggin ('At that time I failed entirely to grasp the extent to which in her eyes Quiggin represented high romance'); and bolts with him shortly afterwards ('I don't think she likes men . . . But I don't think she likes women either. Just keen on herself': Jean Duport). Living with Quiggin in Sussex on Peter's allowance plus £1000 inherited from an aunt who kept a boarding-house in Worthing; divorce pending.

Grown distinctly sluttish and dissatisfied with Quiggin by 1936. Jenkins invited down to their cottage on Erridge's estate to help promote plans for her film career: 'I noted how much firmer, more ruthless her personality had become since I had first met her as Templer's wife, when she had seemed a silly, empty-headed, rather bad-tempered beauty. Now she possessed a kind of hidden force, of which there could be no doubt that Quiggin was afraid'. Bolts again with Erridge on his trip to China that autumn, returning without him a few months later.

Not seen again till she turns up at Erridge's funeral in 1946 as an Air Vice Marshal's lady. Fortyish; rather distinguished; vividly recalls the horrors of travelling dry with Erridge to Hong Kong.

BM At Mr Deacon's party 241–3, 247. AW Married to Templer, her previous career, depth of his feelings for her 40–2; at the Ritz, her manner, speculation on her marriage, asks Jenkins to stay 54–64, 67; her ill-humour, asks Quiggin to lunch 73–81; bewitched by Mrs Erdleigh, ignores Quiggin 84–7, 89, delighted with planchette 91–103; Quiggin's interest in 116–17; pushes St John Clarke's wheelchair in Hyde Park protest march with Quiggin, has left Templer, Jean on their married life

129–34, 136, 138–40; 149, 165–6, 168; Templer on her departure 170–5; 200, 211, 213. LM Divorced, Jenkins asked to stay 99–100; at their cottage, her motives for leaving Templer, her discontent 104–8, 110–12, 115–20, 122–5; at Thrubworth, flirts with Erridge 126–31, 133, 135, 137, 140, 146, 148, 153–4; 186, 190; sailed for China with Erridge 204–6, 209–11; Members' account of their affair 221–3. CCR Has left Erridge 64–6; 71, 77, 80, 92, 114, 131–2, 196, 228. KO 100, 102, 121, 144. MP 132–3. BDFR 49, at Erridge's funeral 54–7; 68, 95, 183.

MONTGOMERY, Field-Marshal Sir Bernard 1887–1976
British Commander-in-Chief during the Allied advance into Germany. Shows Finn's group of military attachés visiting his HQ in November 1944 over his caravans ('a visit personally conducted by the Field-Marshal, whose manner perfectly fused the feelings of a tenant justly proud of a perfectly equipped luxury flat with those of the lord of an ancient though still inhabited historical monument'), and afterwards expounds the course of the war:

'I tried to reduce to viable terms impressions of this slight, very exterior contact. On the one hand, there had been hardly a trace of the almost overpowering physical impact of the CIGS . . . On the other hand, the Field-Marshal's outward personality offered what was perhaps even less usual, will-power, not so much natural, as developed to altogether exceptional lengths. No doubt there had been a generous basic endowment, but not of the essentially magnetic quality. In short, the will here might be even more effective for being less dramatic. It was an immense, wiry, calculated, insistent hardness, rather than a force like champagne bursting from the bottle . . . One felt that a great deal of time and trouble, even intellectual effort of its own sort, had gone into producing this final result.

'The eyes were deepset and icy cold. You thought at once of an animal . . . Did the features, in fact, suggest some mythical beast, say one of those encountered in *Alice in Wonderland*, full of awkward questions and downright statements? This sense, that here was perhaps a personage from an imaginary world, was oddly sustained by the voice. It was essentially an army voice, but precise, controlled, almost mincing . . . There was a faint and faraway reminder of the clergy, too; parsonic, yet not in the least numinous, the tone of the incumbent ruthlessly dedicated to his parish, rather than the hierophant celebrating divine mysteries.'

MP 170–2, 178–85, 191.

MONTSALDY, Captain
Free French officer, a grizzled fifty.

MP 238.

MORELAND, Hugh

Composer. Exact contemporary of Jenkins, and perhaps his closest friend; his view on life and art, love, death, power and the human condition quoted *passim*. First introduced to Jenkins by Mr Deacon in the Mortimer in 1928 or 9:

'He was formed physically in a "musical" mould, classical in type, with a massive, Beethoven-shaped head, high forehead, temples swelling outwards, eyes and nose somehow bunched together in a way to make him glare at times like a High Court judge about to pass sentence. On the other hand, his short, dark, curly hair recalled a dissipated cherub, a less aggressive, more intellectual version of Folly in Bronzino's picture, rubicund and mischievous, as he threatens with a fusillade of rose petals the embrace of Venus and Cupid; while Time in the background, whiskered like the Emperor Franz-Josef, looms behind a blue curtain as if evasively vacating the bathroom. Moreland's face in repose, in spite of this cherubic, humorous character, was not without melancholy too; his flush suggesting none of that riotously healthy physique enjoyed by Bronzino's – and, I suppose, everyone else's – Folly.'

Lives in a garret between Oxford Street and the Tottenham Court Road. Odd jobs as pianist or conductor, provincial engagements, occasional articles. Only child of a music teacher from whom he inherited a tendency to tuberculosis. Orphaned and brought up in lodgings, flitting from Putney to Fulham, by a doting aunt ('keeping solvent in itself rather a struggle') given to spending the rent money on concert tickets. Ed. Royal College of Music, and showed alarming promise from an early age. Friend of Barnby. Horror of musical society. Taste for obscure films, French poets, outmoded popular songs; also for street musicians and mechanical pianos. Especially knowledgeable on the Elizabethan and Jacobean playwrights. Always fond of *The Anatomy of Melancholy*.

Hostile to Honegger and Hindemith, scathing on Brahms. Likes Walton, conducts Debussy, inclined to play Saint-Saëns. Own works include music for Sir Magnus Donners' highbrow film *Lysistrata* (" "I know nothing of music," Barnby had . . . once remarked, "but Hugh Moreland's accompaniment to that film sounded to me like a lot of owls quarrelling in a bicycle factory""); and *Tone Poème Vieux Port* (composed in Marseilles and savagely attacked at its Birmingham performance in the 'twenties by all the critics save Maclintick; admired by both Odo Stevens and General Conyers). Also a symphony completed in 1936. Engaged at various points on an opera, a ballet and numerous slighter works e.g. *Music for a Maison de Passe: A Suite*, *The Firewatcher's March* etc.

Diffident with women, perpetually in love, 'a hopeless addict of what he used to call, in the phrase of the day, a "*princesse lointaine*

127

complex"'. Has made unsuccessful passes at one of Mr Cochran's Young Ladies and the waitress Norma at Casanova's Chinese Restaurant. Marries *c.* 1934 the actress Matilda Wilson, Donners' mistress and Carolo's divorced wife. One child, b. and d. 1936. Hard up. Lung trouble. Depression aggravated that summer by the horrors of his friend Maclintick's marriage, and his own pessimistic views of marriage in general ('"It wasn't for nothing that Petrarch's Laura was one of the de Sade family," said Moreland'). Affair (never consummated) with Priscilla Tolland, made public at Mrs Foxe's party for his symphony and terminated on Maclintick's suicide in the spring of 1937.

Moves with Matilda to a cottage in the country on Donners' estate at Stourwater. Strained, crumpled, unshaven; work block; return of trouble with his lung; tortured by thoughts of Matilda's former relationship with Donners. Makes a hit as Greed in the Seven Deadly Sins tableaux at Stourwater in the autumn of 1938. Returns alone to London in the first week of the war, looking like death; has agreed to allow Matilda to divorce him and marry Donners.

Given up to drink and despair until taken in charge by the dreaded Mrs Maclintick. Living with her in his old flat by 1941 ('It occurred to me she perhaps saw her association with Moreland as a kind of revenge on Maclintick, who had so greatly valued him as a friend. Now, Maclintick was underground and Moreland belonged to her'). Firewatching. Ill, thin, uneasy, dishevelled; claims to have neutralized the death wish for the moment ('Raids are a great help in that'). First signs of an obsession with the old days. Spends much of the rest of the war on government sponsored tours of the provinces.

Turned his back on contemporary life by 1946 ('Life becomes more and more like an examination where you have to guess the questions as well as the answers'). Financial difficulties, worsening health, leading an obscure, secluded life with Audrey Maclintick. Predicts his own death from nostalgia ('All this, and Mopsy Pontner too. I can't bear it') at the Stevenses' musical party in 1959; gives the impression that he has never managed to fall entirely out of love with Matilda. Collapses at the party, and dies in hospital later that year.

CCR Memories of an afternoon with in Gerrard Street, his childhood and background, his flat, his hopeless love affairs 1–9; first encounter with recalled, his unsuccessful rivalry with Barnby for the waitress at Casanova's 12–39; takes Jenkins to see Matilda Wilson in *Duchess of Malfi*, his technique as a lover, subsequent marriage to Matilda 40–56; 57–8, 91; visiting Matilda in nursing home, Widmerpool unimpressed by his claims to fame 98–102; visit to Maclinticks, his cautionary account of their married life and dim view of marriage in general 104–20, 122–3; birth and death of Matilda's child, their unconventional marriage 129–30; courtship of Matilda 133; his symphony performed 133–40; at Mrs Foxe's party afterwards, his affair with Priscilla Tolland 142–5, 148–61, 164, 172–4, 176–7, 179–81, 185, 187–8; subsequent course of this affair hard to chart 193–4; 198; second visit to Maclintick, Maclintick's harrowing remark 202–16; his account of clearing up after Maclintick's suicide, and of ending his affair with Priscilla 217–21; 225; life compared to the Ghost Railway 219 & 229. KO Conversation with at the Hay Loft recalled, on action in relation to art, love, marriage and Sir Magnus Donners, his subsequent marriage to Donners' mistress, his childhood contrasted with Jenkins', their common interests and reminiscences of Dr Trelawney 80–85; moved to the country with Matilda 86; living near Stourwater, attitude to Donners 88–90; at his cottage, lung trouble, low spirits, strained relations with Donners 93–9; instant dislike to Templer 101, 103–6; dinner at Stourwater 108–10, 112–13, 116–18, 120, tormented by thoughts of Matilda's former status there, his performance as Gluttony 122–8, 130, 134–5, 139; 141, 146, 153, 159; on jealousy 162–3; 183, 186–7, 189; Conyers on his *Tone Poème* 211; 214, 217–18, 236; picked up by Lady Molly 231, 238–41; his account of Matilda's leaving him for Donners, his exhaustion 240–5. VB 1, 9, 89, 106, 127–8, 143, 164, 190, 221. SA Edinburgh engagement 4; 6, 73–4; arrangements to dine with 88–90, 92–3; at Café Royal, living with Audrey Maclintick, speculations on their relationship, change in him analyzed 112–25, agitation on meeting Priscilla, charmed by Odo Stevens 128–31, 133–8, 141–8, 150; at his flat, Max Pilgrim on the bomb at the Madrid 151–3, 155–60; 222–3. MP Touring provinces 35; Matilda asks after 208; 212, 218, 227. BDFR 27; friend of Bagshaw 29, 33, 118; 100–2; encounter with 118–20; 191. TK 14, 40, encounter with Glober recalled 67–8, 70–72; ill health, financial troubles 80–1, 90, 153; at Stevens' party, violent attack of nostalgia 227–31, relations with Audrey 238–9, collapse 247–50; his account of subsequent amazing scenes between the Widmerpools 252–4, 256–66; dying in hospital, last talks with, on Candaules, Gyges and the Widmerpools, voyeurism, Donners and Matilda 269–77. HSH 35, his performance as Gluttony recalled 45, 62; 51, 54, 59, 64, 71, 233.

MORGAN, Deafy
Private in Bithel's platoon in N. Ireland in 1940, deaf as a post and none too bright but universally liked for his generosity and sweet temper. Courtmartialled after being ambushed, overpowered and relieved of his rifle by four armed terrorists from over the Border.

VB 65, 68–9, 72–4, 100, 176.

MOSLEY, Sir Oswald b. 1896
Leader of the New Party, a thorn in the flesh of Howard Craggs'
'Smash Fascism' group in the 'thirties.

LM 119.

MOUNTFITCHET, Lord (John)
The Bridgnorths' eldest boy, a great favourite with Sillery, tells hair-
raising stories about Hugo Tolland as an undergraduate. Afterwards m.
the Huntercombes' daughter, Venetia Penistone, and is said to be on
the point of leaving her for Pamela Flitton when he d. in the second
war.

AW 150. LM 34. CCR 43, 90. BDFR 88–9.

MURTLOCK, Leslie ('Scorpio' or 'Scorp')
Drop-out with criminal tendencies and a pronounced appetite for
power. Founder of a neo-Trelawneyist cult in the 'sixties, combining
Gnostic with Mithraic elements. Harmony his watchword. Against
alcohol and drugs, in favour of early rising, physical exercise, fasting,
meditation and obedience ('They sound to me like the good old Simple
Life': Hugo Tolland) but probably not chastity. Camps overnight with
disciples in a horse-drawn caravan at the Jenkinses' in 1968, and is
generally believed to be sleeping with their niece Fiona Cutts (though
not by Hugo Tolland, 'on grounds that, if Murtlock liked sex at all, he
preferred his own'). Early twenties; small and dark with pale, cold,
unblinking eyes. Named for his Zodiac sign. Uncomfortable
personality ('He would have been ominous – perhaps more ominous –
in a City suit, the ominous side of him positively mitigated by a blue
robe . . .').
  Son of a newspaper agent who belonged to a fanatical religious sect
in south London. First developed his remarkable kinetic gifts as a
choirboy ('A beautiful little boy. Quite exceptionally so. And *very*
intelligent. He was called Leslie then') under Canon Fenneau's
guidance. Involved from childhood on in various dubious incidents,
including suicide of the choirmaster during his spell as a scholarship boy
at choir school. Known to have given trouble to a homosexual couple
in the antique trade who rashly employed him as assistant. Once picked
up as an easy lay by Quentin Shuckerley ('Shuckerley had to leave the
country to get Murtlock out of his flat'). May well have been the boy
('Good-looking lad in his way, if you'd cleaned him up a bit': Sunny
Farebrother) who took over milking Jimmy Stripling's money after
Mrs Erdleigh died. Police subsequently investigating his activities at the
not specially famous Stone Age site for which he was heading when
first encountered at the Jenkinses'.

Believes himself to be a reincarnation of Dr Trelawney. TV programme on his cult mooted in Lindsay Bagshaw's *After Strange Gods* series. Anxious to get Widmerpool into his clutches, reported to be engaged in some sort of rivalry with him as underground youth leader. Moves with disciples into Widmerpool's place at Stourwater round about the end of 1969. Their struggle for power eventually decided in his favour at the stag mask dance round the Devil's Fingers the following Midsummer Eve; knifes Widmerpool during sexual rites intended to raise Trelawney from the dead. Rumours of revolting practices at Stourwater thereafter. Has no intention of letting go his hold on Widmerpool's house, goods or money. Refuses permission for Widmerpool to leave the cult in the spring of 1971; and drives him to his death ('It was murder. Nothing short': Bithel) on a naked run through the woods at dawn that autumn.

HSH On crayfishing expedition at the Jenkinses', his disturbing personality, masterful manner and past history 2–10, emergence of the Murtlock standpoint, prophesies concerning Mr Gauntlett's bitch, cross-examines Jenkins on the Devil's Fingers 11–29; 33; his cult a revival of Trelawneyism 35–6; Shuckerley's encounter with, Farebrother on a possible connection with Jimmy Stripling 78–80, 82–3; press report of police interest in 118; Fenneau's not entirely reassuring account of his childhood and subsequent career 129–34; Widmerpool warned against by Fenneau, anxious to meet Widmerpool 136–40; meeting thought to have taken place 141, 143; power struggle in progress, Gwinnett proposing to investigate 147; his powers of second sight, in the matter of Mr Gauntlett's bitch 153; Gwinnett's account of the stag mask dance and his assault on Widmerpool, Beaumont and Fletcher's portrait of 163–9; 174–5; Delavacquerie's account of how and why he got hold of Gwinnett, and of Fiona's escape from 177–85; Fiona's fear of 210, 212; 213; Widmerpool's account of being punished by, his fondness for Bithel 217–21, 224; at Stourwater, compared to Apollyon, reduces Widmerpool to submission 233–9; 247, Henderson's account of his behaviour within the cult, rescue of Bithel and eventual domination of Widmerpool 251, 257–62; Bithel's account of Widmerpool's death at his hands 264–70.

MUSSOLINI, Benito 1883–1945
Italian fascist dictator, Foppa not enthusiastic about.
AW 145–6. CCR 95. TK 58.

NAGY, Imre 1896–1958
Leader of the Hungarian communist party during the uprising of 1956; his trial and execution two years later took place just before the very

similar state trial in E. Europe which was indirectly responsible for Widmerpool's downfall.

TK 188.

NOKES
Walking two hound puppies at Hinton Hoo during the weekend Jenkins spent there with the Walpole-Wilsons, his company much preferred by Eleanor to sir Magnus Donners'.

BM 180.

NORMA
The waitress at Casanova's Chinese Restaurant in the 'twenties who turned down Moreland but not Barnby (' "Rather an old man's piece, isn't she?" he said. "Still, I see your point. Poorish legs, though"'), and afterwards m. a tobacconist in Camden Town. Barnby's nude of her in oils bought by Sir Magnus Donners to hang in the Bailiff's Room at Stourwater; one of his drawings (sold to Sir Herbert Manasch) turns up thirty years later on Rosie Stevens' stairs in Regents' Park.

CCR 29–31, 35–9. KO 109–10. TK 230. HSH 206.

OFFORD
Boy at school who owned an overcoat very like the one which first made Widmerpool conspicuous.

QU 5–6.

OLAF, Prince (later King) of Norway b. 1903
Another of the minor royalty with whom Finn liked to hobnob.

MP 48.

ORCHARD, Miss
The governess shared by various children living near Aldershot who first told Jenkins about the Kindly Ones during a classical mythology lesson in 1914:
'I recalled Miss Orchard's account of the Furies. They inflicted the vengeance of the gods by bringing in their train war, pestilence, dissension on earth; torturing, too, by the strings of conscience. That last characteristic alone, I could plainly see, made them sufficiently unwelcome guests.'

KO 2–3, 18, 51, 80, 148.

ÖRN
Exceedingly tall, gloomy and taciturn Norwegian paying guest of the Leroys at La Grenadière. Loathes the Swede Lundquist, who considers

him wholly lacking in chic and finally exacerbates him beyond bearing by lobbing tactics at tennis ('at that age I was not yet old enough to be aware of the immense rage that can be secreted in the human heart by cumulative minor irritation'). Their rupture healed by a triumph of diplomacy on Widmerpool's part.

QU 114–15, 126–8, 134, 137–44, 146, 148, 151–8. MP 56, 162.

PARDOE, Johnny
Unusually eligible guardsman, popular at dances in Jenkins' Walpole-Wilson phase: 'an agreeable, pink-faced ensign, very short, square and broad-shouldered, with a huge black moustache, brushed out so forcibly that it seemed to be false and assumed for a joke'. Has recently inherited an estate on the Welsh border plus a comfortable income to run it. Loud laugh. No small talk. Speaks in a series of powerful squeaks. An argument with him over bets at Ascot leads to Barbara Goring pouring sugar over Widmerpool at the Huntercombes' ball in 1928 or 9. Engaged to her that autumn ('I could see from Widmerpool's pursed lips and glassy eyes that he was as astonished as myself . . . Among the various men who had, at one time or another, caused me apprehension, just or unjust, in connection with Barbara, Pardoe had never, at any moment, figured in the smallest degree').

M. to Barbara and said to be giving her an awful time by 1934. Has left the Grenadiers, given up shooting and turned into a melancholy recluse, mopes in his library for weeks on end.

Rejoins the army in the second war and is said to have done rather well in Burma.

BM At Walpole-Wilsons' 33–5, 39, 41, 49–50, 52–4; 57, 64; at Huntercombes' 67–8, 73; at Hinton Hoo 176, 180, 183; at Stourwater 200, 209–10, 213, 217–18, 222, 267–8, 271. LM His melancholy 92–3. VB 187. MP 244.

PARKER, Dorothy 1893–1967
American humourist, made a mot on Louis Glober's adventures among dude ranchers in Montana.

TK 164.

PARKINSON
Spotty, sheepish captain of games in Le Bas' house, 'rather a feeble figure who blushed easily'. Misses his Blue at Oxford and rows with Le Bas in a Duffers Eight.

QU 6–7, 53, 222. AW 185, 195. BDFR 233–4.

PARRY
Assistant to Maelgwyn-Jones, expected to replace Jenkins as platoon commander.

VB 8, 225, 231.

PASIONARIA, La (Dolores Ibarruri) b. 1895
Communist deputy celebrated for her oratory in Spanish Civil War, greatly admired by Norah Tolland and Eleanor Walpole-Wilson during their left-wing phase; Gypsy Jones the, of Hendon Central, according to Moreland.

CCR 96. SA 120.

PAT
One of X. Trapnel's mistresses, afterwards m. a sociology don and prefers to forget the past.

BDFR 212. TK 198.

PAUL see FENNEAU, Canon Paul

PAULINE (1)
Girl responsible for precipitating Templer's Vauxhall into a ditch at Oxford, and indirectly for ending his friendship with Stringham.

QU 194–200. AW 42. VB 118. KO 165.

PAULINE (2)
Another of X. Trapnel's mistresses, thought by him to be depraved; afterwards becomes a call-girl catering for the special tastes of clients such as Widmerpool and Ferrand-Sénéschal.

BDFR 212. TK 198–200, 237, 262.

PAUL-MARIE
The older and more precocious of Mme Leroy's two great-nephews at La Grenadière, keeps the household in fits of laughter with his witticisms about women. Resembles Stringham as a small French boy. A corrupt mind, according to Widmerpool.

QU 114–15, 122–3, 128, 137–8, 142, 156, 159, 161.

PAULUS, Field-Marshal Friedrich von 1890–1957
German general who surrendered Stalingrad on 31 Jan., 1943.

MP 72.

PEDLAR, Colonel Eric, MC, Deputy Assistant Adjutant and Quartermaster General ('A & Q', 'Ack-and-Quack')

Dim but dependable, Hogbourne-Johnson's chief butt and Widmerpool's superior officer at Divisional HQ in 1941: 'Colonel Pedlar resembled a retriever, a faithful hound, sound in wind and limb, prepared to tackle a dog twice his size, or swim through a river in spate to collect his master's game, but at the same time not in the top class for picking up a difficult scent'.

VB 240. SA 22–3, 32–41, 51–3, 62–7, 173, 186, 193, 195, 200, 210–11, 213, 225–8.

PENDRY, Sergeant
Jenkins' young platoon-sergeant in N. Ireland, tall, beefy, good-natured, with glittering blue eyes 'like Peter Templer's in the old days'. Utterly undone by his wife's unfaithfulness. Discovered dead in a ditch on sentry duty after a shooting incident, never satisfactorily cleared up, which may have been murder, accident or suicide.

VB 8, 10–11, 18, 41–4, 52, 61, 73–8, 82–3, 85, 88–90, 92–3, 98–102, 141, 191, 198, 211. SA 30.

PENDRY, Cath
Wife of above, carrying on back home with Evans the checkweighman.

VB 55–6, 88, 211.

PENISTONE, Lady Venetia
One of the Huntercombes' daughters, m. John Mountfichet, widowed in second war.

CCR 43, 90. BDFR 88–9.

PENNISTONE, David
Unknown officer who expounds Alfred de Vigny's military philosophy to Jenkins on a night train journey of extreme discomfort in 1940. Tall, thin, rather distinguished, hook nose and fairish hair. Writing 'something awfully boring about Descartes'. Subsequently identified as the supercilious young man with an orchid in his buttonhole at Milly Andriadis' party 'a thousand years before'.

At Cambridge with Bob Duport. No relation to the Huntercombes. Reviews books, thought to live in Venice ('some story of a *contessa*, beautiful but not very young'), once worked in the textile trade in Paris where he met Finn in cosmetics. Lieutenant, General Service badges, transferred to Intelligence Corps, promoted Captain (later Major), in charge of Polish liaison in Finn's section at the War Office. Jenkins posted as his assistant *c*. 1942. Likes thinking about things. Vague on dates and places, uncanny grasp of army lore, brilliant at explaining philosophic niceties or the minutiae of office dialectic. Scores an unprecedented victory over the obstructionist Blackhead:

'Blackhead had written, in all, three and a half pages on the theory and practice of soap issues for military personnel, with especial reference to the Polish Women's Corps. Turning from his spidery scrawl to Pennistone's neat hand, two words only were inscribed. They stood out on the file:

Please amplify. D. Pennistone. Maj. GS. . . .

Blackhead stared down at what Pennistone had written. He was distraught; aghast. Pennistone had gone too far. We should be made to suffer for this frivolity of his. That is, if Blackhead retained his sanity.'

Joins Finn's firm in Paris after the war. Pub. *Descartes, Gassendi and the Atomic Theory of Epicurus* 1947. M. a French girl and succeeds Finn as head of the firm. Working on a book (eventually pub. in the late 'sixties) on Cyrano de Bergerac as philosopher and heresiarch.

BM At Milly Andriadis' party 139–43, 146–7, 193. KO 38. VB 47, encounter with on night train 103–10, 112–13; 125, 148, 233. SA His views on army life 17, 24, 26; encountered in Whitehall, his career and character 98–9, 103–6. MP Jenkins working for, relations with Finn 4–9; on Farebrother 13–14; 16, his flair for military matters 24–6; 28–34, 37; defeat of Blackhead 39, 41–6, 56; 48, 50–1, 54, 56–7, 61, 64–5, 72, 82–5, 88, 91–4, 103, 115, 143, 167, 186, 191, 197, joining Finn's firm 236–7. BDFR 7, 120, 146, 167, 240. TK 202, 217–18. HSH 32.

PEPLOE-GORDON
Contemporary of General Conyers at Sandhurst, splendid rider, first class shot, once led an expedition to Tibet; his marriage annulled on grounds of impotence; had points in common with Widmerpool ('Looking back in the light of what I have been reading, I can see the fellow had a touch of exaggerated narcissism. Is that Widmerpool's trouble?': Conyers).

LM 232.

PERKINS, Lord
Old Labour stalwart, made a peer under first socialist government, wrote about industrial relations and m. as her third husband Peter Templer's elder sister Babs.

AW 79. MP 201, 206.

PHILIDOR, General
French military attaché with a keen sense of farce and a face like a Paris taxi-driver's.

MP 139, 141–3, 152, 159–60, 169. HSH 1, 19–20.

PHILIDOR, Mme
Wife of above.

MP 200, 213.

PHILLPOTS
Candidate to replace Jenkins as platoon commander in 1940.

VB 225, 231. MP 175.

PILGRIM, Max
Pianist and cabaret entertainer, a tall, willowy, bespectacled young man
singing suggestive songs 'in a tremulous quavering voice, like that of an
immensely ancient lady' at Milly Andriadis' party. Later involved in a
violent scene with Mr Deacon. Turns up a few years later at
Umfraville's nightclub with Heather Hopkins ('"A frightfully old-
fashioned couple," said Templer. "The only reason they are here is
because their act was a flop at the Café de Madrid"'). Old friend of
Moreland and Norman Chandler. His mother was a Principal Boy in
pantomime. Songs include 'I'm Tess of Le Touquet, My morals are
flukey'; 'Heather, Heather, She's under the weather'; 'I want to dazzle
Lady Sybil'; 'Di, Di, in her collar and tie, Quizzes the girls with a
monocled eye' etc.
   Living with Hugo Tolland by the late 'thirties. Beginning to date;
cabaret jobs hard to come by; said to be about to join the Baldwyn
Hodges antique business. Comes back into vogue at the beginning of
the war. ENSA tours. Lodges with Moreland and Audrey Maclintick
during his immensely successful season at the Madrid in 1941, and is
one of the few survivors on the night the bomb drops on Bijou
Ardglass's fortieth birthday party. For his lyrics, see Book Index.

BM At Milly Andriadis' party, once gave offence to Deacon 114–15,
118, 120, row with Deacon 148–9, 230; at Deacon's funeral 251, 259.
LM At Café de Madrid 95; and at Umfraville's club 182–3, 185–6, 190,
199, 201. CCR At the Madrid 48, 51–2, 90; 142, 186. KO Living with
Hugo Tolland 145. VB 141. SA Makes a hit at the Madrid 115–17; Odo
Stevens a fan 145–6, 148; his account of the raid on the Madrid 151–9;
180.

PILSUDSKI, Marshal 1867–1935
Polish dictator.

MP 16.

PINKUS, Captain
Adjutant-quartermaster at Castlemallock, looks like something
malignant from the *Morte d'Arthur* ('one of those misshapen dwarfs who

137

peer from the battlements of Dolorous Garde, bent on doing disservice to whomsoever may cross the drawbridge'), and take special pleasure in announcing Gwatkin's downfall: 'He had a voice of horrible refinement, which must have taken years to perfect, and somewhat recalled that of Howard Craggs, the left-wing publisher'.

VB 172, 206, 212–13, 218.

PITT, William 1750–1806
Prime minister, his hat survives under a glass case at Thrubworth Park.

LM 151.

PLYNLIMMON, Lady
At Lady Molly's, won't usually speak to anyone below Cabinet rank but relaxes her rule in favour of Ted Jeavons.

LM 165.

PONSONBY
A damned fellow who trod on General Conyers' gouty toe at a court levee in 1934.

LM 76.

PONTNER
Translator and picture-dealer, frequenter of the Mortimer, musically inclined ('in a manner Moreland could approve, a qualification by no means common'). D. between the wars.

TK 67–9.

PONTNER, Mopsy
Wife of above, quite a beauty in her way; admired by Moreland; once turned Barnby down. Sells a John drawing to Louis Glober who has her on the dinner table afterwards, a story she subsequently confides to Jenkins. M. Lilienthal as her second husband and d. in second war. Mention of her name thirty years after Glober's dinner party brings on Moreland's fatal paroxysm of nostalgia.

TK 67–72, 79–81, 100, 229–30. HSH 63.

POPKISS, Rev. Iltyd
C of E padre in Jenkins' Welsh battalion; small and pale, has a hard time trying to cap the RC chaplain's coprophilic jokes. Preaches on the Valley of Bones from Ezekiel.

VB 19–23, 25, 27–8; his sermon 37–8; 67.

PORTER or TAYLOR, Betty see TAYLOR or PORTER, Betty

PRASAD, Major
Military attaché of an independent Indian state; on trip to continent in
1944; defeats three generals on religious grounds in battle for possession
of the only bathroom.

MP 152, 156, 158–65, 191, 199.

PROGERS
Driver with a lisp and squint in Jenkins' battalion, killed at Dunkirk.

VB 195.

PROTHERO
Replaced by Jenkins as commander of Defence Platoon at Divisional
HQ.

SA 21.

PUGSLEY, Len
Publisher's reader for Quiggin & Craggs. Makes his first, and last, real
step in life by getting a piece about Socialist Realism (*Integral
Foundations of a Fresh Approach to Art for the Masses*) published in *Fission*
on the strength of an affair with Gypsy Craggs. Lives with her after
Craggs' death.

BDFR 151, 209. TK 136–7, 140, 150, 214.

PUMPHREY, Second-Lieutenant
One of Jenkins' regimental room-mates, a red-haired, noisy, rather
aggressive second-hand car salesman inclined to romp with any
available barmaid.

VB 19–22, 24–9, 46, 51, 191.

PYEFINCH
Old Boy in Le Bas' house.

BDFR 233.

QUIGGIN, Ada see LEINTWARDINE, Ada

QUIGGIN, Amanda and Belinda
Identical twin daughters of Ada Leintwardine and J. G. Quiggin, b. c.
1948. No great beauties, almost laughable resemblance to their father, an
embarrassment to their parents from an early age. Ed. Stourwater school
and Widmerpool's newish university. In trouble with the police as
undergraduates (drugs and kicking a policeman respectively). Afterwards

notorious for throwing paint over Widmerpool during his installation as chancellor; letting off a stink bomb of stupefying nastiness while attending the Magnus Donners prize dinner as his guests; and taking part in publicity stunts for the underground magazine *Toilet Paper*.

TK 37, 92, HSH 37–8, 44, 46, 48, 77, 90, 92–6, 101–5, 109, 111–14, 116–17, 121–2, 151, 191.

QUIGGIN, J. G.

Professional reviewer and practising Marxist, 'a kind of abiding prototype of discontent against life'. First encountered as a lean and hungry freshman at one of Sillery's undergraduate tea parties ('Quiggin sat sourly on the extreme edge of the sofa, glancing round the room like a fierce little animal, trapped by naturalists') where he takes an instant dislike to Mark Members. Scholar and exhibitioner reading history at Brightman's college. Squat, balding, looks older than his contemporaries; small, hard, grating North Country voice; grubby starched collar and dilapidated black suit. By no means as under-privileged as he makes out. Mother a town councillor in the Midlands; father (dead) a builder active in municipal politics; uncle a patron of Mr Deacon. Ambitious, self-absorbed and secretive. Hates anything superficial. Envies Stringham his job with Donners Brebner. 'He had something of the angry solitude of spirit that held my attention in Widmerpool.'

Sent down without taking a degree, his scholarship having been withdrawn on grounds of idleness. Helping out in Deacon's shop by the end of the 'twenties, already respected as a writer in left-wing circles and decidedly more self-assured in manner ('there was also his doggy, rather pathetic look about the eyes that had reminded me of Widmerpool, and which is a not uncommon feature of those who have decided to live by the force of the will'). About to bring out a book with the Vox Populi Press. Envies Members his job with St John Clarke. Indissolubly linked to Members as Jenkins to Widmerpool, may possibly be Members' cousin ('the acutely combative nature of their friendship, if it could be so called, certainly possessed all that intense, almost vindictive rivalry of kinship').

Growing literary reputation by 1933, adviser to the publishers Boggis & Stone, book due that spring. Engineers Members' dismissal and his own installation as secretary to St John Clarke, whom he promptly converts to communism. Turns up at the Ritz in a black leather overcoat ('His face wore the set, mask-like expression of an importunate beggar tormenting a pair of tourists seated on the perimeter of a café's *terrasse*'), and at the Templers' in a cruelly blue suit with green knitted tie; has his skull cropped like a convict's later that summer. Willing to go almost anywhere for a free meal. Still collecting material for his survey *Unburnt Boats*. Runs away with Mona Templer, and gets the sack from St John Clarke after Guggenbühl's coup that autumn ('Quiggin laughed . . . Laughter, his manner indicated, was a more civilized reaction than the savage rage that would have been the natural emotion of most right-minded persons on hearing the news for the first time'). *Unburnt Boats* again scheduled for publication.

Moves with Mona to a cottage on Erridge's estate in Sussex, working on plans to found a socially conscious magazine with Erridge's money. No known income save for occasional journalism and intermittent hand-outs from Erridge, whom he has also converted to communism ('When Quiggin ingratiated himself with people – during his days as secretary to St John Clarke, for example – he was far too shrewd to confine himself to mere flattery. A modicum of bullying was a pleasure both to himself and his patrons. All the same, I was not sure that Erridge . . . might not turn out a tougher proposition than St John Clarke'). Beginning to bore Mona by 1936. Publication of *Unburnt Boats* postponed again. Active at protest meetings, committees, anti-fascist demonstrations etc.; writes to the papers in defence of the Stalinist purges; his card-carrying membership of the Communist Party never established for certain (afraid to commit himself, according to Bagshaw). Deserted by Mona for Erridge that autumn.

In low water, professionally dependent on Members for books to review. Disgusted by Erridge's failure to rise to an historic occasion in the Spanish Civil War. Sickened by St John Clarke's choice of Erridge as heir. Demands action over invasion of Czechoslovakia. Affair with Anne Umfraville (née Stepney). Pub. *Unburnt Boats c.* 1939, and abandons authorship as a career. Spends the war caretaking at Boggis & Stone ('I expect that explains why JG dresses like a partisan now, a man straight from the *maquis*, check shirts, leather jacket, ankle-boots': Sillery).

Founds the publishing firm of Quiggin & Craggs and the magazine *Fission* immediately after the war in partnership with Howard Craggs. Means to make money ('He now identified himself, body and soul, with his own firm's publications, increasingly convinced – like not a few publishers – that he had written them all himself'); anxious to avoid a name for peddling the Party line; involved in daily rows with Craggs over choice of books. Drops his para-military style of dress under the influence of Ada Leintwardine. Moves to the board of Clapham's firm on the collapse of Quiggin & Craggs in 1947, m. Ada and is rapidly eclipsed by her in fame. Father of twins. Succeeds Clapham as chairman, and publishes the successful memoirs of a Tory elder statesman. Reluctant to keep St John Clarke in print.

On goodish terms with Members, who turns out to be his second cousin. Looks rather distinguished by the late 'sixties ('Quiggin's dome-like forehead, sparse hair, huge ears, gave him a touch of grotesquerie, not out of place in a prominent publisher'). Increasingly mortified by his daughters' public attempts at revolt, and even more by Members' pity on that score:

' "Poor old JG. The great apostle of revolt in the days of our youth. Do you remember Sillers calling him our young Marat? Marat never had to bring up twins. What a couple.

Did'st thou give all to thy daughters?
And art thou come to this?

It won't be long before JG's out on Hampstead Heath asking that of passers-by.' (Members).

QU At Sillery's tea party 177–83, 185, 187–90; envy of Members and Stringham 201–5; further light on his character and background 209–12. BM At Deacon's party with Members, their bond 237–47. AW At the Ritz, has replaced Members as secretary to St. John Clarke 47–56; Mona Templer impressed by 60–62; and asks him to Sunday luncheon 74–80, his interest stimulated by her indifference 83–90, receives a message from planchette 92–102, 107; Sillery on, his conversion of St John Clarke, Members' account of his treachery 113–27; pushing St John Clark with Mona in Hyde Park demonstration, their possible affair 129–34, 136, 139; 165, 168; living with Mona, sacked by St John Clarke, reconciled with Members 170–5; 178, 183, 213. LM Encounter with in cinema queue, his uneven friendship with Jenkins, his career to date 98–103; weekend visit to his cottage; deteriorating relations with Mona, caginess about his landlord Erridge 104–25; dinner at Thrubworth, relations with his patron, charms Erridge's sisters 126–35, 137–8, 140–2, 144–5, 148–50, 152–4; 164, 186, 201; ditched by Mona for Erridge 203–6, 210–11, Members' account of what happened 221–3. CCR 24, 60; falling behind Members in the literary race, patched things up with Erridge 64–6; relations with St John Clarke 74–5, 80–1, 92–4; 114, 131; with Members 136; his obituary of St John Clarke 192; Erridge in his bad books 196–8, 226, 228. KO 113; dining with Members and Anne Umfraville 249–50. BDFR Founding Quiggin & Craggs, Sillery on 8–9, 21; Ada Leintwardine joining the firm 23, 25; relations with Bagshaw 31, 34–7; at Erridge's funeral 44, 46, 48–51, 53, Mona on 55, 59, 61, 68; and at Thrubworth afterwards 71, recruits Jenkins for *Fission* 73–8, 80, 83; 93, 97, 105–6, his outlook as publisher 110, 114–17; at *Fission* party, various anxieties over authors 122, 123–7, 131, 133, 138; feud with Craggs 142; further trouble with his authors 146, 152–3, 155–8, 168, 183; upheaval at Quiggin & Craggs 184–8, 194; demise of same, m. Ada, job with Clapham's firm 207–11; Quiggin & Craggs last book list 288–9. TK His twins, his marriage 37, 92–3, 129, 131, 133, 135, 137; at Russian

142

embassy with Ada 213, 219–23. HSH His marriage, trouble with his twins, on St John Clarke TV programme 36–40, 48; in poor shape at Donners Prize dinner, further trouble with his twins 93–6, 103, 109, 112–13; Members pities him 121–2; Fenneau's undergraduate reminiscences of 126–7.

RAJAGOPALASWAMI
Undergraduate whose uncle adds an Indian link to Sillery's old boy network.

QU 170.

RAMOS, Colonel
Brazilian military attaché, unequal to wartime food in London.

MP 154–5, 218.

ROBBINS, Private
Replaced by Charles Stringham as waiter in F Mess.

SA 70.

ROBERTS, Field-Marshal Earl ('Bobs') 1832–1914
Hero of the Boer campaign, said to have complimented Aylmer Conyers on his staff work ('Wouldn't be the first time a general got hold of the wrong end of the stick': Uncle Giles).

LM 3. KO 41.

ROBESPIERRE, Maximilien 1758–94
Comes through on planchette after Sunday luncheon at the Templers'.

AW 95.

ROSALIE
Ancient retainer of the Leroys', cheeks cross-hatched with lines and wrinkles like those on the side of Uncle Giles' nose.

QU 108–11, 120–2, 160.

ROSSER, Corporal
Soldier in Gwatkin's company.

VB 219.

ROXBOROUGH-BROWN, Mrs
General Conyers said to have dug his own grave in bed with as a young man in Delhi.

KO 62.

RUBINSTEIN, Ida d. 1960
Dancer and actress, made Sir Magnus Donners weep by her performance in *The Martyrdom of St Sebastian*.
HSH 50.

RUSBY, Sir Horrocks, KC
Fashionable advocate in the 'twenties, anxious for prominence and achieves a great deal of it as counsel in the Derwentwater divorce case; painted by Isbister; forgotten by the late 'sixties when a somewhat pedestrian biography of him gets the Magnus Donners prize off to an unspirited start.
BM 81, 187. AW 109–10. CCR 191. HSH 65.

RUSTY
One of Scorpio Murtlock's disciples on the caravan trip to the Jenkinses' in 1968; air of a young prostitute; looks a battered nineteen and maintains total silence save for intermittent humming. Takes part in the sexual rites at the Devil's Fingers two years later and afterwards defects back to Soho.
HSH 3–6, 11, 15–17, 23, 28, 164, 167, 169, 236.

SALLY
One of X. Trapnel's girlfriends, d. young.
BDFR 190, 212. TK 198.

SALTER, Mrs
Whitehaired and weatherbeaten conservationist armed with a pruning hook, ally of the Jenkinses and others in the great quarry battle of 1968.
HSH 149–52, 160–1, 170, 172.

SALTONSTALL
Diplomat in whose place Sir Gavin Walpole-Wilson attended the Kaiser's court ball in 1913; his portrait by Isbister proves a just retribution for posing all his life as a Man of Taste.
BM 48. AW 108–9.

SALVIDGE, L. O.
Literary critic with a glass eye ('always impossible to tell which') who once devilled for St John Clarke collecting French Revolution material for *Dust Thou Art*. Is among the first to praise X. Trapnel's *Camel Ride to the Tomb* and later writes an introduction to Trapnel's posthumous *Dogs Have No Uncles*. Two volumes of his own essays, *Paper Wine* and *Secretions*, pub. 1947.

BDFR 76, 127, 147, 151, 183, 189, 193, 211, 213, 240. TK 24, 35, 214–15. HSH 39–40, 47–9, 66, 93–4, 96.

SALVIDGE, Mrs L. O.
Produced by above as his fourth wife in 1969; black boots, blue eye make-up, a good deal younger than her predecessors.

HSH 93, 97, 99.

SAM
Hugo Tolland's boy-friend and business partner after the second war, said to have begun life as a sailor; d. by the late 'sixties.

BDFR 39. HSH 8, 251.

SAMSON, Mrs
Gives the other, and probably better, dance in Belgrave Square on the same night as the Huntercombes'.

BM 46, 50, 62–3.

SANDERSON
Lady Molly's vet.

LM 165. KO 231, 238.

SANDWICH, Lord 1625–1672
Pepys' patron at the Admiralty, connected by marriage to the then Lady Sleaford.

LM 11.

SAYCE, Private
Professional trouble-maker of evil disposition and loathsome personal habits in Jenkins' platoon in 1940, steals the Commandant's helmet and is afterwards thought to have flogged the Company's butter ration.

VB 60–5, 69, 79, 82, 96, 108, 210–11, 232. MP 83.

SFORZA, Count 1873–1952
Italian statesman at Paris Peace Conference, another of the men of the middle of the road in whom Sir Gavin Walpole-Wilson senses a fundamental reciprocity of thought.

BM 221.

SHELDON, Nathaniel
All-purpose mass-circulation journalist, probably never read a book for pleasure in his life ('This did not at all handicap his laying down the law in a reasonably lively manner, and with brutal topicality, in the literary

column of a daily paper'). Failed to get Chips Lovell a job on his London evening paper between the wars. Claims some success with Ada Leintwardine at the start of her career. Represents the opposite end of the literary scale from Bernard Shernmaker:

'Publishers, especially Quiggin, endlessly argued the question whether Sheldon or Shernmaker "sold" any of the books they discussed. The majority view was that no sales could take place in consequence of Sheldon's notices, because none of his readers read books. Shernmaker's readers, on the other hand, read books, but his scraps of praise were so niggardly to the writers he scrutinized that he was held by some to be an equally ineffective medium. It was almost inconceivable for a writer to bring off the double event of being mentioned, far less praised, by both of them.

LM 12, 15. BDFR 116, 122–5, 138, 151, 239.

SHERNMAKER, Bernard
Professional reviewer ('one of his goals was to establish that the Critic, not the Author, was paramount. He tended to offer guarded encouragement, tempered with veiled threats, to young writers') who manages to the end to avoid committing himself about X. Trapnel. Practised punch-line killer and saboteur of other people's jokes, specialises in epigram and disobliging innuendo. Said to have had his advances rejected by Ada Leintwardine. His collected essays, *Miscellaneous Equities*, pub. 1947.

Loses his critical nerve in the late 'fifties and begins praising Ada's novels. Puts in an appearance a decade later at the Magnus Donners prize dinner: 'Nightmares of boredom and melancholy oozed from him, infecting all the social atmosphere round about'.

BDFR 76, 122–8, 138, 151, 239. TK 6, 18, 91–2, 99, 214. HSH 93–4, 96.

SHORT, Leonard
Prim but amiable host at undergraduate luncheon parties; has political ambitions and a comfortable income; takes up Jenkins in his first year at University, introducing him to Sillery etc. and afterwards keeping in touch as a civil servant in London. Typifies the unexciting company in which Jenkins spends his time before meeting Barnby and Moreland.

Forms a high opinion of Widmerpool in the war and pulls strings to get him a parliamentary seat in 1946; works for the Minister to whom Widmerpool is Parliamentary Private Secretary. Mild well-behaved air concealing a good deal of quiet obstinacy ('Always of high caste in his profession, now almost a princeling, he stemmed nevertheless from the same bureaucratic ancestry as Blackhead, prototype of all the race of *fonctionnaires*, and, anthropologically speaking, might be expected to revert to the same atavistic obstructionism if roused'). Club Athenaeum. Lives in the same block of flats at Widmerpool and takes X. Trapnel for the porter on the night he runs away with Widmerpool's wife.

Knighted in the 1959 Birthday Honours; last seen forcibly extracting Widmerpool from the rough-house after the Stevenses' party in Regent's Park.

QU At the university, his enthusiastic account of Sillery 167–9, 171, 175; and of Truscott 184–5; 202–3, 208–10, 212. BM 24–5, 131, 240–2. CCR 15, 200. BDFR Gossiping with Sillery after the war 6–10, 12–23, 25–7, 173; horribly embarrassed by Pamela Widmerpool's parting message to her husband 178–81; 183. TK At the Stevens' party 232, 236, 250–2, 254–5, removes Widmerpool 265–6.

SHUCKERLEY, Quentin
Committed poet and novelist ('The new Shuckerley, *Athlete's Footman*, is the best queer novel since *Sea Urchins*': Mark Members), rivals Members himself as a veteran of cultural conferences. A great crony of Ada Leintwardine in the 'fifties ('Ada and Shuckerley sat on the same committees, signed the same protests, seemed to share much the same temperament, except that Ada, so far as was known, required no analogous counterpoise to Shuckerley's alleged taste . . . for being inter-mittently beaten up'). Proves no match for Scorpio Murtlock whom he once picked up in hopes of an easy lay. Battered to death in Greenwich Village in the early 'seventies.

TK 8, 90–2, 95, 99, 116, 159, 214. HSH 58, 78–9, 244.

SIEGFRIED
German prisoner-of-war of rebarbative demeanour and authoritarian outlook detailed for domestic duties at Thrubworth. Personality 'somewhere between that of Odo Stevens and Mrs Andriadis' one-time boy-friend, Guggenbühl'. Takes charge of the household, bullies the mourners at Erridge's funeral and is afterwards reported to be well on the way to seizing control of the village too.

BDFR 66, 69–71, 78–81, 85–6, 132, 169.

SIKORSKI, General 1881–1943
Head of the Polish government in exile during second war, Commander-in-Chief of free Polish forces.

MP 16–17.

SILLERY ('Sillers')
Don with a vocation for interfering in other people's business and an

intelligence network rumoured to stretch from the Vatican to the Trades Union movement. Holds regular Sunday afternoon tea parties for recruiting purposes ('His understanding of human nature, coarse, though immensely serviceable, and his unusual ingenuity of mind were both employed ceaselessly in discovering undergraduate connexions which might be of use to him'). Compared by admirers such as Short to 'a mysterious, politically-minded cardinal of the academic world'; his sphere of influence thought by others to be vastly overrated; held by some to be half-cracked.

Walrus moustache, flowing white locks, generally to be found loitering about his college in aged sack-like clothes and Turkish slippers. Contemporary of Mr Deacon, slightly younger than Le Bas, probably in his middle fifties by 1924, 'merely happening to find convenient a façade of comparative senility'. More interested in power than sensual enjoyment. Touches no strong drink; rooms furnished like a boarding-house parlour; his sexual indiscretions (if any) almost certainly confined to 'a fair amount of arm-pinching and hair-rumpling of the young men with whom he was brought in contact'. Initiates the lifelong rivalry between Mark Members and J. G. Quiggin in their first year at the university, and fixes Stringham's job with Donners Brebner.

Known to have published a slim volume of verse when young; also a politico-economic tract, *City State and State of City*, *c.* 1900. Was on terms with Asquith before the flood, and possibly once hoped for political advancement from that quarter. YMCA work in first war. Keen propagandist for the League of Nations, Czechoslovakia and Mr Gandhi but already veering to the Left by the early 'twenties. Has designs on Prince Theodoric over the Donners Brebner Fellowships. Takes part in the Hunger Marchers demonstration in Hyde Park.

Ardent admirer of Stalin during the war years. May possibly have been a member of the Communist Party. Retires from academic life and accepts a peerage ('It certainly gave some people here furiously to think': Sillery) under the postwar Labour government. Takes a dim view of authorship as a career, never read Jenkins' first novel and mistakes him for a headmaster at their reunion in 1946:

'To enter Sillery's sitting-room after twenty years was to drive a relatively deep fissure through variegated seams of Time. The faintly laundry-cupboard odour, as one came through the door, generated in turn the taste of the rock-buns dispensed at those tea-parties, their gritty indeterminate flavour once more dehydrating the palate . . . In this room, against this background, Sillery's machinations, such as they were, had taken shape for half a century. Here a thousand under-graduate attitudes had been penitentially acted out. Youth, dumb with embarrassment, breathless with exhibitionism, stuttering with nerves, inarticulate with conceit; the socially flamboyant, the robustly brawny, the crudely uninstructed, the palely epicene; one and all had obediently leapt through the hoop at Sillery's ringmaster behest . . .'

Probably still under eighty; 'more simian look than formerly, though of no ordinary monkey'. Contemplating a last bid for power by publication of his secret diaries, and apparently engaged in some sort of flirtation with his secretary Ada Leintwardine. Screws a fat advance out of Quiggin & Craggs that summer. His book, *Garnered at Sunset: Leaves from an Edwardian Journal*, pub. 1947 and generally agreed to be a masterpiece of dullness. Holds his ninetieth birthday party in the late 'fifties; d. by 1968, missing his century by only a year or two.

QU His role in university affairs and beyond, differing estimates of his scope 167–71; his tea-party, relations with Stringham, Quiggin, Members and Truscott 175–90; 201–2; supports Stringham's scheme to leave the university 204–9, and overrides Buster Foxe's opposition 211–19; 223. BM 104; at Mrs Andriadis' party in Charlie Chaplin trousers, relations with Mr Deacon and Prince Theodoric 109–14, 120–5, 130, 132, 137, 139–40, 152, 167; 180, 193–4, 227–8, 238–9, 242, 245, 271. AW His influence on Quiggin and Members 48; compared to Mrs Erdleigh 84; at Isbister retrospective 111–13; marching in Hyde Park 128–30; 150, 152, 155, 180. LM 34, 100, 119. CCR 200. MP 52. BDFR Visit to his rooms in Oxford 5–27; Bagshaw on 36; 46, 51, 115–16, 126, 138; publication of his diaries 210–11, 239; 232, 234. TK His ninetieth birthday celebrations 5, 92, 131, 216. HSH Dead 48–9; 53, his tea-party recalled by Canon Fenneau 124–6.

SIMPSON, Mrs Ernest b. 1896
Brought about the abdication of Edward VIII, afterwards Duchess of Windsor; a meeting with her in the mid 'thirties gives Widmerpool his first and last taste of social success.

CCR 85, 127, 136, 195.

SIMSON
Prematurely bald Old Boy at Le Bas' reunion dinner, keen Territorial, doing well at the Bar; torpedoed on a troop ship in second war.

AW 176–7, 190, 195. BDFR 234.

SKERRETT
Coffin-bearer at Erridge's funeral and gamekeeper on the Thrubworth estate; his face 'of gnarled ivory like a skull' somewhat resembles the carved death's head on X. Trapnel's swordstick.

BDFR 52, 54, 63, 106, 169.

SKERRETT, Mrs
Helps out in the house at Thrubworth.
BDFR 63, 85.

SLADE
Schoolmaster who replaced Jenkins as Pennistone's assistant at the War
Office in 1943; afterwards a headmaster in the Midlands.
MP 72, 91, 199. TK 202.

SLANSKY, Rudolf 1901–1952
Head of the Communist Party in Czechoslovakia, tried and executed
for revisionism in 1952, some years before Widmerpool's entanglement
in another similar debacle in E. Europe.
TK 188.

SLEAFORD, Earl of
Seventeenth-century ancestor of Chips Lovell's uncles, reported by
Pepys to have annoyed Charles II by paying court to Lady Castlemaine;
grandson of the Sleaford who brought the Dogdene Veronese out of
Italy.
LM 11.

SLEAFORD, Earl of
Descendant of above, entertained Byron to supper and had the same
poor taste in food as Chips Lovell's Uncle Geoffrey.
VB 171.

SLEAFORD, Marchioness of (Alice)
Geoffrey Sleaford's wife, the most conventional woman alive but longs
to know someone disreputable. A reluctant hostess, won't use the best
bedrooms and has never so much as tried on the Sleaford tiara. Asks
Mrs Haycock to stay with her fiancé Widmerpool and doesn't notice a
thing during the skirmishings leading up to their disastrous night
together at Dogdene.
LM 39, 57, 214–16, 227–8, 230–1. KO 146, 214.

SLEAFORD, Marquess of (John) Family name Fines
Lady Molly's first husband; Chips Lovell's 'first' Sleaford uncle; a
pompous fellow abominated by Edward VII. Held office under
Asquith and Campbell-Bannerman, resigned at the time of the
Marconi scandal and afterwards devoted himself to charitable works.
Was painted by Isbister in Garter robes and took himself pretty

seriously. Seat: Dogdene. Plenty of money but stingy like all the Sleafords. D. of Spanish 'flu in 1919.

LM 7, 10, 16–18, 32, 78, 158–9, 173, 214. KO 214, 236.

SLEAFORD, Marquess of (Geoffrey)
Chips Lovell's 'second' Sleaford uncle ('a more bone-headed fellow I never came across': General Conyers). ADC in S. Africa at the time of the Boer War, rubbed along in one of the cheaper cavalry regiments, succeeded his brother John in 1919 and 'got married at once, as people do when they come into a peerage, however dim' (Chips Lovell). Destroyed by long dispiriting years as an impoverished younger son. Turns Dogdene into a morgue ('they just potter about and read the newspapers and listen to the wireless': Lovell), gives occasional small luncheon parties (' "shepherd's pie for luncheon," Lovell said, "and not enough sprouts"') and won't have his Veronese cleaned. No children.

LM 12, 16–17, 39, 78, 213–16, 227–9. CCR 194. KO 146.

SLIM, Field-Marshal Sir William, CIGS 1891–1970
Chief of Imperial General Staff from 1948; presents Captain Kernével's MBE and mistakes him for one of the real heroes of the war.

MP 239–41.

SMEETS
Netherlands assistant military attaché who knows his way about, expert on the ladies of Burlington Gardens in wartime.

MP 154.

SMETHWYCK, Michael
Undergraduate at one of Short's luncheon parties, afterwards a museum official, eventually head of his gallery; rather proud of his looks like many of his profession; advises Lord Sleaford to get his Veronese cleaned and points out to Lord Huntercombe that his Van Dyck was painted by Dobson. Regan and Goneril his favourite heroines in fiction.

QU 209, 211. AW 110–13. LM 227. CCR 169. TK 22. HSH 120–2, 124, 195.

SMITH
Erridge's moody alcoholic butler, intermittently on loan to the Jeavonses. Sustains a memorable defeat by Erridge over sherry (' "Sherry, m'lord?" It was impossible to tell from Smith's vacant, irascible stare whether he had never before been asked for sherry since his first employment at Thrubworth; or whether he had himself, quite

simply, drunk all the sherry that remained') and champagne ('Erridge's voice admitted the exceptional nature of the enquiry. He asked almost apologetically. Even so, the shock was terrific. Smith started so violently that the coffee cups rattled on the tray . . . The colourless, unhealthy skin of his querulous face, stretched like a pale rubber mask over the bones of his features, twitched a little. "Champagne, m'lord?"')

Dies of a bite from Lady Molly's monkey Maisky at the end of the 'thirties ('"Smith is the second butler Erry has killed under him," said Norah').

LM At Lady Molly's 20–1, 27–8, 39; 61; at Thrubworth 127–8, 130–4, 142–6; 155, 218, 237–8. CCR 111, 202. KO Dead 144. BDFR 79. MP Jeavons on his nasty nature, ghastly death and dismal profession 78–9.

SNIDER
Advertising agent whose firm employed Mona as model, was entertaining her at a road-house near Staines when she first met Peter Templer.

AW 40.

SOPER, Captain
Bandy-legged Catering Officer at Divisional HQ in 1941, looks like an ape and employs Stringham as Mess waiter.

SA 4, 64–7, 69–71, 76, 167–9, 171, 228. BDFR 7.

SOSNOKOWSKI, General Kazimierz b. 1885
Minister in the Polish government in exile.

MP 16.

SOUNDNESS, Mrs
Once asked Widmerpool to dinner at rather short notice but subsequently failed to send him a card for her dance.

BM 77.

STALIN, Marshal Joseph 1879–1953
Mrs Widmerpool's hero and prospective second husband, known as 'Uncle Joe' to herself and her son; admired in the 'thirties and 'forties by J. G. Quiggin and Sillery.

KO 226. MP 52. BDFR 10, 175. HSH 39.

STANLEY
Audrey Maclintick's brother, a bank clerk keen on Sibelius who

annoyed Gossage by bringing his sister with him to a concert on the black day she and Maclintick first met.

CCR 208–10.

STAUFFENBERG, Colonel C. S. von 1907–1944
Led an unsuccessful attempt to assassinate Hitler on 20 July 1944; fellow guest of Prince Theodoric and Kucherman at a shooting party in Poland before the war.

MP 144.

STEBBINGS, Sydney
Officer in charge of Latin American liaison under Finn at the War Office. Retail fruit trade in civil life. Had a nervous breakdown when his firm went bankrupt at the start of the war; has another and is invalided out of the army; gassed himself by 1945.

MP 30–1, 199.

STELLA
One of Bagshaw's three stepdaughters, found quarrelling with her sister like wild cats outside Russell Gwinnett's bedroom door on the night of Pamela Widmerpool's break-in.

TK 186, 192–5.

STEPNEY, Lady Anne
Daughter of Lord and Lady Bridgnorth, younger sister of Peggy Stepney, distant cousin of Isobel Tolland. First encountered as a truculent debutante in a dress like a done-over nightgown, looking for trouble at the Walpole-Wilsons' dinner table. Same finishing school in Paris as Rosie Manasch. Pretty, grubby, untidy; large dark eyes and reddish hair. Determined to take a different line from her sister; on the side of the People in the French Revolution; sees herself as playing a vehement role in life. Seems to be the only person enjoying herself (as a bridesmaid with her wreath back-to-front) at Peggy's wedding to Stringham that autumn. Her chatter about Braque and Dufy is one of the many points about his in-laws which later gets Stringham down.

Picked up on a train in the early 'thirties by Barnby and declines to tell him her name; leaves him a year later to become the fourth wife of her father's old friend and contemporary Dicky Umfraville. Divorced after twelve months, moves to Paris to paint.

Greatly improved ('She no longer contradicted, as a matter of principle, every word spoken to her') when next encountered as Sir Magnus Donners' current companion at Stourwater in 1938. Plays Anger in the Seven Deadly Sins tableaux, and excels herself as the victim of Peter Templer's Lust. Leaves Donners via Templer for J. G.

Quiggin on the outbreak of war, leaving him in turn for one of the Free French.

Married again by the late 'sixties to a negro psychedelic painter considerably younger than herself; her affair with Templer at Stourwater known at the time to Donners.

BM At the Walpole-Wilsons 33, 38, 41, 44–6, 49, 54, 60–1; 102–3, 188; at her sister's wedding 226; 244, 249. AW Affair with Barnby 70–2; at Foppa's with him, meets Umfraville 148–54, 156, 158–60, 163–4, 166–7, 169; left Barnby 172; married to Umfraville 186–7; Stringham on 199–200; 213. LM 30, divorced 173; Umfraville on 181–2. CCR 175. KO At Stourwater as Donners' châtelaine 110, 113–18, 120, 122–4, 126–33, 138; affair with Templer 170; and with Quiggin 249–51. VB 145, 156. MP 57. BDFR 55. HSH 62.

STEPNEY, Lady Peggy
The Bridgnorths' elder daughter. Fashionable and much photographed beauty, engaged on and off to Charles Stringham whom she eventually m. in 1928 or 9 at a wedding preceded by more than common display of grievance on the part of relatives on both sides. Marriage dies of inanition. Divorced by 1933 and re-married to a cousin ('not the most amusing man you ever met': Stringham) with a haunted Palladian house in Yorkshire. Widowed in the war and married again to Jimmy Klein.

QU Stringham contemplating marriage to 227–9. BM Engagement to Stringham broken off 44–5, 61, 103; about to marry Stringham 187–9, 196–7, 202, 211–12; her wedding 224–6. AW Divorced 43–4, 72, 149–50, 154, 163–4; Stringham on 199–200; 213. CCR Stringham's account of their married life 175–8. KO 99, 113. SA 83, 222. MP 113–14. HSH 205.

STEVENS, Herbert ('Odo')
Short, square, thickset, very young and aggressively cheerful subaltern from Birmingham; on Aldershot training course with Jenkins in 1940 and afterwards breaks up the marriage of Jenkins' sister-in-law Priscilla Lovell. Apprentice in an imitation jewellery firm; gift for languages; knocks off a spot of local journalism ('I saw Stevens would go far, if he did not get killed'). Took his name from a squiggle on an envelope, having got fed up with Bert. Keen on the girls. Something of Chips Lovell about him, also of Dicky Umfraville when young. 'Narcissistic, Stevens was at the same time – if the distinction can be made – not narrowly egotistical. He was interested in everything round him, even though everything must eventually lead back to himself.'

Meets Priscilla through Jenkins on a weekend leave, living with her openly by 1941. Promoted lieutenant, MC ('"Oh, that?" he said. "Pretty hot stuff to have one of those, isn't it?"'), said to have done rather well somewhere, possibly the Lofoten raid. Claims to have been a fan of Moreland from the age of sixteen, also of Max Pilgrim who inspired some unexpectedly melancholy lines of his own called *Guest Night*. His degree of cynicism towards Priscilla hard to estimate; may even be contemplating marriage; apparently unmoved when she walks out on him in the middle of dinner at the Café Royal (Priscilla and Chips Lovell both killed in air raids later that night).

Reputation as rather a tough nut by 1943. Wounded in Middle East, recruited by Farebrother's branch of the secret service, helps spring the professional delinquent Szymanski from detention. Detailed for a dangerous mission in the Balkans. Has an affair with Pamela Flitton and turns up with her on the night of the air raid during which Mrs Erdleigh prophesies. Under Aries, protected by the powerful rays of Mars. Boasts of his distress over Priscilla ('I was determined to endure for as short a time as possible only what was absolutely unavoidable in the exhibition of self-confessed remorse Stevens was obviously proposing to mount for my benefit. He had been, I recalled, unnecessarily public in his carryings-on with Priscilla, had corroded what turned out to be Chips's last year alive . . .'), and of Pamela's prowess in bed. Not noticeably put out when she slaps his face and leaves.

Dropped behind German lines to join Balkan communist partisans, survives the operation in which Peter Templer dies. Known as Odo the Stoat at Intelligence HQ in Cairo. Promoted major, MC and bar, subsequently asked to leave the army; may have played some part in Templer's unexplained death at communist hands (possibly the murder which mucked up Stevens' DSO, and figures prominently in his war memoirs, *Sad Majors*).

Signed up as one of Quiggin & Craggs' new authors after the war. Job with a culture-toting outfit in liaison with Mark Members. Anxious to review for *Fission*. Affair with *Fission*'s well-preserved and wealthy backer Rosie Manasch. *Sad Majors* looked on with disfavour by the Party on account of its revelations about the seamier side of communist resistance in the Balkans ('rather awkward for a firm of progressive tone'); and eventually published elsewhere, on more advantageous terms, after a fierce internal row at Quiggin & Craggs.

Becomes a bone of contention between Rosie and her old enemy Matilda Donners; said to have gone to Ischia with Matilda before succumbing to marriage with Rosie. In his early forties by 1958, two or three children, more than a little in awe of his wife. No regular occupation, hovers on the outskirts of the literary world, rumoured to work part time for the secret service (and has inside information about Widmerpool's espionage activities). Greatly disliked by Isobel Jenkins. See Book Index under *Guest Night* and *Sad Majors*.

VB On Aldershot course 115–17, 120–2, gives Jenkins a lift on leave 134–40, and makes a hit with Priscilla 142–4; 149, 151; flirts with Priscilla 158–9, 163–4, 166–7, 169; 191. SA 37, Chips Lovell's account of his affair with Priscilla 107–10, 112; at Café Royal with Priscilla, his personality and taste for power, speculations on his relations with Priscilla, captivates Moreland and Mrs Maclintick, recites *Guest Night* 124–51; 166. MP His part in the Szymanski affair 91–2; living in Jenkins' block of flats in Chelsea, Pamela Flitton's lover, scene with her, his fortune told by Mrs Erdleigh 123–38; 183; rescued after Balkan operation 188–9; 223. BDFR 70, at *Fission* party, his book 126, 128–31, 138; Rosie Manasch takes a fancy to 143; 149; trouble brewing over *Sad Majors* 168, 187–8, 207–10; 195, 225; *Sad Majors* pub. thanks to Rosie 239–40. TK At Florian's in Venice, m. to Rosie, their marital history, dismayed by Pamela Widmerpool 159–67; 169; 173, 211; host at his wife's Mozart party 225–6, 231–3, 236, 241–9; his version of the scene between the Widmerpools afterwards 252–4, 256–60, 262–6; 278–9.

STEVENS, Rosie see MANASCH, Rosie

STRINGHAM, Amy see FOXE, Amy

STRINGHAM, Boffles
Father of Charles and Flavia, old friend of Dicky Umfraville. Handsome, amusing, looked wonderful on horseback and hadn't a penny to bless himself with when he m. as her second husband the rich and beautiful Lady Warrington in the early years of the century. Grenadier Guards; shrapnel wound in first war; divorced almost immediately after the war in favour of Buster Foxe. M. 2) a small, energetic, rather brassy Frenchwoman whom he met at a tennis tournament in Cannes. Emigrates as a farmer to Kenya where Charles joins him for a holiday on leaving school in 1922. Hard up, drinking heavily, quarrelling with his French wife.

D. by 1939, leaving such money as he had to his widow and narrowly missing Buster Foxe's long awaited downfall ('Boffles Stringham once said: "Mark my words, Dicky, the day will come when Amy will have to get rid of that damned polo-playing sailor." That day has come': Umfraville).

QU 9, 53, 61–2, 175–6, 206. BM 103, 119. AW 152, 154, 206. LM 161, 167. CCR 89–90. KO 215. VB 150, 166. SA 79.

STRINGHAM, Charles
Only son of Boffles Stringham and Amy Foxe (her South African fortune entailed on Stringham), parents divorced. A few months older than Jenkins and a formative influence on him at school. Brought up by his mother ('Of course his upbringing was impossible – always, from

the start,' according to his sister's governess Miss Weedon) and, on her third marriage in 1920, by his stepfather Lt-Commander Buster Foxe, whom he loathes: 'I came in time to regard his circumstances as having something in common with those of Hamlet. His father had, of course, been shipped off to Kenya rather than murdered; but Buster and his mother were well adapted to play the parts of Claudius and Gertrude'.

Messes in his last year at school with Jenkins and Peter Templer:

'He was tall and dark, and looked a little like one of those stiff, sad young men in ruffs, whose long legs take up so much room in sixteenth-century portraits: or perhaps a younger – and far slighter – version of Veronese's Alexander* receiving the children of Darius after the battle of Issus: with the same high forehead and suggestion of hair thinning a bit at the temples. His features certainly seemed to belong to that epoch of painting: the faces in Elizabethan miniatures, lively, obstinate, generous, not very happy, and quite relentless.'

An excellent mimic, noted for his 'ludicrously exact' imitations of Widmerpool (' "That boy will be the death of me," said Stringham'), and a favourite with their housemaster Le Bas (once arrested by the police on information laid by Stringham).

Leaves school at Christmas 1922, and is reluctantly dispatched to his father's farm in Kenya ('the great open spaces, where men are men') where he sleeps with a coffee planter's divorced wife; 'Tuffy' Weedon attributes the subsequent change in him to this trip to Africa. Is laid up after a fall from a horse and misses most of his first year at the university ('he took against the place at once'), seeming already cut off from his school contemporaries by temperament and circumstances: 'Stringham was, in fact, not substantially richer than most undergraduates of his sort, and, being decidedly free with his money, was usually hard-up, but from the foothills of his background was, now and then, wafted the disturbing, aromatic perfume of gold, the scent of which, even at this early stage in our lives, could sometimes be observed to act intoxicatingly on chance acquaintances . . .' Leaves after a single term, in the teeth of Buster's opposition, to become private secretary to Sir Magnus Donners in the autumn of 1924.

Seems to have aged ten years when next encountered in 1928 or 9. Living in West Halkin Street, his engagement to Lady Peggy Stepney long since broken off, already restive in his role as Mrs Andriadis' current lover ('It was . . . clear to me that strangeness was what Stringham now expected, indeed demanded, from life: a need already becoming hard to satisfy'). Leaves Donners Brebner on his marriage to Peggy Stepney that autumn. Divorced by 1931, living alone in his old

* But see footnote in Painting Index under *Alexander receiving the Children of Darius*.

157

flat and drinking heavily like his father. Marked likeness to Umfraville ('The same dissatisfaction with life and basic melancholy gave a resemblance . . .'). Put to bed after a hard bout at Le Bas' Old Boys' reunion by Jenkins and Widmerpool, who struggles with him on his bed till Stringham submits.

An alcoholic, incarcerated by Miss Weedon in her flat from 1936, to Buster's unconcealed delight ('I felt a pang of horror at the way his family now talked of Stringham: as if he had been put away from view like a person suffering from a horrible, unmentionable disease, or become some terrifying legendary figure, fearful as the Glamis monster, about whom it was appropriate to joke as dreadful to behold, but at the same time a being past serious credence'). Teetotal regime, painting in gouache, reading Browning: 'His life with Miss Weedon was impossible to contemplate'. Escapes briefly to his mother's house during Moreland's party, and is recaptured by Miss Weedon acting on a tip-off from Buster.

Later shut up with Miss Weedon at Glimber, his mother's vast uninhabitable unsaleable country house. Hard up, in poor health, cured of drink by 1939. Enlists in the Ordnance Corps ('the point was that Tuffy, like everyone else, had had enough of me. She wanted another sphere in which to exercise her tireless remedial activities. That was why I took the shilling'). Transfers from RAOC to infantry and is posted in 1941 as Mess waiter ('Between you and me, Nick, I think I have it in me to make a first-class Mess waiter. The talent is there. It's just a question of developing latent ability') to the Divisional HQ where Jenkins is already stationed as Widmerpool's assistant. 'War is a great opportunity for everyone to find his own level. I am a major – you are a second lieutenant – he is a private' (Widmerpool). Looks ill, possibly not entirely sane. Transferred on Widmerpool's instructions to a Mobile Laundry Unit conveniently awaiting posting to the Far Eastern front; both Stringham ('Awfully chic to be killed') and Widmerpool remain unmoved at Jenkins' protests.

Captured at the Fall of Singapore in 1942, and d. in Japanese POW camp. Leaves everything, including his mother's South African shares, to his niece Pamela Flitton, Widmerpool's fiancée ('With the right attention, Stringham's estate might in due course be nursed into something quite respectable': Widmerpool).

party 171–6, 178, 180, 185, 187, 189–90; friendship with Templer terminated 190–201; job with Donners Brebner, enlists Sillery to overcome his parents' opposition, leaves Oxford 203–8, 211–22; end of a phase in his friendship with Jenkins 225–9. BM 16, 30–1, 34, no longer engaged to Peggy Stepney 44–5, 61–2; 72; at Hyde Park Corner after the Huntercombes' ball, invites Mr Deacon, Widmerpool etc. on to Milly Andriadis' party 92–5; at Mrs Andriadis': changes in him 101–8, Mr Deacon on, Sillery on 119–23, 126, 132, 134–5, 137, 141–2, row with Mrs Andriadis 144–8; 152; his attitude to women 160–1; 172; at Stourwater, introduces Peggy as his fiancée 186–9, 191, 193–4, 196–202, 209–12, 221–2; their wedding 224–6; 234; leaving Donners 270; 273. AW His divorce 43–5, 72, 112; likeness to Umfraville, drinking hard 149–54, 157, 159–61, 164; at Le Bas' dinner 181–2, 184–5, 190, 192, 195, on his marriage 198–202; his struggle with Widmerpool 203–9; 213–14. LM 52, Miss Weedon on 161–7. CCR 15, 43–4, moved into Miss Weedon's flat 86–9; 93, 123; his mother and Buster on 140–1, 143–6; at their party, swapping marital horror stories with Mrs Maclintick, recaptured by Miss Weedon 161–88; 214. KO 99, 101, 165; caretaking at Glimber, far out-classed by Widmerpool in Templer's estimation 104–6; 113; discharged by Miss Weedon 214–17. VB 110, 118, 138, 146; Umfraville drawn to him in Kenya 150, 155; private in RAOC 157; 160, 164. SA Identified as Mess waiter, his account of his recent history and present state of mind 67–84; 94, 105–6, 121, 129; transferred to Laundry Unit, his motives for enlisting 167–71; rescues Bithel when drunk, teases Widmerpool 175–85; Widmerpool's indifference to his fate 189–93, and refusal to intervene 215; his determination to see the gorgeous East, his views on Browning and the soldier's art, his moorings severed 218–23. MP 23–4, 48, his capture at Singapore announced by Pamela Flitton 59–60; his teasing Le Bas recalled 62–3; 77, 100, 113–14, 197, his capture and death confirmed by Widmerpool 204–6; 221–2. BDFR 40, 48, 51, 53. Left his Modigliani drawing to Pamela 176, its fate 180, 191, 227, 214, 233–4. TK 30; Pamela's feelings for him 102; intimations of experiences endured at Singapore, Cheesman on his behaviour in the camp 204–9; 217, 227. HSH His part in Jenkins' education recalled 188; his sister on his death, and Pamela's passion for him as a child 200–4; final fate of his Modigliani 270.

STRINGHAM, Flavia see WISEBITE, Flavia

STRINGHAM, Lady Peggy see STEPNEY, Lady Peggy

STRIPLING, Babs
Peter Templer's eldest sister. Had a beau who shot himself in Kenya, and afterwards m. 1) an officer in dragoons ('a far from ideal husband')

whom she left in the first war for 2) Jimmy Stripling, divorcing him in turn for 3) Lord Perkins. Tall, good-looking, talks a lot and rather loudly; marked resemblance to Mrs Erdleigh.

QU 68, 80–4, 88–97, 99, 103. AW 76, 79, 102, 142, 184, 174–5. VB 129. MP 201, 234. HSH 81.

STRIPLING, Jimmy
Racing driver m. to Templer's sister Babs, staying with his in-laws for the weekend in 1923 when Jenkins first meets and falls for Jean Templer. Tall, gruff, burly, hair parted in the middle; a grumbler comparable in volume only to Uncle Giles. Poor health, broods incessantly on his inability to take part in first war ('unless – as Peter had remarked – persuading Babs to run away with him while her husband was at the front might be regarded as Jimmy having "done his bit"'). Rags Farebrother and hates his guts, on account of his war record.

Divorced by the early 'thirties; spill at Brooklands; falls under Mrs Erdleigh's thumb. Still perhaps under 40 when next encountered with her at Mona Templer's luncheon party but changed noticeably for the worse, shrivelled, cowed and physically dilapidated with an odd disconcerting stare and starting eyes. Underwriter at Lloyd's ('If there had been any doubt about Stripling's money, his satisfactory financial position could have been estimated from Quiggin's manner towards him, a test like litmus paper where affluence was concerned'). Obsessed, and possibly unhinged, by the occult. Turns out to have been Jean's lover after Babs left him, a revelation with nightmarish implications for Jenkins at the height of his own affair with Jean.

'Double-dealing, stingy, conceited, bad tempered, half cracked,' and a typical specimen of Jean's taste in lovers according to Bob Duport. Mrs Erdleigh still milking him to quite a tune at the start of the second war. Lectures to the troops on the early days of motor-racing.

Turned into an elderly vintage-car-bore by the late 'fifties: 'Tall, shambling, what remained of his hair grey, rather greasy, his bulky figure, which took up more room than ever, was shapeless and bent. Even so, he seemed in certain respects less broken down, morally speaking, than in his middle period'. Attends the Stevenses' party as Mrs Erdleigh's captive, and intervenes ineffectually in the fight between the Widmerpools afterwards.

Falls into the clutches of a young fellow (almost certainly Scorpio Murtlock) who takes over stripping him of his fortune after Mrs Erdleigh's death. D. by 1968, mourned by Farebrother ('Old Jimmy was a highly strung beggar in his way') and a crew of rum characters in robes at his funeral in Kensal Green cemetery.

QU 68, at the Templers' with Babs and Lady McReith, his aggressive manner and hostility to Farebrother 80–4, baulked of revenge on Farebrother in the matter of the collar-turner and the green chamber pot 86–99, 103–5; 145. AW Lunching with the Templers 75–6, 78–9, brings Mrs Erdleigh and insists on planchette 81–4, 87–95, 97–102; 115; revealed by Jean to have been her lover 140–3; 182, 184, 213. KO Duport's account of his affair with Jean 174–9; 191, 197. VB 133. MP 201. TK At the Stevens' party with Mrs Erdleigh, his passion for vintage cars 241–5; after the party 253–4, 256, 258, 264, 266; 277–8. HSH Farebrother's account of his funeral 81–3.

STRYDONCK DE BURKEL, General Victor van b. 1876
Commander-in-Chief of Free Belgian Forces, at wartime performance of *The Bartered Bride* and looks everything he should from his picturesque reputation.

MP 98–101.

SULTAN
The labrador Eleanor Walpole-Wilson was trying to train in Hyde Park on the afternoon Jenkins fell in love with Barbara Goring.

BM 18, 27. AW 108.

SUMMERS-MILLER
Old Boy in Le Bas' house.

BDFR 233.

SUN YAT-SEN, Dr 1867–1925
Founder and first president of the Chinese Republic; news of the Nationalists' capture of Peking reported to him in his coffin on 6 July, 1928, at a ceremony to which Widmerpool was not invited.

BM 51.

SUZETTE
The prettier of Mme Leroy's two nieces ('small and fair, but no beauty', capable of discoursing 'almost as boringly as Widmerpool himself' on Victor Hugo) with whom Jenkins conducts an inconclusive, one-sided affair at La Grenadière in 1923.

QU 113, 116, 120, 123, 126, 137–8, 140, 142, 147–52, 160, 162–6, 172. BM 25, 29, 191, 214.

SZCEPANOWSKI, Dr
Polish paying guest of the Leroys at La Grenadière.

QU 161, 164.

SZYMANSKI alias KUBITSA, BROD, GROZA, DUPONT etc.

Hero of the disgraceful incident which costs Farebrother his job in 1942. A delinquent ('one of those professional scourges of authority that appear sporadically in all armies') of uncertain nationality and outstanding disruptive power. Notorious gambler in peace time. Prudently turned down by the Belgian army on the outbreak of war, later accepted by the Free French in London and gladly ceded by them to the Poles. Question asked about him in parliament. Under surveillance by MI5. Causes endless trouble to Lt-Col Finn's section of the General Staff both before and after his escape from British military detention on forged papers supplied by Farebrother's branch of the British secret service.

Some sort of connection with Pamela Flitton (possibly her lover) in her ATS days. Eventually dropped in German occupied territory in the Balkans with instructions to bump off the head of the Gestapo or some local traitor. Operates independently in the same resistance area as Odo Stevens and Peter Templer, and very probably survives this mission.

SA 94, 103–4. MP 31–2, 63–4(?), 82–4, 91–5, 111, 119, 124, 126–7, 138, 189, 216.

TAYLOR or PORTER, Betty

The adoring girl who turns up at Umfraville's nightclub with Peter Templer ('Rather a peach, isn't she?') soon after Mona left him. Married to, and eventually removed from, a man in jute called something like Taylor or Porter who bored her to death. Responsible for the alarming change in Templer after their marriage. Spends a weekend at Stourwater in 1938 ('I saw at once that something was "wrong" with Betty Templer, not realizing, until I came to shake hands with her, how badly "wrong" things were. It was like trying to shake hands with Ophelia while she was strewing flowers'); brings out a hint of sadism in Sir Magnus Donners (also possibly his voyeuristic instincts); and breaks down during the Seven Deadly Sins tableaux. Pretty, silly, never very bright in the head, driven round the bend by Templer's affair with Anne Umfraville.

Spends the war years in an asylum, emerging after Templer's death to make a successful third marriage to a man in the Foreign Office and become an ambassadress.

LM At Umfraville's nightclub 184, 187, 190, 197–9. KO Templer's wife, brutal change in him 102; at Stourwater, her pitiful state, speculations on the marriage and its consequences 114–22, 125–7, her collapse 130–3, 138–9; Duport's explanation of her breakdown 170. VB 128–30. SA 83. MP 15, Templer on 21–2; 78, 234. HSH 63–4.

TCHAIKOWSKY, Peter Ilich 1840–93
Once drank a glass of wine in Cambridge with the elderly musician
who m. Moreland's aunt.

CCR 4.

TELFORD, Mrs
Adds to Albert's troubles at the Bellevue in wartime by pestering his
girls to join an ambulance class.

KO 154.

TEMPLER, Babs see STRIPLING, Babs

TEMPLER, Betty see TAYLOR or PORTER, Betty

TEMPLER, Jean
Peter's younger sister, Jenkins' mistress. Aged sixteen or seventeen
when Jenkins first sets eyes on her during a visit to her brother between
school and university in the summer of 1923:
'Fair, not strikingly pretty, with long legs and short, untidy hair, she
remained without moving, intently watching us, as Peter shut off the
engine, and we got out of the car. Like her legs, her face was thin and
attenuated, the whole appearance given the effect of a much simplified
– and somewhat self-conscious – arrangement of lines and planes, such
as might be found in an Old Master drawing, Flemish or German
perhaps, depicting some young and virginal saint; the racquet, held
awkwardly at an angle to her body, suggesting at the same time an
obscure implement associated with martyrdom. The expression of her
face, although sad and a trifle ironical, was not altogether in keeping
with this air of belonging to another and better world. I felt suddenly
uneasy, and also interested: a desire to be with her, and at the same
time, an almost paralysing disquiet at her presence.'

Markedly indifferent to Jenkins throughout this stay; his romantic
feelings for her gradually submerged in similar ones for Suzette later
that summer in France. Reported to be in love with a married man
twice her age, simultaneously pursued by Bob Duport. Has become a
dim, if desirable memory by the time of Jenkins' affair with Barbara
Goring. M. to Duport by 1928 or 9, meets Jenkins for the second time
at Stourwater that autumn. Sits next to him at luncheon opposite the
tapestry depicting *Luxuria* in the Seven Deadly Sins; reminds him of
some picture ('Was it Rubens and *Le Chapeau de Paille*: his second wife
or her sister? There was that same suggestion, though only for an
instant, of shyness and submission. . . .'); suspected by him of a lesbian
entanglement with Baby Wentworth. Goes abroad with Duport soon

afterwards. Daughter Polly b. the following spring. Deserted round about this time by Bob for Bijou Ardglass.

Next encountered with Peter at the Ritz the week after Christmas 1932. Thinks Mark Members a goodish poet and St John Clarke a poor novelist; liked *Mädchen in Uniform*; reminds Jenkins for some reason of the woman smoking a hookah in Delacroix's *Femmes d'Alger dans leur appartement* ('Perhaps there was something of the odalisque about Jean, too'). Affair with her begun that weekend at the Templers' house in Maidenhead. Flat in Rutland Gate, games of Russian billiards at Foppa's that summer. Confesses to a previous affair with her brother-in-law Jimmy Stripling ('To think of her as wife of Bob Duport was bad enough, but that she should also have been mistress of Jimmy Stripling was barely endurable'). Leaves Jenkins for her child's sake that autumn to rejoin Duport, sailing with him to take up a new job arranged by Widmerpool in South America ('Rather an odd woman. Moody, I should think. She didn't seem particularly pleased at the reunion. Not at all grateful to me, at least': Widmerpool). Jenkins tormented by memories of her at intervals throughout the next decade.

Spends less than a year with Duport before abandoning him again for good. Divorced by 1938. Settled in South America and remarried to 'a local Don Juan some years younger than herself'. Turns out to have had an affair with Jimmy Brent ('She informed me in bed, appropriately enough. You're not going to tell me any woman would boast of having slept with Jimmy Brent, if she hadn't. The same applies to Jimmy Stripling . . . Both actions strike me as even odder to admit to than to do, if that were possible': Duport). Became Brent's mistress in the middle of her affair with Jenkins ('I thought of that grave, gothic beauty that once I had loved so much, which found fulfilment in such men . . . Perhaps, I thought, her men are gothic too, beings carved on the niches and corbels of a mediaeval cathedral to arouse at once laughter and horror. In any case, I had been one of them. If her lovers were horrifying, I too had been of their order. That had to be admitted.') Turns out still later to have ditched Jenkins only in order to follow Brent ('"You'd never guess," he said apologetically, "but Jean fell for me first"') to South America, where she would have run away with him but for want of enthusiasm on his part.

Unrecognizable when presented to Jenkins by the Latin American attaché, Colonel Flores, as his wife immediately after the second war. Only just short of a perfect stranger ('How could this chic South American lady have shared with me embraces, passionate and polymorphous as those depicted on the tapestry of Luxuria that we had discussed together when we had met at Stourwater?'). Rolls Royce, Paris frocks, address in Knightsbridge, lavish parties: 'It struck me all at once, confronted with this luxuriance, that . . . money was after all what Jean really liked . . .'

Returns with Flores to South America. Delighted by his rise to power as president but would have preferred to do the job herself. Widowed in the 'sixties. Returns to England. Looks like a sad Goya duchess; reunited with Duport; last seen with him in 1971:

'Jean smiled graciously. She held out the hand of a former near-dictator's lady – Carlos Flores cannot have been much short of a dictator at the height of his power – a clasp, brief and light, not without a sense of power about it too. There could have been no doubt in the mind of an onlooker . . . that Jean and I had met before. That was about the best you could say for past love. In fact Jean's former husband, whom I had never much liked, was appreciably less distant than she.'

QU 68; at home, first impressions of 74, 76, 78–82, 88, Jenkins' feelings for crystallised 93–7, 100; Jenkins in love with 106; recalled by Suzette 113, 116, level with Suzette in Jenkins' affections 120, 149–50, eclipsed by Suzette 163, 172; 193. BM 25; m. to Duport 141, 143; conversation with at Stourwater 190–4, 196–7, 213–16, 222; gone abroad, expecting a child 234–5; 274. AW Having trouble with Duport 42–3; at the Ritz, start of Jenkins' affair with 54, 56–66; weekend at the Templers' 73, 79, 83, 86–8, 90–1, 93, 102–5; course of their affair 114, its complexities explored, in deep waters over Stripling 132–44, at Foppa's 146–9, 154–8, 160–1, at Mrs Andriadis' 164, 169; 173, 175–6, 198; appointment with, prospect of parting from 210–11, 213–14. LM Affair with long since over 14–15; Widmerpool on 53–4; Jenkins beginning to recover from loss of 67–8, 99, 136; left Duport 199–200. CCR 6. KO 99–100, divorced 108; Stourwater meeting with recalled 117–18; 154; recalled by encounter with Duport 163–4, 166–9, 172, his account of her affair with Brent 175–81, 191, 194; 246. VB 110; Brent's account of her pursuit of him 119–20, 125–6, 128–33; 140, 169. MP Memories of 152, 225; encounter with as Mme Flores, reflections on the past 232–6. BDFR Her party, Jenkins at last unmoved by 94–9. TK 51, 196, 234–5. HSH 206, at Henderson's gallery with Duport 252–7.

TEMPLER, Mr

Father of Peter, Babs and Jean, 'a wiry, grim little fellow, almost entirely bald'. Widower in his sixties when Jenkins spends a weekend at his house by the sea in 1923. Made his money in cement but recently obliged to retire after an appalling bloomer over steel; his brains still regularly picked by Sunny Farebrother. Not colossally rich but certainly not poor. Painted ('in a style of decidedly painful realism') by Isbister. Keen on keeping fit; boxing fan for forty years; subject to morose fits and gloomy reverie. Holds that an office is the place to learn the realities of life, and has much in common with his son. 'A fine old man. A hard man, but a fine one' (Farebrother).

D. by the early 'thirties, not known how much he cut up for. 'He was an old devil, if ever there was one. Devil incarnate' (Farebrother).

QU His home life, Peter's complaints of 68, 71–2; weekend with, his character, relations with Farebrother and with his son 75–6, 78–9, 81–5, 87–8, 99–100, 103. BM 177. AW His death, Farebrother's *Times* obituary 37; 65–6, 87, 116. LM 53. CCR 71. SA Farebrother's last word on 198. HSH 256.

TEMPLER, Mona see MONA

TEMPLER, Peter
A shade older than Jenkins, messes with him and Stringham in their last year or so at school. Thin face, 'light blue eyes that gave out a perpetual and quite mechanical sparkle', widow's peak and large pointed satyr's ears; dresses like an advertisement for gent's tailoring. Initially mistrusted by Jenkins on account of his boast that he had never read a book for pleasure in his life (but later relaxes this rule in favour of *Sanders of the River*). Claims to have received advances, or at least heavy breathing, from Widmerpool. Smokes, drinks and has his first girl from school while supposedly consulting an oculist in London. Presides with Stringham over the initial stages of Jenkins' worldly education: 'Their behaviour exemplified two different sides of life, in spite of some outward similarity in their tastes. For Templer, there was no truth except in tangible things: though he was not ambitious. Stringham, as I now see him, was romantic'. A scourge to Le Bas, who confidently predicts the worst for him and goes to some lengths to get him removed from school at Easter 1923.

Spends a month or two learning business methods in Holland; sleeps with Lady McReith that summer; already beginning to strike Jenkins as really a more forceful character than Stringham. Turns up at the university a year later with a couple of City friends ('I should have known Brent and Duport anywhere as acquaintances of Peter's. They had that indefinable air of being up to no good that always characterized Peter himself'), and drives his car into a ditch on a disastrous outing which effectively terminates his friendship with Stringham.

Afterwards reported to be thriving as a stockbroker; still exclusively preoccupied with money and girls ('"I have rather suburban taste in ladies, like everything else," Templer used to say'); curious streak of melancholy. M. to the model Mona by 1932, house at Maidenhead, has lost money in the slump and had to sell the Buick. Deeply in love with his wife ('To Templer, accustomed to easy success with women, she had perhaps represented the one absolutely first-rate example of the goods he had so long been accustomed to handle – in the manner that a seasoned collector can afford to ignore every other point in any object he wishes to acquire provided it satisfies completely in those respects most difficult to attain'). Abandoned by her in 1933 for J. G. Quiggin.

Divorced the year after, thinner but more elegant than ever, dazzles Betty Taylor or Porter and removes her from her husband. Has business dealings with Widmerpool and is somewhat less derisive about him than formerly. M. to Betty by 1938 and living with her at Sunningdale. Stringham by now hopelessly eclipsed in his estimation as a friend by Widmerpool. Almost horrifying change apparent in him at Stourwater that autumn: 'He looked hard, even rather savage, as if he had made up his mind to endure life rather than, as formerly, to enjoy it'. Adored by his wife and helplessly aware of the effect on her mental instability of his own attractiveness to other women. Precipitates her collapse during the Seven Deadly Sins tableaux by his spectacular performance with Anne Umfraville as Lust. Has driven Betty off her rocker by his carryings-on with Anne according to Duport, who blames the change in him on business failures in the slump ('Slowed him up for good, so far as being a pal for a night on the tiles').

Job at Ministry of Economic Warfare in second war. Grimmer than before. Curt, preoccupied and profoundly dejected by the failure of both his marriages. Bombed out in 1942; lodges briefly with Ted Jeavons; falls for Pamela Flitton and is tormented by her on the score of age and impotence. Joins Farebrother's secret service outfit. Dropped behind German lines to join Prince Theodoric's Balkan resistance movement ('He was absolutely set on doing that job': Farebrother). Liquidated in mysterious circumstances after the British government's withdrawal of support (Widmerpool, who had recommended this decision possibly at Cabinet level, is afterwards accused by Pamela of Templer's murder).

QU At school 5, first impressions of not wholly favourable 8–10; 12–14, 20–1; harried by Le Bas, his character and temperament, his exploits 28–40, 42–7, 50; contrasted with Stringham 52–3, Stringham on 57, 62–3; his view of Stringham, leaves school, asks Jenkins to stay, his home life 67–76, 79–84, 87–9, 91–2, sleeps with Lady McReith 94–6, 98–102; 116; his dissipation a shock to Widmerpool 130–3; 143, 149, 152, 172–3; his Oxford jaunt 190–201; 207, 222, 228–9. BM 102, 117, 141–3, 161, 190, 192, 208, 211–12, 234. AW 14, at the Ritz, his tastes and character, his marriage, on Stringham and Widmerpool 36–46, 51, relations with Mona 54–67; weekend at his house, conciliatory attitude to Mona 73–81, 83–7, 91–3, 95–9, 102–4; 117; abandoned by Mona for Quiggin 131–3, 136, 138–40; 166; at Le Bas' reunion, collapse of his marriage analyzed 170–3, 175–8, 181–2, 184–5, 192, 195–8; Stringham on 200, 202; 213–14. LM Divorced 52–3; 67–8,

99; Mona's attitude to 104–8, 111, 123–4, 133; 178; at Umfraville's nightclub with Betty, entertaining Widmerpool 184–8, 190, 192, 197–200, 202; 205, 207. KO At Stourwater, his tastes and temperament, change in him, on Stringham and Widmerpool 99–111, painful relations with Betty 114–15, 117–23, his performance as Lust 124–7, 129–33, 135–9; 163, 165–6, Duport on his marriage and the change in him 168–71; 173–4, 181, 197, 250. VB 8, 11, 118–19, 124, 128–30, 141. SA 56, Stringham on 82–3; 124, 196–8. MP At Widmerpool's Cabinet office meeting 14–16, his respect for Widmerpool, angling for a job with Farebrother, on Betty, his black mood 18–24; Jeavons on his unhappiness and determination to find a dangerous job 75–8, Pamela Flitton the cause of his trouble 82; Duport's account of his death 187–90; 197; Farebrother's ditto 201; Widmerpool's ditto 206; Widmerpool accused of murdering him 211–13; reflections on his fate 222; Jean on 234–5. BDFR 51, 53, Jeavons blames Pamela for his death 85; 99, 183, 233–4, 236. TK 73, 92, 102, 153. HSH His photo in Seven Deadly Sins 62–3; 81, 83; his schooldays recalled 188; 192, 256.

TESSA
X. Trapnel's last girlfriend before Pamela Widmerpool, afterwards secretary to the chairman of a merchant bank.

BDFR 159–60, 162, 212. TK 198, 212.

THEODORIC, Prince
Plump youth with a hooked nose, black curly hair and generally Levantine appearance whose presence makes a stir at Milly Andriadis' party in 1928 or 9. Member of a clever royal house, brother to a not wholly satisfactory Balkan king, owes his broadmindedness to a touch of Coburg blood ('One would never guess him descended from Queen Victoria. Perhaps he isn't. But we mustn't be scandalous': Sillery). Charmed by Baby Wentworth. In London to negotiate a deal with Sir Magnus Donners over base metal concessions ('Is it aluminium? Something like that') in return for industrial investment by Donners Brebner and a railway to the coast. His moves on the Balkan chessboard watched with interest from E. European capitals. Is ditched by Mrs Wentworth that summer and settles instead for Bijou Ardglass.

Afterwards m. a Scandinavian princess who keeps him very much in order. Has business dealings at various points with Widmerpool and Peter Templer. Middle of the road in politics; pro-British, hundred per cent anti-Nazi; makes a dramatic escape when the Germans invade his country at the beginning of the war.

Exiled in London. Tall, stoutish, something of the air of a famous tenor. Rumours of an affair with Pamela Flitton. Descended from the Dreyfusard Prince Odoacer who was at the Princesse de Guermantes' party in *Remembrance of Things Past*.★ Delicate and increasingly hopeless diplomatic position. Brings pressure to bear in Whitehall; attempts to organize resistance operations via Farebrother's branch of the secret service; has some hand in the Szymanski affair. Fails to prevent the British switching support from the royalist resistance in his country to the rival communist partisans.

Placed next to the King and Queen of Jugoslavia at the Victory Day service in St Paul's. Permanently exiled after the war (his country now the People's Republic for which Widmerpool becomes an active propagandist); makes a reasonable success of business ventures in Canada; d. towards the end of the 'sixties.

BM In London on business with Donners Brebner 47–8; at Mrs Andriadis' party 111–12, 121–5, 138–9, 146; 166, 172; guest of honour at Stourwater 180–2, 186–7, 194–5, 198–201, 210–11, 215; 221, 235, 242, 253, 271. AW 35, 176, 211. LM 16, 25, 42, 51. KO 99, 118, 141. VB 110. SA 111, 116. MP 20, encounter with in Whitehall 47–53; at *Bartered Bride* 98, with Pamela Flitton 100–2; Szymanski affair 111; Proustian connection 121; political developments in his country 127, 144, 188, 214–15, 221. BDFR 10, 12, 96, 102–3. TK 104. HSH 49.

TODMAN
Man from the Planning Authority, adjudicates between conservationists and quarrymen in the battle for the Devil's Fingers.

HSH 150, 153, 173.

TOKENHOUSE, Daniel McN. (Major, Retd.)
'An eccentric, one in a high class of his category'. Very reasonably successful publisher of art books, text books and topography between the wars. Commissioned St John Clarke's introduction to *The Art of Horace Isbister* (one of his rare miscalculations) and gave Jenkins his first job on coming down from Oxford. Old Sandhurst contemporary of Jenkins' father (and manages to hang on longer than most as one of his very few friends).

Abandoned an unremarkable army career after the first war to enter publishing. Keen amateur painter ('The pictures . . . showed faint but discernible traces of the Camden Town Group. Rising to no great heights as masterpieces of landscape, they did convey an absolutely genuine sense of moral discomfort'). An inveterate puritan with a fanatical hatred of religion in any form and an equal dislike of any hint of sensuality in the arts ('almost to the extent of handicapping a capacity for making money out of them'). No known sex life. Left publishing to become a full time painter in 1938, simultaneously undergoing a violent communist conversion, severing relations with Colonel Jenkins

★ But see footnote in Book Index under PROUST.

169

('When it came to being hasty in temper, idiosyncratic in conduct, my father and Tokenhouse could, so to speak, give each other a game'), and suffering a complete nervous collapse.

Spends the first part of the war in a psychiatric clinic, emerging to settle in Venice ('Better than this country and Attlee's near-fascist Government') where Jenkins looks him up during the writers' conference of 1958. Middle to late seventies:

'Spare, wiry, very upright, he could be thought dried up, wizened, ascetic; considering his years, not particularly old. Hid body seemed made up of gristle, rather than flesh . . . An all-enveloping chilliness of manner hung about him, sense of being utterly cut off from the rest of the world, a personality, even physique, no sun could warm. Unlike Widmerpool, sweltering in his House of Lords suit, the ancient jacket Tokenhouse wore, good thick serviceable tweed, designed to keep out damp wind on the moors, his even older flannel trousers punctiliously pressed, seemed between them garments scarcely substantial enough to prevent him looking blue with cold, in spite of blazing Venetian sunlight outside.'

Characterized by complete absorption in himself and his own doings. High, unamused laugh. Claims to have forged ahead politically and come to see that, for an artist, Naturalism is not enough ('I *must* satisfy my own conviction that a new ideological content had to be infused into painting, one free from all taint of neutrality'). Has jettisoned his former style to become one of the few Socialist-Realists practising in the West, restricting his palette to mud colours, his technique to a sort of neo-primitivism and his subject matter to a straightforward depiction of social injustice under capitalism e.g. *Four Priests Rigging a Miracle*.

Turns out to have been used for years by Widmerpool's Stalinist contact Belkin as convenient cover for passing secret information (and subsequently remains unscathed by, probably unaware of, Widmerpool's exposure for espionage). Only ever sold two paintings, one to Belkin (the army scene, *Any Complaints?*) and one to Louis Glober.

See also Painting Index.

TK His ancient friendship with Jenkins' father, his career and character 54–9, 64–5, 68; 81; reunion with in Venice, displays his paintings and expounds his theory of art, visits the Biennale, charmed by Glober, business with Widmerpool 117–34, 136–7, 139–48, 150; 155, 175–6, 178, 209, 215, 225, 233.

TOLAND, John 1670–1722
Irish deist, author of *Christianity not Mysterious* etc., no relation to Lord Warminster (though Erridge would rather like to have claimed him).

LM 151.

TOLLANDS

Family of the Viscounts Erridge and Earls of Warminster, 'an awfully undistinguished lot on the whole' (Erridge). First appeared as nobody much in the fourteenth century, probably made their money out of the Black Death, came up in the world under Edward IV, were preferred by Henry VIII and out of a job under Bloody Mary, sided with the royalists in the civil war and got their peerage from Queen Anne.

LM 150–1. BDFR 43.

TOLLAND, Hon Alfred

Lonely derelict character invariably present, and always at least twenty years older than anyone else, at Le Bas' reunions for Old Boys. Red face, white moustache and muffled uneasy manner. All but incapable of finishing a sentence. Younger brother of Lord Warminster; uncle to Erridge and his nine brothers and sisters.

Expert on his family history ('and a very great bore on the subject': Erridge). Never goes out except to things like regimental dinners. Employed by Lord Sleaford in charitable works before the first war. Once lay awake almost till dawn after hearing Mrs Patrick Campbell recite; and is similarly stirred long afterwards by a brief encounter with Pamela Flitton ('Confess I like that quiet sort of girl'). Air-raid warden in second war. Chest trouble. Too ill to attend George Tolland's funeral but leaves his sickbed for Erridge's ('"Didn't want to stay away when it came to the head of the family." He spoke as if he would have risen from the dead to reach the funeral of the head of the family. Perhaps he had. The idea was not to be lightly dismissed. There was something not wholly of this world about him').

AW At Le Bas' dinner 181–2, 185–7, 195, 197. LM At Lady Molly's 23–33, 35–8; 75, 77–9, 87–8, 117, 151, 183, 211, 214, 218–20. CCR 69, 76, 199. KO 233–4. BDFR at Erridge's funeral 46–8, 53, 56–9, 61, 63–5, 67, 70–1, 79, 83–4; 96.

TOLLAND, Alfred, Earl of Warminster, Viscount Erridge see ERRIDGE

TOLLAND, Lady Blanche

The dotty one among Lord Warminster's ten children ('When people called Blanche "dotty", no question of incipient madness was implied, nor even mild imbecility . . . Blanche's strangeness, when examined, mainly took the shape of lacking any desire to engage herself in life, to have friends, to marry, to bear children, to go out into the world. Within, so to speak, her chosen alcove, she appeared perfectly happy, at least not actively unhappy'). Six or seven years older than her sister Priscilla to whom she bears a strong resemblance. A respected figure in the world of good works, charities, East End clubs etc., and the favourite of her stepmother Lady Warminster with whom she lives in Hyde Park Gardens.

Residuary legatee under her stepmother's will; afterwards housekeeps for Erridge at Thrubworth. Works for an animal sanctuary after his death, meeting the animals on their own terms and acting as diplomatic link with drug addicts and drop-outs such as her niece Fiona Cutts.

LM 19, 35–6, 42, 75. CCR 57, 60–1, her dottiness analyzed 69–70; 83, 96. KO 116, 143–4, 205. VB 151. BDFR 28, 41, 61, 63–6, 71, 84–7, 131. HSH 7–12, 198.

TOLLAND, Lady Frederica see BUDD, Lady Frederica

TOLLAND, Hon George
Lord Warminster's frightfully correct second son, contemporary of Jenkins at school, resigns from the Coldstream Guards to go into the City. By no means a fool though never at all adept at making money and widely considered a bore. Joins with his sister Frederica in deploring their stepmother's eccentricities, Erridge's shortcomings ('George's line about Erridge was pity rather than blame') etc. M. Veronica Collins in the early 'thirties. Rejoins his regiment on the outbreak of war as captain (later major, lt-colonel, colonel); wounded in Middle Eastern campaign against Rommel; d., after two years in hospital in Cairo, a few months before Erridge. One son, Jeremy, b. posthumously c. 1947.

AW 187. LM 28, 30, 35, 38. CCR 60–1, 66–8, 71–3, 75–7, 84–6, 94–5, 125, 130. KO 239. VB 112. MP 68, 149, 222. BDFR His death and funeral contrasted with Erridge's 38–42, 44–5, 50–1, 53, 58, 86–7; 131, 170.

TOLLAND, Hon Hugo
The youngest, most amusing and, from his family's point of view, least satisfactory of Lord Warminster's sons. Encompassed by a thick sea mist of gossip from an early age. Was sick as a child over St John Clarke. Several times narrowly escapes being sent down in the early 'thirties from the university, where he wears the most extraordinary clothes at a time when aestheticism is hopelessly out of date and becomes the only undergraduate ever known to have got the better of Sillery (by distributing pro-Franco pamphlets to a Labour MP at one of the latter's tea parties). Confounds his relatives by scraping a degree and getting a job with the fashionable antique-and-decorating firm, Baldwyn Hodges Ltd.

Sells a pair of ormolu candlesticks to Max Pilgrim and moves in with him on Lady Warminster's death. Enlists as a gunner in second war; no desire for a commission ('you meet such awful types in the Officers' Mess'); lance-bombardier on S. coast. Opens his own antique shop after the war in partnership with an army friend called Sam. Might have fallen for Pamela Widmerpool, if he were given to falling for women.

Rather a sad figure in the 'sixties after Sam's death, beginning to resemble his aunt Molly Jeavons ('I flatter myself I'm much what she'd have become had she remained unmarried').

LM 33–4, 39. CCR 57, 61, 68, 175, his character and career 199–202, 222–3. KO 97, 143–5, 197, 239. VB 112. SA 78, 153–4. BDFR 10, 38–9, 73–4, 79–80, 83–7, 90, 129, 131, 172. TK 225. HSH 7–11, 25, 35, 198–9, 251.

TOLLAND, Lady Isobel

Eighth of Lord Warminster's ten children, generally agreed to be different from the rest of her family ('I believe she's a bit of a highbrow when she isn't going to nightclubs': Chips Lovell). Meets Jenkins at Thrubworth in 1934, soon after Jean Duport left him ('Would it be too explicit, too exaggerated, to say that when I set eyes on Isobel Tolland, I knew at once that I should marry her?'), engaged to him that autumn, m. shortly afterwards.

Very early twenties; long legs, deep blue eyes, tweed suit; conforms, though less completely than her sister Susan, to the Tolland physical type: 'Tall and thin, all of them possessed a touch of that angularity of feature most apparent in Erridge himself . . . In the girls this inclination to severity of outline had been bred down, leaving only a liveliness of expression and underlying sense of melancholy: this last characteristic to some extent masked by a great pressure of high spirits notably absent in Erridge'. Same age as Matilda Wilson; gets on well with the Morelands; takes a dim view of Widmerpool (one of the reasons for Jenkins' losing touch with him round about this time). Miscarriage in 1936. Plays Pride in the Seven Deadly Sins tableaux at Stourwater. Evacuated to her sister Frederica Budd's house on outbreak of war. Two sons, b. 1940 and 1946.

Sceptical, inquisitive, discreet, well-informed, rarely expresses an opinion. Greatly dislikes Odo Stevens. Authority on the works of St John Clarke, rivals X. Trapnel in knowledge of obscure or forgotten fiction. Under Pisces, and rebels against it.

LM Mention of her name appeals instinctively to Jenkins 19, 36; 92; first sight of at Thrubworth 135–9, 143–6, 148–50, 152–3; Jenkins' engagement to 203, 205, 208, 210; Lady Molly's party for 216, 218–20. CCR 56; in nursing home 62, 70, 72; recovering from a miscarriage, reflections on marriage and the impossibility of writing about it 97, 99; does not care for Widmerpool 85, 102–3; 111; well-disposed towards

Matilda 130, 133–4, 137–8; at Mrs Foxe's party 140, 153, 170, 172–3, 186–7, 189; 198, 204, 216, 223, 227–9. KO 85–6; staying with the Morelands 88–90, 94, 96–7, 99, 101, at Stourwater 106–7, 110, 118, 120, performance as Pride 126, 128–32, 139; starting a baby 146–7; evacuated 204, 206, 213; 223–4, 232, 238–40, 242. VB 16, 39, 110–12; wartime leave spent with 135, 137, 139, 142–8, 150–1, 167; birth of a son, Jenkins missing her 169–72; 196, 206. SA 4–6, 107, 162, 165. MP 20–1, 75, 80–1, 96–101, 200, 209, 213. BDFR 27, at Erridge's funeral 38, 42, 54–9, 63; at Jean's party 94, 97, 101, 124; birth of another son 169–70, 182; 189, 214, 237. TK 153–4, 212, at Stevens' party 225–6, 232, on St John Clarke 234–6, 240, 243, 248, 250–2. HSH Takes part in crayfishing expedition 2–3, 5, 7, 11, 13, 17, 23–4, 28–9; 39–40, 46, her performance as Pride recalled 59–60, 62, 83; at Donners prize dinner 91, 96–8, 105; at quarry meeting 149–50, 152, 160, 173; at Akworth wedding 187, 189, 194–5, 231; 248, 254–5.

TOLLAND, Jeremy see WARMINSTER, Earl of (Jeremy)

TOLLAND, Lady Norah
Only one of Lord Warminster's children who never got on with their stepmother; on especially poor terms with her eldest sister Frederica; swears and dresses like a stable boy, according to her aunt Molly Jeavons. Dark and very pale, narrow face and truculent expression. Capable of making herself disagreeable if she chooses. Sets up a ménage with Eleanor Walpole-Wilson in the early 'thirties, despises the whole male sex and is thrilled by Heather Hopkins.

Takes up politics a few years later, backs the Reds in Spain, no longer on speaking terms with Hopkins. Driver in the women's service run by Gwen McReith in wartime. One of Pamela Flitton's girlfriends and early victims. Looks well in uniform. Thinks Pamela's marriage to Widmerpool a tragic mistake.

Leaves Eleanor after the war, works for a car hire firm as driver (later director), flat in Battersea. Living alone with a pair of pugs bequeathed to her by Eleanor in the late 'sixties.

AW 108, 187. LM 19, 32–3, 84, visits to her and Eleanor's flat 89–97; 117, 135–6, 183, 201, 208. CCR 60, 66–7, 70, 96, 130, 132–3, 198, 200, 222. KO 97, 143–4, 204, 206. VB 138, 187. SA 164. MP 75–6, at Ted Jeavons' party with Pamela Flitton 79–81; 123, 199. BDFR At Erridge's funeral 38, 40, 53–4, 63–4, 73–4, 77, 84–9. HSH 8–11, 198–9.

TOLLAND, Lady Priscilla
Youngest of Lord Warminster's ten children, first realized her eldest brother Erridge was mad when she was seven ('Something about the

way he was eating his pudding. I knew I must be growing up myself when I grasped that'). Blonde and leggy and just left school at the time of Jenkins' engagement to her nearest sister Isobel; Chips Lovell working on plans for her long term seduction.

Job with an organization raising funds for the promotion of opera by 1936. Aged about twenty. Clandestine affair with Moreland who contemplates divorce for her sake but never actually sleeps with her and agrees to part in the spring of 1937. Engaged to Chips Lovell a week later.

Grows quieter, sadder and more beautiful after her marriage to Chips. One daughter, Caroline. Affair with Odo Stevens; turns up with him at the Café Royal and stages a scene in 1941; possibly driven by the need to make men unhappy ('There was something of the kind in her face. Perhaps she was simply tormenting Stevens now for a change; so to speak, varying the treatment. If so, she might have her work cut out to disturb him in the way she was disturbing Lovell; had formerly disturbed Moreland'). Killed in the air raid on her aunt Molly Jeavons' house later that night.

LM Pursued by Chips Lovell 19–20, 36, 42, 49; 75, 89, 91, 117. CCR 57, at home in her stepmother's house 69–70, 92, 96; relations with Moreland 137–40, 142, Matilda on their affair 153–7, 160–1; with Moreland at Mrs Foxe's party 173–5, 178–81, 185, 187, 189; course of their affair 193–4, 204; its termination 219–21; engaged to Chips 224–5, 227, 229. KO Her marriage 86–8; affair with Moreland recalled 97, 105; Moreland on 243–4, 246–7. VB 112, at her sister Frederica's house, meets Stevens 137–9, 142–4, 146–7, 158–9, 164, 166–7, 169. SA Trouble with Chips 74; their marriage 89–92; Chips on her affair with Stevens 106–13, 117; at Café Royal with Stevens, meets Moreland 124–33, scene with Stevens, speculation on their relationship 136–46; 148, 150, 158–9; her death 161–2, 166; 222. MP Stevens' remorse over 124–5; 136.

TOLLAND, Hon Robert

Seventh child and third son of Lord Warminster, b. *c.* 1912, the most congenial of Jenkins' brothers-in-law. Tall, cleanshaven, has his family's blue eyes and characteristic angularity of form. A secretive character with some of Erridge's oddness, much of George's conventionality ('All the same, a faint suggestion of dissipation was always to be found in Robert . . . something that affirmed to those with an instinct for recognizing such things at long range, the existence in the neighbourhood of vaguely irregular behaviour'), and possibly a trace of Blanche's dottiness. Charming manners and faint likeness to Archie Gilbert. Job in export house trading in Far East; lives at home with his stepmother; suspected by Chips Lovell of a taste for nightclub hostesses old enough to be his mother.

Joins up as Lance-Corporal in Field Security, Intelligence Corps ('The army had increased his hungry, even rather wolfish appearance'); starts an affair with Stringham's much older sister Flavia Wisebite; passes up the chance of a commission in favour of wangling an immediate posting to France, and is killed in 1940 fighting before the Channel ports.

LM 36. CCR 43, 57; at his stepmother's luncheon party, his character and secret life 60–3, 67–70, 90; 135–7, 153–4, 161, 188–9, 221–2, 224–5, 227–8. KO 143–4, 239. VB 112, at Frederica Budd's on leave with Mrs Wisebite, speculation on their affair 137–40, 145–8, 157–64, 166–7; his death, reflections on his fate 196–7. SA 78. HSH 201–2.

TOLLAND, Lady Susan

Daughter of Lord Warminster, aged about 24 or 25 in 1934, m. the Tory backbencher Roddy Cutts. Pretty, lively, ambitious like her husband, enjoys giving small political dinner parties at their hideous little mansion flat in Westminster. George's favourite sister. Two sons, Jonathan and Sebastian, one daughter, Fiona. Behaves impeccably over Roddy's wartime romance with a cypherine in Persia and establishes complete ascendancy over him in consequence.

LM 35, newly engaged, with Isobel at Thrubworth 135–41, 143–50, 152–3; 210. CCR 68, 72–3, 77, 85–8. KO 90. VB 112. BDFR 38–40, 78, 80, 87–8, 101, 169–70, 180, 182. HSH 5–7, 10, 78, 195–8, 260.

TOLLAND, Veronica

George Tolland's wife, a big blonde energetic divorcée, somewhat older than her husband; has him to all appearances wholly under her thumb. Two children by her previous marriage to a businessman called Fred Collins. Daughter of a provincial auctioneer near Stourwater, was at school with Matilda Wilson. Widowed in 1946, gives birth to George's son and Erridge's heir, Jeremy, and brings him up at Thrubworth, moving back to London with considerable relief on his coming of age.

CCR 68, 70–2, 75, 85, 130–1. BDFR 29, 39, 131. HSH 192, 194, 200.

TOMPSITT ('Tompy')

Spare man of dubious origins ('Goodness knows where he comes from': Sir Gavin Walpole-Wilson) and unconventional education ('though his air of incivility that so delighted Sir Gavin could no doubt have been inculcated with at least equal success at any public school') at the Walpole-Wilsons' dinner party in 1928 or 9. Large, fair, scruffy in appearance and supercilious in manner. Not particularly enthusiastic admirer of Barbara Goring, bitterly resented by Jenkins as a rival ('his approach to her, or so it seemed to me, was conditioned entirely by the ebb and flow of his own vanity: no inconsiderable element when gauged at any given moment, though laying a course hard for an unsympathetic observe to chart'). Cramming for the Foreign Office, protegé of Sir Gavin who sees in him a newer, and less restricted, vehicle for handling foreign affairs. Almost the first to recognize innate ability in Widmerpool.

Respectable but unglamorous diplomatic post by the time of the second war. Afterwards ambassador to the E. European People's Republic formerly ruled by Theodoric's brother ('The air of disorder, marking out Tompsitt in his early days as a young diplomatist free from the conventionality ascribed to his kind, had settled down into a middle-aged unkemptness, implying chronic irritability, as much as a free spirit').

BM Jenkins' jealousy of 37–9; at Walpole-Wilsons' 41–4, 47–9, 51–4; with Barbara, Jenkins & Widmerpool at the Huntercombes' ball 63–7, 70, 74–5; 88, 122, 133, 153, 268. MP 104–8. TK 232–3, 236.

TOMPSITT, Mrs
Large, ill-favoured, menacing wife of above, Schweizer-Deutsch, rather rich and been married before.

TK 232–3, 236.

TRAPNEL, X. (Francis Xavier)
Novelist of irregular habits, uncompromising ambition and indomitable panache. Makes a startling impact on literary London in 1945 with *Camel Ride to the Tomb*, and is promptly signed up as one of Quiggin & Craggs' new authors. Becomes a frequent contributor to *Fission*. Ranks high in Jenkins' estimation as a writer. Looks about 30. Tall, dark, emaciated, bearded ('even if the beard, assessed with the clothes and the stick he carried, marked him out as an exhibitionist in a reasonably high category, the singularity was more on account of elements within himself than from outward appearance'). Dyed officer's greatcoat, swordstick with carved skull-shaped knob ('This stick clearly bulked large in Trapnel equipment') and general air of the 1890s: 'the final effect had that touch of surrealism that redeems from complete absurdity, though such redemption was a near thing, only narrowly achieved'.

Lapsed Roman Catholic, middle eastern background, only child of an obscure, even faintly shady figure with possible Secret Service connections (who later turns out to have been a perfectly respectable jockey married to an English girl in Egypt). Orderly-room clerk in

RAF Public Relations, New Delhi, in second war. First phase of the Trapnel myth propagated in the semi-autobiographical *Camel Ride to the Tomb*; took his title from a phrase intoned by a turbaned Arab to the Trapnel family party on a childhood outing ('I grasped at once that's what life was. How could the description be bettered? Juddering through the wilderness, on an uncomfortable conveyance you can't properly control, along a rocky, unpremeditated, but indefeasible track, towards the destination crudely, yet truly, stated').

An egotist of the first rank. Habitual role-player, unique in this field for the number and variety of his chosen roles ('they were ... not only hard to achieve individually but, even in rotation, impossible to combine'). Rivals Bagshaw in encyclopaedic knowledge of London pubs; generally to be found in the Hero of Acre, dominating the length of the saloon bar with impersonations of favourite film stars, notably Boris Karloff, or laying down the law on literature in absolutely unstemmable monologue. Panoramic memory for the plots of virtually every English novel published this century. Accomplished parodist (of Evadne Clapham, Alaric Kydd, Widmerpool etc.). Volume of short stories, *Bin Ends*, pub. 1947; working on a major novel, *Profiles in String*; also toys with plans for a critical manifesto to be called *The Heresy of Naturalism* ('I'm in favour of naturalism. I write that way myself. All I want to make clear is that it's just a way of writing a novel like any other, just as contrived, just as selective').

Travels exclusively by taxi on the grounds 'that taxis provided a security, denied to the man on foot, against bailiffs serving writs for debt'. Never known to have failed to extract a loan ('he borrowed literally to keep alive'), even from Widmerpool. Rapid turnover in girlfriends. Lives at the brink of destitution, camping out in borrowed flats, seedy hotels in Paddington or Bayswater, occasionally on the Embankment. Remarkably free for a writer ('let alone a novelist') from self-pity.

Bowled over by a sudden infatuation for Pamela Widmerpool at the beginning of 1947; runs away with her and goes to ground in the semi-derelict area north of Maida Vale. Ill, in debt, goaded by Pamela about his writing. *Profiles in String* nearing completion. Is confronted in his lair by Widmerpool, and draws his swordstick. Tormented by Pamela's insatiable sexual demands, and by fear of losing her. Abandoned by Pamela that summer; finds the manuscript of *Profiles in String* dumped as her parting gesture in the Maida Vale Canal; hurls his swordstick after it.

Drifts downstream thereafter. Goes underground, emerging to haunt an increasingly gruesome and desolate world, and maintaining survival of a sort by intermittent substandard hack work: 'The roving intelligentsia of the saloon bar – cultural nomads of a race never likely to penetrate the international steppe – professional topers, itinerant bores, near-criminals, knew him no more'. Surfaces again in the early 'fifties to spend £100 in notes on a single glorious night at the Hero of Acre ('never had the Hero known a night like that for free drinks'); collapses in the gutter at closing time, and d. in hospital a few hours later.

His early conte, *Dogs Have No Uncles*, pub. posthumously with an introduction by L. O. Salvidge. A biography, *Death's-Head Swordsman*, by the American scholar Russell Gwinnett pub. 1968.

For his views on the art of the novel, see Book Index.

BDFR 24, Bagshaw on his wartime background 33–4; 36, 74; first impressions of, his personality, past history and passionate approach to writing, background of *The Camel* 103–14; 116; at *Fission* party, his doctrine of panache 121–2, 124, makes advances to Widmerpool, takes an instant dislike to Pamela 132–7, 139–40; 141; his life and legend, nature of the odds stacked against him, confesses his love for Pamela 143–68; bolts with Pamela, his parody of Widmerpool pub. in *Fission* 179–87; visit to his flat, relations with Pamela, confrontation with Widmerpool 188–205; 207–8; his views on naturalism, recollections of the night on which Pamela deserted him and destroyed his ms 210–29; 235, 237–8; reflections on his subsequent disintegration 240–1. TK 14, an account of his decline and death, and of Pamela's part in both, prompted by Gwinnett's questioning 23–38, 40–1; 45, 49, 61, 74; Gwinnett's attempts to extract information about him from Pamela 95, 101–3, 112, 116, 134, 149, 152, 156, 158–9, 163, her account of dumping his ms, threatens to destroy his *Commonplace Book* 169–74; Gwinnett's further researches into and attempts to reconstruct his life 176–7, 180–1, 184–6, 189–90, 195, 197–201, 212, 215; his views on naturalism recalled 218–22; 234, 237, 249, 252; Gwinnett's biography shelved 267–8. HSH 32, 41, 43, 54–5, 58, Gwinnett's biography submitted for Donners Prize 67–71, 75–6; his views on biography v. the novel recalled, his own biography assessed and awarded Donners prize 84–6, 88, 91, 94–5, 99, 101, 106–7, 110, 166, 178.

TREADWELL, Corporal
Bottle-nosed NCO in Stringham's Mobile Laundry Unit.

SA 218–18.

TREE, Sir Herbert Beerbohm 1838–1905
See IRVING, Sir Henry.

TRELAWNEY, Dr
Thaumaturge and seer; first encountered running a cult ('of which he

was high priest, if not actually messiah') near Stonehurst in 1914; haunts Jenkins' imagination as a child. No more a doctor than his name is Trelawney (started life as Grubb or Tibbs, according to Moreland). Approaching middle age; silky beard, long hair, white robe, uncomfortably Biblical air; often to be seen out running through the heather at the head of a pack of disciples in pursuit of Oneness. Watchword: 'The Essence of the All is the Godhead of the True'. Response: 'The Vision of Visions heals the Blindness of Sight'. Financed by the Faithful, especially women, and thought by Mr Deacon to be making a good thing out of it. Has long had his eye on General Conyers as a potential recruit to Oneness.

Subsequently moves on from callisthenics, yoga and the Simple Life to more occult concerns. Known by sight to Moreland's aunt at one point*; musical interests of the most banal kind ('I remember the wonderfully fraudulent look on his face as he sat listening to Strauss' *Death and Transfiguration*': Moreland); dresses in black, looks like Rasputin and is said to have enjoyed the favours of succubi on the Astral Plane. Drives a female disciple to suicide at his temple in North Wales, causing public scandal ('There was talk of nameless rites, drugs, disagreeable forms of discipline – the sort of thing that might rather appeal to Sir Magnus Donners': Moreland). Later turns up in Shepherd's Bush as an acquaintance of Maclintick with whom he once attended some German university; and later still crosses swords with Canon Fenneau ('Trelawney was at that time engaged in certain practices to which he did not wish attention to be drawn. He sheered off': Fenneau).

Installed in the Bellevue residential hotel at the time of Uncle Giles' death in 1939. Friend of Myra Erdleigh, fellow guest of Bob Duport. Abandoned by his disciples, unable to pay his bill, suffering horribly from asthma:

'Even the beard, straggling, dirty grey, stained yellow in places like the patches of broom on the common beyond Stonehurst, had lost all resemblance to that worn by the athletic, vigorous prophet of those distant days. Once broad and luxuriant, it was now shrivelled almost to a goatee . . . His sky was dry and blotched. Dark spectacles covered his eyes, his dressing-gown a long blue oriental robe that swept the ground. He really looked rather frightening.'

Prophesies concerning the forthcoming tide of death and destruction. Quasi-hypnotic powers ('His smile was one of the worst things about him'). Depends on Mrs Erdleigh for drugs, and d. when supplies run out in the early years of the war.

* This must have been a few years after his Stonehurst period (see KO 83–5, HSH 34 *et passim*) though KO 83 suggests some slight confusion over dates.

His beliefs revived in the late 'sixties by cult practitioners such as Scorpio Murtlock, who holds himself to be a reincarnation of Trelawney and goes to some lengths organizing rites intended to raise him from the dead.

KO At Stonehurst in 1914, his career and cult 28–33, encounter with General Conyers 63–9, 73–4; Moreland's reminiscences of 82–5; 107; at the Bellevue in 1939 152–4, 162, 174, accidentally locks himself in the bathroom, is rescued by Duport and expounds his philosophy 183–99, 202; 204, 216. VB 39, 113–14, 196. SA 123, 166. MP 35, his death 137; 241. HSH His creed revived 34–6; 86, 117; Canon Fenneau on 128–9; summoned by Murtlock 167, 235.

TRUSCOTT, Bill

Professional charmer and prime favourite of Sillery at the university, 'one of those persons who, from their earliest years, are marked down to do great things'. Tall and dark with wavy hair and regular features caught rather too close together; son of a Harley Street specialist from whom he inherited a respectable capital. Personal assistant to Sir Magnus Donners by 1923, and hanger-on of Mrs Foxe. Five or six years ahead of Jenkins, Quiggin, Members etc., and seems a positively frightening figure in their first year at university; not yet made up his mind whether to become prime minister, lord chancellor or a great poet (possibly all three). Recruits Stringham for Donners Brebner.

Still carving out a career by 1928 or 9, his promise as yet undimmed. Greying round the ears and perilously near thirty. Especially popular with dowagers ('his eyes wandered round the ballroom "earmarking duchesses", as Stringham . . . once called that wistful, haunted intensity Truscott's eyes took on, from time to time') and with elderly bankers. Primarily interested in power. Is among the first to take Widmerpool seriously, and finds a job for him at Donners Brebner.

Promptly recognized as a potential rival by Widmerpool, who engineers his dismissal from the firm in the early 'thirties. Never recovers his status as a coming man, and goes downhill thereafter in by-products of coal. Immured for life after the second war in some dim niche at the Coal Board. Is bitter about not being asked to Sillery's ninetieth birthday party in the late 'fifties but finds some consolation in 'hopes of the very worst for Widmerpool'.

QU At Sillery's tea party, wooed by Quiggin and Members 183–90; selects Stringham for post at Donners Brebner 204–9, 216–7. BM 123, at Mrs Andriadis' party, enlists Widmerpool for Donners Brebner 129–35, 137–9; at Stourwater 186, 188–90, 195–6, 198–202, 205, 210–11; 242, 253, 270. AW Sacked by Donners 46, 205. LM His dim view of Widmerpool 73–5. BDFR Sillery on his blighted promise 8–10, 12. TK 208, last encounter with 215–17, 219. HSH 125.

TUDOR
Clerk to the Jenkinses' local Rural District Council in 1968, key figure in the conservationist campaign against nefarious quarrymen ('Mr Tudor . . . possessed a profile that recalled his shared surname with Henry VII, the same thoughtful shrewdness, if necessary, ruthlessness; the latter, should the interests of the RDC be threatened').

HSH 150, 153, 173.

TURNBULL, WELFORD & PUCKERING
The firm of solicitors in Lincoln's Inn to which Widmerpool was articled on leaving school.

QU 133. BM 32. BDFR 131, 172. TK 142.

UDALL, Jock
Rosie Manasch's first husband, heir apparent to the newspaper proprietor called Udall who is the arch enemy of Sir Magnus Donners; said to have given his wife a good many ups-and-downs before being shot after a mass escape from a German POW camp in second war.

CCR 177. MP 244. BDFR 100.

UDALL, Rosie see MANASCH, Rosie

UDNEY, Jock
Elderly widower, job at court, rumoured to have been turned down by Frederica Budd at Ascot when the Gold Cup was actually being run.

LM 5. VB 137.

UMFRAVILLE, Lady Anne see STEPNEY, Lady Anne

UMFRAVILLE, Dicky
Well-known wit and womaniser, professional cad by his own account, old friend of Boffles Stringham, Eddie Bridgnorth, Hugo Warminster etc., and lifelong enemy of Buster Foxe. Gentleman-rider ('His face, in repose, possessed that look of innate sadness which often marks the features of those habituated to the boundless unreliability of horses'), came second one year in the Grand National. Left Le Bas' house at school under a cloud (though, contrary to rumour, not actually sacked) at least fifteen years before Stringham. Belongs to the generation separated from Jenkins' contemporaries by the first war: 'They partook of both eras, specially forming the tone of the postwar years; much more so, indeed, than the younger people. Most of them, like Umfraville, were melancholy; perhaps from the strain of living simultaneously in two different historical periods . . .'

Spell in Kenya (where he seduced Boffles Stringham's daughter Flavia) during the 'twenties; knew Milly Andriadis in Cuba and Mildred Haycock at Cannes; has spent time in the States and once won a packet on a horse ridden by X. Trapnel's father in Cairo. 'The mystery surrounded him that belongs to strong characters who have only pottered about in life.' Medium height, even rather small; trim, horsey, elegant, irresistibly friendly in manner. His charm heightened by disturbing undercurrents ('There was a suggestion of madness in the way he shot out his sentences; not the kind of madness that was raving, or even, in the ordinary sense, dangerous; but a warning that no proper mechanism existed for operating normal controls'). Probably in his forties when first encountered at Foppa's in 1933. Worried by the lack of parties and the upsurge of dreadfully serious talk about economics or world disarmament; removes Lady Anne Stepney from Barnby. Turns up again a year later, newly divorced, more than usually on the rocks and running the extremely unpromising night club at which Templer entertains Widmerpool.

Son of an improvident breeder of horses who had the presence of mind to marry the daughter of a fairly well-to-do manufacturer of elastic webbing. Scraped a commission in the Brigade of Guards in 1914, fought in Flanders and was all set to become a general when he fell foul of Buster Foxe, who broke up his first marriage and indirectly ditched his army career. M. (1) towards the end of the first war Dolly Braybrooke, who killed herself for love of Buster (2) immediately afterwards Joy Grant, a lady of the town on whose account he was obliged to resign his commission and leave the country (whereupon she bolted with Lord Castlemallock) (3) the wife of a district commissioner in Kenya, who d. of enteric six months later (4) in 1933 Lord Bridgnorth's daughter Anne Stepney, who divorced him after a year ('"Charming child, but the fact was I was too old for her. She didn't like grown-up life – and who shall blame her?" He sighed. "I don't like it much myself," he said') (5) in 1940 Lord Warminster's daughter Frederica Budd ('Took me five attempts, even if I placed the right bet in the end'). No children by any of these marriages; his claim to have fathered Flavia Stringham's daughter, Pamela Flitton, sceptically received by Jenkins.

Railway Transport Officer, London District, in second war; fails to blackmail Buster into getting him a secret job. Promoted Major in charge of a transit camp, later transferred to Civil Affairs. Lt.-Col. with the Control Commission in Germany by 1946. Afterwards land agent at Thrubworth. Retired by 1958; overtaken by all but chronic melancholy ('Christ, what a shambles. Feeling my back too. Trumpeter, what are you sounding now? – *Defaulters*, old boy, if your name's Jerry

Hat-Trick. You know growing old's like being increasingly penalized for a crime you haven't committed'); greatly cheered by Buster Foxe's death. Last seen at a nephew's wedding in 1971, close on eighty, growing deaf, walking with a stick. Has acquired a rather good new impersonation of himself as an old-fashioned drug fiend.

QU Sillery on 176. BM Stringham on 104. AW at Foppa's, his temperament and type, takes a fancy to Anne Stepney and insists on taking the club's entire clientèle to call on Mrs Andriadis 147, 151–65, 167–9; 177; m. to Anne Stepney 185–7, 200; 206, 213. LM At his night club 172–4, 179–83, 185–7, 194, 199, 201–2, 216. CCR 175, 182, 184. KO 81, 101, 106, 113–14, 231. VB 47, at Frederica Budd's house, their engagement 140–2, 144–6, confides the story of his life, his marriages and his hatred of Buster Foxe 149–56, 158–9, encounter with Buster, their mutual loathing 161–4, 166–7; 170, 227. SA 51. MP 74, 115–16, 140, 182, 185. BDFR 38–9, 62–4, 88–90; claims to be Pamela Flitton's father 91–2; 112, 241. TK 2–3, 38, 104. HSH 60–1, at Cutt's wedding 189–91, encounter with Flavia Wisebite (née Stringham) 199–201; 238.

UMFRAVILLE, Lady Frederica see BUDD, Lady Frederica

UMFRAVILLE, R. H. J.
Alfred Tolland's fag at school, not to be confused with Dicky Umfraville.

AW 185. BDFR 64.

UPDIKE, Betty see WILSON, Matilda

UPJOHN, Victor
Widmerpool's notion of a first-rate man; comes to grief through Widmerpool's double-dealing over the Recce Unit command in 1941.

SA 31–2, 203–4.

VAALKIIPAA
Sad and anxious Finn, rather old for an undergraduate, at Sillery's tea party in 1924.

QU 176–80, 183.

VALENTINO, Rudolph 1895–1926
Film star closely resembled by Jean Duport's young second husband Colonel Flores.

KO 181. MP 234. BDFR 96, 112.

VAN DER VOORT, Colonel
Dutch military attaché, looks like a round, red-faced, carousing clown

by Teniers or Brouwer; flies out with Jenkins' party to inspect allied lines in 1944 ('Van der Voort was in his most boisterous form, seeming to belong to some anachronistic genre picture, *Boors at an Airport* or *The Airfield Kermesse*, executed by one of the lesser Netherlands masters').

MP 31, 88–9, 151, 154–5, 178–9, 181, 215.

VAUGHAN, Richard
Shared Jenkins' governess at Stonehurst in 1914, his father killed in the war.

KO 51, 74.

VAVASSOR
Porter at the War Office in Whitehall.

MP 32, 51–4, 236, 239.

VENIZELOS, Eleutherios 1864–1936
Greek patriot and prime minister, hobnobbed with Sunny Farebrother at the Paris Peace Conference.

QU 85.

VERA
Waitress at the Ufford, old enemy of Uncle Giles.

AW 2.

VICTOR EMMANUEL II 1820–78
King of Sardinia and Italy, bore a marked resemblance to Foppa.

AW 145.

VICTORIA, Queen 1819–1901
Related to Prince Theodoric, made Lord Aberavon a peer and placed a touching faith in Uncle Giles' loyalty, courage and good conduct.

BM 80, 122. KO 157–9.

VORTIGERN fl. 450
Ruler of south-east Britain, famed for his supposed treachery and for a union with one of his own daughters; direct ancestor by this incestuous match of Lord Aberavon, Barbara Goring and Eleanor Walpole-Wilson.

VB 188–9.

VOWCHURCH, Lord Family name Blaides
The friend of Edward VII who loosed half a dozen monkeys in tailcoats

and white ties at an ambassadorial ball, and once made the Jenkins'
cook Albert (then a footman) yell by putting a mouse down his sleeve.
As notorious for ill-temper at home as for horseplay abroad. Father of
Bertha Conyers, Mildred Haycock and four other daughters, all of
whom he bullied unmercifully for not having been born boys. See
Painting Index under SPY.

LM 4–5, 7, 23, 34, 87–8, 200–1. KO 10–11, 35–6, 40, 57–8.

VOWCHURCH, Lord
Baby Wentworth's father, cousin of above, comes into the title on his
death.

LM 200.

VOWCHURCH, Lord (Jack)
Baby Wentworth's brother, believed by Mrs Haycock to be rather hell.

BM 125. LM 200.

WAGNER, Richard 1813–83
Another of the famous figures dimly connected to Moreland's uncle,
who once heard him conduct at the Albert Hall.

CCR 4, 101, 104. SA 92. MP Mime in *The Ring* impersonated by the
wizened lieutenant in charge of Signals at the War Office 2–4, 34, 164,
218.

WALPOLE-WILSON, Eleanor
Only child of Sir Gavin and Lady Walpole-Wilson, doing the season at
the time of Jenkins' affair with her cousin Barbara Goring. Detests
dances. Large, brusque, awkward, always more or less of a problem.
Does her hair in a bun behind and keeps a dog-kennel in her parents'
drawing-room (she was always accustomed to act, in principle, as if
London were the country, an exercise of will she rarely relaxed').
Consistently severe towards young men. Disapproving at the Huntercombes' ball, bored to death at Sir Magnus Donners' luncheon party ('I
had . . . by then been wholly converted to Barbara's view that "Eleanor
was not a bad old girl when you know her"'), shipped off with her
Aunt Janet on a banana boat to Guatemala shortly afterwards.

Stuck in the country breeding Labradors until rescued by Norah
Tolland with whom she shares a flat in Chelsea throughout the 'thirties.
Smokes, wears trousers, moves in vastly different circles from her
cousin ('I found myself brought up short . . . like a horse reined in on
the brink of a precipice, at the thought of the astonishing reversal of
circumstances by which Eleanor Walpole-Wilson was now in a
position to feel sorry for Barbara Goring . . .'); plainly on much better
terms with herself, and others, than formerly. No truth in rumours

spread by Lady Molly that she has been seen about in a green pork pie hat and bow tie.

Toys with Roman Catholicism at the time of Heather Hopkins' conversion ('Hugo says that puts Eleanor in a dilemma. She wants to annoy Norah, but doesn't want to please Hopkins'). Enrols as a driver in second war. Middle thirties by 1941: 'she retained an air of never having properly assimilated to either sex. At the same time, big and broad-shouldered, she was not exactly a "mannish" woman. Her existence might have been more viable had that been so'. Afterwards takes to local politics, seat on the Urban District Council. Embarks on a close relationship with a Swedish woman doctor, and d. in Stockholm some time in the 'sixties.

BM Introduces Jenkins to Barbara 16–18; problems posed by, dinner at her parents' house 21–4, 27, 33, 36, 39–42, 49, 54–5; at the Huntercombes' 58–60, 64, 74–5; at home in the country, visit to Stourwater 175–7, 179–84, 187, 195, 200, 202, 209–10, 212, 219–22; 224, 263–4, 266. AW 107–8, 120, 187. LM Living with Norah Tolland 19, 32–3, 84; visit to their flat 89–97; 183, 201. CCR 96, 130, 132, 202. KO 97, 206. SA 132; takes charge after the bomb on the Jeavons' house 161–5. HSH Death 10–11; 250.

WALPOLE-WILSON, Sir Gavin, KCMG

Retired diplomat ('that fellow . . . who made such a hash of things in South America': General Conyers) with a keen sense of grievance and a strong line in nostalgic reminiscence. 'Although not at all inclined to under-estimate the personal part he had played in the Councils of Europe, or, indeed, of the World, Sir Gavin was apt to give the impression that he was always anxious, even in the smallest maters, to justify himself . . .' Marked resemblance in temperament and outlook to Uncle Giles. Large square horn-rimmed spectacles, moustache, slight limp, rather fierce expression like an angry rajah; wears his hair long and favours loose shaggy suits. Makes the most of the captive audience provided by young men like Jenkins and Widmerpool at dinner parties given for his daughter ('His attitude to Eleanor varied between almost doting affection and an approach most easily suggested by the phrase "making the best of a bad job". There were times when she vexed him'). House in Eaton Square, country seat Hinton Hoo.

Especially sensitive on the score of his own inglorious career (junior secretary in the East; Chargé d'Affaires in the Balkans where he was a favourite with Prince Theodoric's father; obliged to resign as minister to a South American republic after a comparatively minor mistake in timing over a coup d'état; voluntary work for refugees at the end of the first war in Paris where he made the acquaintance of Jenkins' parents). Touchy about his family background (landed gentry fallen on hard times who had difficulty scraping together enough money to get him into the Foreign Office). Acquired a fortune on his marriage to one of Lord Aberavon's daughters. Possibly a disappointment to his wife ('it had . . . to be admitted that some fundamental support sustaining the Walpole-Wilson family life had become at some stage of existence slightly displaced, so that a visit to Hinton, as to all households where something fundamental has gone obscurely wrong, was set against an atmosphere of tensity').

Resigned to Eleanor's fiasco on the marriage market by the early 'thirties; looks no older, possibly a shade less sane. D. 1942.

BM 1, 13–15, his history and character 19–20; Jenkins dines with 23–5, 28–30, 35, 37–9, 41–50, 52–4; at the Huntercombes' 56–7, 61; 77–8, 99, 122, 132, 162; weekend spent with, relations with his family, visit to Stourwater 174–88, 196, 210, 215, 217, 221, 223; 265, 271. AW 19, 42, at Isbister exhibition 107–9, 113; 187, 210. LM 5, 30, 33, 84. CCR 9. KO 79, 96–7, 109, 206, 222. VB 186. MP 50, his death 104. BDFR 109. HSH 1, 59, 250.

WALPOLE-WILSON, Janet
Seasoned traveller and woman of wide interests; unmarried younger sister of Sir Gavin; small, defiant and greatly admired by her niece Eleanor:

'She dressed usually in tones of brown and green, colours that gave her for some reason, possibly because her hats almost always conveyed the impression of being peaked, an air of belonging to some dedicated order of female officials, connected possibly with public service in the woods and forests, and bearing a load of responsibility, the extent of which was difficult for a lay person – even impossible if a male – to appreciate, or wholly to understand'.

Seriously concerned with the general welfare of the human race but apt to take exception to individuals such as Sir Magnus Donners, Johnny Pardoe, her brother etc. Makes a living in various capacities (secretary, governess, duenna) through her rich connections. Flat in Chelsea. Old ally of Widmerpool's mother ('there was an area of common ground where disparagement of other people brought them close together, if only on account of the ammunition with which each was able to provide the other: mutual aid that went far to explain a friendship long established'). Active on behalf of Bosnian Moslems for the Minority Problems League; in touch with Sillery over arms embargoes to Bolivia and Paraguay in the mid 'thirties; Women's Voluntary Service in second war.

BM 48, at Hinton Hoo 176–84; at Stourwater 187, 195, 200–2, 210, 215, 217, 220–1; at the Widmerpools' 261–9, 273. AW 113, 210. KO 115, 222–3.

WALPOLE-WILSON, Lady (Daisy)
Wife of Sir Gavin, daughter of Lord Aberavon, suffers from nervous
agitation only less severely than her sister Lady Goring. Dark,
distinguished, with doe-like eyes and a statuesque presence; almost
always especially discomposed at her own dinner parties ('Her own
eagerness of manner always suggested that Lady Walpole-Wilson
would have enjoyed asking congenial people to her parties if only she
could have found people who were, indeed, congenial to her'). Jenkins
decidedly fond of her.

BM 1, 13–15, her temperament and misfortunes, dinner at her house
19–25, 27–8, 32–3, 37–43, 47–50, 54–7, 74; 77–8, 86–7, 99, 122, 152,
162, weekend in the country with, and visit to Stourwater 174–5, 177,
179–84, 195, 218–21. AW 19, 42, 108–9. LM 5, 30, 84. CCR 9. KO
79, 96, 109. VB 186. MP 50. HSH 1, 59, 250.

WARMINSTER, First Earl of, Viscount Erridge, Barron Erridge of
Mirkbooths, GCB, Lieutenant-General etc. (Henry Lucius)
A quarrelsome peer, by no means indifferent to the charms of the fair
sex; considered a damned fool by the Duke of Wellington and likely to
prove a serious liability had he been present on the field of Waterloo.

LM 149. BDFR 43–4, 48.

WARMINSTER, Earl of ('the Chemist-Earl'), FRS
Great-uncle to the ten Tollands and Hugo's favourite forebear; a
scientist of some distinction who specialized in marsh gases and
alcohol-radicles, his work on the deodorization of sewage said to have
been outstanding. D. unmarried in the 1880s.

BDFR 42–3, 68. HSH 191.

WARMINSTER, Earl of (Hugo) Family name Tolland
Amateur explorer and big-game hunter, father of the ten Tollands. M.
(1) a Miss Alford by whom he had issue Alfred ('Erridge'), Frederica,
Norah, George, Susan, Blanche, Robert, Isobel, Hugo, Priscilla (2)
Lady Katherine Jamieson, daughter of the Earl of Ardglass. Seat
Thrubworth Park. Spent much of the latter part of his life abroad,
fishing in Iceland or pig-sticking in Bengal. D. 1928 or 9 of blood-
poisoning while shooting ibex in Kashmir.

AW 187. LM 30, 147, 207–8. CCR 58–9. KO 197. VB 156. BDFR 67.

WARMINSTER, Earl of, Viscount Erridge (Alfred) see ERRIDGE

WARMINSTER, Earl of (Jeremy)
Erridge's heir, only child of George and Veronica Tolland, b. shortly
after the deaths in 1946 of his father and uncle, whom he succeeded.

Turns out to be a throwback to his great-great-uncle the Chemist-Earl; Junior Research Fellow in science at Jenkins' old college by 1971; has plans for turning Thrubworth into a research institute. A rather daunting young man.

BDFR 29, 39, 131. HSH 5, 191–2, 227.

WARMINSTER, Countess of (Katherine)
Widow of Hugo Warminster and stepmother of the ten Tollands; sister to Jumbo, Earl of Ardglass, and Lady Molly Jeavons. 'Smaller, older, quieter in manner and more handsome than Molly Jeavons, she was also much more awe-inspiring. Something of the witch haunted her delicate, aquiline features and transparent ivory skin: a calm, autumnal beauty that did not at all mask the amused, malicious, almost insane light that glinted all the time in her infinitely pale blue eyes.'

An eccentric with a decent regard for eccentricity in others. M. (1) a fairly successful stockbroker with no salient characteristic (2) c. 1921, Lord Warminster. No child by, and apparently no great attachment to, either husband; always hated the country and left it for good on her second husband's death. House in Hyde Park Gardens. Divides her time between her ailments ('real or imaginary – opinion differed within the family on this point') and the writing of biographical studies devoted to the dominating, Amazonian women of history e.g. Catherine the Great; Christina of Sweden; Sarah, Duchess of Marlborough ('volumes rarely mentioned in the press, though usually treated kindly by such critics as noticed them, on account of their engaging impetuosity of style and complete lack of pretension to any serious scholarship'). Working on a life of Maria Theresa left unfinished at her death.

On amicable but not outstandingly warm terms with her stepchildren. Alarmingly well-informed on all topics concerning her relations. Has read one of Jenkins' books and is relatively well disposed towards his engagement to her stepdaughter Isobel in consequence. Occult interests. Horror of drink. Holds regular family Sunday luncheon parties ('she looked as usual like a very patrician sybil about to announce a calamitous disaster of which she had personally given due and disregarded warning'), noted for the nastiness of the wine and her formidable technique in cross-examination:

'Lady Warminster represented to a high degree that characteristic of her own generation that everything may be said, though nothing indecorous discussed openly. Layer upon layer of wrapping, box after box revealing in the Chinese manner yet another box, must conceal all doubtful secrets; only the discipline of infinite obliquity made it lawful to examine the seamy side of life. If these mysteries were observed everything might be contemplated: however unsavoury: however unspeakable.'

D. 1937 or 8, leaving what little money she had of her own to her favourite stepchild Blanche Tolland.

LM 31, 147–8, first meeting with, her house and history, relations with her stepchildren 205–12. CCR Sunday luncheon with, her character and tastes 57–60, 66, 72–4, teasing St John Clarke 76–81 & 83–4, 86–94, 96; 140–1. KO Her death 88, 143, resemblance to her sister 145; 154, Mrs Erdleigh on 197; 209, 235. SA 163.

WARRINGTON, Brigadier-General the Earl of (Piers)
Mrs Foxe's first husband, much older than she was and d. soon after the marriage, leaving her a life interest in his estate, stud and country mansion (Glimber). Collected china. Probably drank, according to Mr Deacon.

QU 20, 60–1. BM 119. LM 167. CCR 43, 89, 169, 174. VB 154.

WARRINGTON, Lady see FOXE, Mrs

WARTSTONE, Miss
Manageress of the block of flats in Chelsea inhabited during the second war by Jenkins, Hewetson, Mrs Erdleigh and Odo Stevens. 'Her outward appearance at once prepared residents for an unusually contentious temperament. Miss Wartstone had, indeed, passed into a middle-age of pathological quarrelsomeness, possibly in part legacy of nervous tensions built up during the early years of the blitz . . .'

MP 69–70, 122, 124, 131.

WEEDON, Geraldine ('Tuffy')
Governess to Charles Stringham's sister Flavia, afterwards stays on as secretary to their mother Mrs Foxe. Tall, dark, beaky-nosed, not overwhelmingly affable. Aged about 30–35 in 1923. Consumed by an unconcealed and unrequited passion for Stringham as a schoolboy; detests his stepfather Buster Foxe.

Comes into a little money and leaves her employer at the end of the 'twenties. Does odd jobs for her old friend Milly Jeavons and means to help Stringham with his drinking ('She gave an impression of complete singleness of purpose: the impression of a person who could make herself very disagreeable if thwarted'). Arctic smile. Living with Stringham in the Jeavonses' top floor flat by 1936 ('Now I saw that restraint, even actual physical restraint, might have been in her mind'). Turns up to reclaim him on the night of Mrs Foxe's party:
'She advanced a little deeper into the room, her mysterious equivocal

presence casting a long, dark shadow over the scene . . . although nothing outward indicated that something dramatic was taking place, Stringham himself . . . had risen from his chair with one of his random easy movements, so that to me it was clear he knew the game was up. He knew he must be borne away by Miss Weedon within the next few minutes to whatever prison-house now enclosed him.'

Removes him from circulation thereafter, to his mother's relief and with Buster's active connivance. Denies him access to money or drink, and discharges him cured on the outbreak of war.

Transformed when next encountered as the radiant bride ('almost girlish in manner') of the octogenarian General Conyers. Honeymoon at the Bellevue. Widowed by 1943. Works for MI5 and m. Sunny Farebrother at the end of the war. D. in the early 'sixties: 'A wonderful woman, Geraldine. Marvellous manager. Knew just where to save . . . Happy years together. Fragrant memories' (Farebrother).

QU At luncheon with Mrs Foxe, her position in the household and relations with Stringham 56, 58–62; 73; compared to Sunny Farebrother 77; Stringham on 174; at Oxford alliance with Sillery against Buster 213–7, 219. BM 103, 225, 273. LM At Lady Molly's, new light on her intimacy with Stringham 161–8; 236–8. CCR Stringham in her clutches 86–9, 141, 145–6, 164; removes him from Mrs Foxe's party 179–88. KO With Stringham at Glimber 104–5; engaged to General Conyers 212–18. VB 158. SA Stringham's account of escaping from 79–80, 169, 182, 218, 222–3. MP 59 In MI5 77; marriage to Farebrother 151, 200–1. TK 30. Farebrother on 212. HSH Dead 83.

WELLINGTON, First Duke of 1760–1842
Took a dim view of the fourth Lord Erridge's abilities as an army commander.

LM 149. MP 185. BDFR 43.

WENTWORTH, Baby (Hon. Mrs)
Sister of Jack Vowchurch, second cousin to Bertha Conyers and Mildred Haycock. Exquisitely fashionable divorcée; small, dark, short curly hair and look of infinite slyness; exemplifies the opposite style in beauty to Bijou Ardglass. Sir Magnus Donners' current companion and presumptive mistress in 1928 or 9; their guilty looks and air of mutual discomfort at Mrs Andriadis' party in Hill Street recall Adam and Eve leaving the garden after the Fall ('I almost expected them to be followed through the door by a well-tailored angel, pointing in their direction a flaming sword').

Pursued by Prince Theodoric that summer, also by Barnby (who has painted her). Recently involved in the Derwentwater divorce case.

Her affair with Cosmo Flitton has already broken up both his marriage to Stringham's sister and her own to Wentworth. Suspected by Jenkins of a lesbian relationship (subsequently denied) with Jean Duport at Stourwater; not even Jean knows what she and Donners did together. Leaves Donners, ditching Theodoric that autumn, for Barnby. M. (2) an Italian film director called Clarini, cloudlessly happy with him in Rome by 1933. Believed never to speak another civil word to a man after taking him as a lover.

In her fifties by 1958, separated from Signor Clarini and staying at the Bragadin palazzo in Venice: 'Her demeanour wafted through the Tiepolo room a breath of the Nineteen Twenties. Like one who hands on the torch of a past era of folk culture, she had somehow preserved intact, from ballroom and plage, golf course and hunting field, a social technique fashionable then, even considered alluring . . .' Pursuing Louis Glober with a view to marriage until cut out by Pamela Widmerpool. Beginning to resemble her cousin Mrs Haycock ('she had developed some of the same masculine hardening of the features, voice rising to a bark, elements veering in the direction of sex-change, threatened by too constant adjustment of husbands and lovers'). Under Scorpio, old friend to Mrs Erdleigh (it was Baby's borrowed planchette that figured in the weekend at the Templers' when Jenkins first slept with Jean Duport).

D. 1968 at Montego Bay shortly after her marriage to (3) a relatively rich Greek.

BM At Mrs Andriadis' party 111–12, 125–6, 132, 135, 138–9; Barnby in pursuit of 165–6, 171–3; at Stourwater 188–90, 194–5, 198–9, 202, 210, 212–15, 221; 235; Barnby's conquest of 252–3, 256. AW Rift with Donners, second marriage 24–5; Jean on 58; 72, 91, Jean's further account of 134–5; 154. LM 68, 199–200. CCR 9, 131, 158. KO 93, 100, 109. VB 146. MP 58. TK At Bragadin palace 103–4, 113–16; 151; Mrs Erdleigh on 242–3. HSH Her death 104–5.

WENTWORTH, Lord and Lady Edward
Guests at the Huntercombes' ball.

BM 57.

WESTMACOTT, Thomas and Henry
Twins who shared Jenkins' governess at Stonehurst in 1914, their father killed in the first war.

KO 51, 74.

WHELAN, Cardinal
His portrait by Isbister ('the only picture I had ever heard Widmerpool

spontaneously praise') exhibited at the Royal Academy at the end of the 'twenties.

BM 87. AW 109.

WHITNEY
Old Boy who had something to say of Tanganyika at Le Bas' reunion dinner.

AW 176, 186, 189–90, 195. BDFR 233–4.

WIDEMAN, Dwight
Undergraduate through whose aunt Sillery gained his hold over the women's clubs of America.

QU 170.

WIDMERPOOL, Kenneth G.
(For convenience' sake this entry is divided into twelve main sections, each headed by the volume to which it corresponds.)

A school contemporary who gradually acquires over the next half century an immutable place as an archetypal figure, 'one of those fabulous monsters that haunt the recesses of the individual imagination', in Jenkins' private mythology; 'I had always felt an interest in what might be called the theoretical side of Widmerpool's life: the reaction of his own emotions to the severe rule of ambition that he had from the beginning imposed upon himself: the determination that existence must be governed by the will'.

QU Two or three years older than Jenkins, a year ahead of him in Le Bas' house at school, makes no great impression until encountered one day returning from a self-imposed and solitary training run:
'It was on the bleak December tarmac of that Saturday afternoon in, I suppose, the year 1921 that Widmerpool, fairly heavily built, thick lips and metal-rimmed spectacles giving his face as usual an aggrieved expression, first took coherent form in my mind . . . Something comfortless and inelegant in his appearance suddenly impressed itself on the observer, as stiffly, almost majestically, Widmerpool moved on his heels out of the mist.'

An innately ludicrous figure, 'so wet you could shoot snipe off him' (Peter Templer). Unremarkable at work or games, notorious only on account of some forgotten peculiarity about his overcoat as a new boy. Wears a cap at least a size too small. Fish-like cast of countenance, thick protesting voice and squeaky boots ('their sullen whining dirge seeming designed to express in musical terms the mysteries of a life of toil and abnegation lived apart from the daily life of the tribe'). Suffers from boils. Given to heavy breathing when worked up or put out.

Brilliantly mimicked by Stringham. Went to some lengths to get a boy named Akworth sacked for making advances to the young Templer (and may even have harboured designs on Templer himself). Reacts with abject devotion when accidentally spattered with banana by Budd, the captain of cricket.

Leaves school in the summer of 1922, articled as a solicitor's clerk to Turnbull, Welford & Puckering. Only child of a widowed mother with whom he lives not far from Victoria Station. Turns up the following summer as Jenkins' fellow pensionnaire at the Leroys' in France; outlines his plans for a career in business and politics ('This all seemed to be such rubbish that I changed the subject'); and shows wholly unsuspected diplomatic skill in reconciling the two mortally opposed Scandinavians Lundquist and Örn: 'There was something about the obstinacy with which he pursued his aims that could not be disregarded, or merely ridiculed. Even then I did not recognize the quest for power'.

BM. Not seen again until the night of the Walpole-Wilsons' dinner party ('We were absolutely at our wits' end for a man tonight, so he had to come') in 1928 or 9. Something indefinably odd about the cut of his white waistcoat. Still working for the same City firm of solicitors; officer in Territorials; makes a point of going down to Barnes and driving a golf ball into a net. Suffers from jaundice and sees himself as a dancing man. Drenched with sugar by Barbara Goring later that night at the Huntercombes' ball. Has loved Barbara since the days when his father supplied hers with artificial manure; prevented from proposing only by lack of funds; determines never to see her again. Is promptly overwhelmed by Gypsy Jones, and pays for her abortion but finds nothing doing in return. Jenkins increasingly taken aback that summer by evidence of his love life, and still more startled to find his business prospects treated seriously by such coming men as Tompsitt and Truscott. Job in the politico-legal department of Donners Brebner fixed for him by Truscott. Reverential attitude to Sir Magnus Donners. Promoted that autumn, and resolves never again to have anything to do with a woman who takes his mind off his work. Reveals his Christian name and invites Jenkins to use it.

AW. Moved on to join a firm of bill-brokers by the early 'thirties, taking a fair proportion of Donners Brebners' business with him. Had gone to some trouble to get Truscott sacked and, becoming too big for his boots, been sacked himself by Donners. Little more than thirty. No longer a subject for laughter to Templer (who hopes to enlist his influence in the City on behalf of Bob Duport). Grown too fat for his dinner jacket when next encountered at Le Bas' reunion for Old Boys; has almost forgotten Jenkins' first name and never heard of his novel.

Makes an uncalled-for speech (on progressive economics, faint Marxist overtones) during which Le Bas passes out and Stringham gets blind drunk. Puts Stringham to bed that night, holding him down in a grotesque wrestling bout until Stringham admits defeat: 'Widmerpool, once so derided by all of us, had become in some mysterious manner a person of authority. Now, in a sense, it was he who derided us . . .'

LM. Engaged to Mrs Haycock by 1934. Looks more than ever like a fish; something a little frightening about him:

'Yet, for some reason, I was quite glad to see him again . . . Widmerpool was a recurring milestone on the road; perhaps it would be more apt to say that his course, as one jogged round the track, was run from time to time, however different the pace, in common with my own. As an aspect of my past he was an element to be treated with interest, if not affection, like some unattractive building or natural feature of the landscape which brought back the irrational nostalgia of childhood.'

Condescending attitude to Sir Magnus Donners. Runs across Templer sometimes in the City (and piques himself on having found work for Bob Duport, thereby patching up Bob's marriage and terminating Jenkins' affair with Bob's wife Jean). Gastric trouble. Violently agitated about his approaching wedding; consults Jenkins as to the advisability of nerving himself to sleep with his fiancée beforehand ('He suddenly began to look wretched, much as I had often seen him look as a schoolboy: lonely: awkward: unpopular; no longer the self-confident business-man into which he had grown'). Moving steadily to the Left, finds much to admire in Hitler, wholly against rearmament. Has given up golf but still finds time for Territorials. Develops jaundice again, grows too thin for his dinner jacket, looks ghastly:

'I thought of Pepys . . . and immediately Widmerpool's resemblance to the existing portraits of the diarist became apparent. He had the same obdurate, put-upon, bad-tempered expression. Only a full-bottomed wig was required to complete the picture.'

Sent packing by Mrs Haycock ('Fellow looked like death. Shaking like a jelly and the colour of wax': General Conyers) after a disastrous failure in bed during their weekend at Dogdene. Turns up shortly afterwards looking more pleased with himself than ever before, applauding his wisdom in having broken off the engagement and freely proffering his advice on marriage to Jenkins.

CCR. Well-disposed towards Russia at the time of the Moscow treason trials. Can talk of nothing but his meeting with Mrs Simpson, sees himself as the Beau Brummel of the new reign. Undergoing treatment for boils. Still a bill-broker. Returns to Donners Brebner in

196

an advisory capacity but is not altogether satisfied with Sir Magnus' attitude. Discounts the possibility of a European war. Sadly put out by the Abdication.

KO. Fairly formidable reputation in the City by 1938: 'I saw that it was no longer a question of Stringham and Widmerpool having drawn level as friends in Templer's mind; the fact was that Widmerpool was now miles ahead'. Drops in at Stourwater during the Seven Deadly Sins revels that autumn, dressed in Territorial kit ('The sight of him in uniform struck a chill through my bones. Nothing, up to that date, had so much brought home to me the imminence, the certitude, of war'); deplores the irregularity of Donners' sex life; reckons that Munich has postponed war for five years at least. Supervises Bob Duport's Turkish dealings for Donners Brebner (with catastrophic consequences for Duport).

Gazetted Captain by the end of 1939. Working night and day to win the war at a top-secret hideout which turns out to be a stuffy back room in his old Territorial HQ. ('The General Staff of the Wehrmacht would be only too happy to possess even a tithe of the information I locked away before we quitted the Orderly Room'). New, enormously hearty voice and offensive line in army slang. Peremptorily refuses to help hasten Jenkins' call-up. Has grave doubts of Donners' fitness for public office. Still sweats at memories of Mrs Haycock; turns pale at sight of the communist agitator Gypsy Jones ('To Widmerpool, she was . . . the ghastly reminder of failure, misery, degradation'). Oppressed by the security risks involved in responsibilities such as his own: 'Widmerpool's view of himself as a man handling weighty state secrets was beyond belief in its absurdity . . .'

VB. Promoted Major by 1940; DAAG (Deputy-Assistant-Adjutant-General) at General Liddament's divisional HQ in Northern Ireland; selects Jenkins as the best of a bad bunch of candidates for the post of his junior assistant.

SA. Proves a hard master on account of his obsessive secretiveness, unflattering estimate of Jenkins' abilities as dogsbody ('his nature was to be appreciated with keener insight from below'), and unremitting industry ('No one but a tireless creator of work for its own sake would have found an assistant necessary in his job'). Takes a dim view of his colleagues from the General downwards. Intrigues ceaselessly against Major Farebrother (an old enemy from Territorials as well as in the City) and Colonel Hogbourne-Johnson (in the matter of the Divisional Recce Command). Is publicly reprimanded by Hogbourne-Johnson, and takes an ample revenge via the Diplock affair. Resents Stringham's turning up in the capacity of Mess waiter as a potential personal embarrassment to himself. Plans and executes the ignominious dismissal of Lt. Bithel from the army. Gets rid of Stringham to a Mobile Laundry Unit destined for the Far Eastern front. Announces his own translation to 'a more lofty – an incalculably more lofty – sphere', namely the Cabinet Offices, and almost immediately comes to grief when outmanoeuvred by Farebrother in the complex series of double-crossings centring on the Recce Command ('I had not seen Widmerpool so upset, so reduced to utter despair, since the day, long past, when he admitted to paying for Gypsy Jones's "operation"'). Ruin of his promotion prospects averted only by the General's providential departure in June 1941.

MP. Military Assistant Secretary at the Cabinet Office, works fourteen hours a day in a basement in Whitehall, has access to the Chiefs of Staff and the Cabinet. Promoted Lt.-Colonel (later Colonel, also awarded an OBE). In a position to influence policy at the highest level (as well as attend to unfinished business of his own, such as arranging for Farebrother to lose his job over the Szymanski affair). Deplores Polish intransigence over the massacre of their officers by the Russians at Katyn ('almost certainly, from what one knows of them, the consequence of administrative inadequacy, rather than wilful indifference to human life and the dictates of compassion'). Claims to have organized a satisfactory sex life round tarts picked up in the blackout; and is shortly afterwards bowled over by Stringham's niece, Pamela Flitton. Engaged to her by the summer of 1945. Announces Stringham's death at the Fall of Singapore, and his fiancée's substantial expectations under Stringham's will. Has plans for a colonial governorship. Accused by Pamela of murdering Peter Templer (and had in fact officially recommended the withdrawal of British support in the Balkans which led incidentally to Templer's death). Marries her that autumn.

BDFR. Labour MP and parliamentary private secretary (to the Minister for whom Leonard Short works) by 1946: 'The House of Commons had already left its indefinable, irresoluble mark. His thick features, the rotundities of his body, always amenable to caricature, now seemed more than ever simplified in outline, positively demanding treatment in political cartoon.' Advocate of Cheap Money; wooed simultaneously by the Labour Party and the City; promising public career threatened only by Pamela's propensity for scandal. His self-assurance greatly reduced by marriage. On board of the new publishing firm Quiggin & Craggs, and seems to have buried his difference with Lady Craggs (formerly Gypsy Jones – 'I'm never quite sure Gypsy hasn't a hold on him of some sort': Bagshaw). Provides part of the backing for *Fission* as an organ for his own political and economic views (article on *Affirmative Action and Negative Values* in its first number). Anxious to promote friendship with the E. European People's Republic formerly ruled by Prince Theodoric's brother, canvasses support from Sillery, Le Bas, the Tory MP Roddy Cutts etc. Possibly a crypto-communist, according to Bagshaw. Lives with his wife in a flat in Victoria Street. Deserted by her for X. Trapnel in the summer of 1947. Said by Pamela to have given up trying to sleep with her after one or two abortive attempts, obtaining a masochistic satisfaction instead from her couplings with other men. Accepts an official invitation to visit E. Europe that autumn; is rejoined by Pamela and receives minor government office on his return; deeply dejected despite both achievements.

TK. Not seen since the night he lost his seat in the General Election of 1955. Reported by Bagshaw to have made advances on both the sexual and political fronts under the tutelage of the French Marxist intellectual Ferrand-Sénéschal. Widely suspected within his own party at one time of secret communist allegiance. The theory that he is actively engaged in sabotage of the capitalist system (as a means 'to be revenged on a world that had found himself insufficiently splendid') persuasively advanced by Bagshaw, and no less authoritatively denied by Roddy Cutts. No truth, according to Cutts, in the rumour that he lent a hand in tipping off Burgess and Maclean in the late 'fifties. Known to have boasted of high jinks in a Parisian establishment catering for Ferrand-Sénéschal's special tastes at the time of Pamela's affair with Trapnel. Has since shown no disposition for divorce in face of Pamela's by now legendary infidelities. Still a fairly prominent public figure. Divides his time between the Westminster flat and his mother's much enlarged cottage at Stourwater. Has made substantial contributions to Labour Party funds and to the growth of trade with E. Europe (said to have made a packet out of cheap Balkan wines). Tends towards fashionable anti-establishment views.

Becomes a life peer under the Conservative government in 1958, and turns up a few weeks later to join his wife in Venice. Overdressed, going bald, looks distinctly elderly. Ugly scene with Pamela in the Candaules and Gyges room at the Bragadin palazzo. First hints of his impending downfall vouchsafed during this Venetian visit by his extreme agitation, part fury, at Pamela's taunts of voyeurism, part fright at the non-appearance of his E. European contact Belkin.

Denounced as a Stalinist-revisionist in the communist press at the time of the State trials in Belkin's country that autumn. Known to have been a client of the call-girl Pauline. Rumours of political scandal circulating pretty freely among informed circles in London by the following spring. Question asked in parliament about his E. European activities. Trial for espionage on the cards; also for tax evasion over his E. European business deals; official enquiry pending. Revenge confidently anticipated by his old enemies such as Sunny Farebrother in the City and Truscott in the civil service.

The case against him inexplicably dropped by early summer. Turns up at the Stevenses' musical party which culminates in an hysterical attack from Pamela who claims that he habitually watched her love-making, and was present on the day Ferrand-Sénéschal died in bed with her; that he regularly passed information to the communists; and that he saved himself from public exposure only by betraying his fellow agent Ferrand-Sénéschal. Cuts short her revelations by seizing her throat (or possibly arm):

'The scene partook, in far more savage temper, of that enacted at the Huntercombes' ball . . . The upshot then had been Barbara pouring sugar over his head. Widmerpool's onslaught this time might be additionally menacing, stakes of the game, so to speak, immensely higher; the physical protest was the same, final exasperation of nerves kept by a woman too long on the edge.'

Next encountered in November a few months after Pamela's death, dressed in deep black ('He showed outward mark of the stresses endured. His body was thinner, the flesh of his face hanging in sallow pouches'), making for the House of Lords and sounding more than a little unhinged.

HSH. Not seen again for almost a decade. Disappeared at the end of 1959 for the best part of a year, surfacing eventually with an academic post in California. His troubles widely attributed in the US to framing by the CIA. Has turned against the parliamentary system; working on a book, *Pogrom of Youth*; his supporters angling for a Nobel citation. Returns to England in the late 'sixties and becomes something of a TV personality. Daubed with paint by student demonstrators (later identified as the Quiggin twins) during his installation as Chancellor of a newish university in 1968. Sunken eyes, gaunt face, bald head.

Centre of a personality cult among the young; already a powerful figure in the student world; styles himself Ken Widmerpool. Makes an unscheduled dinner speech in the name of contemporary counter-culture at the Magnus Donners prize dinner ('Donners represented in public life all that I most abhor. Let me at once go on record as expressing this sentiment towards him'); cut short by a stink bomb thrown by the Quiggin twins. Late sixties, looks older. Dresses like a down-at-heel artist ('whether too big, too small, oddly cut, strangely patterned – his garments had hitherto always represented . . . the essence of stolid conventionality').

Retires to run a centre for dissident youth at his mother's former house near Stourwater, joining forces towards the end of 1969 with Scorpio

Murtlock's cult. Resigns as chancellor that December. Power struggle thought to be taking place between himself and Murtlock. Stabbed by Murtlock after some sort of altercation during the cult's Midsummer Eve sexual rites. Often to be seen running with cult members round Stourwater during the remainder of that year. Encountered in a blue robe on the day of the Akworth wedding at Stourwater in the spring of 1971: 'Widmerpool looked ill, desperate, worn out. The extreme debility of his appearance brought one up short'. Recounts his humiliation at Murtlock's hands after recruitment to the cult of his former army victim, Bithel. Grovels in an act of ritual penance to his former victim at school, the bride's grandfather, Sir Bertram Akworth. Pleads in vain with Murtlock for permission to leave the cult. Submerged from view thereafter. His house and money reported to have been made over to Murtlock; his health failing; his attempts to take the lead on a ritual run at dawn that autumn reported by Bithel:

'It was rather a twisty way through the woods. Nobody could see him, especially in the mist. When they came round a corner, out of the trees, he was lying just in the road.'
'Collapsed?'
'Dead.'

QU First despondent vision of, his school career surveyed 3–7; Stringham's account of his part in the Budd, Templer and Akworth incidents 10–14; 26, 34, 36–8; eye-witness of Le Bas' arrest, leaves school 46–51; 53; at the Leroys' 117–20, his attitude to Stringham and Templer, his dim view of Jenkins' prospects 127–38, his triumph in the affair of Lundquist and Örn, his bitterness at being lampooned in the *cabinet de toilette* 140–2, 151–2, 154–62; 172–3, compared to Quiggin 205, 207, 209, 211, 218; Le Bas on 222–3. BM At the Walpole-Wilsons' 29–34, 36, 39–43, 46–9, 51–4; his father's occupation disclosed, his own acute sensitivity to ridicule 58–60; at the Huntercombes', drenched with sugar by Barbara, confesses his love for her 64–83; takes a fancy to Gypsy Jones 86–90, 92–3; 102; at Milly Andriadis' party 107–8, 122, in pursuit of Gypsy 126–30, joining Donners–Brebner 132–5, 137–8; 150, 153, 159; hanging around Gypsy 168–70, 174; 187, 198; at Stourwater, confesses to having paid for Gypsy's abortion 203–9, 211, 213, wrecks Donners' sunken garden 216–22; Barnby's version of his dealings with Gypsy 231–2; 237, compared to Quiggin 239–40; 242; Gypsy on her dealings with 247–9; 253; supper at his mother's flat, his views on Gypsy and Barbara 260–73. AW Leaving Donners–Brebner to become a bill broker 45–6; 106, 109, 170; at Le Bas' dinner 175–80, his speech 189–97; puts Stringham to bed 201–10. LM 29; at the Jeavons', engaged to Mrs Haycock 40–1, 43–8; confides his anxiety about his fiancée 50–67; apprehensions of his future in-laws 70–5, 77, 82–4; 92, compared to

Quiggin 107–8; 132; Molly Jeavons on his marriage 158–60; Miss Weedon on the same 165–6; 175, 177; at Umfraville's night club with his fiancée, taken ill 184–90, 192, 194–7; 201–2; his engagement broken off 215–17; his fiasco with Mrs Haycock at Dogdene described, and his psychological type diagnosed by Gen. Conyers 227–34; his own rather different version 236–9. CCR 43–4, 79, his sympathy with Russia and obsession with Mrs Simpson 84–6; in nursing home, his contempt for the arts 100–4; luncheon with, his political and economic views 123–8; 194–5, 198, 214. KO Templer's changed attitude to 105–8; at Stourwater on business involving Bob Duport, his disapproval of Donners 133–9; Duport's subsequent account of his treachery 166–8, 172–4, 193, 200–2; in the army, refuses to help Jenkins, deplores Duport's ingratitude 218–26; tormented at sight of Gypsy Jones, his obsession with security 228–31, at the Jeavons' with his mother 235–8, 241–2; 245. VB 89, 119, 222–3, DAAG at Div. HQ, Jenkins posted as his assistant 238–43. SA 4–5, his bitterness against Bithel 9–12; his disagreeable qualities as a superior, his intriguing, initial stages of his feuds with Farebrother and Hogbourne-Johnson 20–34, 36–8, 43–4; publicly humiliated by Hogbourne-Johnson 49–58; plans revenge via Diplock 60–4; attitude to Stringham as Mess waiter 72–4, 76–7, 80; 82–7, 97, 120; transfers Stringham to Mobile Laundry 171; 173–6; enraged by Stringham's attempts to cover up Bithel's drinking, dismisses Bithel from the army, explains his scheme for ditching Stringham, announces his own promotion, ditched by Farebrother, triumphs over Hogbourne-Johnson, his career in jeopardy 178, 181–216, 219–22; disaster averted 225–8. MP In committee at the Cabinet office, his power and influence 9, 11, 14–20; 34, 73, 85; asks the name of Pamela Flitton 99–100; his views on Katyn, his preference for tarts, gloats over the respective downfalls of Farebrother and Hogbourne-Johnson 104–12; promoted colonel, Farebrother's bitterness 115–18; Mrs Erdleigh's prophecy concerning 134; his meeting with Pamela in Cairo 190; his engagement to her 196–7, 199; at Indian embassy party, describes his courtship, announces Stringham's death 201–6, accused by Pamela of murdering Templer, their mutual rage 209–13; 218; laughs off this tiff 230–1; his marriage 244. BDFR Gossip at Sillery's about his election to parliament, his prospects and his wife 12–16, 21–2, 25, 27; with the Craggses at Erridge's funeral 44–50, outraged by Pamela's behaviour 53, 59–65, 69, his relations with Pamela 71–3, connection with Quiggin & Craggs 75–81, 83; 88–9; Bagshaw on his political affiliations 93–4; at Mme Flores' party, boasts of his special relationship with E. Europe 101–3; 105, 117–8; at *Fission* party 128–9, touched by Trapnel for a pound 131–40; Bagshaw on 142–3; 151; Trapnel in love with his wife 164–6; at the House of Commons, invites Jenkins and

Roddy Cutts back to his flat, discovers Pamela's desertion, his reactions, parodied by Trapnel in *Fission* 170–88; his marriage analysed, confronts Pamela and Trapnel in their flat 192, 194–204; 208; his sexual fiasco with Pamela reported by Trapnel 226; his marriage patched up, pays a visit to his old school, his dejection 233–4, 236–8. TK His political sympathies and sexual tastes shared with Ferrand-Sénéschal, Bagshaw on his crypto-communism, his career to date 12–16; 25, 28, his marriage analysed 36–40; 44, 46, 93–5; at Bragadin palace, row with Pamela 103–16; 120; at Tokenhouse's flat in search of Belkin, a second scene with Pamela reported by Ada Leintwardine 140–52; 158, 161–2, Pamela on his spying 167–8; 176–8; denounced in communist press 187–8; his call-girl parties 199–200; 205, 207; Farebrother on his impending ruin 210–11; Truscott on the same 217, 219; 222–3; at Stevens' party, scandal averted 231–3; 236, 246–7, 250–1; final scene with Pamela 255–6, 259, 261–6; 269–70, 273; encounter with after Pamela's death 278–80. HSH His installation as chancellor, his career brought up to date, attacked by student demonstrators 40–8; 57–8, 61, 64, libelled in Trapnel biography 69, 71–7, 79, 87–90; at Donners prize dinner with Quiggin twins 92, 95–6, 100–5, his speech, gloats over the stink bomb 107–17; his standpoint as dropout explored 117–8; at Royal Academy dinner 122–3, anxious to get in touch with Murtlock 134–40; reports of his having joined forces with Murtlock 141–3, 146–8; his row with Murtlock during sexual rites described by Gwinnett 164–9; reflections on this development 173–4; 177, 179–80, 183, 185; his part in Akworth's expulsion from school recalled 188; 197; Flavia Wisebite on his shortcomings as son-in-law 202–4; encountered out running with cult members at Stourwater, his desperate state, his horror of Bithel and remorse over Akworth 211–26; his penance to Akworth, his struggle with and surrender to Murtlock 228–38; 247, 254; his relations with Murtlock described by Henderson 257–62; his death described by Bithel 265–70.

WIDMERPOOL, Mrs
Doting widowed mother of above, lives with her son in a flat near the Roman Catholic cathedral in Victoria and concerns herself with little not directly related to his career. A person of determination. Passionate admirer of Marshal Stalin. Wonderful grasp of business matters, bookish tastes, grows younger year by year, according to Widmerpool ('"I am very much looking forward to your meeting my mother," he said. He spoke as if introduction to his mother was an experience, rather a vital one, that every serious person had, sooner or later, to undergo').

Squarely built, large features, firm teeth, heavy nose. Fringed and flowered velvet bridge coat. Looks no more than in her mid forties by 1928 or 9, though probably older: 'her well-preserved appearance was in striking contrast to Widmerpool's own somewhat decaying youth, so that the pair of them appeared almost more like contemporaries, even husband and wife, rather than mother and son'. Old friend to Janet Walpole-Wilson. Thoroughly approves of her son's choice of a bride in 1934; means to move in with the couple after the marriage ('I thought the two of them, Mrs Widmerpool and Mrs Haycock, were probably worthy of the other's steel'); strongly supports the subsequent ending of the engagement. Her influence, working through the inhibiting action of the incest barrier, put forward by General Conyers as a possible factor in Widmerpool's impotence.

Rents a summer cottage from the end of the 'twenties near Stourwater (thereby acquiring a base from which to molest the Walpole-Wilsons at Hinton Hoo as she had formerly molested the Gorings at Pembringham). Settled there permanently by the late 'thirties, her roses the admiration of the neighbourhood. Malignant smile like the wolf in Red Riding Hood. Tries out Lil Jeavons as lodger on the outbreak of war but decides evacuees would be preferable ('"Has she got evacuees?" "She had some for a short time," said Widmerpool, "then they went back to London. They were absolutely ungrateful"'). Her problems beginning to irritate Widmerpool.

Objects to his marriage to Pamela Flitton in 1945 ('I had quite a scene with my mother, I'm afraid. My mother is getting an old lady now, of course, and does not always know what she is talking about'). Exiled by Widmerpool in consequence. Staying with distant relations in the lowlands near Glasgow; not a success with her hosts; seldom visited by Widmerpool. Immensely gratified by his election to parliament but still inclined to regard a wife as a handicap to a career. D. at a ripe age in 1958 at her cottage in Kirkcudbrightshire, unmourned by Widmerpool ('it was painful to leave a matter like my mother's burial in the hands of a secretary, competent as my own secretary happens to be. Something a little over and above routine competence is required at such a moment. None the less, that was what had to be done').

QU 119, 130, 132–3, 135, 153. BM 31, 60, 77, 205, 208, 219–20; supper at her flat 231–2, 260–7, 269–70, 273. AW 210. LM 50, 54, 192, 232–3, 239. CCR 102, 126, 128. KO 105, 135, 221–4; at the Jeavonses' 230–2, 236–8, 241–2, 253. SA 39, 84. MP 201–2. BDFR 175. TK 106.

WIDMERPOOL, père
Father of Kenneth; son of a Lowland Scottish businessman called Geddes who married above himself and took his wife's name of Widmerpool. Manufacturer of liquid manure. Lived in Nottingham-shire or Derbyshire, and latterly on the Pembringham Woodhouse estate while experimenting with fertilizer on Lord Goring's fruit farm;

d. some time in the 'twenties, leaving his wife and son in low water. His trade a source of excruciating embarrassment to his son, who never mentions him.

QU 132, 135. BM 58–9. LM 84–5, 233.

WILLI
One of Mr Deacon's young men, had points in common with Mrs Andriadis' German lover Guggenbühl.

AW 165.

WILLIAMS, Privates G., G. E., H., I. G., and T.
Soldiers in Gwatkin's company.

VB 10, 29, 31, 97.

WILLIAMS, Mrs Hwfa b. c. 1885
Edwardian hostess who gave the party at which Sillery mingled with Mrs Foxe.

QU 175.

WILLIAMS, Private W. H.
Jenkins' platoon runner, good at running and singing but not otherwise gifted, staggers General Liddament by his dislike of porridge.

VB 4–7, 54–6, 82, 84–5, 95–6.

WILSON, Edward ('Beau') d. 1694
Dandy and big spender in the reign of William and Mary, possibly a collateral ancestor of the Walpole-Wilsons.

BM 178.

WILSON, Field-Marshal Sir Henry Hughes, Bt. 1864–1922
Famous army character, 'one of those talkative beggars who later became generals' (Uncle Giles), probably the fellow who warned Aylmer Conyers to keep away from the women at a vice-regal bunfight in Delhi.

KO 62.

WILSON, General Jumbo (Henry Maitland), First Baron, GCB, etc. 1881–1964
Commander-in-Chief in Middle East; gave Jenkins and Clanwaert something to laugh about in 1943.

MP 102.

WILSON, Matilda
Actress, the jolie-laide who succeeded Baby Wentworth at the end of

the 'twenties as girl friend to Sir Magnus Donners. Plays the Cardinal's mistress in an off-beat production of *The Duchess of Malfi* in 1934 and m. Hugh Moreland a few months later. Tall, angular, fairish hair, green eyes, large mouth; emphatic, forceful personality and dramatic taste in clothes; same age as Isobel Jenkins. Not a very finished actress but decidedly impressive off-stage. Prefers men though often found attractive by her own sex. Understands Moreland pretty well.

Daughter of a provincial chemist near Stourwater, at school with Veronica Tolland ('I just remember her right down at the bottom of the junior school, a little girl you couldn't help noticing. She was called Betty Updike then'). Left home early and m. when very young (1) the violinist Carolo, real name Wilson (or Wilkinson or Parker); divorced after eighteen months. Got her first foothold in the theatre through Norman Chandler. Picked up by Donners while organizing a production of *A Midsummer Night's Dream* put on by her old school at Stourwater ('Sir Magnus, wandering round, came across Matilda Wilson dressing up a lot of little girls as elves. That went pretty well'). Generally agreed to be the only one of his mistresses who refused to cater for his special tastes; not interested in money; turned down Donners' offer of marriage in favour of (2) Moreland.

Capable, decisive, takes over the practical running of Moreland's life. Has a baby that dies at birth in 1936. Behaves impeccably during Moreland's affair with Priscilla Tolland that autumn. Makes a reasonable success as Zenocrate in *Tamburlaine*, acknowledges herself to be a terrible actress and leaves the stage. Thought by Isobel to be quite ambitious. Moves with Moreland to a cottage on Donners' estate round about 1938; plays Envy in the Seven Deadly Sins tableaux at Stourwater; and leaves Moreland on the outbreak of war to marry (3) Sir Magnus Donners.

Takes to the world of politics and big business without regret for her former life. Likes power. Widowed by 1946. Comfortably off, energetic social life, rival hostess to Rosie Manasch; makes off briefly with Rosie's lover Odo Stevens ('more to tease Rosie than because she specially liked Stevens') in the 'fifties. Still fond of Moreland who remains probably a little in love with her to the day of his death ('Something of the sort may have been reciprocally true of herself'). Founds the Magnus Donners literary prize in the 'sixties. Thought by some, though not by Jenkins, to have had an affair with Gibson Delavacquerie. Flat in Eaton Square. Envy not her failing ('Matilda liked her friends to be successful rather than the reverse. That in itself was a rare characteristic'). D. 1970.

AW 25. CCR Moreland contemplating marriage to 7, 40–2; in *Duchess of Malfi*, first impressions of, her marriage to Moreland 44–56; expecting a child 98–9, 104–4, 109, 115, 119, 122–3; death of the child, her married life, some light on her background 129–35; at Mrs Foxe's party 144, 147, uncomfortable conversation with concerning Moreland's affair with Priscilla and her own with Donners 152–61, 187–8; tension with Moreland 193, 202, 205, 213–7; crisis and reconciliation 219–21. KO Relations with Moreland and Donners 78–9; her marriage 85–6; country weekend with, speculation on her current attitude to Donners 89–90, 93–101, 103–5, at Stourwater 107–12, 117–18, 120, 122–3, 126, plays Envy 129–32, 134, 139; 146; leaves Moreland for Donners 238, 242–51. VB 89. SA Effect of her departure on Moreland, compared to Mrs Maclintick 93, 116, 118, 121, 123, 145, 152–3, 159. MP 194, at Indian Embassy party, asks after Moreland 207–9; 212, 232. BDFR 119. TK 17, 67, 153, rivalry with Rosie Manasch 160–1; at the Stevens' party, Moreland's reaction to 228–30, 233, 241; Moreland's last words on 270, 272–3. HSH Her widowhood, founds Donners prize, produces Seven Deadly Sins photos 49–65; 88; at prize dinner 101, 105, 109, 114, 116; her death 189–90; 207.

WILSON, President Woodrow 1856–1924
Somewhat resembled the criminal Braddock alias Thorne.

QU 37.

WISE, Rupert
Male dancer noted for his strict morals and lack of small talk; heart of stone according to Norman Chandler ('He may have a profile like Apollo but he's got a mind like Hampstead Garden Suburb').

CCR 142–3.

WISEBITE, Flavia
Charles Stringham's older sister, has something of his air of liveliness weighed down by melancholy. Was educated by Miss Weedon and came out at the same time as Frederica Budd. Said to have been given absolute hell by her mother till she married the first chap that came along. Lost her virginity in Kenya to her father's old friend Dicky Umfraville (who lays dubious claim to have fathered her daughter Pamela Flitton). M. and div. (1) Cosmo Flitton who left her for Baby Wentworth (2) Harrison F. Wisebite ('Flavia never has any luck with husbands and lovers. Think of being married to Cosmo Flitton and Harrison Wisebite in quick succession. Why, I'd make a better husband myself': Stringham).

Turns up at Frederica's house in 1940 as mistress of Jenkins' much younger brother-in-law Robert Tolland; aged about forty, quiet, reserved, rather sad, fairly peevish; Robert's death in action a few weeks later possibly part of the pattern of her irredeemably bad luck. Nervous trouble after the war, spends much time in and out of nursing homes. Cottage near Glimber and later another near Stourwater. Has a profoundly depressing effect on Umfraville as Clare Akworth's wedding in 1971. Tall, pale, distinguished, rapid trembling voice and tinkly laugh ('She began to speak disjointedly of Stringham. She was, I thought, perhaps a little mad now. As one gets older, one gets increasingly used to encountering this development in friends and acquaintances; causing periods of self-examination in a similar connexion'). Detests her son-in-law Widmerpool and all his works.

QU 9, 59, 69. BM Her divorce 125, 189, 212; at Stringham's wedding 225. LM 161. CCR 87–8, 179. VB At Frederica's house with Robert 138–40, 145–8, Umfraville on 150, 154, on Stringham, relations with Robert 156–8, scene with Buster Foxe 160–7; her part in Robert's death 196–7. SA 74, Stringham on 78–9. MP 58–9, 196, 204. BDFR Umfraville's further confessions about 91–2. HSH At Akworth wedding, her views on Stringham, Pamela and Widmerpool 199–205, her collapse 250–1.

WISEBITE, Harrison F.
Flavia Stringham's second husband, came from Minneapolis and died of drink in Miami. Quite as much of a God-awful heel as Cosmo Flitton but had his good points, according to Umfraville, and mixed a refreshing cocktail of his own invention called Death Comes for the Archbishop.

VB 146, 150, 156. SA 76, 79. MP 58–9, 71, 196. BDFR 92. HSH 200.

WISEBITE, Milton
Harrison's nephew, works for *Time-Life* in New York and counts his brief encounter as an American soldier with Pamela Flitton in wartime the high peak of romance in his life.

MP 71–2.

WREN, Sir Christopher 1632–1723
Told Pepys about the new wing at Dogdene.
LM 11.

ZINOVIEV, Grigory 1883–1936
See KAMENEV, Lev.

Book Index

(including Writers, Plays and Playwrights, Pamphlets, Magazines and
Articles, Publishing Houses and a Literary Prize, together with
sections covering Biblical Texts, Hymns and Popular Songs)

Adam Bede
Novel by George Eliot, 1819–80, see SALTYKOV-SCHREDIN, M. E.

ADAMS, Henry 1838–1918
American historian; Russell Gwinnett half way between him and Charles Addams TK 48–9.

Adolphe
Novel by Benjamin Constant, 1767–1830; X. Trapnel's copy worn to shreds BDFR 191, 202.

Affirmative Action and Negative Values
Article by Widmerpool, see *Fission*.

AGRIPPA, Cornelius 1486–1535
Author of *De occulta philosophiae* etc, his magical writings provide a bond between Moreland and Mrs Erdleigh ('Moreland and Mrs Erdleigh had already reached the Book of Abramolin the Mage, spells for surrounding an enemy with a vision of trellis-work, others for causing the Pope to fall in love with you . . .') TK 254.

'Ah, with the Grape my fading Life provide . . .'
Lines quoted by Stringham with reference to the Green Park, see *Rubaiyàt of Omar Khayyám*.

Aladdin
Bijou Ardglass's father once played Abanazar to Max Pilgrim's mother's Principal Boy in SA 157.

Alcools
See APOLLINAIRE, Guillaume.

Alice in Wonderland and *Alice Through the Looking-glass*
See CARROLL, Lewis.

Anatomy of Melancholy
See BURTON, Robert.

'And I sat by the shelf till I lost myself . . .'
Lines (by J. K. Stephen, 1859–92, from *Lapsus Calami and other verses*) quoted by Le Bas in his annual speech to Old Boys AW 188–9.

Anna Karenin
See TOLSTOY, Leo.

Anthology of Soviet Literature
One of the books on Erridge's shelves at Thrubworth, dating back to his political conversion in the early 'thirties BDFR 68.

Antony and Cleopatra
See SHAKESPEARE, William.

APOLLINAIRE, Guillaume 1880–1918
His *Alcools* one of the few books on Moreland's shelves CCR 5; lines from *Alcools* quoted by Moreland CCR 53–4; HSH 55.

Apple Cart, The
Play by Bernard Shaw, first performed (in August 1929) on the night Books-do-furnish-a-room Bagshaw allegedly made the remark which gave him his nickname BDFR 33.

Arabian Nights, The
AW 212; world to which Sir Magnus Donners really belonged TK 273.

ARIOSTO, Ludovica 1474–1533
Jenkins meditates on themes of madness, loss, mortality, forgetfulness and rediscovery arising from his *Orlando Furioso*: Orlando analyzed as an archetypal drop-out, Ariosto's Time compared to Poussin's, Dr Trelawney's achievements – and St John Clarke's – rescued from Ariosto's waters of Oblivion HSH 30–6, 39; Sir Magnus Donners similarly rescued HSH 50; Widmerpool seen as Orlando HSH 118, 173–4; 247.

Art of Horace Isbister, The
Commissioned at the end of the 'twenties by the art book firm (founded by Daniel Tokenhouse) for which Jenkins works, but never materializes on account of St John Clarke's failure to produce an introduction. For refs, see Character Index under CLARKE, St John, ISBISTER, Horace and TOKENHOUSE, Daniel.

ARNOLD, Matthew 1822–1888
Some lines by (from *The Terrace at Berne*) quoted by Le Bas QU 40–1; Mark Members' Scholar-Gypsy manner AW 123; a last glimpse of X. Trapnel outside the BBC in Langham Place reminds Bagshaw of the Scholar-Gipsy TK 26.

Assumptions of Autarchy v. Dynamics of Adjustment
X. Trapnel's parody of Widmerpool's articles in *Fission*, published shortly after Trapnel's elopement with Widmerpool's wife BDFR 185–8, 193–4, 201–2.

Atheist's Tragedy, The
See TOURNEUR, Cyril.

Athlete's Footman
Quentin Shuckerley's new book in 1958 ('the best queer novel since *Sea Urchins*': Mark Members) TK 8.

'A transient and embarrassed spectre'
Habitually misquoted by Le Bas ('a transient and embarrassed phantom' from *Endymion*) when any boy tries to slip past him without attracting undue attention, see DISRAELI, Benjamin.

Attick and Roman Reckonings of Capacity for Things Liquid and Things Dry reduced to the Common English Mensuration for Wine and Corn. Magnus *opus* of Dr Emily Brightman's ancestor the Revd Salathiel Brightman, thought to have been one of the sources drawn on by Lemprière for his *Bibliotheca Classica*. For refs, see Character Index under BRIGHT-MAN, Revd. Salathiel.

BALZAC, Honoré de 1799–1850
Advanced in self-defence by Jenkins under cross-examination from General Liddament about novels ('Seeking to nominate for favour an author not too dissimilar from Trollope in material and method of handling, at the same time in contrast with him – not only in being approved by myself – in possessing greater variety and range, the *Comédie Humaine* suddenly suggested itself . . . I began to try and recall the plots of all the Balzac books, by no means a large number in relation to the whole, I had ever read') SA 47–8, 86, 95; one of the authors cited by X. Trapnel in support of his theory on the heresy of naturalism BDFR 216; superiority of his novels, and Dickens', to autobiography HSH 84.

BARRIE, J. M. 1860–1937
Associated with Jenkins' mind as a boy with H. G. Wells and St John Clarke, with whom he was once photographed ('The picture had interested me because, although I had already read books by these three writers, all had inspired me with the same sense that theirs was not the kind of writing I liked') AW 20–1. See also Place Index under KENSINGTON GARDENS (Peter Pan statue).

Baroque Interlude
The travel book with which Mark Members recoups his reputation in the 'thirties. For refs, see Character Index under MEMBERS, Mark.

BAUDELAIRE, Charles 1821–1867
VB 9; his *Voyage à Cythère* quoted by Moreland KO 139; TK 50.

BEAUMONT, Francis 1584–1616
HSH 99; and FLETCHER, John 1579–1625, a passage quoted by
Gwinnett from one of their plays (*Cupid's Revenge*) describes Scorpio
Murtlock to the life HSH 168–9.

Bedsores
Ada Leintwardine's fourth novel, the one with which she extracted
herself from threatened literary doldrums. For refs, see Character Index
under LEINTWARDINE, Ada.

Bel-Ami
Novel by Guy de Maupassant, 1850–93; read by Jenkins the summer he
left school QU 143.

BERGERAC, Cyrano de 1619–55
Author of *Histoire comique des états et empires de la lune* etc., and subject
of a book pub. in the late 'sixties by David Penniston ('Penniston was
more interested in his subject as philosopher and heresiarch than space-
traveller . . .') TK 202, HHS 32. See also *Cyrano de Bergerac*.

BIBLICAL QUOTATIONS
'Arise Barak, and lead thy captivity captive, thou son of Abinoam'
(*Judges* V 12). Applied by Captain Gwatkin to his men during a pep talk
about rifles VB 67.

'Be of good courage and let us behave ourselves valiantly for our
people . . .' (*I Chronicles* XIX 13). Inscribed on the First Earl of
Warminster's tomb in Thrubworth church BDFR 43.

'The hand of the Lord was upon me . . .' (*Ezekiel* XXXVII 1–10). Text
of the Rev. Popkiss' sermon on the valley of bones VB 37–8, MP 242.

'The wilderness and the solitary place shall be glad for them . . .' (*Isaiah*
XXXV 1–9). Lesson read at the Victory service in St Paul's, giving rise
to reflections on the fates of various wayfaring men MP 222–4, 231.

'Thou hast a few names even in Sardis which have not defiled their
garments . . .' (*Revelation* III 4). Text inscribed in Gothic letters on the
walls of the Welsh chapel used as a barrack room by Captain Gwatkin's
company in 1940 VB 5; applied by Jenkins to the behaviour of the
Lydian King Candaules and his friend Gyges in Tiepolo's painting TK
86; HSH 35.

'Though I speak with the tongues of men and of angels, and have not
charity, I am become as sounding brass . . .' (*I Corinthians* XIII 1–3).
Lesson read in an appropriately rasping voice by Sir Bertram Akworth
at his granddaughter's wedding HSH 192–3.

Bin Ends
Volume of X. Trapnel's short stories, pub. soon after *Camel Ride to the Tomb*. For refs, see Character Index under TRAPNEL, X.

Bitch Pack Meets on Wednesday, The
Ada Leintwardine's fifth novel, after which she never looked back as a successful writer. For refs, see Character Index under LEINT-WARDINE, Ada.

BLAKE, William 1757–1827
St John Clarke's carefully cultivated resemblance to CCR 79; reflections on his *Jerusalem* during the Victory service at St Paul's ('Blake was as impenetrable as Isaiah; in his way, more so. It was not quite such wonderful stuff as the Prophet rendered into Elizabethan English, yet wonderful enough. At the same time, so I always felt, never quite for me. Blake was a genius, but not one for the classical taste. He was too cranky . . .') MP 223–4, 231; BDFR 127; Mark Members in later life comes to resemble HSH 39.

BOETHIUS, Anicius Manlius Severinus 475–524
Author of *Consolatio Philosophiae* etc., and subject of a controversial study by Dr Emily Brightman. For refs, see Character Index under BRIGHTMAN, Dr Emily.

BOGGIS & STONE
Specialist left-wing publishing firm which takes over Howard Craggs' Vox Populi Press in the early 'thirties, merging after the second war with Quiggin & Craggs AW 49, 118–19, 122; LM 109; CCR 198; BDFR 9, 24, 36. See also Character Index under CRAGGS, Howard, MEMBERS, Mark and QUIGGIN, J. G.

Borage and Hellebore: a Study
Only known title of any of Nicholas Jenkins' works, the book about Robert Burton undertaken at the end of the war as a change from novel writing and published in December 1947 BDFR 2–3, 240; TK 4. See also BURTON, Robert.

Boy's Own Paper
Erridge's favourite reading, together with bound volumes of Chums ('It was Erry's only vice, though one he tried to keep dark, as showing in himself a lack of earnestness and sense of social obligation'), also a consolation to Lt. Bithel in time of trouble LM 129, SA 13–15, BDFR 68.

Bronstein: Marxist or Mystagogue?
The political recantation of Vernon Gainsborough (formerly Guggen-bühl), published in 1947 and favourably noticed along with seven other books on similar subjects in *The Times Literary Supplement*. For refs, see Character Index under GUGGENBÜHL, Werner.

BROOKE, Rupert 1887–1915
Provided a model for Bill Truscott's early verse, according to Mark Members ('Rupert Brooke at his most babbling, Mark used to say, Housman at his most lad-ish') BDFR 8.

Brothers Karamozov,·The
See DOSTOIEVSKY, Feodor.

BROWNING, Robert 1812–89
A legitimate early influence on Mark Members AW 86; Miss Weedon's favourite poet, always makes Stringham feel rather jumpy, his definition of the soldier's art from *Childe Roland to the Dark Tower Came* quoted, Jenkins never quite sure about him SA 79, 218–19, 221–2; his *Grammarian's Funeral* quoted by Mark Members TK 7.

BUNYAN, John 1628–88.
See *Pilgrim's Progress*.

BURTON, Robert 1577–1640
Long a favourite of Jenkins' and subject of his book *Borage and Hellebore*, pub. 1947; reflections on uneasy states of mind, advancing age and loss of friends prompted by his *Anatomy of Melancholy* ('War left, on the one hand, a passionate desire to tackle a lot of work; on the other, never to do any work again. It was a state of mind Robert Burton . . . would have well understood. Irresolution appealed to him as one of the myriad forms of Melancholy, although he was, of course, concerned in the main with no mere temporary depression or fidgetiness, but a "chronic or continued disease, a settled humour". Still, post-war melancholy might have rated a short sub-section in the great work: *The Anatomy of Melancholy . . .*') BDFR 2–4; 11, 19, Erridge a subject for, if ever there was one 27–8; impinges on thoughts of death at Erridge's funeral ('In the end one got back to Burton's "vile rock of melancholy, a disease so frequent, few there are that feel not the smart of it". Melancholy was so often the explanation, anyway melancholy in Burton's terms') 54; Dicky Umfraville a pure Burton type 92; 94; Moreland always fond of his *Anatomy* 118–19; X. Trapnel 'clearly no stranger to what Burton called "those excrementitious humours of the third concoction, blood and tears"' 154–5, 161 & 218; Pamela Widmerpool a melancholic in his definition 196; his account of the ·

216

aberrations of love in the vegetable kingdom quoted with reference to Trapnel 230; Le Bas' view of 234–5; publication of Jenkins' book about 240; TK 4, 87; HSH 30, 99, 144, a torrential passage from the *Anatomy* concludes Jenkins' narrative 271–2. See also entry in Book Index under JENKINS, Nicholas.

BYRON, Lord 1788–1824
CCR 34; his *Don Juan* quoted, his association with Castlemallock, extract from his letter ('said to be of doubtful authenticity'*) to Caroline Lamb at Castlemallock VB 170–1; MP 127; TK 50; HSH 30. See also Character Index under LAMB, Lady Caroline, MALLOCK, Hercules and SLEAFORD, Earl of.

CABELL, James Branch 1879–1958
American novelist to whom Louis Glober offers to introduce Jenkins TK 71.

Cain's Jawbone
Evadne Clapham's thirty-fifth novel, see Character Index under CLAPHAM, Evadne.

Cambises, King of Percia: a Lamentable Tragedy mixed full of Pleasant Mirth
Play ('Not particularly exciting, but does summarize life': Moreland) by Thomas Preston, 1537–98 TK 275.

Camel Ride to the Tomb
Book with which X. Trapnel made his reputation ('the best first novel since the war': Bagshaw). See Character Index under TRAPNEL X.

CARROLL, Lewis (Rev. Charles Dodgson) 1832–98
Author of *Alice in Wonderland, Alice Through the Looking-glass* etc. M. Dubuisson as a French version of the Mad Hatter QU 116; Widmerpool as the Frog Footman BM 60 & BDFR 101–2; AW 97; Mrs Fettiplace-Jones as the Red Queen KO 91; VB 8, Lt. Bithel as a cross between the Walrus and the Carpenter VB 32; Jenkins as Alice SA 2 & MP 241; MP 180, Field Marshal Montgomery as something from *Alice in Wonderland* MP 184.

CASANOVA, Giacomo de Seingalt 1725–1803
For his *Memoirs*, see Character Index under CASANOVA.

* See footnote, p. 246.

Chums
See *Boy's Own Paper*.

City State and State of City
Sillery's only published work, apart from a slim volume of early verse
and the diaries brought out on retirement. See Character Index under
SILLERY.

CLAPHAM, Evadne
Novelist, see Character Index. See also *Cain's Jawbone* and *Golden
Grime*.

CLARKE, St John
Romantic novelist taken reasonably seriously in the early decades of the
century. His work characterized by homosexual undertones ('St J. has
always pooh-poohed the subconscious': Members AW 127), historical
or high society settings, 'windy descriptive passages, two-dimensional
characterization, and . . . the emptiness of the writing's inner content'
(BM 244). Is already largely forgotten by the time of his death in the
'thirties but continues selling fairly well until after the second war. Fails
to make a posthumous comeback on the fashionable wave of
Edwardian nostalgia in the late 'fifties, when Louis Glober's plans to
film his novel, *Match Me Such Marvel* ('How will you handle the scene
where Phyllida and Prosper get lost in the mist on the glacier at
Schwarenbach?' TK 234), come to nothing. Has become an
embarrassment to his publisher, J. G. Quiggin, by the end of the
'sixties.

His novels instinctively disliked by Jenkins as a boy (see BARRIE, J.
M.); later devoured wholesale during Jenkins' last years at school ('I
came round for a time to St John Clarke with that avid literary
consumption of the immature which cannot precisely be regarded
either as enjoyment or the reverse. The flavour of St John Clarke's
novels is hard to describe to those unfamiliar with them, perhaps on
account of their own inexactitudes of thought and feeling' AW 21);
and later still unequivocally repudiated ('I had long preferred to forget
the days when I had regarded St John Clarke's work as fairly daring. In
fact I had become accustomed to refer to him and his books with the
savagery which, when one is a young man, seems – perhaps rightly –
the only proper and serious attitude towards anyone, most of all an
older person, practising the arts in an inept or outworn manner' AW
20).

For a survey of his career, and refs, see Character Index under
CLARKE, St John. For further reflections on his position as a fellow
novelist, see JENKINS, Nicholas; see also *Dust Thou Art, E'en the*

218

Longest River, Fields of Amaranth, The Heart is Highland, Match Me Such Marvel, Mimosa, Never to the Philistines.

COLERIDGE, Samuel Taylor 1772–1834
His evocation of 'sunny domes and caves of ice' (from *Kubla Khan*) used by Quiggin to describe Thrubworth Park LM 137.

Comédie Humaine
See BALZAC, Honoré de.

'Comme le souvenir est voisin du remords'
Line (from *Paroles sur la dune*) quoted by Moreland on revisiting Bloomsbury after the second war, see HUGO, Victor.

'Connaissez-vous la vieille souveraine du monde, qui marche toujours, et ne se fatigue jamais?'
Formula quoted (from *Dogme et Rituel de la Haute Magie*, vol II) by Dr Trelawney to introduce Mrs Erdleigh, see LEVI, Eliphas.

CONRAD, Joseph 1857–1924
See Place Index under UFFORD.

Coral Island, The
By R. M. Ballantyne, 1825–94; Jenkins' animosity towards shared by Moreland as a boy KO 82.

CORELLI, Marie 1864–1924
Her *Sorrows of Satan* one of only four books in the smoking-room bookcase at Stonehurst KO 60.

COWLEY, Abraham 1618–67
One of the poets brought to mind during the Victory service at St Paul's: an outstanding success in his own time unlike Blake, his pointed wit ('In Cowley's quite peculiar grasp of the contrasted tenderness and brutality of love, wit was just the quality he brought to bear with such remarkable effect') and capacity for facing facts illustrated by a quotation (from *The Innocent Ill*) MP 224–5, 231.

CREEVEY, Thomas 1768–1838
Diarist, reported a capital speech★ by the Fourth Lord Erridge BDFR 43.

CROWDING, Malcolm
Committed poet, see Character Index.

★ See footnote, p. 246.

CUMMINGS, E.E. 1894–1962
American poet addicted to lower case letters MP 122.

Cyrano de Bergerac
Play by Edmond Rostand, 1868–1918; the shape of its hero's celebrated nose recalled by Clanwaert's though not by Finn's MP 94.

D'ANNUNZIO, Gabriele 1863–1938
Italian writer and warrior etc.; St John Clarke's much quoted *mot* about ('Gorki is a Russian D'Annunzio') pinched without acknowledgement from Mark Members AW 123.

DANTE Alighieri 1265–1321
Film version of his *Inferno* banned to both Jenkins and Moreland in childhood KO 82; SA 156.

DAVIDSON, John 1857–1909
His lines on Tannhäuser and the Queen of Night (from *A Ballad to Tannhäuser*) brought to mind by Widmerpool and Pamela Flitton MP 203.

'Dearest, our day is over,/Ended the dream divine . . .'
Lines (by Paolo Tosti, 1846–1916) quoted by Moreland to express his own nostalgic feelings at the Stevenses' musical party TK 230.

'Death is the mother of beauty'
Line quoted by Delavacquerie from Wallace Stevens' *Sunday Morning* HSH 76.

Death's-Head Swordsman. The Life and Works of X. Trapnel
Russell Gwinnett's biography, pub. at the end of the 'sixties and awarded the fourth Magnus Donners Memorial Prize. For refs, see Character Index under GWINNETT, Russell and TRAPNEL, X.

DEKKER, Thomas *c.* 1540–1671
See MIDDLETON, Thomas.

DELAVACQUERIE, Gibson
Poet and public relations officer, see Character Index.

DESBAROLLES, Adolphe 1801–86
Parisian chiromancer, author of *Chiromanie Nouvelle: Les Mystères de la Main revelés at expliqués* etc.; quoted by Mrs Erdleigh on the night she reads Pamela Flitton's palm ('your palm makes me think of that passage in Desbarolles, the terrible words of which always haunt my mind when I see their marks in a hand shown to me . . . *la débauche, l'effronterie, la license, la dévergondage, la coquetterie, la vanité, l'esprit léger, l'inconstance, la paresse . . .*') MP 135.

Descartes, Gassendi and the Atomic Theory of Epicurus
Pennistone's book, see Character Index under PENNISTONE, David.

DE TABLEY, Lord 1835–95
Poet and playwright ('A melancholy fellow, but not without merit': Le
Bas), some lines from the chorus of his *Medea* quoted by Le Bas MP
62–3.

DICKENS, Charles 1812–70
Dickensian personage on the door at Umfraville's night-club LM 173;
CCR 18, 96–7; BDFR 68, 141, *Oliver Twist* cited by Trapnel as proof
of the artificiality of naturalism BDFR 216; TK 66; HSH 84.

'Di, Di, in her collar and tie,
Quizzes the girls with a monocled eye,
Sipping her hock in a black satin stock,
Or shooting her cuffs over *pernod* or *bock*.

Like a torpedo, in brogues or tuxedo,
She's tearing around at Cape Cod, or the Lido;
From Bournemouth to Biarritz, the fashion parades
Welcome debonaire Di in her chic tailor-mades . . .'
Song sung by Max Pilgrim at Umfraville's night-club LM 186.

DISRAELI, Benjamin 1804–81
Statesman and novelist, his *Endymion* misquoted by Le Bas BM 104;
another of the novelists cited by Trapnel to demonstrate the heresy of
naturalism BDFR 216.

Dr Zhivago
See PASTERNAK, Boris.

Dogs Have No Uncles
Long short story by X. Trapnel, completed before *Camel Ride to the
Tomb* but delayed by a legal battle over rights and eventually published
after its author's death with an enthusiastic introduction by L. O.
Salvidge. For refs, see Character Index under TRAPNEL, X. and
SALVIDGE, L. O.

Dogme et Rituel de la Haute Magie
See LEVI, Eliphas.

Don Juan
See BYRON, Lord★

★ Other references to Don Juan, comparing and contrasting his prowess as
seducer with Casanova's, seem to be to the hero of Mozart's opera rather than
Byron's poem, see Character Index under CASANOVA.

Don Quixote
By Miguel de Cervantes, 1547–1616; Erridge's gauntness recalls Don
Quixote's LM 135.

DOSTOIEVSKY, Feodor Mihailovich 1821–81
Erridge compared by Quiggin to Prince Myshkin in *The Idiot* LM 153
& CCR 196; the Soviet military attaché General Lebedev refuses to
discuss, recommending instead Nekrasov's truer picture of Russian life
MP 166–7; *The Brothers Karamazov* recalled at Erridge's funeral BDFR
52; cited by Trapnel in support of his theory that there is no such thing
as naturalism BDFR 216–17; *Brothers Karamazov* discussed at Soviet
Embassy, recalling Gen. Lebedev's attitude ('Dostoievsky, impossible
to ignore, equally impossible to assimilate into Communist life, a
monolithic embarrassment to his countrymen, was a tendentious
subject for the present luncheon party') and Trapnel's views on
naturalism, Trapnel seen as Myshkin TK 217–19; HSH 57.

DOWSON, Ernest 1867–1900
Moreland on problems of Time and Space raised by his Cynara (in *Non
sum quails eram bonae sub regno Cynarae*) CCR 34.

Duchess of Malfi, The
Tragedy by John Webster, *c.* 1580–1625; put on at a small theatre in the
early 'thirties, with Matilda Wilson playing Julia to Norman Chandler's
Bosola, shortly before Matilda's marriage to Moreland. For refs, see
Character Index under CHANDLER, Norman, MORELAND,
Hugh and WILSON, Matilda.

Dunciad, The
See POPE, Alexander.

Dust Thou Art
Historical romance by St John Clarke set in the French Revolution.
For refs, see Character Index under CLARKE, St John and
SALVIDGE, L. O.

Dutch Courtesan, The
Play by John Marston, *c.* 1575–1634; its heroine's song applied by
Moreland to Pamela Widmerpool TK 276.

E'en the Longest River
Novel by St John Clarke, generally agreed to rank with *The Heart is
Highland* as a poor second to *Fields of Amaranth*. For refs, see Character
Index under CLARKE, St John.

'Eldorado banal de tous les vieux garçons'
Lines (from *Un Voyage à Cythère*) applied by Moreland to Stourwater
Castle, see BAUDELAIRE, Charles.

ELIOT, T. S. 1888–1965
CCR 33, 54; lines from *The Waste Land* brought to mind during an air
raid SA 18; and again by thoughts of death on Westminster Bridge MP
113.

Engine Melody
See *The Pistons of Our Locomotives Sing the Songs of Our Workers.*

Esmond
See THACKERAY, W. M.

Fabian Essays
Sillery has an inscribed first edition of QU 189.

'Fart upon Euclid, he is stale and antick . . .'
Lines quoted by Moreland (from *The New Inn*), see JONSON, Ben.

FERRAND-SENESCHAL, Léon-Joseph
Prolific French Marxist playwright, novelist and writer of political and
economic tracts ('his early books were ridiculously stilted, his later ones
grossly slipshod': Dr Emily Brightman). See Character Index.

Fields of Amaranth
St John Clarke's most famous novel, takes its title from the legendary
flower which never fades called in English Love-lies-bleeding ('Much
play was made of the two meanings in the story'). For refs, see
Character Index under CLARKE, St John.

FITZGERALD, F. Scott 1896–1940
X. Trapnel on the specialized naturalism of his romantic-hearted
gangster in *The Great Gatsby* BDFR 217.

Fission
Short-lived political and literary weekly of progressive outlook,
founded after the second war by the publishing house of Quiggin &
Craggs with backing from Widmerpool and Rosie Manasch; edited by
Books-do-furnish-a-room Bagshaw who recruits Jenkins as literary
assistant; housed in a sheds at the far side of Quiggin & Craggs'
backyard in Bloomsbury. Starts publication with a bumper first number
(containing short stories by X. Trapnel and Evadne Clapham, a poem
by Malcolm Crowding, an article by Bernard Shernmaker contrasting
Rilke with Mayakovsky, and another by Widmerpool entitled

Affirmative Action and Negative Values) in the second week of October, 1946, and folds the following autumn.* Its conception and prospects BDFR 35–7, Jenkins joins the staff of 75–6, preliminary activity at 93, 97, 101–3, 112–13, 115, 118, inaugural party for 120–3, 127–30, 133, 136–9, trouble at 142–3, 151, Trapnel's treatment of Kydd's *Sweetskin* in 154–6 & 167, 162, Trapnel's parody of Widmerpool in 184–6 & 193–4 & 201, 189, 199, 203, its demise 207–8, 211–13, 237–8; TK Bagshaw's flair as editor of recalled 11–16, 25, 35, 136, 140, 142, 181, 187; HSH 54.

FLETCHER, John 1579–1625
See BEAUMONT, Francis, and *The Humorous Lieutenant*.

'For lust of knowing what we should not know, we take the Golden Road to Samarkand'
A favourite saying (from *Hassan* by James Elroy Flecker, 1884–1915) of Sir Gavin Walpole-Wilson ('This quotation may have offered to his mind some explanation of human adversity, though scarcely applicable in his own case, as he was a man singularly lacking in intellectual curiosity, and it was generally supposed that the inopportune step in his career had been the result of too much caution rather than any disposition to experiment in that exploration, moral or actual, to which the lines seemed to refer') BM 20.

'For some we loved, the loveliest and the best . . .'
Lines quoted by Moreland, see *Rubaiyàt of Omar Khayyàm*.

From Peasant to Collective Farmer
One of the books on Erridge's shelves at Thrubworth, see *Anthology of Soviet Literature*.

GALSWORTHY, John 1867–1933
' "*That* door was banged-to for me at birth," Uncle Giles used to say (in a phrase that I found, much later, he had lifted from a novel by John Galsworthy) when some plum was mentioned, conceived by him available only to those above, or below, him in the social scale.' (From Galsworthy's novel *The Patrician*†) QU 66.

Garnered at Sunset: Leaves from an Edwardian Journal
Volume of selections from Sillery's secret diaries, billed as the scoop of the year by Quiggin & Craggs in 1947 ('They'll be read as the most

* BDFR 121, 211–2, 237; but see BDFR 207, which suggests 'a two-year run'.
† 'He would never have admitted for a moment that certain doors had been banged-to at his birth, bolted when he went to Eton and padlocked at Cambridge.'

notable chronicle of our time': Short) but turns out on publication to be too dull to read. For refs, see Character Index under SILLERY.

GAUTIER, Théophile 1811–72
His treatment of the Candaules and Gyges legend, in a story (*Le Roi Candaule*) portraying the king as a melancholy Ivory Tower aesthete, contrasted by Dr Brightman with André Gide's socially conscious stage version (also called *Le Roi Candaule*) TK 77, 88–9; HSH 57.

GIDE, André 1869–1951
See above.

GISSING, George 1857–1903
His delineation of poverty favourably compared with St John Clarke's in the latter's obituaries CCR 192; more of an authority on starvation than on writing in Trapnel's view BDFR 145.

Goblin Market
By Christina Rossetti, 1830–94; brought to mind by the wizened and fretful War Office Signals officer ('a near-midget, middle-aged and two-pipped, with long arms and short legs attached to a squat frame') who is later identified as the spitting image of Mime in Wagner's *Ring* MP 2.

GOETHE, Johann Wolfgang von 1749–1832
Quoted (*Mignons Lied*) by Members TK 7; HSH 128.

GOGOL, Nikolai 1809–52
Widmerpool never read a line of SA 174; TK 217.

Golden Bough, The
By the anthropologist Sir James Frazer, 1854–1941; Jenkins recalls the fate of temporary kings in TK 7.

Golden Grime
Novel by Evadne Clapham, see Character Index under CLAPHAM, Evadne.

Golden Treasury, The
Ed. F. T. Palgrave, 1824–97, figures in the story of how Books-do-furnish-a-room Bagshaw got his nickname BDFR 32–3.

GORKI, Maxim 1868–1936
See D'ANNUNZIO, Gabriele.

GOSSE, Sir Edmund 1849–1928
Poet, critic and man-of-letters, made Mark Members a name to
conjure with among freshmen of his year by praising the latter's poem
in *Public School Verse* QU 176.

Gothic Symbolism of Mortality in the Texture of Jacobean Stagecraft, The
Book with which Russell Gwinnett follows up his biography of X.
Trapnel, pursuing his researches at the scene of Scorpio Murtlock's cult
activities ('I'd often thought these weirdos linked up with the
seventeenth-century gothicism I was writing about . . . I was right').
See Character Index under GWINNETT, Russell.

Great Gatsby, The
See FITZGERALD, F. Scott.

Green Hat, The
Fabulously successful bestseller (by Michael Arlen, 1895–1956), bought
when it came out in 1924 by Jenkins in his first year at university ('I had
. . . not yet fully digested the subject matter of *The Green Hat*, a novel
that I felt painted, on the whole, a sympathetic picture of what London
had to offer: though much of the life it described was still obscure to
me'), and borrowed by Quiggin who does not expect to like it QU
203–5.

GRILLPARZER, Frans 1791–1872
Austrian dramatist, one of the names bandied by Mark Members in his
Germanic phase LM 221.

GRONOW, Captain 1794–1865
Dandy and duellist chiefly famed for his *Reminiscences*; his account★ of
the first Earl of Warminster's susceptibility to the charms of the fair sex
quoted BDFR 43–4, 48.

GROTE, George 1794–1871
His *History of Greece* once read through by Corporal Curtis MP 28.

Guest Night
Title of some unexpectedly melancholy lines by Odo Stevens, inspired
by his youthful enthusiasm for Max Pilgrim SA 147–8.

HAGGARD, Rider 1856–1925
Mrs Erdleigh compared by Templer to his 'She who must be obeyed'
(in *She*) AW 102.

★ See footnote, p. 246.

Hamlet
See SHAKESPEARE, William.

HARDY, Thomas 1840–1928
QU 182; Mrs Widmerpool keenly looks forward to his widow's articles about in *The Times* (pub. Oct. 22–6, 1928) BM 264; Polly Duport stars in a film version of one of his novels TK 51–2.

HARINGTON, Sir John 1561–1612
Jenkins reads *Orlando Furioso* in his translation, see ARIOSTO.

HAUPTMANN, Gerhart 1862–1946
Ethico-social playwright approved by Werner Guggenbühl ('Drama as highest of arts we Germans know. No mere entertainment, please') AW 166.

H-bomb Ecologue
One of the few poems Mark Members manages to produce in later life. See Character Index under MEMBERS, Mark.

Heart is Highland, The
St John's Clarke's novel, considered by some critics second only to *Fields of Amaranth*. See Character Index under CLARKE, St John.

'Heather, Heather. She's under the weather . . .'
Song of Max Pilgrim's. See Character Index under PILGRIM, Max.

HEMINGWAY, Ernest 1898–1961
Failed to make contact with Erridge in Spain during the civil war CCR 198; would never allow a hero of his to be made a fool of, Trapnel on his impotent good guy (in *The Sun Also Rises*) as a variant of Dostoievsky's Prince Myshkin BDFR 217; punning reference to TK 17.

HENTY, George Alfred 1832–1902
His *For Name and Fame: or, through the Afghan Passes*, one of very few books ever read by Sunny Farebrother KO 24.

'Here upon earth we're kings . . .'
Quoted by Members (from Donne's *The Anniversary*) TK 7.

'Here's to the wings of love'
Toast from *How to Mix Cocktails*, *c.* 1926, sung by Umfraville HSH 199.

HERBERT, George 1593–1633
His lines on death (from *The Temple*) brought to mind at Erridge's funeral, see RALEGH, Sir Walter.

Heresy of Naturalism, The
Trapnel's projected critical manifesto, see TRAPNEL X.

High Tide on the Coast of Lincolnshire
The poem (by Jean Ingelow, 1820–97) Alfred Tolland once heard Mrs Patrick Campbell read aloud LM 37–8.

'His helmet now shall make a hive for bees . . .'
Another of Sir Gavin Walpole-Wilson's favourite quotations (from *Polyhymnia* by George Peele, *c.* 1589–97) BM 223.

Histoire comique des états et empires de la lune
See BERGERAC, Cyrano de.

History of the Great Northern Railway
One of the few books by Moreland's bed CCR 5.

'Honour and Wit, fore-damned they sit'
Line (from *Tomlinson* in *Barrack Room Ballads*) brought to mind by the headless trunks in a theatrical costumier's off Shaftesbury Avenue. See KIPLING, Rudyard.

HOPKINS, Gerard Manley 1844–89
Sillery has a letter from QU 189.

HOUSMAN, A. E. 1860–1936
Not Stringham's favourite poet, his *Lancer* quoted SA 81. See also BROOKE, Rupert.

HOWELLS, William Dean 1837–1920
American novelist, his book about Venice (*Venetian Life*) recommended by Gwinnett TK 61.

'How happy could I be with either . . .'
A variant on this line (from *The Beggars' Opera* by John Gay, 1685–1732) proposed by Moreland TK 90.

HUGO, Victor 1802–85
Tedium of Widmerpool on the subject of QU 114, 151; a line by (from *Paroles sur la dune*) BDFR 119.

Humorous Lieutenant, The
Decidedly obscure Jacobean comedy attributed to Fletcher which is experimentally revived for a limited run in the late 'sixties with Polly Duport as Celia, and greatly enjoyed by Russell Gwinnett ('As a neurotic figure, the Lieutenant is perhaps not altogether unlike Gwinnett': Delavacquerie) HSH 144–6, 176.

By the author of *Seated One Day at an Organ*, title of Moreland's proposed excursion into autobiography BDFR 120.

HYMNS
'Angels in the height, adore him . . .' Brings Stringham to mind when sung at the Victory service in St Paul's ('Hymns always made me think of Stringham, addicted to quoting their imagery within the context of his own life') MP 221.

'As o'er each continent and island . . .' Sung in chapel on Widmerpool's last Sunday at school QU 51.

'Guide me, O thou great Jehovah . . .' Sung by the men of Jenkins' Welsh battalion in 1940 ('This singing on the march, whatever form it took, always affirmed the vicissitudes of life, the changes, so often for the worse, that beset human existence, especially in the army, especially in time of war. After a while they abandoned the hymn, though not those accustomed themes of uncertainty, hardship, weariness, despondency, vain effort, contemplation of which gives such support to the soldier: "We had ter join, We had ter join, We had ter join Belisha's army . . ."') VB 39–40.

'Not for ever by still waters Would we idly rest and stay . . .' Stringham feels just like the hymn CCR 183.

'Now we are come to the sun's hour of rest . . .' Scorpio Murtlock's solo in his choirboy days HSH 131.

'Now thank we all our God . . .' Sung at the Victory service in St Paul's MP 225.

'Open now the crystal fountain . . .' Sung by Welsh soldiers in wartime VB 237, MP 177; and by Bithel at Stourwater more than twenty years later HSH 216.

'Some are sick and some are sad, And some have never loved one well, And some have lost the love they had.' Quoted by Stringham a propos his friends and relations MP 221.

'When I tread the verge of Jordan . . .' Sung by Lance-Corporal Gittins in wartime VB 102; and long afterwards by Bithel at Stourwater HSH 238.

IBSEN, Henrik 1828–1906
Jenkins sees a provincial production of *The Doll's House* as a schoolboy QU 114; *Peer Gynt* brought to mind by the disquieting atmosphere of Stourwater castle ('We passed through room after room, apartments of which the cumulative magnificence seemed only to enhance the earlier

fancy that, at some wave of the wand – somewhat in the manner of Peer Gynt – furniture and armour, pictures and hangings, gold and silver, crystal and china, could turn easily and instantaneously into a heap of withered leaves blown about by the wind') BM 201; and by troll-like air-raid wardens in the blitz SA 160; Dempster distantly related to MP 24 & TK 202; Polly Duport stars in a play by HSH 120, 123–4.

Idiot, The
See DOSTOIEVSKY, Feodor.

If Winter Comes
Bestseller (by A. S. M. Hutchinson), pub. 1921 and read by Jenkins the summer he left school QU 100, 134.

'I'm Tess of Le Touquet,
My morals are flukey,
Tossed on the foam, I couldn't be busier;
Permanent waves
Splash me into the caves;
Everyone loves me as much as Delysia.
When it's wet on the Links, I know where to have a beau
Down in the club-house – next door to the lavabo.

Even the fairies
Say how sweet my hair is;
They mess my mascara and pinch the peroxide.
I know a coward
Would be overpowered,
When they all offer to be orthodox. I'd
Like to be kind, but say "Some other day, dears;
Pansies for thoughts remains still the best way, dears".

I do hope Tallulah
Now feels a shade cooler,
But why does she pout, as she wanders so far off
From Monsieur Citröen,
Who says something knowin'
To Lady Cunard and Sir Basil Zaharoff?
Has someone guessed who was having a beano
At Milly's last party behind the Casino?'

The song of Max Pilgrim's which drives Mr Deacon to frenzy at Milly Andriadis' party. For refs, see Character Index under PILGRIM, Max.

Ingoldsby Legends, The
A favourite book (by the Rev. R. H. Barham, 1788–1845) of Jenkins

as a boy, brought to mind long afterwards in St Paul's by the monuments to Sir Ralph Abercrombie (*sic*) and Sir John Moore MP 216–7.

Indian Crisis, The
Another of the books in Erridge's library, see *Anthology of Soviet Literature*.

Integral Foundations to a Fresh Approach to Art for the Masses
The article in *Fission* with which Len Pugsley makes his first and last real step in life. See Character Index under PUGSLEY, Len.

I Promessi Sposi
Novel (by Alessandro Manzoni, 1785–1873) whose plot provides Moreland with a parallel for Sir Magnus Donners' abduction of Matilda TK 272–3.

Iron Aspidistra
The poem published in *Public School Verse*, and favourably noticed by Sir Edmund Gosse, which first brought fame to Mark Members as an undergraduate. See Character Index under MEMBERS, Mark.

I Stopped at a Chemist
Ada Leintwardine's first novel, published by Quiggin & Craggs in 1947 when it upset several of the more old-fashioned reviewers and inspired a complete change of style in Evadne Clapham; later filmed as *Sally Goes Shopping*. For refs, see Character Index under LEINTWARDINE, Ada.

'I was a king in Babylon, And you were a Christian slave . . .' Subject proposed by Moreland ('not that I can ever see how the couple in question managed to be those utterly disparate things at the same moment in history') for Sir Magnus Donners' photographic tableaux at Stourwater (from *To W. A.* by W. E. Henley, 1849–1903) KO 124.

'I want to dazzle Lady Sybil . . .'
One of Max Pilgrim's songs, possibly inspired by Lady Huntercombe. See Character Index under PILGRIM, Max.

JAMES, Henry 1843–1916
May have been the critic (unless it was Stevenson) who pointed out to Le Bas that the verses he thought frightfully good were, as a matter of fact, frightfully bad QU 32; once stayed at Dogdene before the first world war LM 214; would have made a good job in non-naturalistic terms of Scott Fitzgerald's Gatsby BDFR 217; TK 138.

JENKINS, Nicholas

Novelist. Meditates on writing shortly after the publication of his first novel and before the completion of his second:

'I began to brood on the complexity of writing a novel about English life, a subject difficult enough to handle with authenticity even of a crudely naturalistic sort, even more to convey the inner truth of things observed. . . . Intricacies of social life makes English habits unyielding to simplification, while understatement and irony – in which all classes of this island converse – upset the normal emphasis of reported speech.

How, I asked myself, could a writer attempt to describe in a novel such a young man as Mark Members, for example, possessing so much in common with myself, yet so different? . . . Thinking about Members that evening, I found myself unable to consider him without prejudice . . . Prejudice was to be avoided if – as I had idly pictured him – Members were to form the basis of a character in a novel. Alternatively, prejudice might prove the very element through which to capture and pin down unequivocally the otherwise elusive nature of what was of interest, discarding by its selective power the empty, unprofitable shell making up that side of Members untranslatable into terms of art; concentrating his final essence, his position, as it were, in eternity, into the medium of words.

Any but the most crude indication of my own personality would be, I reflected, equally hard to transcribe; at any rate one that did not sound a little absurd. It was all very well for Mrs Erdleigh to generalize; far less easy to take an objective view oneself. Even the bare facts had an unreal, almost satirical ring when committed to paper, say in the manner of the innumerable Russian stories of the nineteenth century: "I was born in the city of L – , the son of an infantry officer . . ." To convey much that was relevant to the reader's mind by such phrases was in this country hardly possible. Too many factors had to be taken into consideration. Understatement, too, had its own banality; for, skirting cheap romanticism, it could also encourage evasion of unpalatable facts.' (AW 32–4).

Takes stock of his own position a few years later, as a young novelist with two or three books published, in the light of a first meeting with the elderly St John Clarke:

'Mutual relationship between writers, whatever their age, is always delicate, not so much – as commonly supposed – on account of jealousy, but because of the intensely personal nature of a writer's stock in trade. For example, St John Clarke seemed to be a "bad" writer, that is to say a person to be treated (in those days) with reserve, if not thinly veiled hostility. Later, that question – the relationship of writers of different sorts – seemed, like so many others, less easily solved; in fact infinitely complicated. St John Clarke himself had made a living, indeed collected a small fortune, while giving pleasure to many by writing his books (pleasure even to myself when a boy, if it came to that), yet now was become an object of disapproval to me because his novels did not rise to a certain standard demanded by myself. Briefly, they seemed to me trivial, unreal, vulgar, badly put together, odiously phrased and "insincere". Yet, even allowing for these failings, was not St John Clarke still a person more like myself than anyone else sitting round the table? That was a sobering thought. He, too, for longer years, had existed in the imagination, even though this imagination led him (in my eyes) to a world ludicrously contrived, socially misleading, professionally nauseous. On top of that, had he not on this earlier occasion gone out of his way to speak a word of carefully hedge praise for my own work? Was that, therefore, an aspect of his critical faculty for which he should be given credit, or was it an even stronger reason for guarding against the possibility of corruption at the hands of one whose own writings could not be approved? Fortunately these speculations, heavily burdened with the idealistic sentiments of one's younger days, were put to no practical test . . .' (CCR 82–3).

Lays down some general principles a decade or so later, while working on his only non-fiction book, a study (*Borage and Hellebore*) of Robert Burton:

'The period of architecture . . . brought Burton to mind; Burton, by implication the art of writing in general. On this subject he knew what he was talking about:
"Tis not my study or intent to compose neatly . . . but to express myself readily & plainly as it happens. So that as a River runs sometimes precipitate and swift, then dull and slow; now direct, then winding; now deep, then shallow, now muddy, then clear; now broad, then narrow; doth my style flow; now serious, then light; now comical, then satirical; now more elaborate, then remiss, as the present subject required, or as at the time I was affected."
Even for those with a prejudice in favour of symmetry, worse rules might be laid down. The antithesis between satire and comedy was especially worth emphasis; also to write as the subject required, or the author thought fit at the moment. One often, when writing, felt a desire to be "remiss". It was good to have that recommended. An important aspect of writing unmentioned by Burton was "priority"; what to tell first. That always seemed one of the basic problems . . .' (BDFR 206–7).

Further thoughts about books, and the technical, professional and personal problems involved in writing them, include:

On Shakespeare, and the justification for mingling tragedy with farce QU 52

On the gulf between the world of power and the imaginative life BM 253, *et passim*

On the problems posed by women, and compounded by the pernicious influence of homosexual novelists in English AW 69–70, 134.

On objectivity in writing, and the difficulty of portraying marriage CCR 97.

On the inadequacy of accurate factual reporting, the personal colouring imparted to any story by its narrator and the general unreliability of witnesses ('One hears about life, all the time, from different people, with very different narrative gifts . . .') BDFR 107, TK 27–8 & TK 252.

On the compensations of experience ('Each recriminative decade poses new riddles, how best to live, how best to write. One's fifties, in principle less acceptable than one's forties, at least confirm most worst suspicions about life, thereby disposing of an appreciable tract of vain expectation, standardized fantasy, obstructive to writing, as to living . . .') TK 224.

On the sources of imagination ('The Conference settled down in the mind as a kind of dream, one of those dreams laden with the stuff of real life, stopping just the right side of nightmare, yet leaving disturbing undercurrents to haunt the daytime, clogging sources of imagination – whatever those may be – causing their enigmatic flow to ooze more sluggishly than ever, periodically cease entirely') TK 189.

On autobiographies, and their general tendency towards omission or falsification BDFR 3.

On the inadvisability of setting too much store by critics ('So far as I was concerned the juggernaut of critical opinion must be allowed to take its irrefragable course. If too fervent worshippers, like Kydd, were crushed to powder beneath the pitiless wheels of its car, nothing could be done. Only their own adoration of the idol made them so vulnerable') BDFR 157.

On the vagaries of publishers ('It's always a temptation for a publisher to have a go at writing a book. After all, they think, if authors can do that, anyone can') TK 74.

For further views on writers and writing see CLARKE, St John, PROUST, Marcel and TRAPNEL, X.; see also Painting Index under *A Dance to the Music of Time*.

Jerusalem
See BLAKE, William.

'Je suis soumis au Chef du Signe de l'Automne . . .'
Lines quoted by Moreland (from *Signe* in *Alcools*), see APOLLIN-
AIRE, Guillaume.

JONSON, Ben 1573–1637
'He's a sympathetic writer, who reminds one that human life always
remains the same' (Moreland), some lines by (from *The New Inn*)
BDFR 119; more lines by (from *The Devil is an Ass*) quoted by
Moreland TK 229.

JOYCE, James 1882–1941
Maclintick on *Ulysses* CCR 212; technique of *Ulysses* admired by
Trapnel, his analysis of Molly Bloom's sexual musings HSH 85.

KAISER, Georg 1878–1945
Another socially conscious dramatist approved by Werner Guggenbühl,
see HAUPTMANN, Gerhart.

KAFKA, Franz 1883–1924
General Kielkiewicz has heard of MP 33; HSH 54.

Kashmiri Love Songs
See 'Pale hands I loved beside the Shalimar . . .'

KEATS, John 1795–1821
Some lines (from *Endymion*) quoted by Moreland a propos vintage cars
TK 275–6.

'*Kennst du das Land, wo die Zitronen blühn?*'
Quoted by Members (*Mignons Lied*), see GOETHE, Johann
Wolfgang von.

KIERKEGAARD, Sören 1813–55
Taken up a little ahead of the fashion by Mark Members LM 221.

King Lear
See SHAKESPEARE, William.

KLEIST, Heinrich von 1777–1811
Another of the names bandied by Members in his Germanic phase LM
221.

Kleist, Marx, Sartre, the Existentialist Equilibrium
Lecture delivered by Members at the university immediately after the
second war BDFR 21.

KOTECKE
One of the minor celebrities, like Pritak and Ferrand-Sénéschal,
expected to show up at the international writers' conference in Venice
TK 8–9, 18.

KIPLING, Rudyard 1865–1936
M. Dubuisson reading his *Simple Contes des Collines* QU 116–17; CCR
4; Captain Gwatkin's secret weakness for *A Centurion of the Thirtieth* in
Puck of Pook's Hill VB 57–9; and for some lines that make you think
from *A Song to Mithras* VB 90–2, 230 & SA 15 & HSH 134; some lines
by (from *Tomlinson* in *Barrack Room Ballads*) SA 4; Bagshaw not
prepared to be the Gunga Din of RAF public relations in India BDFR
30.

KYDD, Alaric
Novelist, see Character Index. See also *Sweetskin*.

LACLOS, Choderlos de 1741–1803
Barnby compared to Valmont in *Les Liaisons Dangereuses* AW 24; one
of comparatively few novelists admired by Jenkins SA 47; TK 228.

'La mer, la mer toujours recommencée . . .'
Line often quoted by Moreland (from *Le Cimetière marin*), see
VALERY, Paul.

LANG, Andrew 1844–1912
Le Bas quotes some fine lines from (*Ballade to Theocritus in Winter*) QU
39–40, but fails to learn their lesson QU 70; BM 9.

Last Days of Pompeii
Novel by Edward Bulwer-Lytton, 1803–73, see Painting Index under
Pupils of Socrates.

LAWRENCE, D. H. 1885–1930
Banality of *Lady Chatterley's Lover* ('Suburban, narcissistic, daydreams,
a phallic never-never-land for middle-aged women': Moreland) KO
77–8.

Lays of Ind
Another of the four books in the smoking-room of Stonehurst KO 60.

'Leave we the unlettered plain . . .'
Quoted by Members (from *A Grammarian's Funeral*). See BROWNING,
Robert.

LEINTWARDINE, Ada
Bestselling novelist, see Character Index. See also *Bedsores*, *The Bitch Pack Meets on Wednesdays* and *I Stopped at a Chemist*.

LEMPRIERE, John 1765–1824
Classical lexicographer, see *Attick and Roman Reckonings of Capacity etc.*

LERMONTOV, Mikhail Yurevich 1814–41
Another of the comparatively few novelists admired by Jenkins SA 47; BDFR 192.

'Let's have one other gaudy night: call to me/ All my sad captains . . .' The quotation (from *Antony and Cleopatra*) adapted by Odo Stevens for the title of his war memoirs, *Sad Majors* BDFR 138.

LEVI, Eliphas (Alphonse Louis Constant) 1810–75
Mage and ex-abbé, artist, poet, agitator and journalist; author of *Histoire de la Magie* etc. His *Dogme et Rituel de la Haute Magie* thumbed over by Moreland KO 84; his precepts quoted by Dr Trelawney KO 192–3, 196; and by Mrs Erdleigh MP 138; TK 217.

Liaisons Dangereuses, Les
See LACLOS, Choderlos de.

LUTTRELL, Narcissus 1657–1732
Jenkins reads his *Brief Relations* MP 68.

Lysistrata
Film version of, made in France in the 'twenties with backing from Sir Magnus Donners and incidental music by Moreland CCR 15, 26; KO 79, 97.

Magnus Donners Memorial Prize
Literary award founded in the mid 'sixties by Matilda Donners, restricted to biographies of British subjects born no earlier than Sir Magnus, and awarded in its first four years by Jenkins, Members and Dr Brightman as judges to lives of Sir Horrocks Rusby, a general, a homosexual politician and Russell Gwinnett's study of X. Trapnel, *Death's-Head Swordsman*. For refs, see Character Index under DONNERS, Sir Magnus, GWINNETT, Russell, RUSBY, Sir Horrocks and WILSON, Matilda.

MARLOWE, Christopher 1564–93
Matilda Wilson hopes to play Zenocrate in *Tamburlaine the Great*, Moreland on ('"Holla, ye pampered jades of Asia," he cried. "What, can ye draw but twenty miles a day?" That is rather what I feel about

the newspaper criticism of Gossage and Maclintick. I should like them to draw me to concerts, as the kings drew Tamerlaine, in a triumphal coach . . .') CCR 55, 193; Matilda a success as Zenocrate KO 86; Dr Trelawney quotes *Faustus* KO 195.

Marmion
See SCOTT, Sir Walter.

Marx Without Tears
The sort of potted philosophy perused from time to time by Chips Lovell SA 92.

Match Me Such Marvel
Bithel's favourite among St John Clarke's novels, generally agreed to have homosexual overtones; film rights sold in the late 'fifties to Louis Glober who makes abortive plans to star first Pamela Widmerpool ('There's a character just like Pam in *Match Me Such Marvel*. Of course, St John Clarke didn't know anything about women, but a competent script-writer could alter all that': Ada Leintwardine), and later Polly Duport. For refs, see Character Index under CLARKE, St John.

MAYAKOVSKY, Vladimir 1893–30
Contrasted with Rilke by Bernard Shernmaker in *Fission*'s first number BDFR 123.

MEMBERS, Mark
Poet and critic, see Character Index.

MEREDITH, George 1828–1909
Jenkins relegated to Quiggin's bad books after a disagreement over (unless it was Milton) LM 102–3.

MIDDLETON, Thomas *c.* 1520–1627
Some impenetrable lines quoted by Delavacquerie from his and Dekker's *The Roaring Girle* HSH 239–41.

Midsummer Night's Dream, A
See SHAKESPEARE, William.

Middlewatch, The
Play (by Stephen King-Hall and Ian Hay, first performed at the Shaftesbury Theatre in 1929) cited by the elderly assistant in a theatrical costumier's who takes Jenkins for an actor ('I have absolutely no histrionic talent, none at all, a constitutional handicap in almost all the undertakings of life; but then, after all, plenty of actors possess little

enough. There was no reason why he should not suppose the Stage my profession as well as any other. Identification with something a shade more profound than a farce of yesteryear treating boisterously of gun-room life in the Royal Navy might have been more gratifying to self-esteem . . .') SA 2.

MILTON, John 1608–74
Mr Deacon opposed to spelling reform 'on grounds that for him such changes would mar *Paradise Lost*' BM 6; LM 102–3.

Mimosa
One of the more obscure of St John Clarke's novels. See Character Index under CLARKE, St John.

Miscellaneous Equities
Volume of Shernmaker's collected articles, see Character Index under SHERNMAKER, Bernard.

MOLNAR, Ferenc 1878–1952
Hungarian dramatist HSH 123.

MONTAIGNE, Michel de 1533–92
Jenkins is tempted to compose a series of essays in the manner of BM 152.

Morte d'Arthur
By Sir Thomas Malory, fl. 1470. The Castles of Joyous and Dolorous Garde brought to mind respectively by Stourwater and Castlemallock KO 107, VB 172 & 212. See also Place Index under MAIDA VALE CANAL.

Moss off a Rolling Stone
One of the spate of autobiographies ('on the whole unenthralling enough, except insomuch as every individual's story has its enthralling aspect, though the essential pivot was usually omitted or obscured by most autobiographers') pub. immediately after the second war BDFR 3.

MUSIL, Robert 1880–1942
Subject of one of Shernmaker's critical articles HSH 96.

MYSHKIN, Prince
See DOSTOIEVSKY, Feodor and HEMINGWAY, Ernest.

Sung in all three verses at the Victory service in St Paul's ('Repetitive, jerky, subjective in feeling, not much ornamented by imagination nor subtlety of thought and phraseology, the words possessed at the same time a kind of depth, an unpretentious expression of sentiment suited somehow to the moment . . . There must have been advantages, moral and otherwise, in living at an outwardly less squeamish period, when the verbiage of high-thinking had not yet cloaked such petitions as those put forward in the second verse, incidentally much the best; when, in certain respects at least, hypocrisy had established less of a stranglehold on the public mind. Such a mental picture of the past was no doubt largely unhistorical, indeed totally illusory, freedom from one sort of humbug merely implying, with human beings of any epoch, thraldom to another') MP 226–7.

NEKRASOV, Nikolay 1821–78
Novelist approved by Soviet authority, see DOSTOIEVSKY, Feodor.

NEWCOME, Colonel
See THACKERAY, W. M.

Never to the Philistines
Novel by St John Clarke, see Character Index under CLARKE, St John.

NIKLAUS of Damascus fl. BC 20
Herod the Great's secretary, his account of the Candaules and Gyges story illustrates the narrowness of Greek psychology HSH 58.

NIEVO, Ippolito 1831–61
Jenkins reads and admires *The Castle of Fratta* TK 51–2.

NOSTRADAMUS, Michel 1503–66
Confused by Mark Members with Paracelsus in a book review to which Dr Trelawney unwisely takes exception KO 85 & HSH 128.

'Now all strange hours and all strange loves are over . . .'
Lines (from *Ave atque Vale*) quoted by Moreland, see SWINBURNE, Algernon.

'Now we are come to the sun's hour of rest'
Hymn no. 18 from the old *Hymns Ancient and Modern*, by J. Keble from the Greek, composed by Sir J. Stanier, quoted by Fenneau HSH 131.

Oblomov
By Ivan Alexandrovich Goncharov, 1812–91; X. Trapnel's copy worn to shreds BDFR 191, 202.

'Oh, give me a man to whom naught comes amiss, One horse or another, that country or this . . .'
Lines (*Quaesitum Meritis* from *Hunting Songs* by Rowland Egerton-Warburton, 1804–91) quoted by Templer ('As a matter of fact I was thinking of women, really, rather than horses, and taking 'em as you find 'em . . . Of course they are easier to take than to find in my experience . . .') AW 44.

'Oisive jeunesse A tout asservie Par delicatesse J'ai perdu ma vie'
Lines applied by Moreland to himself (from *Chanson de la plus haute tour*), see RIMBAUD, Arthur.

Orlando
Novel (by Virginia Woolf) with which Mrs Conyers can't get on and which Jenkins doesn't greatly like but on which General Conyers ('The woman can write, you know') retains an open mind LM 80–1.

Orlando Furioso
See ARIOSTO, Ludovico.

ORWELL, George 1903–50
Author of *1984*, *Animal Farm* etc. MP 215.

'Pale hands I loved beside the Shalimar . . .'
A Kashmiri song from *The Garden of Kama and other Love Lyrics from India* by Laurence James Hope (Adela Florence Nicolson), 1865–1904. Sung by the blonde woman on crutches beside the bombed-out ruins of the Mortimer in Soho, recalling Moreland's speculations on a previous occasion about the lyric's finer points (' "Whom do you lead on Rapture's roadway far?" What a pertinent question') CCR 1–5, 58 & KO 249.

Paper Wine
One of the two volumes of essays with which L. O. Salvidge brings off a rather notable double in 1947, see Character Index under SALVIDGE, L. O.

PARACELSUS, Philippus (Aureolus Theophrastus Bombastus von Hohenheim) 1493–1541
Physician and alchemist, see NOSTRADAMUS.

PASTERNAK, Boris 1890–1960
Russian novelist prevented by the Soviet authorities from accepting the Nobel Prize in 1958. Ferrand-Sénéschal scheduled to speak on at the international writers' conference in Venice TK 8; Daniel Tokenhouse on the publicity given to *Dr Zhivago* TK 125.

PATMORE, Coventry 1823–96
Said to have influenced the slim volume of verse published by Sillery
when young BDFR 10.

'Pauvre automne Meurs en blancheur et en richesse . . .'
Lines quoted by Moreland (from *Automne Malade* in *Alcools*), see
APOLLINAIRE, Guillaume.

Peer Gynt
See IBSEN, Henrik.

PEPYS, Samuel 1633–1701
Was connected through his patron to one of Chips Lovell's Sleaford
ancestors, Jenkins quotes an extract from his *Diary*★ describing an
encounter on a visit to Dogdene with a great black maid in a closet LM
11–12; Widmerpool's resemblance to Pepys with his wig off ('True,
Widmerpool shared none of Pepys' sensibility where the arts were
concerned; in the aesthetic field he was a void. But they had a common
preoccupation with money and professional advancement; also a kind
of dogged honesty. Was it possible to imagine Widmerpool playing a
similar role with the maid? There I felt doubtful . . .') LM 195

Perfumed Garden of Sheik Nefzaoui or The Arab Art of Love
Uncle Giles' copy of discovered among his effects at the Bellevue,
Jenkins speculates on its origins and ponders its contents KO 160–2,
164, and shortly afterwards gives it to Bob Duport ('To present him
with the book would be small, secret amends for having had a love
affair with his wife . . . It would be better not to draw his attention to
the chapter on the Deceits and Treacheries of Women. He could find
that for himself') KO 181–2; 198–9.

PETRARCH, Francesco 1304–74
A great stay to St John Clarke CCR 84; not for nothing that his Laura
was one of the de Sade family CCR 211–2.

PETRONIUS fl. first century AD
Army Main Group HQ at Brussells compared to the court of a military
Trimalchio (in the *Satyricon*) MP 170; no trace of Trimalchio at Field
Marshal Montgomery's HQ MP 178; X. Trapnel on the irrelevance of
Trimalchio's politics BDFR 216; *Satyricon* the only classical work ever
freely quoted by Trapnel HSH 68.

PHILALETHES, Eugenius
See VAUGHAN, Thomas.

★ See footnote, p. 246.

Pilgrim's Progress, The
By John Bunyan, 1628–88. Brought to mind by the sight of Scorpio
Murtlock crossing the playing field of Stourwater school ('Watching
the approaching figure, I was reminded of a remark made by Moreland
ages before . . . This particular recollection had referred to an incident
in *The Pilgrim's Progress* that had stuck in both our minds. Moreland said
that, after his aunt read the book aloud to him as a child, he could
never, even after he was grown-up, watch a lone figure draw near
across a field without thinking this was Apollyon come to contend with
him. From the moment of first hearing the passage read aloud – assisted
by a lively portrayal of the fiend in an illustration, realistically depicting
his goat's horns, bat's wings, lion's claws, lizard's legs – the terror of that
image, bursting out from an otherwise at moments prosy narrative, had
embedded itself for all time in his imagination. I, too, as a child, had
been riveted by the vividness of Apollyon's advance across the quiet
meadow. Now, surveying the personage in the blue robe picking his
way slowly, almost delicately, over the grass of the hockey-field, I felt
for some reason that, if ever the arrival of Apollyon was imminent, the
moment was this one . . .') HSH 233–4.

Pistons of Our Locomotives Sing the Songs of Our Workers, The
Manuscript submitted to Quiggin & Craggs, causing one of many rows
between Craggs and his partner ('JG's not keen on frank propaganda,
especially in translation . . . He doesn't mind inconspicuous fraternal
writings inculcating the message in quiet ways. He rather likes that.
What he doesn't want is for the firm to get a name for peddling the
Party Line': Bagshaw) BDFR 142; eventually published as *Engine
Melody* BDFR 239.

PLATO BC 427–347
His view of the Candaules and Gyges story TK 87.

POE, Edgar Allan 1809–49
Jenkins' weakness for, some lines (from *To One In Paradise*) quoted
('That verse used to run in my head when in love with Jean Duport –
her grey eyes – though she laid no claims to being a dancer, and Poe's
open-air interpretative choreography sounded unimpressive. However, there were no limits when one was in that state') MP 225; had
points in common with Russell Gwinnett TK 48, 50.

Pogrom of Youth
The book in which Widmerpool proposes putting forward his views
on contemporary counter culture in the 'sixties, see Character Index
under WIDMERPOOL, Kenneth G.

POPE, Alexander 1688–1744
CCR 34; his view of Cowley (from *Imitations of Horace*, Bk II, Ep. I) quoted MP 224; put Dr Brightman's ancestor, the Revd Salathiel Brightman, into the *Dunciad* on account of some forgotten squabble TK 5.

Popular Song from Lilliburlero to Lili Marlene, The
One of Hugh Moreland's projected works BDFR 120.

POPULAR SONGS
'Arm in arm together, Just like we used to be . . .' (words by Jim Church, music by Stan Bradbury, pub. 1940). Sung by Corporal Gwylt on his night out with the barmaid Maureen at Castlemallock VB 228.

'Après la guerre, There'll be a good time everywhere . . .' (words by B. G. Hilliam, 1917, sung by Elsie Janis and her Gang in *Hullo America!*) Snatch hummed by Ted Jeavons when in poor form BDFR 2.

'Dapper Dan Was a Very Handy Man' (words by Lew Brown, music by Albert von Tilzer, pub. 1921). The kind of thing Templer looks as though he might sing, while dancing up and down in front of a row of naked ladies, according to Stringham at school QU 30.

'Everything is buzz-buzz now . . .' (from André Charlot's revue *Buzz-Buzz*, 1918). Record playing on the afternoon Stringham perpetrated the Braddock-alias-Thorne hoax at school QU 44.

'Funiculì-Funiculà'. Composed for the opening of the Vesuvius mountain railway, and sung by the veteran cabaret entertainer at Jenkins' Venetian hotel in the late 'fifties ('A very old man took the floor. Hoarse, tottering, a few residual teeth, arbitrarily assembled and darkly stained, underpinning the buoyancy of his grin, he rendered the song in slower time than ordinary, clawing the air with his hands, stamping the floor with his feet, while he mimed the action of the cable, straining, creaking, climbing, as it hauled upward towards the volcanic crater the capsule encasing himself and his girl . . .') TK 1–4, 44, 59, 83.

'He ran a pin In Gwendolyn, In Lower Grosvenor Place . . .' (first war comic song). Snatch sung by Ted Jeavons at Umfraville's night club LM 201.

'If you were the only girl in the world, And I was the only boy . . .' (from *The Bing Boys are Here*, 1916, lyrics by Clifford Grey, music by Nat Ayer). Sung by Jeavons on the night of his reunion with Mrs Haycock at Umfraville's night club LM 117–18.

'I'm a trooper, I'm a trooper, They call me Gladys Cooper . . .' (sung by Billy Bennett in the 'thirties). Quoted by Jeavons a propos of Hugo Tolland's joining up KO 239.

'In the Mountain Greenery' (from *Garrick Gaieties*, 1925, by Richard Rodgers and Lorenz Hart). Played by one of the two bands in Belgrave Square on the night of the Huntercombes' dance BM 63.

'I Wish It Was Sunday Night' (words by Billy Williams, Fred Godfrey and Hugo Trevor, sung by Billy Williams 1912). Softly hummed by Private Bracey when in good spirits KO 21.

'Molly the Marchioness' (from *A Country Girl* at Daly's Theatre, 1902). Hummed by Chips Lovell's father whenever he hears the name of Molly Jeavons LM 17.

'My Heart Stood Still' (by Rodgers and Hart, 1927). Played on the accordion by the hunchback in a velvet smoking jacket at Milly Andriadis' party BM 105.

'My lips smile no more, my heart loses its brightness . . .' ('The Ashgrove' by John Oxenford, 1812–1877). Sung on the march by Jenkins' Welsh battalion in 1940 VB 45–6; and by Bithel long afterwards at Stourwater HSH 219.

'She'll be wearing purple socks, And she's always in the pox . . .' Sung by Welsh soldiers at Castlemallock in salute to the barmaid Maureen VB 236.

'Softly Awakes My Heart' (from Saint-Saëns' opera *Samson and Delilah*). Played behind the London Pavilion by the street musician with the peg-leg and the patch over one eye SA 114.

'South of the Border Down Mexico Way' (by Jimmy Kennedy and Michael Carr, 1939). Sung by Private Jones, D., in a voice of heartbreaking melancholy in the Welsh chapel Sardis in 1940 VB 4, 7.

'The Man Who Broke the Bank at Monte Carlo' (words by Fred Gilbert, sung by Charles Coborn in the 1890s). Sergeant Ablett's star turn at divisional concert parties in 1941 SA 181.

'There's a long long trail a-winding Into the land of my dreams . . .' (words by Stoddard-King, music by Zo Elliott, 1913). Sung by Ted Jeavons KO 254.

'We had ter join Belisha's army . . .' Second war soldiers' song, sung by Jenkins' battalion on the march in 1940, see HYMNS under 'Guide me, O thou great Jehovah . . .'

'We'll Have a Blue Room' (from *The Girl Friend* by Rodgers and Hart, 1926). Played by the other band in Belgrave Square on the night of the Huntercombes' dance BM 63.

245

'When Father Went Down to Southend'. Music hall song, sung by Ted Jeavons BDFR 90.

'You make fast, I make fast, make fast the dingy . . .' (traditional song of the Royal Engineers). Sung by Sappers at Aldershot in 1941 VB 134.

Prisoner of Zenda, The
Novel by Anthony Hope, 1863–1933; Flavia Stringham possibly named after its heroine ('Mrs Foxe would have been quite capable of that') MP 59.

PRITAK
See KOTECKE

Profiles in String
X. Trapnel's second and last novel, completed in the summer of 1947 and subsequently liquidated by Pamela Widmerpool in the Maida Vale Canal (ten years later Pamela narrowly fails to persuade Louis Glober to film her own version of the story, with herself in the starring role; an outline of the plot, discovered after Trapnel's death in his Commonplace Book, suggests that the novel contained a less than complimentary portrait of Pamela). For refs, see Character Index under TRAPNEL, X., FLITTON, Pamela, and GLOBER, Louis. See also Place Index under MAIDA VALE CANAL.

PROUDHON, Pierre Joseph 1809–65
French political economist BDFR 228, TK 194.

PROUST, Marcel 1871–1922
Bithel's army cap recalls Saint-Loup's in *Remembrance of Things Past* VB 32; Jenkins reading MP 69; extract quoted from *Remembrance of Things Past*,* describing the appearance of Prince Theodoric's ancestor Prince Odoacer at the Princesse de Guermantes' party MP 119–21; MP 146; recalled, on Jenkins' journey through France with the military attachés in 1944, by the name of the party's first stopping place ('As I uttered the last letter, scales fell from my eyes. Everything was transformed. It all came back – like the tea-soaked madeleine itself – in a torrent of memory . . . Cabourg . . . We had just drive out of Cabourg . . . out of Proust's Balbec. Only a few minutes before, I had been standing on the esplanade along which, wearing her polo cap and accompanied by the little band of girls he had supposed the mistresses of professional bicyclists, Albertine had strolled into Marcel's life. Through the high

* This passage, like the extracts quoted elsewhere from Byron's letters, Creevey's papers, Gronow's *Reminiscences* and Pepys' *Diary*, seems to be known only to Nicholas Jenkins.

246

windows of the Grand Hotel's dining-room – conveying to those without the sensation of staring into an aquarium – was to be seen Saint-Loup, at the same table Bloch, mendaciously claiming acquaintance with the Swanns. A little further along the promenade was the Casino, its walls still displaying tattered playbills, just like the one Charlus, wearing his black straw hat, had pretended to examine, after an attempt at long range to assess the Narrator's physical attractions and possibilities. Here Elstir had painted; Prince Odoacer played golf. Where was the little railway line that had carried them all to the Verdurins' villa? Perhaps it ran in another direction to that we were taking; more probably it was no more . . . Proustian musings still hung in the air when we came down to the edge of the water. It had been a notable adventure. True, an actual night passed in one of the bedrooms of the Grand Hotel itself . . . might have crowned the magic of the happening. At the same time, a faint sense of disappointment superimposed on an otherwise absorbing inner experience was in its way suitably Proustian too: a reminder of the eternal failure of human life to respond a hundred per cent; to rise to the greatest heights without allowing at the same time some suggestion, however slight, to take shape in indication that things could have been even better') MP 167–8; Lt Kernével is unimpressed by this incident, having barely heard of Proust MP 191; Kernével looks into the matter and discovers that Proust is not taught in schools ('Kernével looked severe. He implied that the standards of literature must be kept high') MP 238.

PTOLEMY CHENNUS fl. AD 100
Historian, his version of the Candaules and Gyges story HSH 57–8.

Public School Verse
See *Iron Aspidistra*.

Puck of Pook's Hill
See KIPLING, Rudyard.

Purged Not in Lethe
Another postwar autobiography, see *Moss Off a Rolling Stone*.

'Put me To yoking foxes, milking of he-goats . . .'
Quoted by Moreland (from *The Devil is an Ass*), see JONSON, Ben.

QUIGGIN & CRAGGS
Small left-wing publishing firm founded immediately after the second war by J. G. Quiggin in partnership with Howard Craggs. Incorporates the good will of Boggis & Stone; publishes the magazine *Fission*; occupies premises ('an architecturally undistinguished exterior') south

of Tavistock Square in Bloomsbury. List includes X. Trapnel, Alaric Kydd, Ada Leintwardine, Sillery, Vernon Gainsborough etc. Is bedevilled from the start by violent disagreements between its two directors, and swallowed up towards the end of 1947 by Clapham's much larger firm. See BOGGIS & STONE, *Fission*, *Sad Majors*, *Sweetskin*, *The Pistons of Our Locomotives Sing the Songs of Our Workers*; and see Character Index under CRAGGS, Howard, QUIGGIN, J. G., LEINTWARDINE, Ada.

Quo Vadis?
By Henryk Sienkiewicz, pub. 1895. See Painting Index under *Pupils of Socrates*.

RALEGH, Sir Walter *c.* 1552–1618
His apostrophe of Death (in *The History of the World*) brought to mind by some lines from George Herbert at Erridge's funeral ('Reference to bodily corruption was a natural reaction from "Whom none should advise, thou hast persuaded". Ralegh might be grandiloquent, he was also authoritative, even hypnotic, no less resigned than Herbert, as well . . . I thought of the portraits of Ralegh, stylized in ruff, short cloak, pointed beard, fierce look. "All the pride, cruelty and ambition of men". Ralegh knew the form. Still, Herbert was good too. I wondered what Herbert had looked like . . .') BDFR 52–4.

Remembrance of Things Past
See PROUST, Marcel.

RENAN, Ernest 1823–92
Philologist and historian, his theory that complication is anterior to simplicity tested in practice by Pennistone on Mr Blackhead MP 56.

Revenger's Tragedy, The
See TOURNEUR, Cyril.

RILKE, Rainer Maria 1875–1926
See MAYAKOVSKY, Vladimir.

RIMBAUD, Arthur 1854–91
Quoted by Moreland ('*Chanson de la plus haute tour*') KO 84; KO 160; BDFR 138.

Roaring Girle, The
See MIDDLETON, Thomas.

ROBINSON, Edward Arlington 1869–1935
American poet TK 48; some lines quoted by Glober (from *For a Dead Lady*) TK 81.

ROCHESTER, Earl of 1647–80
His disapproval of army life (in lines *Upon Drinking in a Bowl*) brought to mind during Field Marshal Montgomery's disquisition MP 182.

Rosary, The
By Florence Barclay, pub. 1909 CCR 112.

ROUSSEAU, Jean-Jacques 1712–78
Cited by Trapnel in support of his theories about the novel v. autobiography HSH 84.

Rubaiyàt of Omar Khayyám, The
By Edward Fitzgerald, 1809–83. Quoted by Stringham AW 204 & CCR 168; and by Uncle Giles KO 141; once parodied by Col. Hogbourne-Johnson SA 209; quoted by Moreland TK 249 & 275.

RUBEMPRÉ, Lucien de
Character in the *Comédie Humaine*, see BALZAC, Honoré de.

Russia's Productive System
Another of the books in Erridge's library, see *Anthology of Soviet Literature*.

Sad Majors
Odo Stevens' account of his exploits as a British agent with Communist partisans in the Balkans, 'a war book to end all other war books' (J. G. Quiggin). Billed to contain a murder or two and some rather spicy political revelations. Commissioned by Quiggin & Craggs, and subject of one of the many internal rows which contribute to that firm's collapse. Turns out to cast such a damaging light on the Communist Party, especially in connection with the mysterious liquidation of another British officer working with the rival Balkan royalist group, that the manuscript is eventually eliminated together with its carbon copy by Lady Craggs (née Gypsy Jones), causing Stevens to leave the firm and his mistress, Rosie Manasch, to withdraw her financial backing. Subsequently published elsewhere (from a second carbon in Rosie's keeping) on more advantageous terms after successful serialisation in Fleet Street. For refs, see Character Index under STEVENS, Odo, JONES, Gypsy, MANASCH, Rosie and TEMPLER, Peter.

SALTYKOV-SCHREDIN, Mikhail Eugrafovitch 1826–89
Jenkins reads *The Golovlyov Family* on fire duty at the War Office ('a
more trivial choice would have been humiliating because Corporal
Curtis . . . had *Adam Bede* under his arm') MP 146, 149.

SALVIDGE, L. O.
Literary critic, see Character Index.

Sanders of the River
See WALLACE, Edgar

SANTOS
See KOTECKE.

Satyricon
See PETRONIUS.

Scholar Gypsy, The
See ARNOLD, Matthew.

SCOTT, Sir Walter 1771–1832
Stourwater Castle seen as a vision from his pages, or Tennyson's ('the
Middle Age . . . at its most elegant; all sordid and painful elements
subtly removed') BM 185; some lines from (*Bonny Dundee*) quoted by
Stringham SA 81; more lines from (*Marmion*) VB 12; Dr Trelawney as
the wizard lord in *Marmion* KO 187.

Sea Urchins
See *Athlete's Footman*.

Secretions
The other one of the pair, see *Paper Wine*.

'Seduction is to do and say/The banal thing in the banal way'
Spoof quotation invented by Moreland CCR 34.

SHAKESPEARE, William 1564–1616
Justification for his mingling comedy with tragedy QU 52; Stringham
as Hamlet QU 73; Mr Deacon looks as if made up to play Prospero BM
10; Deacon as Lear on the heath, with Gypsy Jones as the Fool BM 84;
Maclintick quotes *Henry IV, Part I* CCR 38; Matilda Wilson picked up
by Sir Magnus Donners during a school production of *A Midsummer
Night's Dream* at Stourwater CCR 131; Betty Templer as Ophelia KO
115; Jimmy Brent's attraction for Jean Duport recalls Bottom and
Titania VB 128; his dying words MP 53; some evidence suggesting that
he must have served in the army MP 170; Howard Craggs in old age

recalls Deacon as Lear BDFR 45, 49; Hamlet on fellow-travellers BDFR 94; title of *Sad Majors* adapted from a line in *Antony and Cleopatra* BDFR 138; Dr Emily Brightman's hair style recalls the Dark Lady's in sonnet CXXX TK 19; X. Trapnel's downfall compared to the god Hercules deserting Antony TK 29; Scorpio Murtlock floored by a quotation from sonnet CVII HSH 20; ghosts of Dr Trelawney and Mrs Erdleigh return like Hamlet's father's HSH 36; Members compares Quiggin's daughters to King Lear's HSH 121–2; Mr Deacon quotes some lines from *Pericles* on picture-framing HSH 247.

She
See HAGGARD, Rider.

SHERNMAKER, Bernard
Highbrow literary critic, see Character Index.

SHELDON, Nathaniel
Lowbrow literary critic, see Character Index.

SHUCKERLEY, Quentin
Poet and novelist, see Character Index.

SIDNEY, Sir Philip 1554–86
A sympathetic figure, his death on a Flanders battlefield not far from Allied lines recalled in 1944, Spenser's elegy for quoted MP 181–2.

Slow on the Feather
Another postwar autobiography, see *Moss Off a Rolling Stone*.

'So let each cavalier who loves honour and me . . .'
Quoted by Stringham (from *Bonny Dundee*), see SCOTT, Sir Walter.

Some Things That Matter
Only book Uncle Giles ever seen reading QU 230.

SPENSER, Edmund 1552–99
His *Astrophel* quoted, see SIDNEY, Sir Philip.

STENDHAL (Henri Beyle) 1783–1842
Barnby's technique as a lover seen in terms of Stendhal's power-conscious heroes AW 24; his thoughts on marriage KO 77; Captain Gwatkin also cast as a Stendhalian hero VB 13, 218; took a dim view of the monuments in St Paul's MP 216; Nievo an antidote to TK 51. See also Painting Index under MEISSONIER, Ernest.

'Stetson! You who were with me in the ships at Mylae . . .'
Lines brought to mind on Westminster Bridge (from *The Waste Land*), see ELIOT, T. S.

251

STEVENSON, Robert Louis 1850–94
Jekyll and Hyde aspect of Umfraville's impersonations BDFR 91; Louis Glober as Long John Silver in *Treasure Island* TK 229. See also JAMES, Henry.

'Still are thy pleasant voices . . .
Lines quoted by Stringham (from *Heraclitus* by William Cory, 1823–92) in a successful bid to soothe Le Bas QU 141.

STIFTER, Adalbert 1805–68
Another of the names bandied by Members in his Germanic phase LM 221.

STIRNER, Max (Kaspar Schmidt) 1805–56
Bagshaw's favourite political philosopher, would have understood Widmerpool BDFR 13, TK 16.

Stockbroker in Sandals
Another postwar autobiography, see *Moss Off a Rolling Stone*.

STRINDBERG, August 1849–1912
Jenkins has heard of QU 144; CCR 7; Polly Duport stars in a play by HSH 252.

STUBBS, Bishop 1825–1901
Constitutional historian, his *Select Charters* read by Jenkins as an undergraduate QU 223.

'sunny domes and caves of ice'
Line (from *Kubla Khan*) applied by Quiggin to Thrubworth Park, see COLERIDGE, S. T.

SVEVO, Italo 1861–1928
Another of Jenkins' admired novelists, see LACLOS, Choderlos de.

Sweetskin
Alaric Kydd's much vaunted and supposedly erotic novel, pub. by Quiggin & Craggs in 1947 ('Even Quiggin was known to have reservations about the novel's merits . . . On the one hand, the novel might be suppressed, the firm fined, a director possibly sent to gaol; on the other, alleged lubricities being in themselves not sufficient to guarantee by any means a large sale, *Sweetskin* might easily not pay off its considerable advance in royalties'), and subsequently unsuccessfully prosecuted for obscenity. For refs, see Character Index under KYDD, Alaric.

SWINBURNE, Charles Algernon 1837–1909
His lines about 'wandering water sighs where the sea sobs round Lesbian promontories' (from *Ave atque Vale*) applied to Gypsy Jones by Mr Deacon ('In fact restriction to such a coastline was almost a condition of our association') BM 113; *Ave atque Vale* quoted by Moreland KO 124; TK 50.

SYMONS, Arthur 1865–1945
Evadne Clapham's coiffure recalls his line, 'And is it seaweed in your hair?' (from *Stella Maris*) BDFR 138.

Tamburlaine the Great
See MARLOWE, Christopher.

TENNYSON, Alfred, Lord 1809–92
The Lady of Shalott quoted a propos Stourwater Castle BM 185; SA 79; his lines on Lazarus (from *In Memoriam*, XXXI) TK 31; HSH 6.

THACKERAY, William Makepeace 1811–63
Colonel Newcome (in *The Newcomes*) recalled by the young Sunny Farebrother ('Years later, when I came to know Sunny Farebrother pretty well, he always retained for me something of this first picture of him; a vision . . . that suggested an almost saintly figure, ill-used by a coarse-grained world: some vague and uncertain parallel with Colonel Newcome came to mind, in the colonel's latter days in the Greyfriars almshouses, and it was easy to imagine Mr Farebrother answering his name in such a setting, the last rays of the sunset falling across his, by then, whitened hair . . .') QU 78; QU 182; Maclintick's likeness to caricatures of Thackeray CCR 18; Jenkins reads *Esmond* VB 168, 200; Farebrother's increased resemblance in middle age to Colonel Newcome SA 195–6.

Thin Man, The
Novel by Dashiel Hammett, X. Trapnel's copy worn to shreds BDFR 191, 202.

'the head to which all the ends of the world are come, and the eyelids are a little weary'
Walter Pater's description of the Mona Lisa (in *The Renaissance*), applied by Pennistone to the Civil Affairs branch of the War Office MP 115.

'the sound of horns and motors, which shall bring Sweeney to Mrs Porter in the spring'
Lines (from *The Waste Land*) brought to mind after an air raid, see ELIOT, T. S.

Time and Western Man
By Percy Wyndham Lewis, 1882–1957; Chandler reading CCR 48.

Toilet Paper
'Underground' magazine associated with the Quiggin twins in the early 1970s HSH 91.

TOLSTOY, Leo 1828–1910
Mona Templer as Anna Karenin AW 171; an inordinately brilliant but ultimately unsatisfactory naturalistic writer in Trapnel's view BDFR 215–6; TK 217.

TOURNEUR, Cyril *c.* 1575–1626
Moreland in search of a copy of *The Atheist's Tragedy* TK 67; couplet from *The Revenger's Tragedy* prefixed to Gwinnett's life of X. Trapnel HSH 71, 76; HSH 167; quoted by Delavacquerie on lust HSH 240.

Towards the Understanding of Karl Marx
Another of the works in Erridge's library, see *Anthology of Soviet Literature*.

TRAPNEL, X.
Perhaps the most promising novelist of the postwar generation which includes Ada Leintwardine, Evadne Clapham, Alaric Kydd etc. 'A very good writer' in Jenkins' view, and one more or less immune to censorship ('Trapnel's writing was not of the sort to be greatly affected by prohibitions of language or subject matter. He was competent to express whatever he wanted in an oblique manner' BDFR 133). Is the only person with whom Jenkins regularly discusses the art of the novel ('"Reading novels needs almost as much talent as writing them", he used to say' TK 219).

Apt to get worked up and carried away by favourite themes, such as naturalism in writing ('People can't get it right about Naturalism. They think if a writer like me writes the sort of books I do, it's because that's easier, or necessary nowadays. You just look round at what's happening and shove it all down. They can't understand that's not in the least the case. It's just as selective, just as artificial, as if the characters were kings and queens speaking in blank verse. . . . What I'm getting at is that if you took a tape-recording of two people having a grind it might truly be called Naturalism, it might be funny, it might be sexually exciting, it might even be beautiful, it wouldn't be art. It would just be two people having a grind . . . There are certain forms of human behaviour no actor can really play, no matter how good he is. It's the same in life. Human beings aren't subtle enough to play their part. That's where art comes in . . . What I mean is that if, as a novelist, you put over something that hasn't been put over before, you've done the trick. A novelist's like a fortune-teller, who çan impart certain information, but not necessarily what the reader wants to hear. It may be disagreeable or extraneous. The novelist just has to dispense it. He can't choose . . . Naturalism's only "like" life, if the novelist is any good. If he isn't any good, it doesn't matter whether he writes naturalistically or any other way. What could be less "like" life than most of the naturalistic novels that appear?' BDFR 214–6).

Holds fiction superior to biography in point of truth ('People think because a novel's invented, it isn't true. Exactly the reserve is the case. Because a novel's invented, it is true. Biography and memoirs can never be wholly true, since they can't include every conceivable circumstance of what happened. The novel can do that. The novelist himself lays it down. His decision is binding. The biographer, even at his highest and best, can only be tentative, empirical. The autobiographer, for his part, is imprisoned in his own egotism. He must always be suspect. In contrast with the other two, the novelist is a god, creating his man, making him breathe and walk. The man, created in his own image, provides information about the god. In a sense you know more about Balzac and Dickens from their novels, than Rousseau and Casanova from their Confessions . . . a novel can imply certain truths impossible to state by exact definition. Biography and autobiography are forced to attempt exact definition. In doing so truth goes astray. The novelist is more serious – if that is the word' HSH 84–5).

See Character Index. See also *Bin Ends*, *Camel Rides to the Tomb*, *Dogs Have No Uncles*, *The Heresy of Naturalism* and *Profiles in String*.

Treasure Island
See STEVENSON, R. L.

Triads, The
Subject of a well-known work by Dr Emily Brightman. See Character Index under BRIGHTMAN, Dr Emily.

TRIMALCHIO
See PETRONIUS.

TRISMEGISTUS, Hermes
Legendary, pre-Pythagorean Egyptian magician and sage, reputed author of the *Ritual of the Dead* etc., quoted by Mrs Erdleigh TK 246.

TROLLOPE, Anthony 1815–82
Greatly admired by General Liddament, who is driven to the brink of violence when Jenkins rashly admits his own want of enthusiasm for ('I tried to think of an answer. From the past, a few shreds of long forgotten literary criticism were just pliant enough to be patched hurriedly together in substitute for a more suitable garment to cover the dialectical nakedness of the statement just made. ". . . the style . . . certain repetitive tricks of phrasing . . . psychology often unconvincing . . . sometimes downright dishonest in treating of individual relationships . . . women don't analyse their own predicaments as there represented . . . in fact, the author does more thinking than feeling . . . of course, possessor of enormous narrative gifts . . . marshalling material . . . all that amounting to genius . . . certain sense of character, even if stylised . . . and naturally as a picture of the times . . ." "Rubbish," said General Liddament') SA 45–7, 51, 79, 86; TK 202. See also BALZAC, Honoré de.

Ulysses
See JOYCE, James.

Unburnt Boats
J. G. Quiggin's first and only book, a 'documentary' alternately scheduled for and withdrawn from publication throughout the 'thirties and eventually brought out just before the outbreak of war ('A literary Caesarian was all but required for that infant of long gestation, *Unburnt Boats*': Sillery). For refs, see Character Index under QUIGGIN, J. G.

Uncle Tom's Cabin
Novel by Harriet Beecher Stowe, 1812–96 CCR 212.

VALERY, Paul 1871–1945
Quoted by Moreland (*Le Cimetiére marin*) VB 1–2 & KO 217.

VAUGHAN, Thomas (Eugenius Philalethes) 1621–66
Alchemist and hermetic philosopher; his name invoked by Dr Brightman TK 87; his spirit moving in Venice during the international writer's conference, according to Mrs Erdleigh TK 242–3; quoted by Mrs Erdleigh ('Where, as again Vaughan writes, the liberated soul ascends, looking at the sunset towards the west wind, and hearing secret harmonies . . .'*) TK 246; his words recalled by Jenkins HSH 36, and quoted again by Canon Fenneau HSH 134.

* This passage appears to be a paraphrase of ideas taken from Trismegistus and interpreted in *Monas Hieroglyphica* by Vaughan's fellow magician John Dee, 1527–1608; Mrs Erdleigh's next image – of the world as 'an outdoor theatre, in whose wings the Dead wait their cue for return to the stage' – comes from Vaughan's *Lumen de Lumine*.

VERLAINE, Paul 1844–96
Said to have influenced an early volume of verse published and
afterwards disowned by Ferrand-Sénéschal TK 18.

VIGNY, Alfred de 1797–1863
David Pennistone expounds his austere view of the soldier's calling as
laid down in *Servitude et Grandeur Militaire*, Jenkins quotes a line from
(*Le Cor*) VB 107–9; his military philosophy recalled VB 172; Gwatkin's
indifference to his views 233–4; Jenkins finds consolation in his
philosophy SA 24; Field Marshal Montgomery essentially the kind of
soldier he had in mind MP 182; BDFR 51; TK 29.

VOX POPULI PRESS
Small publishing business producing books and pamphlets of an
insurgent tone run by Howard Craggs from a seedy office next door to
Mr Deacon's shop; extinct by the early 'thirties but partly
reincorporated as Boggis & Stone BM 163, 233, 245–6, 259; AW 49,
118–9; KO 227; BDFR 142.

WALLACE, Edgar 1875–1932
Peter Templer relaxes his rule of never reading for pleasure in favour
of *Sanders of the River* QU 46 & AW 44.

War Never Pays!
Pacifist broadsheet, price one penny, distributed in the late 'twenties by
Mr Deacon and his colleague Gypsy Jones (who leaves her copies
behind at Mrs Andriadis' party) BM 83, 88, 91, 99, 108, 147, 150, 167;
AW 96; CCR 11; BDFR 45.

Waste Land, The
See ELIOT, T. S.

WEBSTER, John *c.* 1580–1625
Always a favourite of Moreland, see *Duchess of Malfi*.

WELLS, H. G. 1866–1946
J. G. Quiggin in his black leather overcoat recalls a Wellsian man of the
future AW 47. See also BARRIE, J. M.

'When Roland brave, and Olivier, And every paladin and peer, On
Roncesvalles died!'
From *Marmion*, see SCOTT, Sir Walter.

WHITMAN, Walt 1819–92
Mr Deacon's spiritual father BM 236 & KO 80.

WILDE, Oscar 1856–1900
Some lines from (*Theocritus*) quoted by Stringham to tease Le Bas QU
41, 43; CCR 173.

'Within those woods of Arcadie . . .'
From *Astrophel, an Elegie*, see SPENSER, Edmund.

WOOD, Anthony à 1632–95
Jenkins reading *Athenae Oxonienses* in wartime MP 68.

WOOLF, Virginia 1882–1941
See *Orlando*.

Painting Index

(including Painters, Sculptors, Works of Art, Collections, Galleries, Exhibitions etc.)

ABERAVON collection
See Character Index under ABERAVON, Lord.

ADDAMS, Charles b. 1912
Cartoonist, see Book Index under ADAMS, Henry.

Agony in the Garden, The
Tiepolo's painting (Hamburg Kunsthalle) in which 'the soldier who so much resembles General Rommel' may also have been the model for Gyges in the ceiling at the Bragadin Palace TK 85.

Alexander receiving the Children of Darius after the Battle of Issus
For Stringham as a younger version of Alexander★ in Veronese's painting, see Character Index under STRINGHAM, Charles.

ALMA-TADEMA, Sir Lawrence 1836–1912
Mr Deacon's style a cross between his and Burne-Jones' BM 2.

Angry Seas off Land's End
One of the less passable seascapes in the Robert Duport collection HSH 245, 257.

ANGONI, Pietro b. 1910
A reproduction of his portrait of the Queen replaces the Seven Deadly Sins tapestries in the dining room at Stourwater school HSH 206.

Any Complaints?
Army scene ('a typical mess-room injustice about rations') by Daniel Tokenhouse. For refs, see Character Index under TOKENHOUSE, Daniel McN.

BARNBY, Ralph
Prolific and increasingly successful painter in the 'thirties; his name regularly put forward as a rather daring alternative to Isbister for portraits of such establishment figures as Sillery and St John Clarke; belongs to the modern school of painting ('"I can see Ralph has talent," [Moreland] said of Barnby, "but why use combinations of colour that make you think he is a Frenchman or a Catalan?"') to whose existence Mr Deacon prefers to close his eyes. For a description of his work and refs, see Character Index under BARNBY, Ralph.

★ Cecil Gould in his National Gallery catalogue (*The Sixteenth Century Venetian School*, 1959, pp. 144–5) admits it to be an arguable point that the central figure in this painting – the character in crimson, pointing with his left hand, whom Stringham resembles – is not in fact Alexander at all but his bosom friend Hephaestion; Goethe certainly held this view but Anthony Powell (*Infants of the Spring*, Heinemann, 1976, pp. 99–100) remains unconvinced.

BAYEUX tapestries
Le Bas 'holding up both his hands, one a little above the other, like an Egyptian god or figure from' QU 221.

BEARDSLEY, Aubrey 1872–98
HSH 54.

BERNINI, Gianlorenzo 1598–1680
See *Truth Unveiled by Time*

Bolton Abbey in the Olden Time
An engraving of Landseer's painting is the only picture hanging in the Ufford's lounge ('Beneath this crowded scene of medieval plenty – presenting a painful contrast with the Ufford's *cuisine* – a clock . . . stood eternally at twenty minutes past five') AW 4; MP 62.

BONINGTON, Richard Parkes 1801–28
HSH 257.

BONNARD, Pierre 1867–1947
Unlikely to make you any happier than Bouguereau, if you are not really interested in pictures AW 27.

BOSCH, Hieronymus *c.* 1450–1516
KO 124.

BOTTICELLI, Sandro 1445–1510
Only painter tolerated by Anne Stepney in the 'twenties BM 46.

BOUCHER, François 1703–70
Flattered his women like Reynolds and nearly all novelists AW 69.

BOUGUEREAU, William 1825–1905
See BONNARD.

Boyhood of Cyrus
Possibly Mr Deacon's best-known work, 'a group of rather woodenly posed young Medes (possibly young Persians)' set against an ambitious rendering of the gardens of Babylon. Purchased from the artist by Lord Aberavon, it proves unsaleable when bequeathed to the Walpole-Wilsons and hangs high · up at the back of their hall, acquiring a special significance for Jenkins at the time of his affair with their niece Barbara Goring in the 'twenties. Singled out for critical acclaim at the Bosworth Deacon retrospective in 1971, and sold within an hour of the show's opening. For refs, see Character Index

under DEACON, Edgar Bosworth and GORING, Barbara.

Boyhood of Ralegh
Millais' painting which provides Mark Members with a favourite pose in his romantic phase at university QU 179, 181.

Boyhood of Widmerpool
Hypothetical work from Mr Deacon's hand BM 30.

BRAQUE, Georges 1882–1963
One of Anne Stepney's heroes in her art student phase AW 199; CCR 175.

BRONZINO, Alessandro Allori 1503–72
For Moreland's resemblance to his Folly in the National Gallery, see Character Index under MORELAND, Hugh.

BROUWER, Adriaen *c.* 1606–38
See MEMLING, Hans.

BRUEGHEL, Pieter 1525–69
His *Hunters in the Snow* almost Jenkins' favourite picture, Pennistone very fond of his *Two Monkeys* VB 106; Sillery in later life closely resembles these apes BDFR 7.

BURNE-JONES, Sir Edward 1833–98
See ALMA-TADEMA, Sir Lawrence.

By the Will of Diocletian
One of Mr Deacon's larger canvases (painted during his Roman Catholic period) in which the younger of the two torturers bears a marked likeness to Scorpio Murtlock. For refs, see Character Index under DEACON, Edgar Bosworth; and see also *Pupils of Socrates*.

CALLOT, Jacques 1592–1635
See Place Index under HOUSE OF COMMONS.

CANALETTO 1697–1768
Brought to mind on the way home from Milly Andriadis' party by an encounter with Uncle Giles in Shepherd Market:
  'Now, touched almost mystically, like another Stonehenge, by the first rays of the morning sun, the spot seemed one of those clusters of tumble-down dwellings depicted by Canaletto or Piranesi, habitations from amongst which arches, obelisks and viaducts, ruined and overgrown with ivy, arise from the mean houses huddled together

below them . . . As I penetrated farther into the heart of that rookery, in the direction of my own door, there even stood, as if waiting to greet a friend, one of those indeterminate figures that occur so frequently in the pictures of the kind suggested – Hubert Robert or Pannini – in which the architectural subject predominates. This materialization took clearer shape as a man, middle-aged to elderly, wearing a bowler hat and discreetly horsy overcoat, the collar turned-up round a claret-coloured scarf with white spots. He leant a little to one side on a rolled umbrella, just as those single figures in romantic landscapes are apt to pose; as if the painter, in dealing with so much static matter, were determined to emphasize "movement" in the almost infinitesimal human side of his composition.' BM 153–4.

Candaules and Gyges
Virtually unknown ceiling painted by Tiepolo in the Bragadin palazzo in Venice. This painting, never photographed and not open to the public, caused a scandal when it was first unveiled (on account of its reference to the sexual habits of some local dignitary); and it causes another during the Widmerpools' visit to Venice in 1958, when its disturbing – possibly even unhinging – effect on Pamela plays a crucial part in her destruction of Widmerpool and in her own suicide a year later. It depicts the Lydian king, Candaules, exhibiting his naked wife to his friend Gyges:
'Miraculous volumes of colour billowed, gleamed, vibrated above us . . . subtle yet penetrating pinks and greys, light blue turning almost to lavender, rich saffrons and cinnamons melting into bronze and gold . . . The scene above was enigmatic. A group of three main figures occupied respectively foreground, middle distance, background, all linked together by some intensely dramatic situation. These persons stood in a pillared room, spacious, though apparently no more than a bedchamber, which had unexpectedly managed to float out of whatever building it was normally part – some palace, one imagined – to remain suspended, a kind of celestial "Mulberry" set for action in the upper reaches of the sky. . . . Meanwhile, an attendant team of inter-mediate beings – cupids, tritons, sphinxes, chimaeras, the passing harpy, loitering gorgon – negligently assisted stratospheric support of the whole giddy structure and its occupants, a floating recess perceptibly cubist in conception, the view from its levels far outdoing anything to be glimpsed from the funicular . . .
. . . A cloaked and helmeted personage was slipping swiftly, unostentatiously, away from the room towards a curtained doorway behind the pillars, presumably an emergency exit into the firmament beyond. At that end of the sky, an ominous storm was plainly blowing

up, dark clouds already shot with coruscations of lightning and tongues of flame (as if an air-raid were in progress), their glare revealing, in the shadows of the bedchamber, an alcove, where this tall onlooker had undoubtedly lurked a moment beforehand. Whether or not the lady was categorically aware of an intruding presence threatening the privacy of sexual embrace, whether her suspicions had been only partially aroused, was undetermined . . . The calmly classical treatment of the scene, breathtaking in opulence of shapes and colour, imposed at the same time a sense of awful tension, imminent tragedy not long to be delayed.'*

First mention of, as one of the treats in store for delegates to the writers' conference in Venice TK 42–3, 51; first sight of 75–7; described, its history and themes, its various legends expounded by Dr Brightman and its practical aspects by Pamela Widmerpool 81–90; 92, 95–6, used by Pamela as a means of taunting Widmerpool 110–12; 114–16, another scene between the Widmerpools on the score of 147, 150; its effect on Pamela 196; Moreland on the legend, and its bearing on the Widmerpools 269–70, 276; Dr Brightman on the same HSH 57–8.

CEZANNE, Paul 1839–1906
Considered a bourgeois by St John Clarke in his left-wing phase AW 126.

CHARDIN, Jean-Baptiste-Simeon 1699–1779
Anne Stepney interested only in his highlights AW 150.

CLAUDE Lorraine 1600–82
'At first sight the Templers' house seemed to be an enormously swollen villa, red and gabled, facing the sea from a small park of Scotch firs: a residence torn by some occult power from more appropriate suburban setting, and, at the same time, much magnified. It must have been built about twenty or thirty years before, and, as we came along the road, I saw that it stood on a piece of sloping ground set about a quarter of a mile from the cliff's edge. The clouded horizon and olive-green waves lapping against the stones made it a place of mystery in spite of this outwardly banal appearance: a sea-palace for a version of one of those embarkation scenes from Claude Lorraine – the Queen of Sheba, St Ursula, or perhaps the Enchanted Castle – where any adventure might be expected.' QU 73.

* Space permits only a fragmentary quotation from Jenkins' detailed description of this painting which takes on a significance in the last two volumes comparable only with Deacon's *Boyhood of Cyrus* at an earlier stage in *A Dance to the Music of Time*.

Clergyman Eating an Apple
One of Isbister's early genre paintings, possibly modelled by St John
Clarke who may or may not have been the artist's lover. For refs, see
Character Index under ISBISTER, Horace, RA.

CONDER, Charles 1868–1909
Represented in Sir Magnus Donners' collection at Stourwater KO 109.

CONSTABLE, John 1776–1837
His painting of Dogdene ('the mansion itself lying away in the middle
distance, a faery palace set among giant trees, beyond the misty water-
meadows of the foreground in which the impastoed cattle browse') in
the National Gallery LM 10; TK 22.

COROT, Camille 1796–1875
Brought to mind by the Normandy countryside in 1944 ('In one of
these secluded tracts, a Corot landscape of tall poplars and water
meadows executed in light greys, greens and blues, an overturned staff-
car, wheels in the air, lay sunk in long grass . . .') MP 157.

Countess of Ardglass with Faithful Girl, The
Portrait of Bijou ('Isbister had painted her in an open shirt and riding
breeches, standing beside the mare, her arm slipped through the reins:
with much attention to the high polish of the brown boots') for which
Jumbo Ardglass never managed to raise the money AW 113–14.

Dance to the Music of Time, A
Poussin's painting (Wallace Collection, London). Brought to mind at
the start of Jenkins' narrative by workmen round a bucket of coke in
falling snow:
'For some reason, the sight of snow descending on fire always makes
me think of the ancient world – legionaries in sheepskin warming
themselves at a brazier: mountain altars where offerings glow between
wintry pillars; centaurs with torches cantering beside a frozen sea –
scattered, unco-ordinated shapes from a fabulous past, infinitely
removed from life; and yet bringing with them memories of things real
and imagined. These classical projections, and something in the
physical attitudes of the men themselves as they turned from the fire,
suddenly suggested Poussin's scene in which the Seasons, hand in hand
and facing outwards, tread in rhythm to the notes of the lyre that the
winged and naked greybeard plays. The image of Time brought
thoughts of mortality: of human beings, facing outward like the
Seasons, moving hand in hand in intricate measure: stepping slowly,
methodically, sometimes a trifle awkwardly, in evolutions that take

recognizable shape: or breaking into seemingly meaningless gyrations, while partners disappear only to reappear again, once more giving pattern to the spectacle: unable to control the melody, unable, perhaps, to control the steps of the dance.'

Recalled long afterward by Ariosto's lunar allegory in *Orlando Furioso*: 'Ariosto's Time – as you might say, Time the Man – was, anthropomorphically speaking, not necessarily everybody's Time. Although equally hoary and naked, he was not Poussin's Time, for example, in the picture where the Seasons dance, while Time plucks his lyre to provide the music. Poussin's Time (a painter's Time) is shown in a sufficiently unhurried frame of mind to be sitting down while he strums his instrument. The smile might be thought a trifle sinister, nevertheless the mood is genial, composed.

Ariosto's Time (a writer's Time) is far less relaxed, indeed appallingly restless . . .'

Recalled again by another autumn bonfire at the narrative's close:
'The thudding sound from the quarry had declined now to no more than a gentle reverberation, infinitely remote. It ceased altogether at the long drawn wail of a hooter – the distant pounding of centaurs' hoofs dying away, as the last note of their conch trumpeted out over hyperborean seas. Even the formal measure of the Seasons seemed suspended in the wintry silence.'

First reference to QU 2; Poussin's Time compared with Ariosto's HSH 33; the whole scene compared with Widmerpool's naked ritual dance HSH 173; final reference to HSH 272.

Dante and Beatrice
Painting (by Henry Holiday, 1839–1927) always to be found on the walls of boarding houses, and not without appeal for Maclintick in whose life pictures play no part CCR 212.

DAUMIER, Honoré 1808–79
Conjured up by army billets in a Welsh chapel in 1940 ('At first sight it was not easy to discern what lay about us in a Daumier world of threatening, fiercely slanted shadows, in the midst of which two feeble jets of bluish gas, from which the pungent smell came, gave irregular, ever-changing contours to an amorphous mass of foggy cubes and pyramids . . .') VB 4.

DEACON, Edgar Bosworth
Intended by nature to be in some manner an adjunct to the art movement of the 1890s but somehow missed that spirit in his youth. Painter of 'not utterly unsympathetic' canvases belonging to a 'school

267

of large, untidy, exclusively male figure compositions, light in tone and mythological in spirit: Pre-Raphaelite in influence without being precisely Pre-Raphaelite in spirit: a compromise between, say, Burne-Jones and Alma-Tadema, with perhaps a touch of Watts in method of applying the paint. One of them – ripping away from its stretcher at the top – was dated 1903. A decided weakness of drawing was emphasized by the certitude – which overtakes, after all, some of the greatest artists – that none of Mr Deacon's pictures could possibly have been painted at any epoch other than its own: this hallmark of Time being especially attributable to the painter's inclination towards large, blank expanses of colour, often recklessly laid on . . .

. . . I could not help pondering once again the discrepancy that existed between a style of painting that must have been unfashionable, and at best aridly academic, even in his early days; and its contrast with the revolutionary principles that he preached and – in spheres other than aesthetic – to some considerable extent practised. . . . Undoubtedly his painting, in its own direction, represented the farthest extremity of Mr Deacon's romanticism, and I suppose it could be argued that upon such debris of classical imagery the foundations of at least certain specific elements of twentieth-century art came to be built. At the same time lack of almost all imaginative quality in Mr Deacon's painting resulted, finally, in a product that suggested not "romance" – far less "classicism" – as some immensely humdrum pattern of everyday life: the Greek and Roman episodes in which he dealt belonging involuntarily to a world of cosy bar-parlours and "nice cups of tea" . . . In short, the pictures recalled something given away with a Christmas Number, rather than the glories of Sunium's marbled steep . . .'

Follower of Simeon Solomon. Sickert the only person, apart from Jenkins, ever known to have found anything to say in his favour as a painter.

His works virtually unsaleable from the 'twenties onwards until rediscovered in 1971 at a centenary exhibition acclaimed by the younger critics ('. . . albeit his roots lie in Continental Symbolism, Deacon's art remains unique in itself. In certain moods he can recall Fernand Khnopff or Max Klinger, the Belgian's near-photographic technique observable in Deacon's semi-naturalistic treatment of more than one of his favourite renderings of Greek or Roman legend. In his genre pictures, the academic compliances of the School of Vienna are given strong homosexual bias – even Deacon's sphinxes and chimaeras possessing solely male attributes – a fearless sexual candour that must have shocked the susceptibilities of his own generation, sadomasochistic broodings in paint that grope towards the psychedelic . . .'). For further comments on his work and refs, see Character Index under

DEACON, Edgar Bosworth; see also *Boyhood of Cyrus*, *By the Will of Diocletian*, *Pupils of Socrates* and Place Index under EUSTON ROAD.

DEGAS, Edgar 1834–1917
Foppa belongs, aesthetically speaking, to the world of Degas or Guys AW 146.

DELACROIX, Eugène 1798–1863
Jean Duport recalls the woman smoking a hookah in his *Femmes d'Alger dans leur appartement* AW 58.

DERAIN, André 1880–1954
An unsatisfying painting, in the manner of, exemplifies Bob Duport's abysmal taste in pictures BM 136.

DOBSON, William 1610–46
Painted the Hundercombes' Van Dyck, see *Prince Rupert Conversing with a Herald*.

DUFY, Raoul 1877–1953
Another of Anne Stepney's heroes in her art student phase AW 199; CCR 175.

DUPORT, Robert, collection of Victorian seascapes
Rather a job lot, picked up over the years for practically nothing by Bob Duport★ and sold off when the going is good in 1971 at the same gallery as the Bosworth Deacon retrospective, attracting only slightly less enthusiastic reviews ('here too, as with the Deacons, an exciting revival had taken place of a type of painting long out of fashion with yesterday's art critics ...'). For refs, see Character Index under DUPORT, Bob

Dying Gladiator, The
Another of the poses adopted by Mark Members as an undergraduate at Sillery's tea party QU 181.

★ And said to have been reluctantly stored by Peter Templer at Maidenhead when Duport sold his own Hill Street house in the early 'thirties (HSH 252, 256–7); but some at the least of the 'very indifferent nineteenth-century seascapes' at Maidenhead had in fact come from Templer's family home by the sea (AW 80). No doubt Duport acquired them at a knockdown price on the death of Templer senior, when Peter was also trying unsuccessfully to flog his father's Isbister portrait.

EGYPTIAN GODS
Le Bas adopts the pose of QU 221; Colonels Hogbourne-Johnson and
Pedlar as Horus and Anubis to General Liddament's Pharaoh SA 35.

ENSOR, Baron James 1860–1940
His *Entry of Christ into Brussels* re-enacted by Jenkins' party of military
attachés in 1944 MP 169–70.

EPSTEIN, Sir Jacob 1880–1959
Too sentimental to do justice to Mona as model BM 243; AW 74.

ERNST, Max 1891–1976
See VENICE BIENNALE.

FOUJITA, Tsuguharu Leonard 1886–1968
One of the moderns admired by the diplomat Saltonstall who always
posed as a Man of Taste but settled in the end, when it came to his own
portrait, for Isbister AW 109.

Four Priests Rigging a Miracle
One of Daniel Tokenhouse's socialist realist paintings in almost regular
monochrome picked out with passages of heavy flat black, mistaken at
first sight by Jenkins for a garage scene. For refs, see Character Index
under TOKENHOUSE, Daniel McN.

FROMENTIN, Eugène 1820–76
Brought to mind by Uncle Giles' copy of *The Perfumed Garden or the
Arab Art of Love*, 1886, translated from the French version of a Staff
Officer in the French Army in Algeria: 'I pictured this French Staff
Officer sitting at his desk. The sun was streaming into the room
through green latticed windows of Moorish design, an oil sketch by
Fromentin or J. F. Lewis. Dressed in a light-blue frogged coatee and
scarlet peg-topped trousers buttoning under the boot, he wore a
pointed moustache and imperial. Beside him on the table stood his
shako, high and narrowing to the plume, the white puggaree falling
against the scabbard of his discarded sabre . . .' KO 160.

GAINSBOROUGH, Thomas 1727–1778
Lady Huntercombe's features and dress designed to recall his Mrs
Siddons BM 199, 226.

Gannets Nesting
Another of the Victorian seascapes in the Robert Duport collection
HSH 245.

GAPONENKO, T. G. b. 1906
Socialist Realist painter, featured with Svarogh and Toidze in Len Pugsley's *Integral Foundations of a Fresh Approach to Art for the Masses* TK 136–7, 140.

GAUGUIN, Paul 1848–1903
Abandoned business for art, unlike Rimbaud and J. G. Quiggin BDFR 138.

GERICAULT, Théodore 1791–1824
A possible Free French version of his *Raft of the Medusa* MP 140.

GIORDANO, Luca 1632–1705
Painted frescoes for the Bragadin palazzo TK 75.

GLEIZES, Albert 1881–1953
Ranks low, with Lhote and Barnby, in Moreland's choice of portrait painters for his girl CCR 36.

GLOBER, Louis, collection of twentieth-century primitives
Includes one of only two Tokenhouses ever sold, depicting capitalist exploitation of the poor on a Venetian vaporetto. For refs, see Character Index under GLOBER, Louis.

GOYA, Francisco 1746–1828
Gypsy Jones, after seduction, recalls his *Maja nude* BM 258; the muffled trio in his *Winter* recalled by Debussy's *Iberia* CCR 63; Jean Duport in old age looks like one of his sad duchesses HSH 252–3.

GOZZOLI, Benozzo *c.* 1421–97
A Bond Street dealer caught napping by Lord Huntercombe in the matter of a Virgin and Child by CCR 143;

GRECO, El 1541–1614
VB 2.

GREUZE, Jean Baptiste 1725–1805
A Greuze and a Richard Wilson hang among the gimcrack furnishings of the Jeavonses' drawing-room, both probably carried off from Dogdene LM 21, 158; SA 163.

GUARDI, Francesco 1712–93
His sister m. Tiepolo and may have been the model for the Queen in the *Candaules and Gyges* ceiling TK 38.

HAIG statue
The design (by A. F. Hardiman 1891–1949), for this equestrian effigy of the Field Marshal has become 'almost the chief enigma of contemporary aesthetic' by the time Jenkins dines at the Walpole-Wilsons, an issue hotly debated by Widmerpool, Anne Stepney and Eleanor Walpole-Wilson, and subject of a letter from St John Clarke in *The Times*★ BM 39–41.

HALS, Franz 1533–1666
Isbister the British AW 30.

HENDERSON, Barnabas, gallery
Near Berkeley Square, inaugurated in the autumn of 1971 with the Bosworth Deacon Centenary Exhibition, together with a smaller show of marine paintings mostly from the Robert Duport collection. For refs, see Character Index under HENDERSON, Barnabas.

HOLBEIN, Hans 1497–1543
One of his portraits of Erasmus hangs in the Long Gallery at Stourwater BM 183, 186.

HOLLAR, Wenceslas 1607–77
Stringham possesses an engraving of his mother's house, Glimber, in the style of AW 206.

Hopeless Dawn, The
By Frank Barmley, 1857–1915 CCR 212.

Hunters in the Snow
See BRUEGHEL, Pieter.

Iphigenia (the Dogdene Veronese)
Veronese's painting, imported from Italy by one of Chips Lovell's Sleaford ancestors and viewed by Pepys ('a most rare and noble thing') at Dogdene LM 11; still at Dogdene in the 1930s when Geoffrey Sleaford won't hear of having it cleaned LM 227; sold after the second war to pay for the house's upkeep TK 21–2; re-sold at a record price HSH 225–6.

★ *Times* leader Aug. 8, 1929: 'hundreds of letters pouring into this office, nearly all . . . finding fault with the design . . . It is obvious that the design is overwhelmingly and passionately disliked . . . It is not on such grounds as the length of a boot or the make of a bit that the work of an able and earnest young sculptor is to be condemned . . .'

Iphigenia, The Sacrifice of
Tiepolo's painting (Villa Valmarana, Vicenza), not unlike his *Candaules and Gyges* in composition TK 22, 43, 77.

ISBISTER, Horace, RA
Portrait painter in great demand both before and after the first war. Holds a peculiar fascination for Jenkins:
'Such a taste is hard to justify. Perhaps the inclination is no more than a morbid curiosity to see how far the painter will give himself away. Pictures, apart from their aesthetic interest, can achieve the mysterious fascination of those enigmatic scrawls on walls, the expression of Heaven knows what psychological urge on the part of the executant; for example, that for ever anonymous drawing of Widmerpool in the *cabinet* at La Grenadère.

In Isbister's work there was something of that inner madness. The deliberate naïveté with which he accepted his business men, ecclesiastics and mayors, depicted by him with all the crudeness of his accustomed application of paint to canvas, conveyed an oddly sinister effect. Perhaps it would be more accurate to say that Isbister set out to paint what he supposed to be the fashionable view of such people at any given moment. Thus, in his early days, a general, or the chairman of some big concern, would be represented in the respectively appropriate terms of Victorian romantic success; the former, hero of the battlefield: the latter, the industrious apprentice who has achieved his worthy ambition. But as military authority and commercial achievement became increasingly subject to political and economic denigration, Isbister, keeping up with the times, introduced a certain amount of what he judged to be satirical comment. Emphasis would be laid on the general's red face and medals, or the industrialist's huge desk and cigar. There would be a suggestion that all was not well with such people about. Probably Isbister was right from a financial point of view to make this change, because certainly his sitters seemed to grow no fewer. Perhaps they too felt a compulsive need for representation in contemporary idiom, even though a tawdry one. It was a kind of insurance against the attacks of people like Quiggin: a form of public apology and penance. The result was certainly curious. . . .'

For a list of portraits and refs, see Character Index under ISBISTER, Horace. See also *Clergyman Eating an Apple*, *The Countess of Ardglass with Faithful Girl*, *The Old Humorists* and *Merville, December 1st 1914*.

JOHN, Augustus 1878–1961
A cut above the painters who used Mona as model AW 74; represented in Donners' collection at Stourwater KO 109; a drawing of his bought by Louis Glober TK 66–70, 79–80.

KHNOPFF, Fernand 1849–1906
See DEACON, Edgar Bosworth (Painting Index).

KITCHENER bust
By Sir William Reid Dick, RA, 1879–1961; stands on the stairs at the
War Office ('I left . . . quickly passing Kitchener's cold and angry eyes,
surveying with the deepest disapproval all who came that way') MP 51,
54.

KLINGER, Max 1857–1920
See DEACON, Edgar Bosworth (Painting Index).

LANDSEER, Sir Edwin 1802–73
See *Bolton Abbey in the Olden Time.*

LAVERY, Sir John 1856–1941
Painted Lady Walpole-Wilson in a white dress and blue sash at the time
of her marriage BM 28.

LAWRENCE, Sir Thomas 1769–1830
Painted the fourth Lord Erridge and the first Earl of Warminster LM
149, 151.

LEGAT, Nicholas 1869–1937
Moreland's London flat decorated with prints from his and his brother's
The Russian Ballet in Caricature CCR 5.

LELY, Sir Peter 1618–80
Smethwyck caught napping by Lord Huntercombe over a supposed
portrait of Judge Jeffreys attributed to CCR 169.

LEONARDO da Vinci 1452–1519
See *Mona Lisa.*

LEWIS, J. F. 1805–76
See FROMENTIN, Eugène.

LEWIS, Percy Wyndham 1884–1957
Drew Sir Magnus Donners HSH 50.

LHOTE, André 1885–1962
See GLEIZES, Albert.

LIPCHITZ, Jacques b. 1891
Sufficiently angular in style, like Zadkine, to do justice to Mona as
model BM 243.

Long Engagement, The
By Arthur Hughes, 1832–1915 CCR 212.

LONGHI, Pietro 1702–85
Mrs Erdleigh a subject for CCR 197; caricatures by in the ballroom at
the Bragadin palace TK 76, 90, 95.

MANET, Edouard 1832–83
Gypsy Jones recalls his *Olympia* BM 258.

MARINETTI, Filippo Tommaso 1876–1944
TK 4.

Mars and Venus
Tiepolo's painting (Villa Valmarana, Vicenza), has points in common
with his *Candaules and Gyges* ceiling TK 77.

MATISSE, Henri 1869–1954
St John Clarke thought he was a *plage* AW 123.

MEISSONIER, Ernest 1815–91
'I suspected [Gwatkin] saw himself in much the same terms as those
heroes of Stendhal . . . an aspiring, restless spirit, who, released at last
by war from the cramping bonds of life in a provincial town, was about
to cut a dashing military figure against a backcloth of Meissonier-like
imagery of plume and breastplate: dragoons walking their horses
through the wheat, grenadiers at ease in a tavern with girls bearing
flagons of wine . . .' VB 13.

MEMLING, Hans *c.* 1433–94
'On the whole, a march-past of Belgian troops summoned up the
Middle Ages or the Renaissance, emaciated, Memling-like men-at-
arms on their way to supervise the Crucifixion or some lesser
martyrdom, while beside them tramped the clowns of Teniers or
Brouwer, round rubicund countenances, haled away from carousing to
be mustered in the ranks. These latter types were even more to be
associated with the Netherlands contingent . . . Colonel Van der Voort
himself an almost perfect example.' MP 88.

Merville, December 1st, 1914
Painting (by Herbert A. Olivier, 1861–1952) in the War Office in
Whitehall: 'Outside the Army Council Room, side by side on the
passage wall, hung, so far as I knew, the only pictures in the building,
a huge pair of subfusc massively framed oil-paintings, subject and
technique of which I could rarely pass without re-examination. The

murkily stiff treatment of these two unwontedly elongated canvases, although not in fact executed by Horace Isbister RA, recalled his brushwork and treatment, a style that already germinated a kind of low-grade nostalgia on account of its naïve approach and total disregard for any "modern" development in the painter's art. The merging harmonies – dark brown, dark red, dark blue – depicted incidents in the wartime life of King George V . . .' MP 37–8.

MESTROVIČ, Ivan 1883–1962
Anne Stepney's candidate as sculptor for the Haig statue BM 41, 46.

MICHELANGELO 1475–1564
Brought to mind by the octogenarian General Conyers ('there was a restless strength, a rhythm, about his movements that made one think of the Michelangelo figures in the Sistine chapel. The Cumaean Sybil with a neat moustache added? All at once he leant forward, turning with one arm over the back of his chair, his head slightly bent, pointing to another picture hanging on the wall. I saw he was an unbearded Jehovah inspiring life into Adam through an extended finger') KO 209.

MILLAIS, Sir John Everett 1829–96
Boyhood of Raleigh QU 179; *Bubbles* BM 163.

MODIGLIANI, Amedeo 1884–1920
Stringham's signed drawing of a nude by hangs in his London flat in the 'thirties, passing on his death in turn to Pamela Flitton (Stringham's niece, who takes it with her during her disastrous union with X. Trapnel), Widmerpool (Pamela's husband, who manages to hang on to it even when stripped of virtually all other personal possessions in the last months of his life), Scorpio Murtlock (who consigns it to the bonfire after Widmerpool's death) and Bithel (who furtively retrieves it from the flames), and coming finally to rest in the hands of the art dealer Barnabas Henderson AW 260; BDFR 176, 180, 191, 227; HSH 270.

Mona Lisa
Anne Umfraville (née Stepney) was once told she looked like KO 123; provokes a characteristic response in Jenkins' father TK 53.

MONET, Claude 1840–1926
QU 190.

MORO, Antonio 1519–75
Likened to Isbister by the Warden of Sillery's college AW 112.

Moses Saved from the Water
Painting by Tiepolo (National Gallery of Scotland, Edinburgh) who obviously used the same model for Pharaoh's daughter as for the Queen in *Candaules and Gyges*, and the lady in the *Antony and Cleopatra* frescoes (Palazzo Labia, Venice), TK 77.

MURILLO, Bartholomé Esteban *c.* 1617–82
BM 67.

Needles: Schooner Aground, The
One of the more passable seascapes in the Robert Duport collection HSH 245, 257.

Old Humorists, The
Another of Isbister's early genre paintings. For refs, see Character Index under ISBISTER, Horace RA.

Omnipresent, The
The coloured reproduction (of a painting called *Den Allestedsnaervaerende* by Baron Arild Rosenkrantz b. 1870) which hangs in Widmerpool's mother's flat, and depicts three robed figures on the brink of a precipice BM 261; Widmerpool in his final phase as a cult member comes to resemble one of these figures HSH 213.

OROZCO, José Clemente 1883–1949
A possible influence on Daniel Tokenhouse TK 141.

PANNINI, Gian Paolo 1691–1764
See CANALETTO.

PERUGINO 1450–1523
Painted more than one of the Raphaels in the Louvre, according to Mr Deacon BM 10–12, 84. See also *St Sebastian*.

Pharisee, The
A late eighteenth-century coloured print of this racehorse and another of *Trimalchio*, both with blue-chinned jockeys, hang in Stringham's room at school and later in his London flat QU 9, 191, AW 205.

PICASSO, Pablo 1881–1973
Norman Chandler and Matilda Wilson as subjects for CCR 52–3; Moreland on CCR 212; KO 124.

PIRANESI, Giovanni Battista 1720–78
See CANALETTO, and Place Index under HOUSE OF COMMONS.

POUSSIN, Nicolas *c.* 1594–1665
Ranks with Tiepolo as one of Jenkins' most admired masters TK 43.
See also *A Dance to the Music of Time*.

Prince Rupert Conversing with a Herald
The Huntercombes' Van Dyck (the herald in question being Lord Huntercombe's direct ancestor), afterwards prudently re-attributed by its owner to Dobson BM 58; CCR 169.

PRUNA, Pedro b. 1904
Another of the moderns admired by Saltonstall, see FOUJITA, Tsuguharu Leonard.

Pupils of Socrates
Brought to mind by the late Roman décor of a pub off the south side of Oxford Street: 'It was the kind of place my old, deceased friend, Mr Deacon, used to call "a gin palace" . . . The bar, built in the shape of an L, took up most of the two sides of this saloon, of which the pillars and marbled wall decoration again recalled Mr Deacon's name by their resemblance to the background characteristic of his pictures: *Pupils of Socrates*, for example, or *By the Will of Diocletian*. No doubt this bar had been designed by someone who had also brooded long and fruitlessly on classical themes, determined to express in whatever medium available some boyhood memory of *Quo Vadis?* or *The Last Days of Pompeii*'. For refs, see Character Index under DEACON, Edgar Bosworth.

PUVIS DE CHAVANNES, Pierre 1824–98
Only painter, apart from Simeon Solomon, who has Mr Deacon's unqualified approval BM 5.

RACKHAM, Arthur 1867–1939
His goblin-haunted illustrations brought to mind by the gnarled and twisted, ivy-strangled elder trees round the Devil's Fingers HSH 161.

RAPHAEL 1483–1520
Jenkins' and Moreland's common prejudice when young against *La Madonna della Sedia* in framed oval reproduction KO 82. See also PERUGINO.

RENOIR, Pierre Auguste 1841–1919
Recalled by the clientèle of the Ritz ('a sea of countenances, stamped like the skin of Renoir's women with that curiously pink, silky surface that seems to come from prolonged sitting about in Ritz hotels . . .') AW 34; his technique analyzed by Barnby to demonstrate the superiority of painters over writers when it comes to telling the truth about women AW 69.

REYNOLDS, Sir Joshua 1723–92
See BOUCHER, François

RIVERA, Diego 1889–1921
An influence not denied by Tokenhouse TK 141.

ROBERT, Hubert 1733–1808
See CANALETTO.

RODIN, Auguste 1840–1917
'The mere fact of a woman sitting on a man's knee, rather than a chair, certainly suggested the Templer *milieu*. A memorial to Templer himself, in marble or bronze, were public demand ever to arise for so unlikely a cenotaph, might suitably take the form of a couple so grouped. For some reason – perhaps a confused memory of *Le Baiser* – the style of Rodin came to mind. Templer's own point of view seemed to approximate to that earlier period of the plastic arts. Unrestrained emotion was the vogue then, treatment more in his line than some of the bleakly intellectual statuary of our own generation.' AW 213.

ROMNEY, Sir George 1734–1802
A portrait by hangs in the library of Mrs Foxe's London house QU 55, CCR 140, 144.

ROUSSEAU, Douanier 1844–1910
Captain Soper's resemblance to the homely apes in his *Tropiques* BDFR 7.

RUBENS, Sir Peter Paul 1577–1640
Jean Duport recalls his second wife or her sister in *Le Chapeau de Paille* ('There was that same suggestion, though only for an instant, of shyness and submission. Perhaps it was the painter's first wife that Jean resembled, though slighter in build. After all, they were aunt and niece. Jean's grey-blue eyes were slanting and perhaps not so large as theirs') BM 216 & AW 58; KO 124.

St Sebastian
Perugino's painting in the Louvre, in front of which Mr Deacon was
once discovered by the Jenkinses ('Mr Deacon showing an unexpected
grasp of military hierarchy – at least of a somewhat obsolete order – by
pointing out that the Saint, holding as he did the rank of centurion –
and being, therefore, a comparatively senior non-commissioned or
warrant officer – probably possessed a less youthful and altogether more
rugged appearance than that attributed to him by Perugino: and,
indeed, commonly by most other painters of hagiographical subjects')
BM 10–12, 14.

SARGENT, John Singer 1856–1925
One of the many points on which Dicky Umfraville failed to hit it off
with his fourth wife Anne Stepney ('She was always tremendously keen
on her painting. I fell rather short on that score too. Can't tell a Sargent
from a "Snaffles."') LM 181.

SCHWITTERS, Kurt 1887–1948
See VENICE BIENNALE.

Sea Giving Up the Dead that were in It, The
Painting (by Lord Leighton, PRA, 1830–96) in the Tate, likened by
Mark Members to the scene of Mr Deacon's birthday party BM 242.

Seven Deadly Sins tapestries
Sixteenth-century tapestries hanging in Sir Magnus Donners' dining-
room at Stourwater Castle:
'I supposed that they might be Gobelin from their general appearance,
blue and crimson tints set against lemon yellow . . . I found myself seated
opposite *Luxuria*, a failing principally portrayed in terms of a winged and
horned female figure, crowned with roses, holding between finger and
thumb one of her plump naked breasts, while she gazed into a looking-
glass, supported on one side by Cupid and on the other by a goat of
unreliable aspect. The four-footed beast of the Apocalypse, with his
seven dragon-heads, dragged her triumphal car, which was of, great
splendour. Hercules, bearing his clubs, stood by, somewhat gloomily
watching this procession, his mind filled, no doubt, with disquieting
recollections. In the background, the open doors of a pillared house
revealed a four-poster bed, with hangings rising to an apex, under the
canopy of which a couple lay clenched in a priapic grapple. Among
trees, to the right of this composition, further couples and groups, three
or four of them at least, were similarly occupied in smaller houses and
Oriental tents; or, in one case, simply on the ground.'

First encountered at the luncheon party in 1928 or 9 when Jenkins discusses *Luxuria* with Jean Duport. Not seen for another ten years ('More gorgeous, more extravagant than ever, they engulfed my imagination again in their enchanting colours, grotesque episodes, symbolic moods . . .') until the night of the dinner party at which Sir Magnus photographs Isobel and Nicholas Jenkins, Matilda and Hugh Moreland, Anne Umfraville, Betty and Peter Templer impersonating respectively Pride, Sloth, Envy, Gluttony, Anger, Avarice and Lust.

First sight of BM 189–92; second sight of KO 117–18, proposed by Jenkins as a subject for photography 124, 126, 130; recalled on meeting Jean again after the war MP 235; Matilda Donners produces the photographs originally inspired by HSH 56, 61–3; replaced at Stourwater by a reproduction of a portrait of the Queen by Annigoni HSH 206.

SICKERT, Walter Richard 1860–1942
Said to have put in a good word for Mr Deacon's work BM 167 & HSH 247–8; a couple of Sickerts in Donners' collection KO 109.

SNAFFLES (Charles Payne) b. 1884
Popular painter of fox-hunting and military scenes, see SARGENT, J. S.

SOLOMON, Simeon 1840–1905*
Regarded by Mr Deacon as his master BM 5.

SPY (Sir Leslie Ward) 1851–1922
His caricature of Lord Vowchurch, in the *Vanity Fair* series, hangs in the damp deserted billiard room at Thrubworth, 'depicting this high-spirited peer in frock-coat and top hat, both grey: the bad temper, for which he was as notorious at home as for his sparkle in Society, neatly suggested under the side-whiskers by the lines of his mouth' LM 4.

STEEN, Jan 1626–79
His florid round-faced clowns reincarnated in the person of Colonel Van der Voort MP 154.

STEER, Philip Wilson 1860–1942
Represented in Donners' collection at Stourwater KO 109.

* The friend of Swinburne, Burne-Jones and Rossetti, admired by Walter Pater. Son of a Jewish hatter, born in Bishopsgate and showed great promise from an early age (exhibiting, among other scriptural or Hebraic canvases at the Royal Academy, *A Deacon* in 1864). Later switched to classical themes (*Bacchus*, *Toilet of Roman Lady*, *A Greek Acolyte* etc.) before going spectacularly downhill. Arrested for homosexual offences in 1871, and d. of drink in St Giles workhouse after an unsuccessful spell as a pavement artist in Bayswater.

SVAROGH, Vassily Semeonovich 1883–1946
Another socialist-realist painter (his name misremembered by Ada
Leintwardine as Svatogh), see GAPONENKO, T. G.

TENIERS, David 1610–90
See MEMLING, Hans.

TIEPOLO, Giovanni Battista 1696–1770
Ranks with Poussin as one of Jenkins' most admired masters TK 42–3.
See also *The Agony in the Garden, Candaules and Gyges, Mars and Venus,
Moses Saved from the Water*.

TOIDZE, Irakliy Moiseevitch b. 1902
Art worker of RSFSR (Russian Soviet Federated Socialist Republics),
see GAPONENKO, T. G.

TOKENHOUSE, Daniel McN.
Socialist-realist painter of amateur status, unshakeable communist
convictions and strictly limited imaginative faculty. Former art-book
publisher who painted indifferent landscapes as a hobby until redeemed
by a political conversion at the end of the 'thirties. Recants thereafter
from Formalism ('The Camden Town Group had been wholly
superseded, utterly swept away, so far as the art of Daniel Tokenhouse
was concerned'), going on to experiment with such unsatisfactory and
ultimately discarded techniques as industrial realism, politico-
symbolism etc. ('Most of his pictures, Formalist or Reformed, were apt
to end up a superfluity of brownish-carmine tones. This latest canvas,
vermilion and light cobalt, showed . . . what were evidently factory
workers, stripped to the waist, pushing over a precipice a disordered
group of kings and bishops, easily recognizable by their crowns and
mitres. Perhaps deliberately, treatment of posture and movement was a
trifle wooden, but the painter had clearly taken a certain pleasure in
depicting irresolute terror in the features of monarchs and ecclesiastics
toppling into the abyss'). Has moved on by the late 'fifties to a
systematic exposure in monochrome of the evils of capitalism ('You
meditate along the correct political lines, the picture almost paints
itself'). For a further analysis of his work and refs, see Character Index
under TOKENHOUSE, Daniel McN. See also *Any Complaints?* and
Four Priests Rigging a Miracle.

TOULOUSE-LAUTREC, Henri de 1864–1901
Painted the black sheep of the Manasch family slumped in the
background to a café scene, and would have done justice to Rosie
Manasch as well ('At forty or so, she herself was not unthinkable in

terms of Lautrec's brush, more alluring certainly than the ladies awaiting custom on the banquettes of the Rue des Moulins, though with something of their resignation') BDFR 101–2.

Trimalchio
See *The Pharisee.*

TROOST, Cornelis 1697–1750
General Conyers owns a painting by ('The scene was a guard room in the Low Countries. "Undisciplined-looking lot," General Conyers went on. "No joke soldiering in those days"') LM 227, KO 209–10.

Truth Unveiled by Time
A reproduction of the group in the Villa Borghese picked up in the Caledonian Market by Norman Chandler, and purchased from him by Mr Deacon ('I must say that in the original marble Bernini has made the wench look as unpalatable as the heartless quality she represents') in the Mortimer a week before his fatal accident CCR 13–14, 21–2; turns up after Deacon's death in Mrs Foxe's drawing room CCR 144, 169; HSH 253.

VAN DONGEN, Kees 1877–1968
St John Clarke's modernist phase initiated by his learning to tell the difference between a Van Dyck and a Van Dongen AW 25.

VAN DYCK, Sir Anthony 1599–1641
See *Prince Rupert Conversing with a Herald*, and VAN DONGEN, Kees.

VAN GOGH, Vincent 1853–90
Moreland in a strong position for imagining what it felt like to be the man on the threshold of eternity in the Van Gogh pictures TK 271.

VAN TROOST
See TROOST, Cornelis.

VENICE BIENNALE
Toured in 1958 by Jenkins, Tokenhouse ('We'll look at everything. Just to get an idea how low the art of painting has fallen in these latter days of capitalism . . . I can guarantee that the only sanctuary from subjectless bric-à-brac will be in the national pavilions of what you no doubt term the Iron Curtain countries'), Louis Glober and Ada Leintwardine ('"Why, hullo," she said. ". . . We're having such an argument about the things on show, especially this one. Mr Glober sees African overtones, influenced by Ernst. To me the work's more

redolent of Samurai armour designed by Schwitters'") TK 118, 124, 127–9, 132, 141, 143.

VERONESE, Paolo *c.* 1528–88
TK 20, 40, 147. See *Alexander Receiving the Children of Darius After the Battle of Issus* and *Iphigenia* (the Dogdene Veronese).

VUILLARD, Edouard 1868–1940
Brought to mind by the solitary outline of a military policeman jogging his horse across the heath near Stonehurst, 'a heavy brushstroke of dark blue, surmounted by a tiny blob of crimson, moving in the sun through a Vuillard landscape of pinkish greys streaked with yellow and silver' KO 21.

WATTEAU, Antoine 1684–1721
Brought to mind by the unalluring décor of Casanova's Chinese Restaurant CCR 28, 30.

WATTS, George Frederick 1817–1904
A touch of his method discernible in Deacon BM 2.

Where Belgium Greeted Britain
The other one of the pair by Herbert A. Olivier, see *Merville, December 1st, 1914*.

WHISTLER, James Abbot McNeill 1834–1903
Admired by Jenkins' father TK 54; Mrs Erdleigh in old age resembles a nocturne in portraiture by TK 241–2.

WILSON, Richard 1714–82
See GREUZE, Jean Baptiste.

ZADKINE, Ossip 1890–1967
See LIPCHITZ, Jacques.

ZOFFANY, Johann 1733–1810
Portrait of one of Sir Gavin Walpole-Wilson's naval forbears attributed to BM 177.

Place Index

Note. This index is by no means exhaustive. Where references are not given, page numbers will generally be found in the Character Index under names mentioned in the relevant entry. Fictional places are distinguished from actual ones by double asterisks.

ACE OF SPADES
Road-house near Maidenhead where Peter Templer once had a disagreeable experience AW 103.

ALBERT MEMORIAL
Where Jenkins fell in love with Barbara Goring on a Sunday afternoon walk in June when Eleanor Walpole-Wilson was training her dog in Hyde Park ('Sparkles of light radiated this way and that from the clusters of white statuary and nodular gilt pinnacles of the Albert Memorial, towards which we were steadily moving . . . We ascended the steps of the Albert Memorial and inspected the figures of the Arts and Sciences loitering in high relief round the central mass of that monument. Eleanor . . . made some comment regarding the muscles of the bearded male figure belonging to the group called "Manufacturers" which caused Barbara to burst out laughing. This happened on the way down the steps at the south-east corner, approaching the statues symbolizing Asia, where, beside the kneeling elephant, the Bedouin forever rests on his haunches in hopeless contemplation of Kensington Gardens' trees and thickets, the blackened sockets of his eyes ranging endlessly over the rich foliage of these oases of the mirage') BM 17–18; revisited by Jenkins eighteen months later ('Now, like scraps of gilt peeled untidily from the mosaic surface of the neo-Gothic canopy, the leaves, stained dull gold, were blowing about in the wind, while, squatting motionless beside the elephant, the Arab still kept watch on summer's mirage, as, once more, the green foliage faded gradually away before his displeased gaze . . .') BM 224; AW 120.

ALDERSHOT
A 'uniquely detestable town' where Jenkins' father is stationed in 1914, and where Jenkins himself attends an officers' training course in 1940 with Odo Stevens and Jimmy Brent. See also STONEHURST.

BAG OF NAILS
Night club to which Stringham proposes taking Audrey Maclintick on the night he gave Miss Weedon the slip to attend his mother's party for Moreland's symphony CCR 182, 184.

BAYSWATER
Territory principally associated with Uncle Giles, who puts up when in London at one or other of its seedy residential hotels; also with the exiled Poles who make their official headquarters there in the second war ('Some of the big houses here had been bombed and abandoned, others were still occupied. Several blocks that had formerly housed Victorian judges and merchants now accommodated refugees from

Gibraltar, whose tawny skins and brightly coloured shirts and scarves made this once bleak and humdrum quarter of London, with its uncleaned or broken windows and peeling plaster, look like the back streets of a Mediterranean Port. Even so, the area was not yet so squalid as it was in due course to become in the period immediately following the end of the war, when squares and crescents over which an aroma of oppressive respectability had gloomily hung, became infested at all hours of day and night by prostitutes of the lowest category' MP 60–1). See also HYDE PARK GARDENS, UFFORD, DE TABLEY, TITIAN.

BELGRAVE SQUARE
The Huntercombes' London address, where Jenkins attends the dance at which Barbara Goring throws sugar over Widmerpool.

BELLEVUE, THE★★
Small private hotel on the south coast run by the Jenkinses' former cook Albert, where Uncle Giles dies in 1939 ('Like the Ufford, its exterior was painted battleship-grey, the angle of the building conveying just the same sense of a hopelessly unseaworthy, though less heavily built vessel, resolutely attempting to set out to sea . . . even though I ought to have been prepared for a house of more or less the same sort, this miniature, shrunken version of the Ufford surprised me by its absolute consistency of type, almost as much as if the Ufford itself had at last shipped anchor and floated on the sluggish Bayswater tide to this quiet roadstead. Had the Ufford done that? Did the altered name, the new cut of jib, hint at mutiny, barratry, piracy, final revolt on the high seas – for clearly the Bellevue was only awaiting a favourable breeze to set sail – of that ship's company of well brought up souls driven to violence at last by their unjustly straitened circumstances? Here, at any rate, Uncle Giles had died. By the summer sea, death had claimed him, in one of his own palaces, amongst his own people, the proud, anonymous, secretive race that dwell in residential hotels'). Patronized also by Dr Trelawney, Bob Duport and General Conyers on his second honeymoon. KO 141–2, its likeness to the Ufford 146–9, 151, 153–4, 165, 168, 172, 174, 182–3, 188, 190, 215–16; MP 137.

BERKELEY SQUARE
Stringham's mother's house is in the neighbourhood of.

BLOOMSBURY
Occupied at various points by Barnby, who moves into a studio not far from Fitzroy Square in the 'thirties; by the publishing firm of Quiggin & Craggs, snapping up a cheap lease after the second war near

Tavistock Square in an area of 'sad streets and squares, classical façades of grimy brick, faded stucco mansions long since converted into flats'; and by X. Trapnel, camping out with successive mistresses in bleak hotels under perpetual threat of eviction by the management on account of unpaid bills. See also CHARLOTTE STREET.

BOADICEA Statue
Spot on the embankment where Jenkins encounters Widmerpool during a vintage car rally at the height of the latter's private and public misfortunes in the late 'fifties TK 277.

BRIGHTON
Where Jenkins' parents made the acquaintance of Mr Deacon, possibly at a Pavilion concert, when Captain Jenkins was stationed nearby immediately before the first war ('During that period a call was certainly paid on Mr Deacon in his studio: several small rooms converted to that use at the top of a house in one of the quiet squares remote from "the front". He had chosen this retired position because the sight of the sea disturbed him at his work: a prejudice for which psychological explanation would now certainly be available') BM 5, 7.

BRONZE MONKEY★★
Shady night club, newly opened and in danger of imminent closure, where Mr Deacon receives a fatal injury falling downstairs on the night of his birthday party in 1928 or 9 BM 229–30; its licence removed after a police raid two or three weeks later CCR 9; its name misremembered by Chandler as the Brass Monkey HSH 256.

CABOURG
See Book Index under PROUST, Marcel.

CABINET OFFICES
Scene of Widmerpool's official activities 1941–5, where Jenkins twice attends committee meetings as representative of Finn's War Office section ('I followed the marine down flight after flight of stairs. It was like the lower depths of our own building, though more spacious, less shabby. The marine, who had a streaming cold in the head, showed me into a room in the bowels of the earth, the fittings of which were also less down-at-heel than the general run of headquarters and government offices . . . It was impossible to remain unaware of an atmosphere of exceedingly high pressure in this place, something much more concentrated, more intense, than that with which one was normally surrounded . . . In this brightly lit dungeon lurked a sense that no one could spare a word, not a syllable, far less gesture, not of direct value in

289

implementing the matter in hand. The power principle could almost be felt here, humming and vibrating like the drummings of the teleprinter. The sensation that resulted was oppressive, even a shade alarming') MP 11–12.

CAFE DE MADRID★★
Where Max Pilgrim regularly performs in cabaret during the 'thirties, notably on the occasion when his act with Heather Hopkins proved such a flop that he was reduced to appearing at Umfraville's night-club. Subsequently destroyed by a bomb which falls directly over Bijou Ardglass's table on the night of her fortieth birthday party in 1941. LM 95, 190; SA 111–12, 115–16, 132, 142, 155–8, 165, 222; MP 208.

CAFE ROYAL
Quiggin and Members occasionally to be found skulking there between the wars; scene of some curious exchanges between Priscilla Lovell and her lover Odo Stevens when Jenkins dines there with Moreland on the same night as the raid on the Madrid.

CASANOVA'S CHINESE RESTAURANT★★
Italian restaurant in Soho, newly taken over by Chinese personnel from the Amoy up the road, to which Moreland introduces Jenkins in 1928 or 9 and where Barnby promptly helps himself to the waitress Norma. Decorated with scenes from its namesake's career ('Along the walls frescoes tinted in pastel shades, executed with infinite feebleness of design, appealed to Heaven knows what nadir of aesthetic degradation') CCR 3, 5, 27–30, 210, 215–16, 218; KO 110; TK 230; HSH 206.

CASTLEMALLOCK★★
Victorian neo-Gothic pile housing the Corps School of Chemical Warfare to which Jenkins is briefly posted during his battalion's spell in N. Ireland in 1940. Erected by a rich linen draper on the site of the Palladian mansion put up by the Castlemallocks and visited by Lady Caroline Lamb in the aftermath of her affair with Byron ('An air of thwarted passion could well be imagined to haunt these grass-grown paths, weedy lawns and ornamental pools, where moss-covered fountains no longer played . . . there was an undoubted aptness in this sham fortress, monument to a tasteless, half-baked romanticism, becoming now, in truth, a military stronghold, its stone walls and vaulted ceilings echoing at last to the clatter of arms and oaths of soldiery. It was as if its perpetrators had re-created the tedium, as well as the architecture of medieval times . . . This impression – that one had slipped back into a nightmare of the Middle Ages – was not dispelled

by the Castlemallock "details" on parade. There were warm summer nights at Retreat when I could scarcely proceed between the ranks of these cohorts of gargoyles drawn up for inspection for fear of bursting into fits of uncontrollable demoniac laughter'). VB 155, 168, 170–2, 200–1, 206, 215, 218, 225, 235; SA 10, 188; MP 174–5.

CENOTAPH
Saluted by Sunny Farebrother on the occasion when he narrowly avoided the humiliation of paying the same tribute to Col. Widmerpool MP 116–17.

CHARLOTTE STREET
'Charlotte Street, as it stretches north towards Fitzroy Square, retains a certain unprincipled integrity of character, though its tributaries reach out to the east, where, in Tottenham Court Road, structural anomalies pass all bounds of reason, and west, into a nondescript ocean of bricks and mortar from which hospitals, tenements and warehouses gloomily manifest themselves in shapeless bulk above mean shops. Mr Deacon's "place" was situated in a narrow by-street in this westerly direction: an alley-way, not easy to find, of modest eighteenth-century – perhaps even late seventeenth-century – houses, of a kind still to be seen in London, though growing rarer, the fronts of some turned to commercial purpose, others bearing the brass plate of dentist or midwife. Those that remained private dwellings had three or four bells, one above the other, set beside the door at a height from the ground effectively removed from children's runaway rings. Mr Deacon's premises stood between a French polisher's and the Vox Populi Press. It was a sordid spot . . .' BM 162–3.

CHELSEA
Where Miss Janet Walpole-Wilson lives; and where Eleanor Walpole-Wilson sets up a ménage with Norah Tolland in the 'thirties ('we had arrived before a dilapidated stucco façade in a side street, a house entered by way of a creaking, unlatched door, from which most of the paint had been removed. The hall, empty except for a couple of packing cases, gave off that stubborn musty smell characteristic of stair-cases leading to Chelsea flats: damp cigarette smoke: face powder . . .' LM 89); and where Jenkins spends much of the second war in a tenement block inhabited also by Odo Stevens and Mrs Erdleigh.

DEACON'S SHOP★★
Situated not far from Moreland's flat, between Oxford Street and the Tottenham Court Road, with Mr Deacon's living quarters above it and Barnby's studio in the attic ('the shop was shut. Through the plate glass,

obscured in watery depths, dark green like the interior of an aquarium's compartments, Victorian work-tables, *papier-mâché* trays, Staffordshire figures, and a varnished scrap screen – upon the sombrely coloured *montage* of which could faintly be discerned shiny versions of *Bubbles* and *For He Had Spoken Lightly Of A Woman's Name* – swam gently into further aqueous recesses that eddied back into yet more remote alcoves of the double room: additional subterranean grottoes, hidden from view, in which, like a grubby naiad, Gypsy Jones . . . was accustomed, from time to time, to sleep, or at least to recline, beneath the monotonous, conventionalized arabesques of rare, if dilapidated, Oriental draperies. For some reason, the thought rouses a faint sense of desire. The exoticism of the place as a bedroom was undeniable') BM 91, 163–4; scene of its owner's last birthday party BM 235–6; Jenkins sleeps with Gypsy Jones at the back of BM 255–6; CCR 9–10. See also CHARLOTTE STREET.

DE TABLEY★★
Hotel across the road from the Ufford in Bayswater, occasionally patronized by Uncle Giles in fits of pique AW 2, MP 27; requisitioned in wartime as a local branch of the Food Office MP 62.

DEVIL'S FINGERS, THE★★
Minor archaeological site just over the hill from the Jenkinses' house in the country and under threat of encroachment from the neighbouring quarry; consists of two stone uprights, possibly remnants of a neolithic grave, thought to have been left behind by the devil while attempting to lay hands on a girl out courting with her lover, and credited locally with various magical properties. Visited by Scorpio Murtlock on his caravan jaunt in 1968, and re-visited on Midsummer Eve two years later for the naked ritual dance in the course of which Murtlock stabs Widmerpool and Dr Trelawney fails to rise from the dead. HSH 23, its historical origins and legendary properties, Murtlock's interest in 25–8, local conservationists gather at on Midsummer Day 148–9, 151, Ernie Dunch's distressing experience at the night before, Gwinnett's account of the previous night's rites 153–64, 170–4, 182, 184–6, 189, 212–3, 266.

DOGDENE★★
The Sleafords' magnificent country mansion, one of the first houses in England to be built as a nobleman's castle rather than a fortified keep according to Christopher Wren; visited by Pepys, also by George IV, and painted by Constable; renowned for its Veronese, its architectural splendours and its fine parterres. Home of Lady Molly Jeavons (who entertained royalty there as well as Henry James, St John Clarke and Dicky Umfraville at house parties before the first war) during her first

marriage to the Marquess of Sleaford. Requisitioned as a military hospital in the first war, and afterwards inherited by Geoffrey Sleaford who lets all but the gardens go to pot. Scene of Widmerpool's catastrophic night with his fiancée Mrs Haycock in the 'thirties. Houses an evacuated girls' school in second war, and is later thrown open to the public in an attempt to defray the expense of basic upkeep. LM 7, 9–13, Pepys' visit to 11–13, 17, 18, 42, 57, 159, 173, 175, 194–6, its glorious past 213–6, Widmerpool's visit to 227–31, 237; CCR 80, 191, 194; KO 146, 214; SA 222; TK 21–2. See also Painting Index under CONSTABLE, John.

DONNERS BREBNER BUILDING★★
Opposite Millbank, dominating the southern shore of the Thames like a vast penitentiary ('the innate dejection of spirit of that part of London was augmented by regarding its landscape from this huge and shapeless edifice, recently built in a style as wholly without ostensible order as if it were some vast prehistoric cromlech') QU 225; its entrance hall decorated with murals by Barnby AW 24; CCR 9, 123; sustains a direct hit in the blitz SA 5; MP 113.

EATON SQUARE
The Walpole-Wilsons' London address.

EUSTON ROAD
Northern boundary of the haunts of Mr Deacon, four of whose paintings are knocked down long after his death at an auction room in the neighbourhood of ('On these particular premises almost every man-made thing seemed represented. Comparatively new mowing machines: scabbardless and rusty cavalry sabres: ebony fragments of African fetish: a nineteenth-century typewriter, poised uncertainly on metal stilts in the midst of a tea-set in Liverpool ware, the black-and-white landscapes of its design irreparably chipped. Several pillows and bolsters covered with the Union Jack gave a disturbing hint that, somewhere beneath, a corpse awaited burial with military honours. Farther off, high rolls of linoleum, coloured blue, green and pink, were ranged beneath the wall like pillars, a Minoan colonnade, from which wicker arm-chairs and much-used pieces of luggage formed a semicircle. Within this open space stood the washstand round which the pictures were grouped. On its marble top rested an empty bird-cage, two men-at-arms in lead, probably German, and a dog-eared pile of waltz music. In front of a strip of Axminster carpet, displayed like faded tapestry from the side of a near-by wardrobe in pitch pine, a fourth painting stood upside down . . . the pictures . . . were not utterly unsympathetic in that situation. Even the forest of inverted legs,

moving furiously towards their goal in what appeared to be one of the running events of the Olympic Games, were manifested to what might easily have been greater advantage in that reversed position, conveying as they did, an immense sense of nervous energy, the flesh tints of the athletes' straining limbs contrasting strangely with pink and yellow contours of three cupids in debased Dresden who tripped alongside on top of a pedestal cupboard.') BM 1–3.

F MESS★★
Billets to which Jenkins is assigned ('F is low, but not the final dregs of the Divisional Headquarters staff, if they can be so called. The Mobile Bath Officer, and his like, are in E Mess': Widmerpool) during his attachment to General Liddament's HQ in a N. Ireland coastal town in 1941 ('The Mess was situated in a red-brick, semi-detached villa . . . Entering the front door, you were at once assailed by a nightmare of cheerlessness and squalor, all the sordid melancholy, at its worst, of any nest of bedrooms where only men sleep; a prescript of nature unviolated by the character of solely male-infested sleeping quarters established even in buildings hallowed by age and historical associations. F Mess was far from such . . .'). VB 242; SA 5, 18–19, 64–5, 72–3, 75–6, 83, 167, 169–70, 175, 177, 182, 220, 228.

FOPPA'S★★
Small, smoky Soho club above a restaurant with a peculiarly Italian smell on the stairs ('minestrone: salad oil: stale tobacco: perhaps a faint reminder of the lotion Foppa used on his hair'). For its character and clientèle, see Character Index under FOPPA.

FORTY-THREE
Night club considered too stuffy, in all senses, by Stringham when in the mood for haunts of vice BM 144–5.

FRENCH-POLISHERS' ARMS★★
One of the three pubs cleared of customers by X. Trapnel on the night he bought free drinks for all comers at the Hero of Acre. See HERO OF ACRE.

GERRARD STREET
Where Jenkins and Moreland heard the bald prima donna on crutches singing 'Pale hands I loved beside the Shalimar' CCR 1–4.

GHOST RAILWAY★★
Jenkins and Moreland once took a trip on, rushing downhill in total darkness and crashing through closed doors towards a body lying across

the line, which both agreed was very like everyday life CCR 5, 219.

GLIMBER★★
Stringham's mother's seventeenth-century home, inherited for her lifetime from her first husband Lord Warrington; pretty but too big and much too draughty in the winter; gone over by Widmerpool as a schoolboy with his mother on one of the days it was open to the public. Let to an Armenian at the end of the 'twenties, later inhabited by Miss Weedon and Stringham in the final phase of his alcoholic cure ('It's huge, uninhabitable, entailed, nobody wants to rent it': Templer). Taken over by an evacuated government office in second war; and returned to the Warringtons on Mrs Foxe's death. QU 59, 62, 68–9, 130, 174; BM 103; AW 206; KO 104–5, 215; SA 79.

GLOUCESTER ROAD
See SCARLET PIMPERNEL and SOUTH KENSINGTON

GREAT WEST ROAD
Traversed by Jenkins and Jean Duport en route for Maidenhead in the back of Peter Templer's car on the weekend which sees the start of their affair in 1933 ('On either side of the highway, grotesque buildings, which in daytime resembled the temples of some shoddy, utterly unsympathetic Atlantis, now assumed the appearance of an Arctic city's frontier forts. Veiled in snow, these hideous monuments of a lost world bordered a broad river of black, foaming slush, across the surface of which the car skimmed and jolted with a harsh crackling sound, as if the liquid beneath were scalding hot . . . The exact spot must have been a few hundred yards beyond the point where the electrically illuminated young lady in a bathing dress dives eternally through the petrol-tainted air; night and day, winter and summer, never reaching the water of the pool to which she endlessly glides. Like some image of arrested development, she returns for ever, voluntarily, to the springboard from which she started her leap. A few seconds after I had seen this bathing belle journeying, as usual, imperturbably through the frozen air, I took Jean in my arms . . . To what extent the sudden movement that brought us together was attributable to sentiment felt years before; to behaviour that was almost an obligation within the Templer orbit; or, finally, to some specific impetus of the car as it covered an unusually bad surface of road, was later impossible to determine with certainty . . .') AW 64–5, 136; VB 154; MP 152.

GRENADIERE, LA★★
Home of the Leroys in Touraine where Jenkins and Widmerpool spend some weeks learning French in the summer of 1923.

GROSVENOR PLACE
See QUADRIGA

HAY LOFT★★
Place off the Tottenham Court Road, dispensing rather especially good bacon-and-eggs at any hour of the night, where Jenkins discussed action and its bearing on Sir Magnus Donners at the end of the 'twenties with Moreland KO 75, 78–9; HSH 55.

HERO OF ACRE★★
X. Trapnel's favourite London pub, noted for the boreal chills of its saloon bar. Scene of Trapnel's final apotheosis on the night he returned like Lazarus from the dead to spend one hundred pounds in notes: 'The Hero, one of those old-fashioned pubs in grained pitchpine with engraved looking-glass (what Mr Deacon used to call a "gin palace", was anatomised into half a dozen or more separate compartments, subtly differentiating, in the traditional British manner, social divisions of its clientèle, according to temperament or means: saloon bar: public bar: private bar: ladies' bar: wine bar: off-licence: possibly others too. Customers occupied in these peripheries were all included in the Trapnel largesse, no less than those in the saloon bar, where he had manifested himself. Swept in, too, were several birds of passage, transients buying half-a-bottle at the off-licence. The fountains ran with wine, more precisely with bitter and scotch. News of this munificence got round immediately, not only emptying The French-polishers' Arms opposite – according to Crowding, lately a serious rival to The Hero in draining off a sediment of discontented intellectuals – but also considerably reducing numbers in The Marquess of Sleaford round the corner, where intellectuals were virtually unknown. Not only were these two latter pubs practically cleared of customers, but what Crowding called a "thirsty concourse" poured into The Hero from The Wheelbarrow . . . Not only Crowding, but many others, agreed The Hero had never known such a night'. BDFR 145, 147–9, 152, 156, 158–9, 160, 167–8, 183; TK 23, 26, Trapnel's last night in 30–4.

HILL STREET
Scene of the party given by Milly Andriadis in 1928 or 9 on the same night as the Huntercombes' dance ('The house, which had the air of being rented furnished only for a month or two, was bare; somewhat unattractively decorated in an anonymous style which, at least in the upholstery, combined touches of the Italian Renaissance with stripped panelling and furniture of "modernistic" design, these square, metallic pieces on the whole suggesting Berlin rather than Paris. Although smaller than the Huntercombes', my uncle would have detected there a decided suggestion of wealth, and also . . . an atmosphere of frivolity.

. . . The comparative formality of the scene to be observed on our arrival had cast a certain blight on my own – it now seemed too ready – acceptance of Stringham's assurance that invitation was wholly unnecessary; for the note of "frivolity", to which Uncle Giles might so undeniably have taken exception, was, so I could not help feeling, infused with an undercurrent of extreme coolness, a chilly consciousness of conflicting egoisms, far more intimidating than anything normally to be met with at Walpole-Wilsons', Huntercombes', or, indeed, anywhere else of "that sort"') BM 94, 98–9, 109, house rented from Bob Duport, its décor deplored by David Pennistone ('these appalling Italianate fittings – and the pictures – my God, the pictures') BM 140–1, and by Jean Duport, who proposes suing Mrs Andriadis for breaking a looking glass and burning the boiler out BM 193–4, 229–30, 234; house sold at the time of Duport's financial crash AW 160, Mrs Andriadis apologizes for raising hell in it AW 164; VB 110, its décor evinced by Jimmy Brent as evidence of Duport's flawless artistic taste VB 125.

HINTON HOO**
The Walpole-Wilsons' place in the country, near Stourwater and not far from Widmerpool's mother's cottage, a small red-brick Queen Anne manor house where Jenkins spends a weekend in the summer of 1928 or 9.

HOUSE OF COMMONS
Jenkins dines at with Roddy Cutts in 1946 ('We rose from the table, exchanging the claustrophobic pressures of the hall where the meal had been eaten, for a no less viscous density of parliamentary smoking-rooms and lobbies, suffocating, like all such precincts, with the omnipresent and congealed sense of public contentions and private egotisms; breath of life to their frequenters . . . Callot-like figures pervaded labyrinthine corridors. Cavernous alcoves were littered with paraphernalia of scaffolding and ropes, Piranesian frameworks hinting of torture and execution, but devised only to repair bomb damage to structure and interior ornament') BDFR 169–70.

HYDE PARK
Where Jenkins encounters a protest demonstration on a dank misty afternoon in 1933, convened to meet Hunger Marchers from the Midlands and consisting mostly of heterogeneous intellectuals such as Sillery, and St John Clarke pushed in a wheel chair by J. G. Quiggin and Mona Templer AW 120, 122, 127–32, 136. See also ALBERT MEMORIAL.

HYDE PARK CORNER
Coffee stall at, where Stringham turns up on the night of the Huntercombes' dance and invites Jenkins, Widmerpool, Mr Deacon and Gypsy Jones on to a low party at Milly Andriadis' BM 83, 89–92.

HYDE PARK GARDENS
Home of Lady Warminster and her unmarried stepchildren Blanche, Robert, Priscilla and Hugo Tolland ('Life at Hyde Park Gardens might be ruthless, but it was played out on a reasonably practical basis, in which every man was for himself and no quarter was given; while at the same time a curtain of relatively good humour was usually allowed to cloak an inexorable recognition of life's inevitable severities'). Atmosphere of quiet melancholy; rich, rather too heavy furnishings; deceptively ordinary interior, 'expressing almost as profound an anonymity as Uncle Giles' private hotel, the Ufford . . .' LM 49, 92, 147, first visit to 206–8; CCR Sunday luncheon at 57–8, 60, 88, 193; KO 143–6.

KENSINGTON GARDENS
St John Clarke a keen supporter of the Peter Pan statue in, and a vigorous opponent of Rima in the bird sanctuary AW 19, CCR 192. See also ALBERT MEMORIAL

MADRID, THE★★
See CAFE DE MADRID.

MAIDA VALE CANAL
X. Trapnel goes to ground with Pamela Widmerpool in 1947 in an apparently uninhabited house to the north of ('Before the war, the indigenous population, time-honoured landladies, inveterate lodgers, immemorial whores, long undisturbed in surrounding premises, had already begun to give place to young married couples, but buildings already tumbledown had now been further reduced by bombing. The neighbourhood looked anything but flourishing') BDFR 189–91; and later finds the manuscript of his *Profiles in String* dumped by Pamela in the waters of ('Then an extraordinary thing happened. Trapnel was still standing by the edge of the water holding the dripping sheet of foolscap. Now he crushed it in his hand, and threw the ball of paper back into the Canal. He lifted the swordstick behind his head, and, putting all his force into the throw, cast it as far as this would carry, high into the air. The stick turned and descended, death's-head first. A mystic arm should certainly have risen from the dark waters of the mere to receive it. That did not happen') BDFR 220–1.

MAIDENHEAD
Where Peter Templer lives at the time of his marriage to Mona in a

grotesquely gabled house not unlike his father's former home by the sea, set among pine and fir plantations and shielded from other similar houses by thick laurel bushes ('This was, no doubt, a settlement of prosperous businessmen; a reservation, like those created for indigenous inhabitants, or wild animal life, in some region invaded by alien elements, where they might live their own lives, undisturbed and unexploited by an aggressive outer world. In these confines the species might be saved from extinction') AW 65–8.

MARQUESS OF SLEAFORD★★
Another of the three pubs emptied by X. Trapnel, see HERO OF ACRE.

MERRY THOUGHT★★
Where Gypsy Jones attends a fancy-dress party as Eve to Howard Craggs' Adam, and Heather Hopkins plays the piano most nights in the early 'thirties BM 127, 153, 255; LM 95; KO 134, 228.

MORTIMER★★
Soho pub where Jenkins first met Moreland at the end of the 'twenties, noted for its depressing musical clientèle, indifferent beer and draughty saloon bar. Bombed out in the second war ('A direct hit had excised even the ground floor, so that the basement was revealed as a sunken garden, or site of archaeological excavation long abandoned, where great sprays of willowherb and ragwort flowered through cracked paving stones; only a few broken milk bottles and a laceless boot recalling contemporary life. In the midst of this sombre grotto five or six fractured steps had withstood the explosion and formed a projecting island of masonry on the summit of which rose the door. Walls on both sides were shrunk away, but along its lintel, in niggling copybook handwriting, could still be distinguished the word *Ladies*. Beyond, on the far side of the twin pillars and crossbar, nothing whatever remained of that promised retreat, the threshold falling steeply to an abyss of rubble; a triumphal arch erected laboriously by dwarfs, or the gateway to some unknown, forbidden domain, the lair of sorcerers'). Afterwards rebuilt, becoming a favourite haunt of X. Trapnel. CCR Its ruin 1–2, its former character, meeting with Moreland recalled 9–10, 16, 20–2, 24–6, 47, 130, 144, 216; TK 23, 67, 69.

MOUNTFICHET★★
Lord Bridgnorth's country seat, makes a dim impression on his son-in-law Charles Stringham AW 199.

NAG'S HEAD★★
Pub where all the tarts go in Pimlico, Maclintick's local CCR 150, 152, 204.

1917 CLUB
(Haunt of Bloomsbury intellectuals in Gerrard Street, founded by Leonard Woolf and others in 1917 and named for the Russian revolution). Gypsy Jones said to be the toast of BM 171; Howard Craggs had the girls from, in the days when he was young and running the Vox Populi Press BDFR 142.

NOTTINGHAMSHIRE
Widmerpool's place of origin, vouchsafed by Jenkins under cross-examination from Widmerpool's prospective sister-in-law Mrs Conyers ('I felt that the least I could do for an old acquaintance in these circumstances was to suggest, however indirectly, a soothing picture of generations of Widmerpools in a rural setting: an ancient, if dilapidated, manor house: Widmerpool tombs in the churchyard: tankards of ale at the "Widmerpool Arms"') LM 83.

NORMANDY
Jenkins experiences a sense of occasion while travelling through, on the way to inspect allied lines in 1944 MP 156–7, 217.

OLYMPIA
Where Jenkins collects his demob outfit at the end of the war, and runs into Archie Gilbert MP 241–1, 244.

PADDINGTON
One of the traditional Trapnel areas of bivouac BDFR 148, 190.

PARK LANE
Milly Andriadis' address at the time of her Trotskyite conversion LM 160–3.

PEMBRINGHAM WOODHOUSE★★
Lord Goring's estate, where Widmerpool fell in love with Barbara Goring in the days when his father supplied hers with liquid manure BM 59, 80–1.

PICCADILLY
Scene of Stringham's collapse after some hard drinking at Le Bas' reunion for Old Boys LM 201–4.

PIMLICO
Territory occupied by Maclintick ('He says his mood is for ever Pimlico'), 'a vast, desolate region of stucco streets and squares upon which a doom seemed to have fallen. The gloom was cosmic. We traversed these pavements for some distance, proceeding from haunts

of seedy, grudging gentility into an area of indeterminate, but on the whole increasingly unsavoury complexion . . . The house, when we reached it, turned out to be a small, infinitely decayed two-storey dwelling that had seen better days; now threatened by a row of mean shops advancing from one end of the street and a fearful slum crowding up from the other' CCR 106–7, 117–18, 205, 216.

PORTOBELLO ROAD
Street market where X. Trapnel bought his death's-head swordstick BDFR5 108, 190.

PRIMROSE HILL
Where Books-do-furnish-a-room Bagshaw finally abandons a vagrant's life on his third marriage to settle for domesticity in a dilapidated house later broken into by Pamela Widmerpool.

QUADRIGA
Statue at Hyde Park Corner where Jenkins and Widmerpool encounter Mr Deacon and Gypsy Jones after the Huntercombes' dance ('By this time we had come to Grosvenor Place, in sight of the triumphal arch, across the summit of which, like a vast paper-weight or capital ornament of an Empire clock, the Quadriga's horses, against a sky of indigo and silver, pranced desperately towards the abyss') BM 82.

REGENT'S PARK
Rosie and Odo Steven's address, scene of Pamela Widmerpool's final assault on her husband after the Mozart party at their house in 1959.

REGENT'S PARK CANAL
See MAIDA VALE CANAL.

RITZ, THE
Jenkins keeps an appointment with Mark Members among a large party of South Americans camped out in the palm court, and meets Jean Duport for the third time AW 30–2, 34–6, 41, 46–7, 49, 56, 63, Le Bas holds a reunion for Old Boys at AW 170; SA 69, 71; Colonel Flores once stayed there with all his family MP 232, 235.

RUTLAND GATE
Jean Duport has a flat somewhere beyond, at the time of her affair with Jenkins.

ST PAUL'S
Jenkins attends the Victory Service, and ponders on the tombs in MP 214–18, 221, 227, 229; Widmerpool would prefer to be buried in, rather than Westminster Abbey MP 230.

SARDIS★★
Nineteenth century Welsh chapel where Captain Gwatkin's company is billeted when Jenkins joins his regiment in 1940 VB 3–5; TK 86.

SCARLET PIMPERNEL★★
Restaurant near the Jeavonses' house in Gloucester Road, where Jenkins dines with Moreland in 1939 KO 241, 243, 250.

SCHOOL★★
Its setting, historical exhalations and present sombre aspect ('As winter advanced in that river valley, mist used to rise in late afternoon and spread over the flooded grass; until the house and all the outskirts of the town were enveloped in opaque, chilly vapour, tinted like cigar-smoke. The house looked on to other tenement-like structures, experiments in architectural insignificance, that intruded upon a central concentration of buildings, commanding and antiquated, laid out in a quadrilateral, though irregular, style. Silted-up residues of the years smouldered uninterruptedly – and not without melancholy – in the maroon brickwork of these medieval closes . . . Running westward in front of the door, a metalled road continued into open country . . . fields: railway arches: a gas-works: and then more fields – a kind of steppe where the climate seemed at all times extreme: sleet: wind: or sultry heat: a wide territory, loosely enclosed by inflexions of the river, over which the smells of the gasometer, recalled perhaps by the fumes of the coke fire, would come and go with intermittent strength . . .') QU 2–3, interior of Le Bas' house, its characteristic smell QU 7, its passages and boot-room QU 24–5, its hall as setting for Widmerpool ('He stood there in the shadowy space by the slab in a setting of brown-paper parcels, dog-eared school books and crumbs . . . his appearance suggesting rather some unusual creature actually bred in those depths by the slab, amphibious perhaps, though largely belonging to this land-world of blankets and carbolic: scents which attained their maximum density at this point, where they met and mingled with the Irish stew, which, coming from the territories of laundry baskets and coke, reached its most potent force on the first step of the stairs') QU 46–7, school chapel QU 49–50; revisited half a century later BDFR 206–7, 230–1, 237.

SHAFTESBURY AVENUE
Where Jenkins and Moreland bought the bottle labelled *Tawney Wine*

(*port flavour*) which even Moreland was later unwilling to drink CCR 2, 5; and where Jenkins purchases his military greatcoat at a theatrical costumier's on the outbreak of war VB 1–4, MP 241.

SHEPHERD MARKET
Where Jenkins lives on first coming to London in rooms between an all-night garage, a sandwich bar and a block of flats inhabited by peculiarly rowdy and aggressive prostitutes ('As I reached the outskirts of Shepherd Market, at that period scarcely touched by the rebuilding, I regained once more some small sense of exultation, enjoyed whenever crossing the perimeter of that sinister little village, that I lived within an enchanted precinct. Inconvenient, at moments, as a locality: noisy and uncomfortable: stuffy, depressing, unsavoury: yet the ancient houses still retained some vestige of the dignity of another age; while the inhabitants, many of them existing precariously on their bridge earnings, or hire of their bodies, were – as more than one novelist had, even in those days, already remarked – not without their own seedy glory') BM 76, 153–4; MP 109. See also Painting Index under CANALETTO.

SKINDLES
Hotel at Maidenhead where Peter and Mona Templer dined exactly 1,027 times AW 103.

SLOANE SQUARE
General and Mrs Conyers' flat is in the neighbourhood of.

SOHO
See CASANOVA'S CHINESE RESTAURANT, FOPPA'S, TROUVILLE and UMFRAVILLE'S NIGHT CLUB.

SOUTH KENSINGTON
Where the Jeavonses live in a large, disorganized, chronically untidy, over-ornamented, dark red brick house ('the architecture of which sounded a distant, not particularly encouraging, echo of the High Renaissance') near Gloucester Road underground station.

STONEHURST★★
Red-tiled, possibly haunted, furnished bungalow near Aldershot, built by a retired Indian army officer *c*. 1900 and rented by Jenkins' parents in the summer of 1914. Not far from the pebble-dashed, gabled establishment in which Dr Trelawney and disciples pursue the Simple Life. Scene of Jenkins' childhood wargames, also of the Conyerses' visit and the breakdown of the parlourmaid Billson on the afternoon of the

assassinations at Sarajevo ('Its configuration suggested a long, low Noah's Ark, come uncomfortably to rest on a heather-grown, coniferous spur of Mount Ararat . . . The final limits of the Stonehurst estate, an extensive wired-in tract given over to the devastations of a vast brood of much interbred chickens, bordered on the heath, which stretched away in the dim distance, the heather rippling in waves like an inland sea overgrown with weed . . . Dark, brooding plantations of trees; steep, sandy slopes; soft, velvet expanses of green moss . . . Here, among these woods and clearings, sand and fern, silence and the smell of pine brought a kind of release to the heart, together with a deep-down wish for something, something more than battles, perhaps not battles at all; something realized, even then, as nebulous, blissful, all but unattainable: a feeling of uneasiness, profound and oppressive, yet oddly pleasurable at times, at other times so painful as to be almost impossible to bear'). KO Its buildings, estate and setting 4–5 & 7–9, its domestic personnel 11–12, 15, 18–19, 21–2, 25, its nearness to Trelawney's establishment 27–8, 31–2, the Conyerses' visit to 34–5, 41, 43, 50, 54, 60, Trelawney's appearance at 63, 66, 74–5, 80–1, 86–7, recollections of quarter of a century later 107, 133, 140, 150–2, 155, 159, 186, 189, 201, 208, 254; VB 114, 119, 120, 172, 193; MP 216; TK 196, 277; HSH 34, 128.

STOURWATER CASTLE★★
Home of Sir Magnus Donners (who purchased it from Rosie Manasch's Uncle Leopold) and his magnificent art collections, an almost perfectly preserved, late medieval castle of little or no historical interest. Scene of the luncheon party in 1928 or 9 at which Jenkins meets Jean Duport for the second time ('Mounted effigies in Gothic armour guarded either side of the door by which we entered the Great Hall; and these dramatic figures of man and horse struck a new and somewhat disturbing note; though one at which the sunken garden had already hinted. Such implications of an over-elaborate solicitude were followed up everywhere the eye rested, producing a result altogether different from the cool, detached vision manifested a minute or two earlier by grey walls and towers rising out of the green, static landscape. Something was decidedly amiss . . . The impression was of sensations that might precede one of those episodes in a fairy story, when, at a given moment, the appropriate spell is pronounced to cause domes and minarets, fountains and pleasure-gardens, to disappear into thin air; leaving the hero – in this case, Sir Magnus Donners – shivering in rags beneath the blasted oak of a grim forest, or scorched by rays of a blazing sun among the rocks and boulders of some desolate mountainside').

Revisited by Jenkins a decade later on the occasion when Donners organizes tableaux after dinner, recreating the subjects of the Seven Deadly Sins tapestries in his dining room ('Cardboard was . . . the material of which walls and keep seemed to be built, as we rounded the final sweep of the drive, coming within sight of a large castellated pile, standing with absurd unreality against a background of oaks, tortured by their antiquity into elephantine and grotesque shapes . . . In my memory the place had been larger, more forbidding, not so elaborately restored . . . Now, Stourwater seemed nearer to being an architectural abortion, a piece of monumental vulgarity, a house where something had gone very seriously wrong'). Requisitioned by the government in second war; becomes a fashionable girls' school in the 'fifties after Donners' death; and is the scene of the Cuttses' wedding, and of Widmerpool's cult activities, in the early 'seventies. BM Its past history, luncheon party at, first impressions of 180–1, 183–6, the Seven Deadly Sins tapestries 189–92, Donners' tour of the dungeons 200–5, 209–11, its sunken lawn wrecked by Widmerpool 215–19, 221; AW 58, 134–5, 154; LM 50; CCR 130–1; KO 89–90, 95–100, 102–3, dinner party at, its Wagnerian and Arthurian overtones, disappointing second impressions of 105–10, Seven Deadly Sins tableaux 114–18, 120, 135, 138–9, 166, 170, 172–3, 225–6, requisitioned 250; VB 119, 172; MP 15, 21, 50; turned into a school TK 36–7, 153; HSH 45, 187, 191, Cuttses' wedding at 194–5, 200, 203, tour of 205–10, 212, 214–15, 219–20, 222, Murtlock's arrival at 232–3, 238–9, 247, 263, 266. See also Painting Index under SEVEN DEADLY SINS and Book Index under IBSEN, Henrik and *Pilgrim's Progress*.

STRASBOURG, THE★★
Restaurant frequented by the Jenkinses and Morelands as an alternative to Foppa's in the 'thirties CCR 130, 133; KO 85; VB 129.

THRUBWORTH PARK★★
Country seat of Lord Warminster (Erridge), a seventeenth-century brick mansion of no great architectural distinction, where Jenkins first sets eyes on his future wife, Isobel Tolland, during a weekend spent with the Quiggins at their cottage on Erridge's estate. Kept under dustsheets, with the state rooms shut off, by its owner who lives in a state of discomfort bordering on squalor in servants' quarters at the back. Requisitioned in the second war as a Corps HQ, later occupied by a top-secret inter-service organization, and later still converted into a camp for German prisoners-of-war. Destined to become a scientific research institute in the hands of Erridge's heir, Jeremy Warminster. LM 4, 21, 27–8, 93–4, 97, 121–2, dinner at, its cavernous gloom, Erridge's living room 124–30, tour of the house 134, 147–52, 203, 205, 210; CCR 59, 63, 66–8, 78, 92, 202, 223, 227–8; KO 143–4, 204–5; VB 150–1, 160,

164, 166; MP 78; BDFR 28, 38, 55, visited after Erridge's funeral, his room and its accumulated lumber 65–9; 117, 131, 169; TK 2; HSH 192.

TITIAN★★
Bayswater hotel, Edwardian in tone, once visited by Uncle Giles; headquarters of the exiled Polish army in the second war MP 27, 29, 31, 65–6; BDFR 100–1.

TOTTENHAM COURT ROAD
See CHARLOTTE STREET, DEACON'S SHOP and the HAYLOFT.

TROUVILLE★★
Uninviting Soho restaurant patronized by Uncle Giles QU 220, 230, LM 173.

UFFORD★★
Recognized as the nearest thing to a home by Uncle Giles ('This private hotel in Bayswater . . . occupied two corner houses in a latent, almost impenetrable region west of the Queen's Road. Not only the battleship grey colour, but also something at once angular and top-heavy about the block's configuration as a whole, suggested a large vessel moored in the street. Even within, at least on the ground floor, the Ufford conveyed some remainder of life at sea, though certainly of no luxuriously equipped liner; at best one of those superannuated schooners of Conrad's novels, perhaps decorated years before as a rich man's yacht, now tarnished by the years and reduced to ignoble uses like traffic in tourists, pilgrims, or even illegal immigrants; pervaded – to borrow an appropriately Conradian mannerism – with uneasy memories of the strife of men. That was the feeling the Ufford gave, riding at anchor on the sluggish Bayswater tides') BM 155; AW tea with Uncle Giles and Mrs Erdleigh in its deserted lounge, its character, appointments and mysterious, sombre ambiance 1–6, 17, 81, 88, 102, 182, 212; LM 69; CCR 58, 98, 141; KO 141, compared with the Bellevue 149, 153–6, 162, 197; MP converted into a semi-secret Polish headquarters in second war, unrecognised at first by Jenkins 61–3, 131; BDFR 148. See also the BELLEVUE.

UMFRAVILLE'S NIGHT CLUB★★
In Soho, nearly opened on the night in 1934 when Peter Templer entertains Widmerpool there, and Ted Jeavons is reunited with Widmerpool's fiancée Mrs Haycock ('The entrance of the club was concealed in an alleyway, by no means easy to find . . . At the end of a narrow, dimly-lit passage a villainous-looking fellow with watery eyes

and a nose covered with blue veins sat behind a rickety table . . .
Nothing about the club suggested that Umfraville's fortune would be
made managing it'). LM Visited with Jeavons 172–4, 181; CCR 184;
KO 101, 106, 114, 231; VB 140; MP 21; BDFR 85.

UNIVERSITY★★
Revisited by Jenkins immediately after the war ('Reverting to the
university at forty, one immediately recaptured all the crushing
melancholy of the undergraduate condition. As the train drew up at the
platform, before the local climate had time to impair health, academic
contacts disturb the spirit, a more imminent gloom was re-established,
its sinewy grip in a flash making one young again') BDFR 1.

VICTORIA
Where Widmerpool lives with his mother in a block of flats near the
Roman Catholic cathedral ('That region has an atmosphere peculiar to
itself, separated in spirit as far from the historic gloom of Westminster's
more antique streets as from the *louche* seediness and Victorian decay of
the wide squares of Pimlico beyond Vauxhall Bridge Road. For some
reason, perhaps the height of the tower, or more probably the prodigal
inappropriateness to London of the whole structure's architectural
style, the area immediately adjacent to the cathedral imparts a sense of
vertigo, a dizziness almost alarming in its intensity: lines and curves of
red brick appearing to meet in a kind of vortex, rather than to be
ranged in normal forms of perspective. I had noticed this before when
entering the terrain from the north, and now the buildings themselves
seemed that evening almost as if they might swing slowly forward from
their bases, and downward into complete prostration') BM 273–4; and
where he afterwards moves on his marriage to a service flat in Victoria
street BDFR 173.

WAR OFFICE
Nights spent in the Duty Officer's room at ('Endemic as ghouls in an
Arabian cemetery, harassed aggressive shades lingered for ever in such
cells to impose on each successive inmate their preoccupations and
anxieties, crowding him from floor and bed, invading and distorting
dreams. Once in a way a teleprinter would break down, suddenly
ceasing to belch forth its broad paper shaft, the column instead
crumpling to a stop in mid-air like waters of a frozen cataract . . .
Outside in the corridor, diffused in clouds by the brooms of the
cleaners' dawn patrol and smarting to the eye like pepper, rose the dust
of eld. Messengers in shabby blue uniforms, a race churlish almost to a
man, were beginning to shuffle about, yawning and snarling at each
other . . .') MP 1, 3–4; nature and position of the office allotted to

Finn's section in MP 25; basement of ('The new flight of stairs led down into the bowels of the earth, the caves and potholes of the basement and sub-basement . . . Here . . . the unsleeping sages of Movement Control spun out their lives, sightless magicians deprived eternally of the light of the sun, while, by their powerful arts, they projected armies or individual over land and sea or through the illimitable wastes of the air. The atmosphere below seemed to demand such highly coloured metaphor . . . Like a phantasm in one of Dr Trelawney's own narcotically produced reveries, I flitted down passage after passage, from layer to layer of imperfect air-conditioning, finding the right door at last in an obscure corner') MP 34–5; Blackhead's lair in ('The stairs above the second floor led up into a rookery of lesser activities, some fairly obscure of definition. On these higher stories dwelt the Civil branches and their subsidiaries, Finance, Internal Administration, Passive Air Defence, all diminishing in official prestige as the altitude steepened. Finally the explorer converged on attics under the eaves, where crusty hermits lunched frugally from paper bags, amongst crumb-powdered files and documents ineradicably tattooed with the circular brand of the teacup. At these heights, vestiges of hastily snatched meals endured throughout all seasons, eternal as the unmelted upland snows. Here, under the leads, like some unjustly confined prisoner of the Council of Ten, lived Blackhead . . .') MP 38, 42; fire duty, and air raid, on the roof of MP 147–8.

WEST HALKIN STREET
Where Stringham has a bachelor flat before and after his marriage to Peggy Stepney.

WHEELBARROW**
Another of the three pubs cleared of customers by X. Trapnel, see HERO OF ACRE.

Synopsis

A Note on Dating

This rough synopsis is intended chiefly to give some indication of the chronological framework of *The Music of Time*. Dates or major public events explicitly mentioned by Jenkins are given in the margin. Supplementary dates in brackets are my own deductions from the text, and should not be taken as an attempt to marry fictional time too strictly to factual time: they simply provide a convenient shorthand alternative to the cumbersome process of dating one event by another (so that, for reference purposes, 1933 stands throughout the year of Jenkins' affair with Jean Duport, 1934, for the year of Widmerpool's engagement to Mrs Haycock and Jenkins' to Isobel Tolland, etc.).

Jenkins' time is of course consistent within itself, given the odd discrepancy arising from vagueness or lapse of memory on the part of his informants, and can generally be dated with reasonable accuracy. The only serious snag concerns volume two, *A Buyer's Market*, in which Jenkins' time describes a kind of loop round actual or other people's time. *A Buyer's Market* covers the year in which he dines at the beginning of the summer with the Walpole-Wilsons', going on the same night to the Huntercombes' ball and Mrs Andriadis' party; meets Barnby later that summer; attends Stringham's wedding in the second week of October, on the very day that Mr Deacon dies; and dines with the Widmerpools on the evening of Mr Deacon's funeral. Among the various topics discussed at the Walpole-Wilsons' dinner table are the controversial design for the Haig statue (public debate about this design began in July, 1929, and raged for the rest of the summer), and the Chinese Nationalists' recent victory at Peking (which took place in June, 1928); while, at the Widmerpools', Mrs Widmerpool discusses some forthcoming articles by Thomas Hardy's widow in *The Times* (a series published between October 22 and 26, 1928). The matter is further complicated by a flashback three volumes later, in *Casanova's Chinese Restaurant*, when Jenkins first meets Moreland in the Mortimer a week before the accident which brought about Mr Deacon's death: on the evening in the Mortimer Maclintick and Gossage talk about the Delius festival at the Queen's Hall (held in September, 1929). For simplicity's sake, therefore, I refer to this crucial composite year as '1928 or 9' throughout.

A Question of Upbringing

A Buyer's Market

Chapter One

313

The Acceptance World

314

At Lady Molly's

315

Casanova's Chinese Restaurant

reveals that Moreland has fallen in love with Priscilla Tolland 154–61 – Stringham turns up unexpectedly and takes a fancy to Mrs Maclintick, Matilda's disclosure is borne out by the behaviour of Moreland and Priscilla 161–78 – Stringham is forcibly removed by Miss Weedon with the connivance of Buster Foxe 179–87 – and Matilda goes home alone 188–9.

The Kindly Ones

318

pool's mother is negotiating terms for an evacuee 231–9, and a homeless stranger picked up by Lady Molly turns out to be Moreland 240–1 – who gives an account over dinner of Matilda's decision to leave him for Donners 242–8 – encounter with Members, Quiggin and Anne Umfraville 249–51 – return to the Jeavonses' where Ted's brother offers to fix Jenkins' call-up and commission 251–4.

The Valley of Bones

encounter in London with Barnby in RAF uniform
110-3 - arrival at Aldershot, encounter with Odo
Stevens 114-7 - and with Jimmy Brent 118-20 -
Stevens' character 120-2 - Brent's account of his affair
with Jean causes yet another drastic reassessment of
Jenkins' relationship with her 123-33 - Stevens gives
Jenkins a lift on his way to spend a weekend leave at
Frederica Budd's house 134-6 - inexplicable change in
Frederica, affair between Robert Tolland and Stringham's sister Flavia Wisebite 136-40 - Dicky Umfraville
produced as Frederica's fiancé 140-2 - Priscilla Lovell
makes a hit with Stevens 142-4 - Isobel fills in the
background to recent family developments 145-8 -
Umfraville confides the story of his life and ancient feud
with Buster Foxe 149-56 - Flavia's melancholy manner
and unfathomable relationship with Robert 157-8 -
Robert's leave cancelled, unexpected arrival of Buster
Foxe, his and Umfraville's mutual detestation 159-65 -
scene of confusion and distress cut short by Stevens'
arrival to collect Jenkins 166-7.

Chapter Four

Churchill becomes
Prime Minister;
Germany invades
The Netherlands
(May 10, 1940)

Italy joins the war
(10 June 1940)

Jenkins rejoins his regiment at Castlemallock, history
and Byronic aspects of the mansion, its present grim
atmosphere and drab occupants 168-74 - change for the
worse in Gwatkin, his unrequited passion for the
barmaid Maureen 175-93 - reappearance of Bithel 194-6
- Robert Tolland killed in France 196-7 - forebodings
about Gwatkin's affair with Maureen 197-8 - Gwatkin
has Bithel arrested for kissing a private 198-206 - and is
severely reprimanded for a balls-up over code words
207-12 - and is further reprimanded for the arrest of
Bithel 213-5 - and is relieved of his command 216-21 -
Jenkins instructed to report to the DAAG at Divisional
HQ 222-4 - Gwatkin accepts his military downfall but
is buoyed up by love 225-8 - and finds himself betrayed
by Maureen with another 229-30 - Jenkins makes his
farewells to the company 231-6 - and arrives at Div.
HQ where the DAAG turns out to be Widmerpool
237-43.

The Soldier's Art

Chapter One

(*Beginning of 1941*)

Chapter Two
British withdrawal in Greece
(*April 1941*)

evening in which Bijou and all her guests died at the Madrid 151–9 – Jenkins sets out for the Jeavonses' to tell Priscilla of Chips' death and, finding the Jeavonses' house also bombed that night in a raid which killed Priscilla and Lady Molly, imparts his news to Eleanor Walpole-Wilson 160–6.

Chapter Three

Germans invade
Crete
(May 21, 1941)

Jenkins returns to Div. HQ to find Stringham transferred on Widmerpool's instructions to a Mobile Laundry Unit 167–71 – Widmerpool's various plots concerning Diplock, the Recce corps and his own promotion 172–4 – Stringham enlists Jenkins' help in an attempt to cover up Bithel's drunkenness, their rescue plans foiled by Widmerpool 175–85 – Widmerpool arranges Bithel's dismissal from the army, congratulates himself on having engineered Stringham's posting abroad and announces his own promotion to the Cabinet Offices 186–93 – Farebrother brings news of imminent disaster awaiting Widmerpool over the Recce Unit affair 194–207 – Hogbourne-Johnson and the culmination of the Diplock affair 208–14 – Widmerpool reduced to utter despair 214–5 – Jenkins tries unsuccessfully to persuade Stringham to leave the Laundry before

Day on which
Germany invades
Russia
(June 22, 1941)

it moves to the Far East 216–24 – Biggs hangs himself, Widmerpool's career is reprieved in the nick of time and Jenkins is instructed to report to the War Office 225–8.

The Military Philosophers

Chapter One

Early spring (1942)
Five or six weeks
after the Fall of
Singapore (attack on
Singapore
February 8, 1942)

Wagnerian aspects of night duty at the War Office in Whitehall 1–4 – Jenkins' present position as Pennistone's assistant, looking after Poles in Allied Liaison under Finn 4–9 – Cabinet Office meeting chaired by Widmerpool and attended by Farebrother and Templer 10–18 – conversation with Templer, his distant manner and extreme

Chapter Two

Chapter Three

Chapter Four

Proust's Balbec, reflections on this revelation 166–8 – Brussels and Army Main Group HQ 169–71 – encounter with members of Jenkins' former Welsh battalion 172–7 – inspection by Field-Marshal Montgomery, musings on his military predecessors and his own singular brand of willpower 178–85 – meeting with Bob Duport in Brussels, his account of Templer's death in the Balkans 186–90 – return to London, Jenkins solves the problem of the Belgian resistance army 191–5.

Books Do Furnish a Room

Temporary Kings

Chapter One
Summer (1958)

Evening after dinner at Jenkins' Venetian hotel during international writers' conference. Reflections on Venice and the passing of time 1–4 – Dr Emily Brightman 4–5 – Members on the conference 6–8 – Ferrand-Sénéschal, his equivocal career, political and sexual connections with Widmerpool, and recent death 8–18 – arrival of Russell Gwinnett, prospective biographer of X. Trapnel 19–22 – recollections of Trapnel, his disintegration, apotheosis and death, Pamela Widmerpool's part in his downfall and her subsequent married life 23–40 – Gwinnett produces sensational press report linking Pamela with Ferrand-Sénéschal's death 41–7 – Dr Brightman on Gwinnett's character and history 48–51 – Jenkins, in bed that night, recalls his parents' visit to Venice and ancient friendship with Daniel Tokenhouse 52–4 – Tokenhouse's career, collapse and withdrawal to Venice 55–9.

Chapter Two

Visit to Bragadin palace next day. Previous encounter thirty years before with Bragadin's house-guest Louis Glober recalled 60–74 – the Tiepolo ceiling 75–6 – Pamela Widmerpool and Glober discovered gazing at it 77–81 – *Candaules and Gyges*, Dr Brightman's theoretical and Pamela Widmerpool's practical exposition of its themes 82–90 – Ada Leintwardine 91–5 – Glober and Gwinnett 96–9 – Gwinnett approaches Pamela about Trapnel 100–3 – arrival of Widmerpool and Baby Wentworth, row between the Widmerpools 104–12 – Glober and Mrs Wentworth, Gwinnett and Pamela 113–6.

Chapter Three

Visit to Tokenhouse the following Sunday, his painting in theory and practice 117–26 – on to the Biennale, luncheon with Ada and Glober, his film plans 126–40 – further viewing of Tokenhouse's paintings cut short by Widmerpool's arrival 141–7 – Ada's account of Glober's designs on Pamela, and Pamela's obsession with Tiepolo's *Candaules* 148–53 – dinner with Gwinnett, his

327

Hearing Secret Harmonies